Race, Class, and the World System: The Sociology of Oliver C. Cox

Herbert M. Hunter and Sameer Y. Abraham, eds.

Race, Class, and the World System: The Sociology of Oliver C. Cox

Monthly Review Press
New York

The editors would like to thank the following, who have kindly given permission for the use of copyrighted material: University of North Carolina Press for "The Modern Caste School of Race Relations," which appeared in *Social Forces* 21 (December 1942): 218–26; *Journal of Negro Education* for "An American Dilemma," which appeared in *Journal of Negro Education* 14 (Spring 1945): 132–48; University of Chicago Press for "Race and Caste: A Distinction," which appeared in *American Journal of Sociology* 50 (March 1945): 360–68; Wayne State University Press for "Significance of Rural Culture for Race Relations," "The Ghetto," "Negro Protest and the Subculture," and "The Road Ahead," all from *Race Relations: Elements and Social Dynamics*, copyright © 1976 by Wayne State University Press; *Race and Class* and the Institute of Race Relations, London, for "The Question of Pluralism," which appeared in *Race* 12, no. 4 (April 1971): 386–400; The American Sociological Association for "Estates, Social Classes, and Political Classes," which appeared in the *American Sociological Review* 10 (1945): 464–69; Philosophical Library for "Capitalist Cities," "Venice the Progenitor," and "Economic Underpinning of Venice," all from *The Foundations of Capitalism*, copyright © 1959 by Oliver C. Cox, and for "Assumption of Leadership," from *Capitalism and American Leadership*, copyright © 1962 by Oliver C. Cox; and Monthly Review Press for "Race Relations," "The Political Class," "Facets of the Modern Political-Class Struggle," and "Modern Democracy and the Class Struggle," all from *Caste, Class, and Race*, copyright © 1948 by Oliver Cromwell Cox, and for "Structure of the System," "Imperialism," and "Movements Toward Change," all from *Capitalism as a System*, copyright © 1964 by Oliver C. Cox.

Library of Congress Cataloging in Publication Data

Race, class, and the world system.

  Bibliography: p.
  1. Cox, Oliver C. (Oliver Cromwell), 1901–1974.
2. Afro-American sociologists—United States—Biography.
3. Sociology—United States.   4. Race relations.
I. Hunter, Herbert M.   II. Abraham, Sameer Y.
HM22.U6C697 1987   301'.092'4   86-28635
ISBN 0-85345-683-6
ISBN 0-85345-684-4 (pbk.)

Monthly Review Press
155 West 23rd Street, New York, N.Y. 10011

10 9 8 7 6 5 4 3 2 1

To the memory and intellectual spirit of Oliver C. Cox

Contents

Paul M. Sweezy

Foreword

Reviewing Oliver Cox's *Caste, Class, and Race* more than thirty-five years ago (*Monthly Review*, June 1950), I wrote:

> American academic social science has a long and inglorious tradition of evading the burning social issues of the day. The powers-that-be hold the purse strings and on occasion crack the whip; the social scientists, bowing respectfully, either elaborate justifications of the existing social order or else escape into the innocuous study of other times and other systems.
>
> But there have always been a few who have insisted on dealing with the crucial issues of their times and on telling the truth as they see it, regardless of whose toes may be stepped on or whose sensibilities may be injured. They have prevented the complete stultification of academic social science and in the long run have exercised an influence on American life out of all proportion to their numbers.
>
> Such a one is Oliver Cromwell Cox, a professor of sociology, formerly at Tuskeegee Institute, now at Lincoln University in Missouri. Oliver Cox's book, *Caste, Class, and Race* . . . is unquestionably an outstanding product of American sociology. And yet packed away in its long words and copious footnotes there is plenty of dynamite—and no pulled punches.
>
> It has been my experience that very few people, even among social scientists, have heard of Cox's work. This is perhaps not surprising. *Caste, Class, and Race* is the kind of book publishers bury as quickly as they can; while the sociologists, unable to answer it, seem to have found it most expedient to ignore it. Nevertheless, its message is of vital importance, not only to scholars and students but to the whole American progressive movement.

If I were rewriting the review today, I would not have to change much. The original publisher (Doubleday) did bury the book, allowing it to go out of print when the first printing was sold out hardly more than a year after it was published (it was reprinted in

1959 by Monthly Review Press and has been kept in print ever since). Many more people of course know about and appreciate Cox's work than did so thirty-five years ago, but it is still ignored by most of his professional colleagues. As far as what I wrote then about Cox himself and the substance of the book, I would not change a word.

During the last twenty-five years of his life (he died in 1974), the center of Cox's attention shifted from race relations in the contemporary world to the origins and development of capitalism. He published three major works in this hitherto much neglected field: *The Foundations of Capitalism* (1959), *Capitalism and American Leadership* (1962), and *Capitalism as a System* (1964). These studies display the same careful and broad-ranging scholarship and the same qualities of original and critical thought as *Caste, Class, and Race.* However, they deal with a set of problems that spread-eagle all the social sciences and hence lay outside both the interest and the competence of American sociologists of that period. It is hardly surprising, therefore, that this whole aspect of Cox's work went almost entirely unnoticed at the time of publication and for the most part has still to be discovered by a later generation of sociologists, many of whom are no longer confined within the narrow limits of an artificially restricted (and impoverished) "discipline." Particularly noteworthy is the fact that after Cox's death a whole new branch of historical sociology, generally known as world systems theory, opened up and rapidly grew in the Americas, under the leadership of such eminent scholars as Immanuel Wallerstein, Andre Gunder Frank, and Samir Amin. Both chronologically and logically, Oliver Cox deserves to be considered not only a forerunner but a founding father of this relatively new and welcome departure in American sociology. I hope and trust that the publication of this selection from his major works, carefully chosen and helpfully introduced by Herbert Hunter and Sameer Abraham, will go far toward achieving this result.

One factor in evaluating the importance of thinkers and scholars is of course the prestige accorded them by their peers. In the case of Oliver Cox, however, this criterion is manifestly inapplicable. In Cold War America, the time and place in which he did his work, his peers—or those who ought to have been his peers—either knew nothing about him, did not understand him, or rejected his work on irrelevant ideological grounds. I think this is changing and will change even more in the future, but in the meantime we must judge him by other criteria.

For my part, I prefer what some may think too subjective a

yardstick, i.e., the influence he has had on my own intellectual development. And by this standard I can only rank Oliver Cox as one of a small group of great American social scientists. On race relations, I am quite simply his pupil. Before *Caste, Class, and Race,* I had never really thought about the theoretical issues involved. I found his refutation of caste theory, so popular in the United States at the time, totally persuasive; and his linking of capitalist exploitation and modern race relations provided the necessary historical perspective. On the origins and development of capitalism, subjects on which I had discussions and occasionally disagreements with him during his lifetime—the differences related to the relative importance of commercial and capital-labor relations in the early period—I have come more and more to appreciate and make use of his contributions in my own work. This holds especially of what I now consider to be the extraordinary importance of his analysis of the role of medieval Venice and a few other Italian city-states in creating and shaping the bourgeois institutions and mentality without which capitalism would have been very different from what it has been during its period of world dominance.

In conclusion, one question to which Hunter and Abraham rightly devote attention in their introduction: Was Oliver Cox a Marxist? There is no right or wrong answer. Once again, I can only give my own: Yes, he certainly was a Marxist. He made no effort to minimize or disguise his intellectual debt to Marx. He thought like a Marxist. The revolutionary conclusions to which his work led, even if not always explicitly spelled out, were basically the same as Marx's. This last point for me is the decisive one. If I had my way, I would deny the honorific title of Marxist to anyone who denies or repudiates the rock-bottom revolutionary content of Marx's thought. By this standard, Oliver Cox clearly qualifies as a Marxist. If he often felt it necessary to deny that he was a Marxist, this was because what most American social scientists, not to mention the public at large, understood by Marxism was (and unfortunately still remains) a vicious caricature of the real thing.

Preface

Of the many sociologists one could select to pay tribute to in a volume such as this, Oliver C. Cox might appear to be an unlikely candidate. An older generation of sociologists might not consider Cox one of the premier figures of twentieth-century sociology, while younger sociologists might not recognize his name—let alone his contributions. Only a small handful of sociologists would argue that Cox belongs to an illustrious group of sociological thinkers who have served as the faithful opposition to the sociological establishment. It is part of the purpose of this volume, then, to establish a firm basis for granting Cox his deserved place in U.S. sociology.

Two implicit, perhaps even unconscious, questions have guided us in the preparation of this volume: Why Cox? and, Why Cox now? Although prodigious in his learning and prolific in his scholarship, Cox was not rewarded with a commensurate position at one of the nation's leading universities. He was influential as a critic of establishment ideas, particularly in the field of race relations, but never played a significant role as an "insider" in academic sociology. In today's parlance, Cox was not someone who was "networked" into mainstream sociology. Instead, he was cast in the role of a sort of intellectual pariah, which made it easier to avoid, evade, and neglect his contribution. In addition, his "outsider" status deprived him of the institutional prestige and, more important, of the contact with graduate students that is so essential to leaving an imprint on the profession. This is not to argue that a Coxian "school of thought" might have developed under more favorable conditions, but only to underscore the fact that as a critic on the periphery of the institutional system, Cox had little impact on the next generation of students in the discipline. The fact that he was one of the few black sociologists eminently qualified for a post at a major university but, to our knowledge, was never offered such a position, is further testimony to the numerous impediments that obstructed his career. It was another generation before black sociologists were to reap the benefits of the civil rights movement.

These few reasons alone might be sufficient to award Cox his deserved place on the sociological landscape. Others of his generation have received greater homage for much smaller contributions. But there are other compelling intellectual reasons for bestowing this tribute. Anyone reading Cox for the first time cannot help but be immediately struck by the breadth, depth, and power of his learning. His erudition was profound. Both of us have read and reread Cox's work on many occasions; each time we have encountered something new—a previously unrecognized point of theoretical emphasis, another approach to a recurring problem, or the concise formulation (or reformulation) of a research question. Above all else, Cox had a penetrating analytical mind. He refused to look at issues narrowly; he was unmercifully critical in his questioning, whether directed at the establishment or its opponents, meticulous in his documentation, uncompromising in debate, and resilient and resourceful when under attack. Perhaps most important, he was intent on connecting what on the surface appear to be disparate and isolated fragments of knowledge. To journey with Cox into the topic of race relations is to travel in time and space, from the sixteenth to the twentieth centuries, from India, Africa, and Europe to the Americas and beyond. Whether searching for the origins of capitalism or carefully slicing through the encrusted layers of the concepts of caste and class, Cox works his subject with the agility of a master artisan. The study of an issue is never confined to the narrow limits of a single discipline, but always encompasses political economy and social history, as well as sociology. We follow a first-rate intellectual and scientific mind at work. Even if we do not agree with the results, it is difficult not to be impressed by the careful and comprehensive consideration with which Cox literally lays seige to his subject.

Cox exhibits a number of qualities that imbue him with an intellectual appeal similar to that of C. Wright Mills and Thorstein Veblen, the premier critics and independent radicals of the U.S. sociological profession. Like them, Cox was a scholarly critic and an independent radical. Modelling himself on the "classical" thinkers, he focused on the big questions and controversial issues. His criticism was aimed at the dominant voices in sociology and at the established ways of an unjust and capitalist society. He published critical works during the McCarthy era and was labelled a Marxist at a time when it was risky to be a member of the opposition. Operating under these constraints required not only intellect and

conviction, but also courage, for a black scholar who openly acknowledged his intellectual debt to Marx even though he disassoci-
ated himself from most "Marxists." In temperament and philosophy, Cox was not one to "play along," ideologically or politically,
for the sake of personal convenience or comfort. This may help to
explain why he appeared content to teach in small black colleges: if
"playing the career game" meant compromising his independence,
as some of his noteworthy black peers had done, Cox would have
no part of it. And his distance from the academic mainstream did
not seem to affect the quality of his scholarship, even though it
probably meant that his works faded into relative obscurity sooner
than they might otherwise have done. Cox's character should appeal to many who still believe in the old-fashioned notion that
scholarship should be judged on its own merits and not on the
pretense or institutional affiliation of its author. But then again,
ideas are not unattached in the real world; nor do they possess
equal "exchange value" on the open market of ideas. That is all the
more reason for preserving Cox's life and work, and for bringing it
before a larger public.

In answering our second question, Why Cox now?, the answer is
that the various issues that Cox spent a lifetime researching and
writing about continue to be intensely debated both inside and
outside the social sciences. Witness the heated exchanges surrounding race and intelligence; the debates over changing patterns of
race relations, ghetto life, and the black "underclass"; the unending
discussion of definitions of social class; the international pursuit of
a comprehensive world systems theory; and the quest for an over-
arching theory that explains the origins, development, and transformation of capitalism. Cox has much to say about these and other
topics, whether directly or indirectly. In some instances his work
should lay to rest controversies that ought to have been buried long
ago. In other instances he provides a clarity that is often difficult to
achieve in the whirlwind of debate. He refuses to be part of sociology's ahistorical tendency to deny or forget history, including
the history of sociology itself. Of all the disciplines, then, it is
perhaps sociology that has the most to gain from Cox, because at
bottom he was a sociologist and demonstrates so well the value of a
sociohistorical, cross-cultural, and economic approach to many of
the issues sociology faces today.

This is the first published anthology on the life and work of
Oliver C. Cox, and a few words need to be said about how it is
organized. We have tried to bring together, in one volume, representative selections from Cox's published articles and books in
order to meet three critical needs: (1) to provide social scientists,

particularly sociologists, with a concise review of the intellectual contributions of a leading, but largely neglected, critical black sociologist; (2) to enrich current debates on race relations, capitalism, and the political economy of world systems theory by offering a wide range of Cox's writing on these subjects; and, finally, (3) to lay to rest some of the ambiguity and debate surrounding Cox's life and work. We have organized the selections into four main sections according to analytical subject matter rather than chronology of publication. Like all editors of collections, we spent countless hours discussing which article to select or excerpt, how each would contribute to the book, which would best convey the full range of Cox's thinking without compromising the depth of his analysis of a particular issue, and which would provide material that would be relevant to the ongoing debates in the social sciences. All of these considerations had to take place within the larger calculus of the constraints of time and money that are a part of present-day publishing. We took great care to keep as much of the original material as possible, primarily eliminating repetitous and digressive material (such as lengthy quotations and explanatory footnotes). Readers interested in any of these omissions should consult the bibliography at the end of the volume in order to locate the original work. Perhaps the gravest limitation we faced was that we were not able to locate Cox's unpublished manuscripts or correspondence, which we suspect have not been preserved.

While space does not allow us to acknowledge all who have provided assistance in various ways, special thanks are due to the following: Cox's niece, Juliet A. Uibopuu, was instrumental in putting one of us in touch with members of Cox's family in Trinidad and the United States, while Stella Awon Cox and Aldwin Vidale helped in key interviews with the Cox family and provided deeply appreciated hospitality. Other interviews and background material were provided by some of Cox's former colleagues and students, including Lewis Wade Jones, Lorenzo Greene, Gordon Morgan, G. Franklin Edwards, Charles Gomillion, Nathan Hare, Elmer P. Martin, Butler Jones, Charles Key, Alwin W. Rose, Bruce Williams, Herbert Blumer, Everret C. Hughes, Hylan Lewis, Noel P. Gist, and Edgar T. Thompson.

We would also like to thank Monthly Review Press for being receptive to the idea of publishing a volume of this kind, and especially Susan Lowes, who provided us with invaluable editorial feedback on early drafts of the manuscript.

—Herbert M. Hunter
Sameer Y. Abraham

September 1986

The Life and Career of Oliver C. Cox

The Early Years

Oliver Cromwell Cox was born on August 24, 1901, in Port-of-Spain, Trinidad, the son of Virginia Blake and William Raphael Cox.[1] His family was economically stable and was less impoverished than the majority of Trinidadians. His father, a "wavy-haired," light-skinned man, was able to achieve middle-class status for his relatively large family by working as the captain of a revenue schooner, a government ship that sailed around the island enforcing the sea laws,[2] and then as a customs and excise officer, collecting duties and checking for contraband and pilferage for the British colonial authorities. William Cox owned a home in Port-of-Spain and a small "estate" or farm in Tabaquite village in the center of the island, where the family had a summer home and grew cocoa beans.[3] Correct in his treatment of his business affairs and strict in family matters, William Cox was a demanding father and encouraged all nine of his children (six sons and three daughters) to be thrifty, hard working, and disciplined.[4]

William Cox's work and the time spent managing the estate did not allow him to be as attentive to his children as he might have liked, and it was his brother, Reginald V. Vidale, who—in the words of his son Aldwin—"took the Cox boys by the hand and inspired them toward study." Vidale was at first a schoolteacher and later the headmaster of St. Thomas Boys' School, where Oliver Cox received his primary education.[5] Aldwin, who was Oliver Cox's cousin and lifelong friend, reports the impression his father made on the young Cox:

> He [Cox] kept telling me that his uncle was so sound, so dignified; you noticed how choice his language is. And then he would laugh and say

what a disciplinarian! At times I was a bit baffled at his attitude towards his uncle's wraft without question. Whatever his uncle said was okay. Oliver appeared to me that he was focusing all along on his uncle as a guideline for his achievements.[6]

Vidale was a worthy role model for Cox. A Catholic, he was well known as a teacher and was highly respected in the community. He became inspector of schools in 1943 and then a city councilman, alderman, and finally mayor of Port-of-Spain.[7]

Cox's father had an unremitting determination to further his children's education, and insisted that they (especially the males) go to the United States to prove themselves. Cox's older brother Ethelbert went first, to study medicine, and was followed by Reginald, who wanted to be a dentist. In 1919 Oliver went too, planning to become either a doctor or lawyer, and then to return home, marry, and live happily ever after.[8] All three sons received financial support for the initial passage, but it was only the eldest—his father's favorite—who received assistance while attending school. Once in the United States, the young Oliver was on his own.[9]

The experience of growing up in the West Indies under the British colonial system in the first two decades of the twentieth century provided Oliver Cox with a cultural heritage that was to be unique among black American sociologists of his generation. In Trinidad, Cox was far removed from the racial discrimination and hostility that characterized race relations in the United States, and in addition had experienced living in a country where whites were a minority and considered outsiders. Poverty, illiteracy, and exploitation were common, but unlike in the United States, where blacks were a minority in a white majority society and culture, living primarily in racially segregated communities maintained by force, Cox was a member of the majority group. Without explicit legal restrictions or a rigidly defined color bar separating the races, there were opportunities for Trinidadians who had the appropriate skin color, wealth, education, and/or family status—it was the interplay among these factors that set the pattern of power and privilege in the native population.[10] While it is difficult to know the extent to which an individual's background influences his or her later development, it can be argued that Oliver Cox was able to develop an independent path in his life and work in part at least because he was freer intellectually to see the problems of black America in a manner not typical of U.S. social scientists, who tended to be preoccupied with the racial victimization of blacks by race prejudice, discrimination, and segregation.

Cox's Education and Intellectual Development in the United States

When Oliver Cox arrived in the United States, he was eighteen years old. The following year he began to prepare for college by attending the Central YMCA High School in Chicago, from which he graduated in 1923. He then spent two years at Lewis Institute, majoring in history and economics, and received his associate degree in 1927. In the fall of that year he entered Northwestern University to study law, and received his Bachelor of Science in Law degree in 1929. He still expected to become a successful lawyer and return to his native country, but suddenly his plans were destroyed when he was stricken with poliomyelitis. With full recovery in doubt—he walked with crutches for the rest of his life—he was forced to rethink his plans. He felt that he would not be mobile enough to be a lawyer, and that he would neither be able to marry nor to make Trinidad his permanent home.

He was nevertheless determined to survive despite his disability, and in 1930, after a year and a half spent recovering, he entered the department of economics at the University of Chicago, believing that academic work "would not require too much footwork."[11] While there he studied economic history, economic theory, and labor problems under John U. Nef, Frank H. Knight, Jacob Viner, and Harry A. Millis.[12] Although this was a well-known and esteemed coterie of intellectuals, Cox never reported that they had any great influence on him. Even so, it was probably through Knight that Cox learned the value of Max Weber's comparative and historical approach to studying world civilizations, an approach he later used in his own work. It was during this period that Cox developed an analytic approach that later placed him at odds with the ahistorical and empiricist approach of many of his sociological contemporaries.

In June 1932 Cox completed his M.A. thesis, which was entitled "Workingmen's Compensation in the United States, with Critical Observations and Suggestions."[13] Demonstrating his skills as both a lawyer and an economist, he examined the history of employer liability for industrial accidents and the development of workingmen's compensation. He used a number of legal cases to show how the law, and legislative bodies at various levels, had dealt with the problem. Perhaps his own disability had sensitized him to some of the issues in this area. He argues, for instance, that compensation for total disability should be for life; that rehabilitation to make the injured party reemployable should be part of any program;

and that workers' compensation should cover all categories of workers.[14]

Cox did not stay in economics, however, but shifted to sociology. He explained this as being in part because of the inability of the Chicago economists to explain adequately the Great Depression of the 1930s. According to Cox himself, "I felt that if economics did not explain what I wanted to know; if economics did not explain the coming of the depression; if economics did not help me to understand that great economic change, then I felt I did not need it. Thus, I changed over to sociology."[15]

While the reasons for moving away from economics may be clear, the reasons for moving into sociology are less so. Certainly, the department of sociology at the University of Chicago played a leadership role in U.S. sociology during the 1920s, under the guidance of Robert E. Park, Ernest W. Burgess, and Ellsworth Faris. Cox could not have made a better choice if he was looking for a department that would bring him into contact with some of the most prominent and influential personalities in sociology. But as eminent as these men were, there was little in their work that could have provided Cox with the critical perspective he ultimately developed. It may have been that sociology offered a wider framework for analysis and theorizing than did economics; further, if Cox wanted to study race relations, as he ultimately did, there was no better place then this department of sociology, which had an ongoing teaching and research program and attracted more black graduate students than that of any other academic institution in the United States.

On the recommendation of Ellsworth Faris, an influential sociological figure of the day, Cox enrolled in courses in preparation for the doctorate. His first introductory course covered the work of Park and Burgess, whose *Introduction to the Study of Sociology* had become the established primer for introductory courses across the country. He also attended courses given by such prominent Chicago sociologists as William F. Ogburn, Herbert Blumer, Faris, and others, and was exposed to the historical approach to social problems and institutions adopted by Louis Wirth.

Cox wrote his dissertation, entitled "Factors Affecting the Marital Status of Negroes in the United States," under Ogburn. In it he concentrated "on those aspects which are amenable to quantitative techniques" by demonstrating the effect of demographic variables—such as sex ratios, urbanization, population increase, age, employment status, school attendance, and farm tenancy—on marital status.[16] The study abounds with charts and tables, with simple and partial correlations, scattergrams, and other statistics that, contrary to later criticism of Cox's methodology, show that he was knowledgeable about quantitative methods.[17] Unlike virtually all of his fellow black students who had been trained in the department of sociology at Chicago, Cox was attracted to the quantitative methods emphasized by Ogburn and Samuel Stouffer, rather than the more qualitative case-study method and ecological approach developed by Park, Burgess, Blumer, and their students.[18] Thus in the introduction to the dissertation he called E. Franklin Frazier's *The Negro Family in Chicago* "an ecological study that presented crude data on Negro marriages," and referred to Charles S. Johnson's *The Present Status and Trends of the Negro Family* as being much the same as Frazier's work. He then wrote:

> Of a different nature is the work of William F. Ogburn. His is by far the greatest contribution to the analysis of marriage statistics in the United States. The present writer has found considerable help in Groves and Ogburn, *American Marriage and Family Relationships,* and "Recent Changes in Marriage" by Ogburn. Although Professor Ogburn did not study Negro marriage specifically, his general work has been so thorough our obligations are too many to mention individually.[19]

On August 26, 1938, two days after his thirty-seventh birthday, Cox received his doctorate in sociology. For seven years, including summers, he had been in school, taking off only one or two quarters during the entire period. The only employment he had undertaken was a job as senior statistician for the Chicago Park District in 1936, and a position as assistant professor of sociology at Louisville Municipal College for nine months in 1936–37. His childhood socialization to the values of hard work, discipline, and thrift appear to have been his guides, as, with great persistence and little financial help, he achieved the education that he had come to the United States to pursue.

Teaching in a Black College

Like many of his black contemporaries, Cox was now well prepared for a career as an academic. With graduate degrees in economics and sociology from a leading university, he was in a position to teach both disciplines, which should have considerably widened his employment opportunities. Despite this, he was unable to secure a position in any of the larger white institutions, with their greater resources, and instead—as was customary for even the brightest young black scholars well into the 1950s—was forced to seek employment in a black college, where the teaching load was heavy, the salary low, and there were few graduate students or resources for carrying out research.[20] In fact, Cox was destined to spend his career in both intellectual and geographical isolation, not only working within a framework that removed him from the mainstream of academic sociology but working in institutions where few of his colleagues could match his academic credentials and scholarly accomplishments and that were in geographical isolation, far from the intellectual centers of activity. Despite these problems, however, he was able to surmount the intellectual limitations imposed on racially segregated southern black colleges. He attended professional meetings around the country, and traveled during the summer months and during sabbatical years. He maintained contact with the scholarly world through reading and by contributing to the most important journals in his field. As we shall see, most of his major works were produced while teaching in black schools, where he spent most of his years as a sociologist.

Cox's first major teaching position was at Wiley College, a small Methodist school in Marshall, Texas.[21] There he taught economics and was director of the Bureau of Social Research, a position he shared with his friend and colleague V. E. Daniels from 1939 to 1944. He also benefited greatly from the "very fruitful relationships . . . with members of the faculty." It was at Wiley that he developed a lifelong friendship with the renowned black poet Melvin Tolsom.[22]

While at Wiley, Cox began his critique of the "caste school of race relations," a theory that was rapidly gaining popularity among social scientists. The conceptualization was first initiated by the social anthropologist W. Lloyd Warner, in his article "American Caste and Class," which appeared in the *American Journal of Sociology* in 1936. Here Warner brought together the concepts of caste and class to explain the social organization of the U.S. South in terms of a biracial system of social stratification. He argued, accordingly, that while caste and class were two concepts often thought to be antithetical, they could nevertheless operate within a single community. Thus whereas class describes a situation where intergroup movement, including marriage, is possible, caste describes a situation where both social mobility and intermarriage between blacks and whites are restricted through extralegal codes of behavior and patterns of deference between the races. According to Warner, in the U.S. South, caste and class structures could coexist and accommodate themselves to internal conflict and hostility because both the dominant white group and the subordinate black group participated in maintaining the caste system.

Cox's critique of Warner and his associates and students first appeared in 1942 in the journal *Social Forces,* in a piece entitled "The Modern Caste School of Race Relations" (included in this volume). Although not recognized as such at the time, it was this article that established Cox as one of the first U.S. sociologists to present an alternative to the accepted proposition that black-white relations in the United States constituted a caste system similar to that found in Hindu society. Cox found this analogy completely unacceptable because it ignored the historical differences between the two societies and discounted the political and economic imperatives undergirding race relations in the United States. His article was only the first salvo in what was to become a comprehensive critique of the conceptual framework of the entire field of race relations and social stratification—a critique that emerged in a number of articles and culminated, in 1948, in the magnum opus *Caste, Class, and Race.*

The working conditions at Wiley were unsatisfactory to a scholar of Cox's ability. In 1944, because of the low salary and the absence of any prospect for advancement, he decided to accept an offer from Tuskegee Institute, the most celebrated black vocational school in the South, founded by Booker T. Washington, and located in the heart of the Alabama Black Belt. At the time, Tuskegee was still committed to Washington's industrial education program of uplifting the black masses through training in the trades and technnical professions, and did not place a great deal of emphasis on the liberal arts. Indeed, it is not clear why Cox chose to seek employment at Tuskegee (given his scholarly proclivities) rather than go to one of the other black institutions (such as Howard, Fisk, or Atlanta), where a liberal arts education, particularly in the social sciences, was more central to the curriculum. His decision may have been prompted in part by the fact that a number of graduate programs had recently been established at Tuskegee. Addie Louise Joyner Butler, in her analysis of Tuskegee Institute, has noted that at that point,

> In addition to the organization of the School of Veterinary Medicine, 1944 was significant in the history of Tuskegee as the year that graduate instruction was initiated. By 1944, the state colleges were fairly well supported and they offered standard training on the undergraduate level in a number of areas. Thus, Tuskegee's graduate program was instituted to "serve the region on the graduate level in

terms of its efforts to meet the graduate and professional needs of Negro youth." Graduate training was offered in the fields of rural education, home economics and agriculture. The opening of the Veterinary School and the initiation of graduate instruction contributed to increased institutional complexity in terms of bigness and levels of study.[23]

Cox thus went to Tuskegee during a period of institutional expansion. He had also written several articles while at Wiley on the demographics of black and white marriages in rural and urban communities, and in one had examined the relationship between farm tenancy and rates of marriage. These research interests coincided with Tuskegee's needs in the area of rural education. Cox was undoubtedly an attractive candidate to the Tuskegee faculty. As Charles Gomillion, a former colleague, reports, "Cox was scholarly and it was felt that he could bring prestige to the school in research and teaching. His publication record was impressive and he was thought highly of by his peers."[24] Since few teachers in black colleges at that time had either Ph.D.'s or even M.A.'s, it was felt that the new Division of Education would be greatly enhanced by someone of Cox's stature and credentials.

While at Tuskegee Cox primarily taught economics and sociology. He taught a graduate course on race and culture that, according to the school's bulletin, focused on "racial theories of culture as a factor determining race relations in different situations," a concern Cox also addressed in his writings. He also taught a course on the socioeconomic problems of the rural South, which was directed particularly at the predominantly rural and southern Tuskegee student, as well as basic economics and courses on labor problems, consumer economics, and the U.S. economy—all subjects in keeping with his training at Chicago. But since Tuskegee was primarily a vocational institution, Cox had few students who were interested in graduate study in sociology, or even in sociological theory; they preferred to concentrate on the practical applications of sociological research that they could use after graduation. This created some problems for Cox: Gomillion reports that he was scholarly and better suited to teach graduate students in sociology, so that some students had difficulty following him.[25]

Cox's reputation as a sociologist continued to grow while he was at Tuskegee, and it was at this point that his radical critique of the prevailing notions of caste, class, and race relations began to gain him the label of "Marxist." But although those of his writings on race relations published between 1944 and 1948 were powerful critiques of mainstream theories, they were probably read by a relatively small number of people: Many appeared in *The Journal of Negro Education*, which was read by few social scientists. With the publication of *Caste, Class, and Race* in 1948, however, Cox's label of Marxist sociologist was well established, as the many reviewers ideologically opposed to his ideas dismissed his work as "Marxist dogma" and "Communist propaganda," pernicious labels that were to shadow him throughout the rest of his career and deny him the scholarly recognition he deserved.

Given that this was a time when Marxism and Communism were both anathema to post-World War II America, it was not surprising that Cox's approach clashed with a "conservative religious-oriented black school which spent a great deal of its time trying to present a positive image to powerful white capitalist philanthropists who kept the school financially alive."[26] In a letter to F. D. Patterson, president of Tuskegee, Cox apparently felt it necessary to clarify his political beliefs: "As you know, my interest in the major tendencies of modern civilization and its discontents is that of a student and teacher with major interests in teaching. As a citizen, however, I am in sympathy with the philosophy and practice of the late President Franklin D. Roosevelt."[27]

Other evidence suggests, however, that Cox's growing reputation as an intellectual and ideological radical had little effect on his position at Tuskegee. He had many friends, and there was great respect for his ideas—which in any case often seemed more radical than he was. He was personally austere and conservative in his ways, and did not espouse a particular political philosophy publicly. Moreover, the advocacy of political and civil rights, which had been deemphasized under the leadership of Washington and his successor Robert Russa Moton, played a much larger role under Patterson. Gomillion organized the Tuskegee Civic Association in 1947 and launched a program of political activism in the town and surrounding rural areas. As Butler A. Jones points out, "The near miraculous quality of this feat is highlighted by the fact that it occurred in the face of violent opposition from the local white citizenry, in defiance of legislative action at the state level designed to outlaw the movement and stymie its leadership, and over the unrelenting opposition of the governor of the state."[28] Gomillion reports that the state legislature tried to pressure the Tuskegee president into prohibiting Gomillion's involvement in civil rights activities, but that the president resisted, and even when rumors were circulated that Gomillion was a Communist, he refused to issue a reprimand.[29]

Neither Gomillion nor Jones has any recollection of Cox's being pressured to leave Tuskegee because of his so-called Marxism. In fact, since many black civil rights organizations were considered—by white politicians—to be "Communist-inspired," even Patterson could be considered something of a radical for serving as an adviser to the militant Southern Negro Congress.[30] Cox's own intellectual radicalism certainly went far beyond the civil rights activities of many of his Tuskegee colleagues, but the alleged conservatism at Tuskegee in the late 1940s was not so pervasive that Cox's ideas could not be tolerated.

If Cox was condemned at all, it was for his attack on the school's founder and idol, Booker T. Washington, for being a "quisling," a term Cox used to describe those individuals who aligned themselves with the white ruling class.[31] The "old-timers" at the school, who firmly supported Washington's philosophy of vocational education and self-help and who were proud of their founder's success in the white world, were furious at Cox's attack. Indeed, according to Lewis Wade Jones they became so upset that they made Cox come to the auditorium and defend his statement, "which he did, but not to their satisfaction."[32]

Cox did not relent, however, and in a paper entitled "The Leadership of Booker T. Washington," which was read before the annual meeting of the Association of Social Science Teachers—a primarily black group—in Jefferson City, Missouri, in 1949, Cox reiterated that Washington was a class collaborator and that his leadership was "spurious":

> He was not a leader of the masses in the Garvian sense; his function was rather that of controlling the masses. He deflated and abandoned their [the Negroes'] common cause. He demanded less for the Negro people than that which the ruling class had already conceded. And because he was in reality sent with a mission to subdue the spirit of protest in the masses instead of his arising among them as a champion of their cause he was frequently insulting and harsh towards them.[33]

Cox continued to develop this theme in several articles written in the early 1950s.

When Cox left Tuskegee, in the spring of 1949, it was not because of these tensions but because of the inadequate support he thought the school was giving to the social sciences. He wanted to teach in a university that would support his research. This was made clear, for instance, in a letter he wrote to Sherman D. Scruggs, president of Lincoln University in Jefferson City, Missouri, in applying for a job: "I am now employed as head of the

Department of Social Science at Tuskegee Institute; but since there has been an increasingly inconsequential emphasis on the social sciences here, I should be happy to make a change."[34]

Cox was now forty-eight, and his academic record was so impressive that he should have been able to obtain a position wherever he chose. He had published more than twenty articles in the major professional journals in his field, including the *American Journal of Sociology,* the *American Sociological Review,* and *Social Forces.* He was a member of a number of professional organizations, including the Society for Social Research, the Southern Sociological Society, the American Sociological Society, and the National Educational Association. *Caste, Class, and Race,* although never accepted into the mainstream of sociological thought, did earn him recognition outside the sociological fraternity. In 1948, the book's publisher, Doubleday and Company, awarded Cox the George Washington Carver Award. In addition, he was in the process of preparing a second major volume, to be titled *The Foundations of Capitalism,* a study of the historical origins, growth, and development of the capitalist world system.

But there were still few opportunities for a man like Cox in predominantly white colleges and universities, and in July 1949 he therefore accepted a position as associate professor at Lincoln University. There he lived in Allen Hall, the men's dormitory, which was not only inexpensive but put him close to the library, classrooms, and his office—an advantage given his physical disability. Life in a dormitory full of younger men proved something of an ordeal, however; and Cox often complained to the administration about the excessive noise and profanity, which he felt demonstrated a reversion to ghetto behavior that was not conducive to academic excellence. Cox was an articulate and proper man, and the youthful antics of the college dormitory tenants only served to confirm his intellectual understanding of such behavior—a view articulated intellectually in articles published somewhat later that criticized the lifestyle of the black lower class and such black nationalist leaders as took up their cause (see Part 2). Although Cox was a radical in his approach to sociology, he was clearly far more conservative in his personal life.

At Lincoln Cox continued to develop his reputation as a demanding teacher who took his scholarship seriously and expected the same from his students—or those who were brave enough to enroll in his courses. He was known as a perfectionist who published books and gave mostly Cs, and, according to one student, many students deliberately "tracked themselves away from his courses."[35] He believed in upgrading his students' vocabulary through the use of appropriate language, and had a disdain for those who slouched or dozed in their seats. At times his thoroughness made for a slow and ponderous teaching style—sometimes he would take an entire semester to cover two or three chapters in an assigned text. "He would deal with the material comprehensively," recalls one former student, "looking at the same thing from so many different perspectives."[36] On the other hand, many students found him informed and intellectually stimulating.

Institutional constraints gave Cox a teaching load of twelve to fifteen hours a week, which left little time for research and writing. Yet the university administration understood Cox's research needs and also knew that his success as a scholar would bring prestige to the university. Thus, although he funded much of his own research and travel expenses, the university supported him by granting him sabbaticals with half pay, and providing funds for travel to conferences and for typing manuscripts. Nevertheless, while many of his sociological peers, both black and white, served on study commissions and received foundation support for their research, Cox received no such institutional amenities.[37]

Given the resources at his command, the scholarly record Cox established at Lincoln University was remarkable. During his twenty-one years there, he published articles in professional journals and completed his trilogy on capitalism—*The Foundations of Capitalism* (1959), *Capitalism and American Leadership* (1962), and *Capitalism as a System* (1964). Together, these volumes reexamined the historical origins and development of the world capitalist system and provided the basis for an explanation of the political economy of race relations. Cox argued that a significant feature of European capitalist societies, beginning with early Venetian capitalism of the thirteenth century, was the commercial relations they fostered with "backward" areas in the world system. Racial antagonisms found throughout the world were not the cause but the effect of capitalist domination of the less-developed countries. As the articles in Part 4 illustrate, in arguing that for a capitalist nation to dominate in the world capitalist system it had to maintain uneven patterns of development, Cox was introducing a world-system perspective that predated by at least a decade the work of Immanuel Wallerstein and his followers.[38]

In March 1970, nearing the mandatory retirement age of seventy (set by the state of Missouri) Cox informed Walter Daniels, president of the university, that he had decided to retire. He left very quietly, declining festivities and testimonials.[39] He debated moving back to Trinidad, but, as he wrote to his sister, "Too many problems seem to come to mind—not money, but other problems"[40]—a probable reference to his physical condition. At the invitation of Alvin W. Rose, chairman of the department of sociology at Wayne State University in Detroit, Michigan, he accepted the post of Distinguished Visiting Professor of Sociology. He would only have to teach one seminar a semester and assist doctoral students with their dissertation research in the area of race relations. Rose thought Cox would benefit from having a larger audience, advanced graduate students, and a large faculty with whom to discuss his ideas:

> I think he was lonely and very glad that I had invited him. . . . It was a push, more than a pull, in the sense that Lincoln was barren intellectually for his purposes. There wasn't a community of sociologists there at Lincoln and I wanted the students, both black and white, to have a chance to see a good sociologist in seminars and to have him on campus.[41]

As it turned out, however, Wayne State proved to be a disappointment to Cox. He in fact had limited contact with his colleagues, and most of the graduate students were either not interested in his courses or, once again, unprepared to meet his rigorous standards. His classes were therefore small, and few students stayed for more than one semester.

In addition, the climate of the times had changed dramatically. No longer was Marxism necessarily something to be avoided—indeed, it was often forcefully defended. Ironically, this created something of a problem for Cox. In some of his classes he came into conflict with black Marxists who adhered to a rigid analysis of capitalism and who went so far as to accuse him of being "an apologist for the system."[42] But Cox refused to engage in polemics or speak from a "soap box," and he constantly asserted that he was not a Marxist. He insisted on examining both the positive and negative aspects of Marx's thought, as well as of capitalism in general. As one student, Bruce Williams, reports:

> I specifically remember in his course on the sociology of capitalism, Cox was attempting to establish the positive contributions of capitalism, i.e., that capitalism had brought the world into a unified, interdependent system—ending isolation; that it replaced mysticism with science and rational thinking. . . . The black Marxists in the class (three) cursed him out, stormed out and dropped the class, accusing him of being a traitor to the revolution. . . . Those who stayed received one of the best analyses of the system available.[43]

While Cox did not influence a large group of students, he did influence individuals at all the places he taught. As Williams put it, "The brilliance of the man would eventually be demonstrated if one had the patience to wait and listen closely. Thus the key to being a student in his class was to be patient and keep your ears open. You could only do this if you gave him his due as a genius and a scholar."[44]

Back at Wayne State University, Alvin Rose also remembers Cox's teaching differently:

> His lectures were some of the best I ever heard. He always came very well prepared and he took an interest in his teaching. Usually, we would bring twenty graduate students to a class and there was a pattern of students visiting his classes. His mind was so loaded with information that it did turn out sometimes where one question would take him at least one hour to explain, but nonetheless it was very interesting.[45]

Cox's students went on to pursue a variety of careers in academia, social work, and business—many not realizing the richness of his teaching until long after they had left their alma maters.

At Wayne State, Cox continued to write and to generate controversy. He published several articles in the early 1970s, as well as his last major book, *Race Relations: Elements and Social Dynamics* (1976). Much of this work was in response to the reemergence of the black nationalist movement in the late 1960s, and to the resurgence of ethnic consciousness among whites that followed, and was significantly encouraged by the writings of Michael Novak, Andrew Greeley, and others. A strong proponent of assimilation, especially among blacks, Cox was opposed to ethnic solidarity movements of any type, and was critical of those sociological perspectives that were linked with such movements. In one article, published in the British journal *Race* (to which he was a contributing editor for many years), Cox challenged what he believed to be an imprecise use of the term "pluralism." As he noted, the term had been given at least three inconsistent meanings in the social science literature: It had been used as (1) a political concept, in order to discuss the concentration and dispersal of power in society; (2) a legal concept, in order to identify the aims of minority groups in protecting their civil rights and heritage through judicial means; and (3) an economic concept, in order to analyze the larger societal process of colonialism, where capitalism came to dominate and disrupt indigenous native cultures. This debate on ethnic pluralism was not unconnected to Cox's earlier opposition to, and debates with, the

We did not attach to it any great importance and weight like it subsequently . . . gathered in the scholarly world . . . as a really outstanding bit of analysis—quite apart, let us say, from what was a central stream of scholarly tradition in this country on the part of sociologists dealing with this matter of race. You have to realize that in many ways the real center of scholarly, scientific work—sociological work—done in the field of race here in the United States was done in the Department of Sociology at the University of Chicago, going back to the time when Park was there, when Park had developed a distinct reputation and accordingly was attracting young Negro intellectuals here in the United States, as represented by Charles S. Johnson and E. Franklin Frazier and a number of others. That was a tradition at Chicago and it represented, as a group, an approach to the study of race relations along the lines of Park's whole scheme of analysis.

Now Oliver's book was not in that tradition. A very different approach. And what is of interest, too, is the fact that when Oliver was there in the Department of Sociology, he was not participating in this group that was preoccupied with this whole topic of race as a scientific problem, as it had been developed by Park and carried on by Wirth and some of the rest of us.

Q. Was the book ignored? Well, I wouldn't say it was ignored. I would say, to use the term—which perhaps should not be misunderstood but is perhaps applicable—it was kind of downgraded. It wasn't scholarly; it was regarded as kind of a doctrinaire sort of an approach, over against what I have been emphasizing here as a sort of—presumably—a kind of scientific detachment.

Q. Did anybody see a need to respond to Cox?

No, I don't think there was any response. I don't recall, for example, that Wirth, who was at the forefront of this, took any particular interest in that work of Cox. So it is in this sense that it was not ignored, but sort of minimized. . . .

[The reaction was] it's a work, it's all right, it's nothing outstanding, and it doesn't really represent the direction that real sociological scholarship should follow in dealing with the matter of race. I am inclined to think—and I am putting this in my own words here at the moment—but I am inclined to think that there was the judgment on the part of people like Wirth, Burgess, and others that Oliver was coming in with a kind of political motivation and political slant in his work over against the essence of how Park and the students of Park were approaching this whole matter of race.[64]

One student of Park's, Everett C. Hughes, wrote a review of the book in the journal *Phylon*. He centered his attack on what he saw as Cox's deceptive reasoning. Coming to the defense of caste theory, Hughes argued that Cox's argument was both inadequate and unacceptable: ". . . the utmost sophistry that he [Cox] turned his whole work, by colossal verbal twist, into an argument *ad hominum;*

that he aggravates all of this by freely using without credit such of his opponents' ideas as he approves of, while he names them only for purposes of attack."[65] The "verbal twist" was Cox's use of the term "caste," and his failure one of method: "Instead of using it [caste] as a concept to refer to some group of social phemonena whose limits and likenesses and differences are to be discovered by careful comparative analysis, he uses the term as the proper name of the social system of India."[66] This completely ignored, of course, the very basis of Cox's analysis, which was to contrast India with the United States.

Hughes refused to acknowledge Cox's method as valid, instead calling him doctrinaire: -

> I, Cox, elect to say that caste is the proper name of the social system of India as I conceive it to have been sometime or other. I will not tolerate that anyone should use a comparative concept. In India—at least in my idealized India—all those who suffer status disabilities glory in their misery. (Although, of course, they live right that they may do better in another incarnation.) Therefore, anyone who uses this term to refer to American race relations says that American Negroes also glory in their misery. Such people are blind to the aspirations of the American Negro, and assume that the color bar will always remain as it is—as I, Cox, assume will be the case with the caste system in India, barring *force majeur* applied from without.[67]

Cox responded:

> It seems that Dr. Hughes read chapter 22, "The Modern Caste School of Race Relations," and, finding it positively opposed to his own views as a member of that School, decided it was sufficient to comment upon its content with scarcely a condescending glance at the other twenty-four chapters. Since "The Modern Caste School of Race Relations" appeared essentially as it now stands under the same title as an article in *Social Forces*, Dec., 1942, the editor might have sent Professor Hughes that article for review instead of the book. *At any rate, until now the article has not been answered by any member of the caste school.*[68]

Cox's black peers gave him no more recognition than his white ones. They too had largely been trained at Chicago and while their minority status compelled them to be critical of racial segregation and discrimination, they were less critical of research in this area than was Cox. As Charles Smith and Lewis Killian have written in their analysis of social protest in the writings of the black sociologists of this generation, these scholars did not attack white American civilization and its values to the extent that we would expect today from those associated with black cultural and/or revolutionary nationalism.[69] Cox, in contrast, was openly suggesting that fundamental political and economic problems had to be resolved in order for race relations in the United States to change.

One result of the neglect of Cox's work is that there are few discussions of his ideas in the works of the black sociologists of the 1940s and 1950s, and he received few invitations to lecture from those black institutions that had attained some visibility and prestige in the social sciences. As Alvin Rose reports:

> Cox had no choice but to stay on the fringes of scholarship because the centers of scholarship as far as the Black community was concerned were at Atlanta, Fisk, and Howard. That was it, and those were people Cox did not identify with. Johnson and Frazier, not the Black institutions, would determine who came to Fisk or Howard. Johnson brought people from all over the world to Fisk, but never invited Cox; nor do I believe that Cox was ever invited to Howard. I was surprised when Ira Reid left Atlanta and was replaced by Mozell Hill. The attitude in those days, simply put, was that Cox was not to be taken seriously. I know it was Frazier's attitude and I know it was Johnson's. I remember sitting up one night talking with Frazier and I think Frazier viewed Cox as a person with problems that we just had to understand.[70]

For his part, of course, Cox had little time for people like Johnson and Frazier. Butler Jones had written that "Oliver Cox, the theoretician among black sociologists, but never a serious threat to Johnson's status, has at times spoken of Johnson with what can be judged as contempt."[71] Cox was even more critical of Frazier and his attachment to Park and the Chicago School. Writing retrospectively, he observed:

> It was Frazier's lot to be a student at the University of Chicago when three great sociologists, Ellsworth Faris, William F. Ogburn, and Robert E. Park, dominated the department. I have become convinced, from my personal association with and study of these men, that they were profound liberals in the sense in which that term is currently defined by direct-action leaders. They were men possessed of praiseworthy attitudes toward Negroes, but still strongly opposed to any definition of them as fully equal to whites; they were willing to do many things *for* Negroes but sternly opposed to Negroes taking such initiative as would move them along faster than a *proper* pace; and they would rather turn conservative than tolerate independent thinking or acting Negroes.[72]

Frazier, Cox believed, had promoted his career through compromise with the sociological establishment. He wrote:

> One can discern most clearly the hand of Park on the intellectual life of Frazier. . . . His professional career had to be contrived on the

tightrope set up by the associational establishment. He won many prizes and honors, but the exigencies of winning involved his soul and his manhood. Sometimes *Black Bourgeoise* is compared to the *Theory of the Leisure Class* and to *White Collar*. It is, in my opinion, nothing of the sort. Had Frazier assumed the posture of Veblen or Mills, he would doubtless have been even more completely consigned to outer darkness, to endure in silence the agony of his ways. He hardly confronted even tangentially a real power structure.[73]

Cox avoided what he perceived to be white intellectual paternalism, which locked many black sociologists into the prevailing view of the race problem. Aware of the professional rewards to be accrued by those closely associated with the institutional establishment in sociology, he was nevertheless uncompromisingly critical of those whites he believed were perpetuating a conservative view of race relations behind the facade of value neutrality and scientific objectivity. For Cox, the race problem in the United States could not be solved with moralistic arguments proving that society was wrong, or by pursuing a detached "science" that did not raise structural issues and place intellectual problems in the context of the wider society.

The Continuing Neglect of Cox's Work

Caste, Class, and Race was allowed to go out of print as soon as the first edition was exhausted in 1949.[74] It was ten years before it was reissued, a task undertaken by Monthly Review Press, at that time a small enterprise publishing only a few books a year. Regardless of the rationale underlying Doubleday's decision—whether it was the result of succumbing to Cold War hysteria or because of lack of sales (an indication of a wider neglect)—the fact remains that Cox's ideas continued to be disregarded, even when they were read. This pattern of neglect was even more glaring in the case of the trilogy on capitalism than the work on race—particularly given the recent upsurge in interest in world-systems theory. Cox was, moreover, omitted altogether from John H. Bracy, August Meier, and Elliot Rudwick's *The Black Sociologists*, one of the first anthologies to present selections from the writings of black sociologists. In their introduction, the editors defend their omission by claiming that "Cox, an independent thinker, stood apart from the dominant tradition in the sociology of American race relations, and exerted little influence on later scholars."[75] And in Morris Janowitz and James E. Blackwell's *The Black Sociologists*, the scant three pages devoted to Cox are completely overshadowed by full-length articles on Johnson, DuBois, and Frazier, whom the authors call the "founding figures" among black sociologists.[76] Had Blackwell and Janowitz been objective, they would have acknowledged that after the death of Frazier in 1962 there was no other black sociologist equal in stature to Cox.

On those occasions when Cox is cited in the literature on social stratification or race relations, he receives only the most perfunctory treatment. He is usually referred to simply as a major opponent of caste theories of race relations and the originator of a classical Marxist class analysis of racial exploitation. His contributions to world-systems theory are ignored altogether.

What little recognition Cox has received has come from a group of younger black social scientists, themselves often outside the mainstream of the discipline. The Association of Social and Behavioral Scientists, composed largely of black scholars, awarded Cox its first W. E. B. DuBois Award in 1968 for his contribution in the field of race relations. A few years later, as black sociologists saw the need to rediscover the contribution of older scholars, Cox was (ironically) the first to receive the newly established DuBois-Johnson-Frazier Award (in 1971), sponsored by the Caucus of Black Sociologists.

Cox's association with Marxism has both facilitated and hindered his subsequent recognition by young sociologists. On the one hand, as Marxism has emerged as a valid alternative perspective within U.S. sociology in general, both Marxist and non-Marxist writers interested in the role of class conflict and power in race relations have begun to reexamine Cox's work. On the other hand, as mainstream sociology continues to consider Marxism a "limited" way of interpreting class, Cox continues to be branded a Marxist and dismissed. On both counts, the critique has in part been the result of a narrow reading of Cox's work, with *Caste, Class, and Race* the only work considered (and not all of it at that), while the writings on capitalism are ignored.

Cox: A Marxist Intellectual or an Intellectual Radical?

This is, then, a good place to consider what Cox's theoretical orientation really was. Cox's approach to Marx, and to Marxist theory in general, often seems inconsistent, and Marxists and non-Marxists alike have engaged in much argument over the precise nature of his theoretical orientation.[77] Cox relied unabashedly on

Marx for much of his critique of capitalist society, and recognized the outstanding contributions of Marx's theory to the study of society in general. On the other hand, he firmly objected to being affiliated with what he called the "religious Marxists" because of their rigid adherence to a dogmatic brand of Marxism. Moreover, he criticized some of Marx's essential theoretical precepts, and disavowed Marx himself whenever that name was associated with unscientific thinking. Thus he criticized Marx's theory of class, which he argued failed to offer a precise enough definition of classes themselves; and, as noted below, when he analyzed the historical origins, growth, and development of capitalism as a world system, he repudiated Marx's labor theory of value, arguing that surplus value was derived not simply from the exploitation of labor in the sphere of the factory (within the nation-state), but also in trade among nations in the larger world economy.

It might seem, then, that Cox was a "plain" Marxist, as C. Wright Mills used the term. He argued that one could work openly and flexibly with Marx's ideas without embracing all that Marx said.[78] Yet Cox's acceptance of Marx and Marxist theory was a cautious one, an acceptance predicated on two essential factors: First, Cox did not embrace Marxist theory out of direct theoretical and political conviction, but rather as the end result of a process of independent investigation and theoretical elimination. Second, Cox was primarily concerned with Marx's method, and rejected outright any ideological commitment that might be associated with an adherence to Marxism. Thus in the preface to *Caste, Class, and Race*, he declared that his attachment to Marxist theory rested on its greater explanatory power when compared to other theories: "If, therefore, parts of this study seem Marxian, it is not because we have taken the ideas of the justly famous writer as gospel, but because we have not discovered any other that could explain the facts so consistently." He drew a distinction between Marx and the "religious marxists," disclaiming any association with the latter:

> At best, Marxian hypotheses are "servants, not masters." Indeed, it has been said that Karl Marx himself was not a Marxian because in his studies he strived to understand modern society, while religious Marxists, in their exegetical discussions, center their attention not upon the ongoing social system but rather upon an explanation and criticism of Marx—a sort of rumination of his conclusions, incidental errors and all.[79]

In other words, independent thinkers should be free to draw on any body of knowledge as long as it proved scientifically sound—

one need not be a Marxist in order to benefit from Marx's approach.

Cox leaned on two principal aspects of Marx's methodology. First, like Marx, his approach was historical, and his research into the actual conditions of human social life was anti-idealist, fundamentally materialist, and historically specific. Thus, to give but one example, he challenged the widely accepted notion that racism had existed throughout history, instead arguing that it emerged with the advent of capitalism and colonialism.

Cox followed Marx in another significant respect. He, like Marx, placed a great deal of emphasis on the significance of labor and on the centrality of class divisions in the development of racism. Thus, after discussing the spread of European capitalism, he demonstrated the role of African slaves and black tenant farmers in the system of capitalist production relations. On the basis of economic interests, he argued, the "white ruling class" developed a corresponding ideology in order to justify and rationalize existing relations of production. The resulting "political-class struggle" is inextricably connected to racial antagonism and constitutes its central dynamic core.

Thus in methodological approach, conceptual language, and mode of analysis, Cox seems to us today to be very much a Marxist. Indeed, any reader of *Caste, Class, and Race,* Marxist or non-Marxist, can hardly come to any other conclusion. Yet in his trilogy on capitalism, Cox is not content to accept Marx's theory of capitalism at face value. He finds it necessary to rediscover and rethink the origin of capitalism from its early beginning in Venice. One of the most controversial points he makes in *The Foundations of Capitalism,* for example, is that capitalism originated in Venice as a result of chance circumstances that led the city-state to rise to prominence. He then argues that an unbroken process of growth links the "infant" capitalism of Venice to the "mature" capitalism of the United States. Venice prospered and gained influence throughout Europe and the East through the development of foreign trade—a pattern that was followed by other Italian city-states, by the Hanseatic League, and by Holland. Cox thus argues two related points: that capitalism has always expanded and developed on the basis of foreign trade; and that capitalist societies have been from their inception part of a world system and thus by nature open and dynamic, not closed. This argument directly challenged both Marx and those of his followers who argued that capitalism grew out of the declining feudal order, and developed in the closed system of

English industrial capitalism.[80] Cox further argues that even the amendments to Marx's theory made by Lenin, Rosa Luxemburg, and Maurice Dobb, while placing more emphasis on the imperialistic strivings of the capitalist nations, do not correct the fundamental errors in Marx's theoretical conception of capitalism:

> Having accepted the fundamental Marxian postulates on the nature of capitalist society, Marxists cannot go back to Venetian, Hanseatic, Dutch or even early English imperialism for the essential concepts of the components of that phenomenon. It thus becomes a crucially limiting position which entails procrustean operations in the handling of the facts of modern social change as they relentlessly impose themselves upon us. The rigid ideas concerning the role of industrial workers in modern revolutionary movements, and the earlier Marxian predictions giving precedence to the more advanced capitalist nations in the succession of socialist revolutions, are all derivatives of the theory.[82]

But it is one thing to point out Marx's shortcomings—many Marxists, after all, do that, placing Marx in the context of the time in which he lived and developed his theory. It is quite another to claim that Marxism, as practiced by Marx's followers, is simply the "ideological" consequence of political practice—and this is what Cox argues in *Capitalism as a System:*

> But Marx and his immediate colleague, Frederick Engels, were also major leaders of anti-capitalist action groups; and, in that capacity, they assumed the normal charismatic aura of outstanding leadership. The completely rational analysis of society formulated by these thinkers can scarcely be expected of their followers [*sic!*]. To be sure, this is also true—in reverse fashion, so to speak—of the capitalist leadership and its dedicated scholars: a diabolical image tends spontaneously to be evoked whenever any Marxian concept is brought into their purview. They do not allow critical thinking free play. Moreover, because the preponderance of power rests in the existing elite, we should expect and find more flagrant and effectual manifestations of intolerance on their side.[83]

According to Cox, Marx's theory is not based on a scientific analysis, as one ought to expect, but appears as a theoretical justification that is used to cloak his "proletarian ideology." To quote Cox once again:

> He [Marx] contrived with remarkable success to become the ideological leader of this [proletarian] class; and then devoted the rest of his intellectual life mainly to a study of the economics and sociology of capitalism in order to provide a theoretical foundation for his proletarian ideology. It goes without saying that if Marx's preoccupation

had originally been the *scientific* study of capitalism as a form of social organization, with only a derived interest in the contemporary class struggle, his entire theoretical work would have been differently informed.[84]

Two related points should be noted about this passage. First, assuming that Marx did indeed seek a theoretical foundation for his proletarian ideology, there is no reason to conclude that such a pursuit would of necessity be *unscientific*. After all, Marx's theorizing and political praxis went hand in hand. Second, Cox suggests that had Marx remained detached from the ongoing class struggle, he would have developed a different (a Coxian?) view of capitalism. Here he reveals his own view of science while simultaneously failing to grasp an essential aspect of Marx's theory: the notion of social praxis.[85]

Cox objected to being called a Marxist, and certainly was not perceived as such by his closest associates and friends.[86] In his posthumously published volume, *Race Relations,* he not only explicitly challenged Marxist theory but also noted that he had been falsely "accused" of being a Marxist: "They have accused the writer of 'economic determinism,' 'Marxism,' or of seeking to explain race relations 'solely,' 'only,' 'merely,' 'exclusively' on the basis of economics."[87] A footnote refers the reader to a section of *Capitalism as a System* in which Cox elaborated on his most pungent criticism of Marxist theory.[88]

Cox's intellectual independence has been commented on by many writers. In his Foreword to *The Foundations of Capitalism,* Harry Elmer Barnes distinguished between two extremes in scholarship, "libertarians" and "radical collectivists," and concluded that Cox belonged to neither. Rather, he put Cox in a third group, the "realistic scholars"—a group that Barnes might well have included himself in as well. Barnes's reasoning is worth quoting at length:

> Libertarians, not unduly alarmed by the current trends toward collectivism and state action, even in the so-called free nations, ardently urge a return to the free enterprise of the days of the Physiocrats, Adam Smith and David Ricardo. The radical collectivists assume that the days of capitalism are numbered if, indeed, they do not view the system as a sort of economic antiquity or museum piece. Realistic scholars, not committed in advance to either extreme, are seeking to understand its origins, nature, present state, and future trends. They recognize that the economic world was never in a more fluid or unpredictable condition than it is today. So far as I can judge by this first volume of Professor Cox's projected three-volume work on the history and theoretical analysis of capitalism as a social system, the author belongs to this third group.[89]

As this passage indicates, Barnes believed that a safe and scholarly middle ground exists wherein one can avoid the ideological battering that accompanies the struggle between Left and Right.

If Cox did not consider himself a Marxist, but nevertheless borrowed heavily from Marxist theory and method—which was, after all, not uncommon at the time—then how is he to be situated theoretically? Perhaps the best way to describe Cox is as a critical theorist, one who draws on a number of "classical" thinkers (including Weber, Sombart, Marx, Durkheim, to name only a few) to pursue a line of inquiry using a historical materialist and comparative approach. But it is important to point out that Cox was not eclectic in his approach, even though he was influenced by a number of thinkers with opposing views (e.g., Durkheim and Marx). Rather, Cox always began with a historically specific society viewed as a system—be it the Venetian city-state, the Hanseatic League, Hindu caste society, or U.S. capitalism:

> After addressing themselves in this fashion to the economic aspects of race relations, these scholars usually move on to emphasize certain startling psychological or political incidents, implying that these are at least as significant for an analysis of the society. Such approaches may seem to satisfy the requirements of a detached eclectism, but they can hardly arrive at a conception of race relations as societally determined, that is, if we think of society as a definable pattern of social relations. The economics of all societies are socially defined, but social factors do not limit the operation of the economic order in the same way in all societies.[90]

Cox's respect for, and dependence on, the classical sociological thinkers puts him in the company of C. Wright Mills, another contemporary sociologist who was often disparagingly labeled a radical. Both men shared a respect for the classical tradition in sociology and saw themselves as a part of it. Both men respected Marx and used his insights, and both were repeatedly accused of dogged adherence to simple economic and political formulas and interpretations. With Cox, in particular, a concern for societal and controversial issues was interpreted as Marxist; a creative application of certain aspects of Marx's theory and method was seen as confirming their dogmatism; and, finally, a respect for Marx's colossal intellectual production was reason for excommunication from the sociological community. Cox was then a radical intellectual in the classical tradition of both C. Wright Mills and Thorstein Veblen. He thought of himself as an independent thinker, a scholar, and a social scientist. As an intellectual craftsman, he pursued a line of inquiry reminiscent of an earlier period of classical thinkers. Like them, he preferred to tackle the most controversial issues of the day. Unlike many of his contemporaries, he refused to sidestep or blindly malign Marx (even though he disagreed with some essential aspects of Marx's theory) in order to demonstrate his orthodoxy in the sociological fraternity and thus gain success and fame in official circles. He was a rebel and an iconoclast at a time when it was fashionable to vociferously pronounce one's anti-Marxism and adherence to official canon. He paid dearly for his unwillingness to conform. His works were relegated to relative obscurity in the sociological profession and he was never offered an academic post commensurate with his achievements. He refused to compromise his integrity as a scholar, even when he was roundly criticized for his Marxist borrowings. He openly declared his intellectual debt to Marx, but freely renounced those aspects of Marx's theory that he found dogmatic or incompatible with the historical dynamics of capitalism as a world system and the transition from capitalism to socialism. He may have seen himself as an "independent" radical thinker, but in today's class-and-race-divided world, Oliver C. Cox can justifiably be considered a distinguished and creative fellow-traveler among Marxists, albeit an independent one.

Notes

1. Some of the material included in this introduction has appeared in a previously published article and has been revised for this book; see Herbert M. Hunter, "Oliver C. Cox: A Biographical Sketch of His Life and Work," *Phylon* 44, no. 4 (December 1983): 249–61.
2. Elmer P. Martin, "The Sociology of Oliver C. Cox: A Systematic Inquiry" (Master's Thesis, Atlanta University, 1971), p. 12.
3. Interview with Stella Awon-Cox, Port-of-Spain, Trinidad, May 18, 1978.
4. Virginia Blake Cox gave birth to six children, four sons and two daughters. Through a second marriage, to Louisa Cox, two additional sons and a sister were added to the Cox family. Several of Oliver Cox's brothers and sisters died at a relatively early age; one brother, Ethelbert Cox, and a sister, Stella Awon-Cox, are still living.
5. Interview with Aldwin Vidale, Petel Valley, Trinidad, May 19, 1978.
6. Ibid.
7. Ibid.
8. Interview with Stella Awon-Cox.
9. Ibid.
10. See Jan Knippers Black et al., *Area Handbook for Trinidad and Tobago*

(Washington, D.C., 1976), p. 78. For an analysis of the socioeconomic conditions of Trinidad in the early twentieth century see also Eric Williams, *Inward Hunger: The Education of a Prime Minister* (London, 1969).

11. Interview with Oliver C. Cox by Elmer P. Martin, November 19, 1970.
12. Harry Elmer Barnes, "Foreword," in Oliver C. Cox, *The Foundations of Capitalism* (New York, 1959), p. 11.
13. Oliver C. Cox. "Workingmen's Compensation in the United States, with Critical Observations and Suggestions," (Master's Thesis, The University of Chicago, 1932).
14. Ibid., p. 117.
15. Interview with Oliver C. Cox by Elmer P. Martin.
16. Oliver C. Cox. "Factors Affecting the Marital Status of Negroes in the United States," (Ph.D. diss., The University of Chicago, 1938).
17. For example, if Allison Davis's criticism that as a sociologist Cox had "done no sustained empirical research on human communities" is meant to equate quantitative methods with empirical research, it should be noted that Cox continued to demonstrate his training and skill in statistical analysis after leaving the University of Chicago (see Allison Davis, "Mystical Sociology," *The Journal of Negro Education* 17 [Spring 1948]: 161). In this connection we refer to several statistical studies published by Cox in the early 1940s: "Sex Ratio and Marital Status among Negroes," *American Sociological Review* 5 (December 1940): 937–47; "Farm Tenancy and Marital Status and Employment of Women," *Sociology and Social Research* 25 (December 1940): 155–65; "Sex Ratio and Marriage in Rural Communities," *Rural Sociology* 5 (June 1940): 222–27; "Provisions for Graduate Education among Negroes," *Journal of Negro Education* 9 (January 1940): 22–31; and "Employment, Education and Marriage," *Journal of Negro Education* 10 (January 1941): 39–42. Of course Cox's theoretical arguments are also firmly based on empirical data.
18. For a brief discussion of an early debate about statistics and the case study method among Chicago sociologists, see Robert E. L. Faris. *Chicago Sociology: 1920–1932* (San Francisco, 1967), pp. 114–15.
19. See Cox, "Factors Affecting the Marital Status of Negroes," p. 11.
20. An excellent analysis of the experiences of black social scientists teaching in black colleges may be found in Butler Jones, "Tradition of Sociology Teaching in Black Colleges: The Unheralded Professionals," in *Black Sociologists: Historical and Contemporary Perspectives,* ed. James E. Blackwell and Morris Janowitz (Chicago, 1974), pp. 121–63.
21. In Hunter, "Oliver C. Cox: A Biographical Sketch of His Life and Work," Wiley College is identified as a Baptist school. It has since been brought to our attention that the religious denomination of Wiley College is Methodist. We are indebted to Darnell D. Thomas of Texarkana, Texas for this correction.
22. Martin, "The Sociology of Oliver C. Cox," p. 16.

23. Addie Louise Joyner Butler, *The Distinctive Black College: Talladega, Tuskegee and Morehouse* (Metuchen, N.J., 1977), p. 90.
24. Telephone interview with Charles G. Gomillion, Washington, D.C., May 23, 1978.
25. Interview with Gomillion.
26. Martin, "The Sociology of Oliver C. Cox," p. 17.
27. Letter from Oliver C. Cox to F. D. Patterson, president of Tuskegee Institute, September 15, 1945, quoted in ibid.
28. Butler Jones, "The Tradition of Sociology Teaching in Black Colleges," p. 153.
29. Interview with Gomillion.
30. In fact, one author has referred to the Southern Negro Congress as a "communist front organization"; see William A. Nolan, *Communism Versus the Negro* (Chicago, 1951), p. 578.
31. See footnote in Oliver C. Cox, *Caste, Class, and Race* (New York, 1970), p. 578.
32. Interview with Lewis Wade Jones, Tuskegee Institute, Tuskegee, Alabama, January 4, 1978.
33. See Oliver C. Cox, "The Leadership of Booker T. Washington," *Social Forces* 30, no. 1 (October 1951): 95. See also "The New Crisis in Leadership Among Negroes," *Journal of Negro Education* 19 (Fall 1950) 459–65; "Leadership Among Negroes in the United States," in *Studies in Leadership*, ed. Alvin Gouldner (New York, 1950), pp. 228–71; "The Programs of Negro Civil Rights Organizations," *Journal of Negro Education* 20 (Summer 1951): 354–66.
34. Letter from Oliver C. Cox to Sherman D. Scruggs, April 26, 1949.
35. Interview with Charles Key, University of Massachusetts, Amherst, March 10, 1978.
36. Ibid. Another student who attended Cox's classes at Lincoln University provides additional insight into Cox's slow and ponderous manner of teaching by noting that "Dr. Cox was more concerned with a student's substantive comprehension of an idea, concept or paradigm than he was with how much material was covered in a given time frame." (correspondence from Joseph Henry, graduate student in American Studies, The University of Iowa, October 8, 1984).
37. Cox did seek support for his research from the Carnegie and Ford Foundations during his career, but in both cases his proposals were rejected.
38. Cf. Immanuel Wallerstein, *The Modern World System* (New York, 1974), and Barbara Hockey Kaplan, ed. *Social Change in the Capitalist World Economy* (Beverly Hills, Calif., 1978).
39. Interview with Lorenzo Greene, Lincoln University, Jefferson City, Missouri, February 17, 1978.
40. Letter from Oliver C. Cox to Stella Awon-Cox, June 8, 1970.
41. Interview with Alvin W. Rose, University of Miami, Coral Gables, Florida, May 16, 1980.

42. Correspondence with Bruce Williams, Vanderbilt University, Nashville, Tennessee, March 16, 1980.
43. Ibid.
44. Ibid.
45. Interview with Alvin Rose.
46. Oliver C. Cox, "Jewish Self-interest in Black Pluralism," *The Sociological Quarterly* 15 (Spring 1974): 183–189.
47. "Comments on Cox," *The Sociological Quarterly* 16, no. 1. (Winter 1975):131–134.
48. Geoffrey Perrett, *A Dream of Greatness: The American People, 1945–1963* (New York, 1979), p. 72.
49. Cabell Phillips, *The 1940s: Decade of Triumph and Trouble* (New York, 1975), p. 364.
50. David Caute, *The Great Fear: The Anti-Communist Purge under Truman and Eisenhower* (New York, 1978), p. 404.
51. Ibid.
52. Cox, *Caste, Class, and Race*, p. 223.
53. Letter from Howard Becker to Oliver C. Cox, August 23, 1946; quoted in Martin, "The Sociology of Oliver C. Cox," p. 85.
54. Letter from William B. Selgby, editor, Public Affairs Press to Oliver C. Cox, August 26, 1960; quoted in Martin, "The Sociology of Oliver C. Cox," p. 22.
55. Letter from Paul M. Sweezy to Oliver C. Cox, July 20, 1949; quoted in Martin, "The Sociology of Oliver C. Cox," p. 80.
56. Letter from Benjamin J. Davis, Jr., to Oliver C. Cox, September 9, 1948; quoted in Martin, "The Sociology of Oliver C. Cox," pp. 79, 80.
57. Quoted ibid., p. 2.
58. Quoted in ibid., p. 83.
59. Ibid.
60. See Roscoe C. Hinkle, Jr., and Gisela J. Hinkle, *The Development of Modern Sociology* (New York, 1954), p. 47.
61. Interview with Alvin W. Rose.
62. See Winifred Raushenbush, *Robert E. Park: Biography of a Sociologist* (Durham, N.C., 1979), p. 197.
63. James T. Carey, *Sociology and Public Affairs: The Chicago School* (Beverly Hills, Calif., 1975), p. 155.
64. Interview with Herbert Blumer, University of California, Berkeley, California, January 9, 1978.
65. Everett C. Hughes, Review of *Caste, Class, and Race* by Oliver C. Cox, *Phylon* 9 (March 1948): 66.
66. Ibid., p. 67.
67. Ibid.
68. Oliver C. Cox, Rejoinder to Everett C. Hughes's review of *Caste, Class, and Race, Phylon* 9 (June 1948): 171; emphasis added.
69. Charles U. Smith and Lewis Killian, "Black Sociologists and Social Protest," in *Black Sociologists*, p. 199.
70. Interview with Alvin Rose.

71. Jones, "Tradition of Sociology Teaching in Black Colleges, p. 163.
72. Oliver C. Cox. "Introduction," in Nathan Hare, *The Black Anglo Saxons* (New York, 1970), p. 28.
73. Ibid., p. 30.
74. This section draws on an earlier paper by Sameer Y. Abraham, "Oliver C. Cox's (Neglected) Contributions Toward a Theory of Race Relations," presented at the annual meeting of the North Central Sociological Association, Dayton, Ohio, May 1–3, 1980.
75. John H. Bracy, Jr., August Meier, and Elliot Rudwick, *The Black Sociologist: The First Half Century* (Belmont, Calif., 1971), p. 12.
76. Blackwell and Janowitz, eds., *Black Sociologists*, p. xii.
77. This section draws on an earlier paper by Sameer Y. Abraham, "Oliver C. Cox: An Independent Contribution to Marxist Theory," presented at the Fourth Annual Conference on the Current State of Marxist Theory, University of Louisville, November 15–17, 1979. Also see Herbert M. Hunter, "Oliver C. Cox: Marxist or Intellectual Radical?" *Journal of the History of Sociology* 5, no. 1 (Spring 1983): 1–27.
78. C. Wright Mills was accused by many of being a Marxist, although many thought him un-Marxist or even anti-Marxist. In 1957, he said he had never been a Marxist; in 1962 he wrote as a "plain Marxist" in criticizing "vulgar" and "sophisticated" Marxists for trying to rationalize and repair Marx's outmoded model rather than using Marx's method to construct a new and credible picture of a changed reality. See *The Marxist* (New York, 1962), pp. 96–104.
79. Cox, *Caste, Class, and Race*, p. xi.
80. Marx's view of the subject can be located in Eric J. Hobsbawm, *Karl Marx: Pre-Capitalist Economic Formations* (New York, 1964), and Maurice Dobb, "Marx and Pre-Capitalist Economic Formations," *Science and Society* 30 (Summer 1966): 1–11.
81. Cox specifically refers to the following Marxists here: Vladimir Lenin, *Imperialism: The Highest Stage of Capitalism* (Peking, 1967); Maurice Dobb, *Political Economy of Capitalism* (London, 1937); and Rosa Luxemburg, *The Accumulation of Capital* (New Haven, 1951).
    It appears odd that so thorough a scholar as Cox would deliberately neglect key works in this area, namely, Nikolai Bukharin, *Imperialism and World Economy* (New York, 1929); idem, *Imperialism and the Accumulation of Capital* (New York, 1973); and Paul Baran, *The Political Economy of Growth* (New York, 1962). This seeming neglect points to Cox's superficial reading of the Marxist literature.
82. Cox, *Capitalism as a System* (New York, 1964), p. 218.
83. Ibid., p. 210.
84. Ibid., p. 212.
85. For a discussion of social praxis, the reader is referred to Karl Korsch, *Three Essays on Marxism* (New York, 1972), and Shlomo Avineri, *The Social and Political Thought of Karl Marx* (New York, 1968).
86. See Morgan, "In Memoriam: Oliver Cox," 1901–1974," *Monthly Review* 28, no. 1 (May 1976), p. 35. One of Cox's former classmates and long-

time friends, Charles Parrish at the University of Louisville, in a recent conversation reaffirmed the fact that Cox was not a Marxist.

87. Oliver C. Cox, *Race Relations: Elements and Social Dynamics* (Detroit, 1976), p. 6.
88. See Cox, *Capitalism as a System,* pp. 212–18.
89. Harry Elmer Barnes, Foreword to Cox, *The Foundations of Capitalism,* pp. 5, 6.
90. Oliver C. Cox, *Race Relations,* p. 6.

1

A Critique of the Caste School of Race Relations

Caste interpretations of black-white relations in the United States gained considerable popularity among social scientists, particularly social anthropologists, in the late 1930s and throughout the 1940s. Armed with the notion that certain characteristics found in non-Western caste systems were applicable to the U.S. race problem, these observers argued that the unequal distribution of rights and privileges found in the southern United States provided evidence of a racial caste system that structured relationships between a dominant white caste and a subordinate black caste. According to this view, race was an ascriptive and unchangeable feature of racial caste, so that although individuals might change their socioeconomic status, they would always remain members of their racial caste; restrictions on intermarriage were considered analogous to endogamous marriage patterns in traditional caste systems; and it was believed that a whole system of attitudes and practices was enforced to relegate blacks to an inferior position in society. A few investigators, including W. Lloyd Warner, also sought to show how caste and class, two concepts often thought to be mutually exclusive, in fact operated within a single community.

Oliver Cox became the leading opponent of the caste-class model of race relations, and waged a systematic and single-handed assault on its basic tenets. He argued that race relations in the United States were qualitatively different from caste relations, which were unique to India. It was his selective use of a Marxian historical materialist approach, which analyzed social life in terms of a particular time and place, that distinguished him from his more liberal contemporaries.

1

This section includes representative articles and excerpts that illustrate Cox's criticism of the caste school. The first selection, "The Modern Caste School of Race Relations," was Cox's initial effort to debunk the work of social scientists influenced by Warner's conception of class and caste. Cox argues that the caste concept can be applied only to Hindu society in India, a unique social system that be believed U.S. social scientists had not studied systematically and did not understand. He also thought that the basic concepts Warner employed were logically inconsistent and lacked sufficient supporting evidence for the analogies being proposed. For one thing, unlike racial divisions in the United States, Indian caste society "carries within itself no basic antagonism," according to Cox, since its members are fully assimilated into the society. The application of the caste model to the United States therefore mystified both the process and origins of race relations, which resulted from labor exploitation under capitalism, a point elaborated in the fourth selection.

In the second selection, "An American Dilemma: A Mystical Approach to the Study of Race Relations," Cox criticizes Gunnar Myrdal's classic book, *An American Dilemma,* published in 1944. Here he argues that while Myrdal's work was impressive and the product of considerable scholarly collaboration among liberal social scientists, it suffered from two major problems: First, it ignored the fundamental class struggle between the southern oligarchy and black and white workers, and second, it settled for an acceptable normative interpretation of race relations. Cox argues further that Myrdal's approach was unavoidable given his reliance on a caste analysis and his failure to recognize the more critical social determinants of race relations in the United States. He deplores Myrdal's argument that poor whites played a key role in the oppression of blacks, and that sexual relations involving white women and black men were the primary motivation behind white discrimination. He also rejects Myrdal's theory that white prejudice and the economic status of blacks are inversely related, creating a "vicious circle" whereby white prejudice increases as the economic situation of blacks improves. He instead argues that these are dependent variables, "produced by the calculating economic interest of the southern oligarchy."

In the third selection, "Race and Caste: A Distinction," Cox takes his analysis of U.S. race relations a step further by comparing different features of caste society in India with race relations in capitalist society. Caste society, he argues, is ancient, nonconflictual, occupationally limited, hypergamous, and endogamous. Capitalism, in contrast, is a modern, profit-oriented system that is exploitative and based on a mobile wage-labor force that is restricted by the controllers of labor, who seek to inhibit the assimilation of subordinate groups such as blacks.

The conceptual distinctions that Cox introduced into this debate not only contributed to the clarification of an often muddled analysis, but also helped to shape the thinking of a growing number of sociologists. In addition, Cox analyzed in depth the growth of racial anatagonism in modern capitalist societies. This analysis appeared briefly in the critiques of the caste school, but was extended in the fourth selection, "Race Relations: Its Meaning, Beginning, and Progress." Here the central hypothesis is that "racial exploitation and race prejudice developed among Europeans with the rise of capitalism and nationalism, and that because of the worldwide ramifications of capitalism, all racial antagonism can be traced to the policies and attitudes of the leading capitalist people, the white people of Europe and North Amercia." Cox argues that racial prejudice is not to be found in earlier civilizations, where cultural and religious differences determined situations of superiority and inferiority among groups. Only with the emergence of a capitalist economy based on "labor-capital-profit relationships" did race relations emerge as an integral part of the class struggle. Thus Cox argues against the misconceived notion that it was due to their complexion that peoples of color throughout the world were made objects of exploitation and enslavement; on the contrary, racial prejudice became an "attitudinal instrument of modern human, labor exploitation." Caste prejudice—to close the circle—is therefore cultural prejudice and cannot be viewed as analogous to racial prejudice.

1

The Modern Caste School
of Race Relations

During the last decade a prolific school of writers on race relations in the United States, led mainly by social anthropologists, [has] relied religiously upon an ingenious, if not original, caste hypothesis. Professor W. Lloyd Warner is the admitted leader of the movement, and his followers include scholars of considerable distinction.[1] We propose here to examine critically the position of this school.

The Hypothesis

Strictly speaking, the school has no hypothesis, but we shall quote liberally so that the authors might have an opportunity to speak for themselves about the things [. . .] they believe. The school is particularly interested in race relations in the southern states of the United States, and its members believe that they have struck upon an unusually revealing explanation of the situation. In the South, they maintain, Negroes form one caste and whites another, with an imaginary rotating caste line between them. "The white caste is in a superordinate position and the Negro caste in a subordinate social position." The following definition of caste has been most widely accepted:

> Caste . . . describes a theoretical arrangement of the people of a given group in an order in which the privileges, duties, obligations, opportunities, etc., are unequally distributed between the groups which are considered to be higher and lower. . . . Such definition also describes class. A caste organization . . . can be further defined as one where marriage between two or more groups is not sanctioned and where there is no opportunity for members of the lower groups to

5

rise into the upper groups or of members of the upper to fall into the lower ones.[2]

A class system and a caste system "are antithetical to each other. . . . Nevertheless they have accommodated themselves in the southern community." The caste line is represented as running asymmetrically diagonally between the two class systems of Negroes and whites as in Figure 1.

It is assumed that during slavery the caste line AB in Figure 1 was practically horizontal, but that since then with the cultural progress of Negroes it has rotated upward. It may become perpendicular so that it coincides with the line DE; indeed, though unlikely, it may swing over toward the whites. The point here is that it would be possible for the line to take a vertical position while the caste system remains intact. It is thought further that the social disparity between Negro classes and white classes is particularly disconcerting to upper-class Negroes. . . .

It is believed that in many countries of the world besides India there are developed caste systems, but the school has never found it convenient to demonstrate this proposition. . . . Thus the caste system in India has been taken as the criterion; nowhere has the school relied upon any other system.

On the crucial question of marriage among castes Warner and Davis give Émile Senart credit for the belief that castes "isolate themselves to prevent intermarriage" while they regard hypergamy as an example of "variations from the caste ideal."[3] Kingsley Davis, however, thinks that hypergamy distinguishes two major types of caste systems. In India hypergamy is possible because the Indian caste system is a "nonracial caste system"; in the United States and South Africa, on the other hand, hypergamy is impossible because there are in these situations "racial caste systems."[4] Warner and Davis depend further upon Senart and Bouglé for their significant conclusion that *"no one occupation has but one caste assigned to it."*[5]

Considerable emphasis is put upon the fact that a Negro or a white person, who was born Negro or white, could never hope to be anything but Negro or white. . . . Further, this biological fact of inheriting racial marks strikes Kingsley Davis as providing an ideal foundation for a caste system. . . .

Estimate of Basic Principles

Although the school has relied completely on references to the caste system in India for its authority, it has nowhere made any-

FIGURE 1

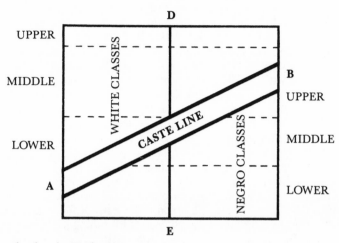

After the chart by W. Lloyd Warner, "American Caste and Class," *American Journal of Sociology* (September 1936): 235.

thing approaching a careful study of the caste system. Yet, even so, it has been difficult to determine which of their selected "essences" of the caste system will be controlling in given situations. For example, after one tentative discussion of caste in India, the conclusion was reached that "there has been no attempt in these last few paragraphs to demonstrate that our caste structure and Indian caste structure are exactly the same, but rather we have attempted to show that they are the same kind of social phenomena."[6]

At this point the question may easily devolve upon the meaning of the expression *same kind*. We have had considerable difficulty also in finding clear-cut statements of principle. Usually some such phrase as "for our purpose," "as here used," or "generally" limits statements that are forthwith given universal applicability. Of course one could hardly question such a contrivance; it may be likened to the researcher who says: "This animal before us is not a horse, but *for our purpose* it is convenient to call it a horse; if you examine it closely you will discover that it is a water-buffalo. That does not matter, for we are not going to use it in the water-buffalo sense. Of course, you cannot say this animal is not a horse; after all, it has four legs; and what does it matter in any event whether we say horse or water-buffalo?"

At points where clarity is most needed the school invariably becomes impressionistic and circuitous. It has been accepted that the form of social organization in Brahmanic India constitutes a caste system. This system has certain distinguishing characteristics; hence we shall consider these the norm.

. . . It should be emphasized that a definition of "a caste" does not describe "the caste-system." We have shown elsewhere that upper-caste men in India have always been able to marry women of lower castes without disturbing the caste system, a procedure which could not be sanctioned in the South. Endogamy may be an isolator of social classes, castes, tribes, sects, or any other social groups which think they have something to protect; hence, the final test of caste is not endogamy but the social values which endogamy secures. . . .

Probably the most insidious analogy between race and caste relations rests in the idea of life membership in each group. The identity of the phenomena, however, is only apparent. It must be obvious that a man born in a certain race cannot have the choice of leaving it and going into another race. This biological affiliation has not been the position of one caste man with respect to another in India. In fact, this very distinction should raise the suspicion that different social forces are operating in the caste system from those in situations of racial adjustment. But what really do we mean by saying that a white man cannot fall into the Negro group? To the extent that he can have sex relations with Negro women he can "fall" biologically. The mixed-blood children that are born are, in the long run, the most potent equilibrator of the races; and the lawmakers of the South are by no means unmindful of this fact. The Negro may "rise" biologically if he is able to pass.

From too much preoccupation with the unchangeableness of physical inheritance, the conclusion is reached that the social status of Negroes and whites in the South may become identical yet they will continue to constitute two castes. In explaining his diagram, Professor Warner holds that there is a theoretical possibility of Negroes' advancing to the point where they may become the dominant caste. And this makes his theory particularly illogical and sterile. So far as its logic is concerned, it asserts that Negroes may become equal to whites, evidently in wealth, in learning, in opportunity to control the government of the state—in short, culturally equal. Yet Negroes and whites will still be unequal; unequal, obviously, in color. For a person born white could never have the privilege of becoming black. Clearly it must be on the grounds of this latter disability that his caste system will still be maintained. And since, so far as we know, time will not alter the possibility of a man's changing his racial marks, we must expect the white caste and the black caste to remain indefinitely intact—an ideal leopard-and-spots theory of race relations.

The theory goes happily past the meaning of the racial dichotomy in the South. It makes it appear that the white man is protecting his color and that the Negro is equally interested in protecting his; so that with the ballot in the hands of Negroes and with the opportunity for cultural participation open to him as a normal citizen, the black code which keeps the races segregated will still be the law of the South. . . . The theory sees a caste system set up in the South in the interest of the white man's color and, for that matter, the Negro's also. Nonetheless it may be shown that the white man has no such obsession about his color. He will protect it only so long as it helps him to reserve a calculable cultural advantage.

The caste interpretation of race relations in the South does not see that the intermarriage restriction laws are a social affront to Negroes; it cannot perceive that Negroes are smarting under the Jim Crow laws; it may not recognize the overwhelming aspiration among Negroes for equality of social opportunity; it could never realize that the superiority of the white race is due principally to the fact that it has developed the necessary devices for maintaining incontestable control over the shooting iron; and it will not know that "race hatred" may be reckoned in terms of the white man's interest. Hence it is possible for the school to imagine the anomaly of Negroes fully assimilated culturally and yet living symbiotically apart from whites on the basis of some unexplained understanding that their colors should never be mixed. In other words, the races will, as Warner and Davis believe "isolate themselves to prevent intermarriage!"

In order that the authors might come to terms with the disturbing question of the relationship of occupation and caste, it is concluded that even in India there is no identification of every occupation with a caste. It is argued, in other words, that since many castes have the same occupation, occupation is no significant factor in the system. The point to remember here, however, is that every caste has a traditional occupaiton, and not that every occupation has a caste.

Considerable importance is given to interracial etiquette in the South as a factor supporting the caste hypothesis.

. . . However, in the South, there is also an etiquette intended to keep poor whites at a proper distance from upper-class whites, and it is probably more severely nonreciprocating there than in other parts of the country. To upper-class Negroes, also, lower-class Negroes are unusually respectful. Indeed, a system of social etiquette which distinguishes superior persons or classes is no exclusive trait of the caste system. It is found in armies, churches, among social classes, as well as among peoples and races who live in relationship of subordination and superordination.

Personality of Upper-Class Negroes

It is a common belief, not peculiar to the caste school, that upper-class Negroes are especially maladjusted. The biracial system in the United States, it must be admitted, is a pathological situation, and insofar as this is so, it affects adversely the personalities of both whites and blacks. But sensitivity to social wrongs need not imply derangement or an "off-balance" personality. We may mention at this point that although this assertion calls for explanation, the caste theorists evidently do not realize that it is most damaging to their hypothesis. A person belonging to a lower caste is not "constantly butting his head against the caste line." In fact, the absence of such a phenomenon is so vital to the persistence of a caste order that it would hardly be inaccurate to maintain that it is definitely incompatible with a caste system. Caste barriers in the caste system are never challenged; they are sacred to caste and caste alike. The personalities developed in the caste system are normal for that society.

Negroes are moving away from a condition of extreme white domination and subjection to one of normal citizenship. The determinant of unrest or social dysphoria among a people is not so much their *state* of subjugation or seeming oppression; it is rather the process of changing from some accommodated stage of well-being to one of subservience. Since the Civil War the situation among Negroes in the South has been opposite to this. Hortense Powdermaker makes the significant observation that it is not difference in class so much as difference in age which determines the attitude of Negroes toward whites. "Among the younger [Negro] generation, those in their teens, twenties, and thirties, resentment is keen and outspoken."[7] Older Negroes were reared in an earlier school of racial beliefs; and, indeed, the younger are not infrequently very impatient with their compromising attitudes toward whites. Among Negroes in the South the "Uncle Toms" are distributed through all the social classes.

Of course militance in the interest of racial progress should not be mistaken for personality imbalance. In fact, dissatisfaction with the status quo is the common preoccupation of all Negro leaders. There is, furthermore, some compensation to upper-class Negroes. Frequently they meet whites under flattering conditions, mostly in business relations. They have considerable prestige among their own people, sometimes even more than that which whites of similar attainments can hope for within their own group. This windfall may not only compensate for loss of respect from low-class whites, but it may even result in a sort of grandiose importance inconsistent with reality. The "big Negro," a recognized personality type, is usually indelicate and grossly lacking in humility; yet, he is not pathological.

Upper-class Negroes do not envy poor whites in the South because the latter are beyond the purview of the black code. One might as well argue that some human beings suffer severe personality traumas because the dogs and cats of the rich have certain advantages that they do not have. The resentment of upper-class Negroes is rather against the ruling class, the guardians of the status quo. Enlightened Negroes recognize clearly the cultural inferiority of the poor whites. As a youth, W. E. B. DuBois says of himself: "I cordially despised the poor Irish and South Germans, who slaved in the mills, and annexed the rich and well-to-do as my natural companions."[8] Thus, bitter as it is, the real conflict is usually between Negroes and their cultural equals or superiors. [. . .]

The Social Organization of Negroes

[. . . One] way of looking at a society is in terms of its capacity to perpetuate itself. Hinduism or the caste society of India is a powerful form of social organization which may go on self-satisfiedly, so to speak, forever. It carries within itself no basic antagonisms. But the social aims and purposes of whites and Negroes in the South are irreconcilably opposed. If such a situation could be termed a society at all, it must be a society divided against itself. Sapir has used this idea in his analysis of culture. Thus he writes: "The genuine culture is not of necessity either *high or low;* it is merely inherently harmonious, balanced, self-satisfactory. . . . If the culture necessitates slavery, it frankly admits it; if it abhors slavery, it feels its way to an economic adjustment that obviates the necessity of its employment."[9]

In like manner we may think of the larger American society as fundamentally antipathetic to the non-Christian, nondemocratic, biracial system in the South; hence it is continuously "feeling its way" to something else. To put such a situation easily into a typology of societies which includes the caste system in India, indeed, to identify it with the caste system, must be misleading to say the least. The caste system of India is a minutely segmented, assimilated social structure; it is highly stable and capable of perpetuating itself indefinitely.

When two racial or nationality groups become more or less isolated from each other because of some continuing conflict situation or basic repugnance, we do not refer to them as forming a social-status hierarchy even though their relationship is one of superordination and subordination or of conqueror and conquered. As an illustration, Adolf Hitler in his *My Battle* says: "It must be held in greater honour to be a citizen of this Reich, even if only a crossing-sweeper, than to be a king in a foreign state."[10] Suppose now that this philosophy be made a reality in future German-Polish relationships; all Poles will then be considered inferior to the least of Germans, and an etiquette will be developed to implement the attitude. But there will be here no social status hierarchy; neither would Hitler there and then have enacted a caste system. The Poles will seek a *modus vivendi* in some sort of society of their own, and the intergroup relationship will most likely be one of antagonism, a latent power group relationship.

So, too, Negroes and whites in the Deep South do not constitute an assimilated society. There are rather two societies. Thus we may conceive of Negroes as constituting a quasi or tentative society developed to meet certain needs resulting from their retarded assimilation. Unlike the permanence of a caste, it is a temporary society intended to continue only so long as whites are able to maintain the barriers against their assimilation.[11] It provides the matrix for a universe of discourse in which members of the group give expression to their common sympathies, opinions, and sentiments, and in which their primary social institutions function. The political and economic structure is controlled by another and larger society to which the whites are assimilated and toward which all Negroes are oriented.

The "public" of the white society includes Negroes only in the broadest sense; and when Negroes in their institutional functions declare that "everybody is invited," white people who turn up must assume the role of strangers. The "we feeling" of the white and of the Negro society tends to be mutually exclusive. Says Robert E. Park: "Gradually, imperceptibly, within the larger world of the caste theorists. For Cox, a concept of ethnic pluralism that lends support to the revitalization of black urban ghettos, or to separate political, economic, and cultural development for blacks, was not dissimilar to the earlier attempts to explain race relations within the framework of a caste system—both concepts paradoxically implied that blacks should remain estranged from the larger U.S. social system.

Cox triggered further controversy in an article entitled "Jewish Self-interest in 'Black Pluralism'" (1974), published shortly before his death. Here he noted that anti-Semitism was an ancient social attitude, related to the rise of Jewish identity, and that it would therefore arise wherever Jews asserted this identity. He believed that Jewish support for the notion of pluralism, used to enhance Jewish self-respect and survival, was similar to certain elements of black nationalism, but that neither blacks nor Jews had anything to gain from the strategy. Black self-interest, therefore, should lead to support for integration and assimilation. Cox's observation, in a footnote to the article, that Andrew Greeley, one of the foremost proponents of ethnic pluralism, "is a converted Irish ethnic contributing to publications of the American Jewish Committee"[46] brought forth a chorus of scathing and critical rebuttals, from Greeley and other readers of Cox's paper. Cox was accused of not offering empirical evidence for many of his assertions and of addressing important issues with generalities and stereotypes about an unfounded Jewish conspiracy to promote ethnicity. Greeley wrote the following: "I can only use the word flabbergasted to describe my reaction to Oliver Cox's article in your spring issue. Such a piece might have been acceptable in Nazi Germany in the middle 1930s, but it surely is not acceptable in a responsible social science publication in the middle 1970s. It is a tendentious, wandering, vicious diatribe and you should be ashamed of yourself for publishing it."[47] Cox died on September 4, 1974, before he was able to reply to his critics.

A Neglected Scholar

Oliver Cox's writing was never incorporated into the mainstream of sociological thinking, even after the publication of *Caste, Class, and Race* in 1948. To be sure, the economic and political milieu in the United States at the end of World War II was far from propitious for the kind of Marxist-inspired analysis that Cox was engaged in. The prosperity generated by the New Deal and the war appeared to have laid to rest any fears about the viability of capitalism. A consumer-oriented society was launched with the $100 billion that Americans had saved during the war.[48] When Stalin announced in 1946 that there would be no long-term relations between the "young, dynamic world of socialism and the dying, corrupt world of capitalism," the stage was set for a wave of virulent anti-Communism that would last a decade. The House Committee on Un-American Activities (HUAC), which had gone into eclipse during the war, was reinvigorated and granted the status of a standing committee of the Congress. Its members saw a vast conspiracy across the nation.[49] Few academicians who expressed disapproval of U.S. society could escape the hysteria:

> Pressures on colleges and universities tended to be implicit when federal, explicit when locally instigated; although explicit enough was HUAC's letter of June, 1949, to eighty-one colleges and high schools, demanding lists of textbooks in use in the fields of literature, economics, government, history, political science, social science and geography.[50]

Serious constraints were placed on academic freedom "as communists and socialists were thought to be lurking in all the dark corners of academe."[51] Even the accusation of being associated with the Communist party or harboring radical ideas could mean being passed over for promotion—or the loss of a job and "blacklisting" from future employment.

Thus there were few people—either social scientists or ordinary citizens—who were prepared to embrace the concept of class struggle or endorse a probing critique of capitalist society. Nor were the times conducive to the publication of a sociological treatise that asserted—as did *Caste, Class, and Race*—that "from the standpoint of degrees of development in democracy in the three great nations of the world—the United States, England, and Russia—the United States is probably most backward and Russia farthest advanced,"[52] or argued that racial prejudice was used by the ruling class to prevent the unification of black and white workers.

Cox was never called before the House Un-American Activities Committee, but he was not immune from the pressures of the times. At least one prominent sociologist, Howard Becker, refused to write an introduction to the book because of its putative "Marxist" orientation, and one publisher turned it down because the ideas were reminiscent of "Communism." In a letter to Cox, Becker wrote:

After much soul-searching and a very painstaking second perusal of your transcript, I am compelled to say that it will be absolutely impossible for me to write an introduction to your book which would not do more harm than good. Your Marxism is so undiluted, especially in the part on class and in the conclusion, that I should have to dissociate myself completely from these proportions.

He added: "I don't know who your publisher is, but I should be greatly surprised—assuming that his office reader is prudent—if he accepted the book without modification."[53] Indeed, one editor provided the following assessment:

Dear Professor Cox:
   It's no use, I can't stomach the communist line.

Sincerely Yours,
Wm. B. Selgby[54]

When Cox consulted Paul Sweezy, editor of *Monthly Review,* an independent socialist magazine, about publishing some of his work, Sweezy wrote: "Needless to say, we are very well aware of the fact that many people can't write what they want to these days, and we are perfectly willing to publish articles anonymously where protection is needed."[55]

After the book was published, Cox received letters that further show the extent of the hysteria rampant at the time. Benjamin J. Davis, a former black Communist councilman from Harlem, wrote the following:

Some of them [critics of *Caste, Class and Race*] in deference to their millionaire employers, would obviously like to skin you alive, or bring you before the House UnAmerican committee. . . .One can be a murderer, lyncher, exploiter or bankrobber—or even starve little children to death—but if one is anti-communist, all is forgiven, such is the pass to which decadent capitalism has come.[56]

The reviews of the book in scholarly journals, magazines, and newspapers were mixed. Some reviewers believed that it was a significant contribution and placed Cox among the ranks of such leading scholars as Ruth Benedict, Gunnar Myrdal, Aldous Huxley, and Ashley Montagu.[57] Few failed, however, to label Cox a "Marxist sociologist." For instance, Elmer P. Martin has reported that out of one hundred reviews on Cox's books, between 75 and 80 percent referred to Cox as a Marxist. There were some reviewers who expressed a reluctance to make a statement about Cox's work because, as one put it, it "is so deeply steeped in Marxism that it may do interracial relations more harm than good." Others believed that although Cox's writings were Marxist, his approach "differed from the exponents of Marxism" in not taking an orthodox approach to race relations.[58] And even those reviewers who praised Cox's erudition and the "freshness" of his approach expressed a concern that he was advocating political action within the Marxist framework, rather than producing a scientific study of human society.[59]

Those few who responded directly to Cox's arguments were also concerned with his inattention to the rules of science (as they were defined at the time). While the question of the relation between values and scientific sociology had come to the fore in the 1940s, as sociologists became involved in applied research,[60] most still believed that an "objective" or "value-free" sociology was possible. Thus while Cox's Marxism was the issue for some, for others the criticism was expressed in more "scientific" terms. Cox's entire theoretical orientation was considered unscientific, deterministic, polemical, and incapable of addressing the complex problems of a modern industrial society. Alvin Rose has commented on the atmosphere of the time:

> I think that exacerbated the problem for him. Marxism in those days was a dirty word. Sociologists generally believed that Marx was naive. The assumption that there are really only two important social classes was seen as a gross oversimplification. They did not blame Marx. Marx wrote in another time. But they thought that it was naive for people in this day to be spouting that out as contemporary sociology. The class system was seen as being much more complex.[61]

A similar view was expressed by many of the sociologists who, like Cox, had been trained in sociology and anthropology at the University of Chicago. For example, Robert Park, a leading mentor of many Chicago sociologists, was at the forefront in the quest to make sociology "scientific," and he impressed upon his students a view of the scientific role of the sociologist.[62] Furthermore, Park believed that "one's personal status depended on one's ability to gain access to unusual research sites and establish rapport with key respondents," which he saw as the opposite of adhering to a particular ideological framework.[63] Thus going into the field, collecting data, and having group discussions of research results were all part of a work style that was believed to be conducive to developing and producing a community of sociologists that would be maintained after their graduate education.

Herbert Blumer, one of Park's students, describes how *Caste, Class, and Race* was regarded by his fellow students:

white man, a smaller world, the world of the black man, is silently taking form and shape[12][. . .]

One device for retarding Negro assimilation, which does not have to be resorted to in the caste system, is the policy of guarding against any development of an overt expression of indispensability of Negroes within the social organization. Whatever their de facto importance, they must never appear as an integral part of the society. Instead, they pay little taxes; hence little or none of certain public expenditures should be diverted to their benefit. The theory of taxation according to ability to pay and expenditure according to need does not include them. Crime, sickness, death, and poverty almost characterize Negroes; hence they are a drag on "society" and may be ostensibly sloughed off to advantage. Whites are generally protected from contact with cultured Negroes. The successful practice of this contrivance tends to give the Negro a sense of worthlessness and unwantedness, which contributes finally to the retardation of his assimilation. In Brahmanic India, however, where the population is assimilated to the caste culture, it is openly admitted that low-caste men are indispensable to the system, and this admission does not conduce to any advancement in the latter's social status.

By using the caste hypothesis, then, the school seeks to explain a "normal society" in the South. In short, it has made peace for the hybrid society that has not made peace with itself, and insofar as this is true its work is fictitious.

Contribution of the School

A remarkable characteristic of this caste school of race relations is its tendency to conceive of itself as being original.[13] It believes that it has made a discovery. It is difficult, however, to determine wherein rests the originality. We do not know who made the first analogy between race relations and the caste system of India, but it is certain that the idea was quite popular during the middle of the last century. One of the most detailed and extended discussions of this hypothesis is that of the Hon. Charles Sumner published in 1869.[14] Since then, many textbooks have accepted the idea.[15] Some students, like Sir Herbert Risley, have used the hypothesis as the basis of extensive research.[16] Many writers such as E. B. Reuter and Charles S. Johnson have applied the term casually to the racial situation in the United States.[17] [. . .]

With respect to the scientific precision of the word "caste" the school argues that "by all the physical tests the anthropologists might apply, some social Negroes are *biologically* white," hence the word "race" cannot have meaning when applied to Negroes.[18] We should remember here, however, that the racial situation in the South never depended on "physical tests of anthropologists." It developed long before anthropometry came of age. The sociologist is interested, not in what the anthropometrists set up as their criteria of race, but in what peoples in interaction come to accept as a race. It is this latter belief which controls their behavior and not what the anthropometrist thinks. But in reality the term "caste" does not economize thinking on this subject. It is always necessary first to say what kind of people belong to the Negro caste before we can know what the Negro caste means. Therefore in the process of defining Negro caste we have defined Negro race, and the final accomplishment is a substitution of words only. One may test this fact by substituting in the writings of this school the words "Negroes" or "white people" wherever the words "Negro caste" or "white caste" are used, and observe that the sense of the statement does not change.

For this reason the burden of the productions of this school tends to be old wine in new bottles. In other words, much that has come to us by earlier studies has taken on the glamour of caste, and the school seldom refers to the contributions of outgroup students.[19] One could hardly help recalling as an analogous situation the popularity which William McDougall gave to the instinct hypothesis. Without making any reference to William James, Lloyd Morgan, and others who had handled the concept with great care, McDougall set out with pioneering zeal to bend all social behavior to his instinct theory. It was not long, however, before reaction came. And so too, until comparatively recently, the race-caste idea had a desultory career. It has now been made fashionable; yet, already, students who had once used the term "caste" begin to shrink from it.[20] But we should hasten to add that this school has none of the anticolor complexes of the instinct school. Its leadership merely lacks, as Robert E. Park might say, a sociological tradition.

Notes

1. See the leading hypothesis: W. Lloyd Warner, "American Caste and Class," *American Journal of Sociology*, 42 (September 1936): 234–37. See also, by the same author, "Social Anthropology and the Modern Com-

munity," ibid. 46 (May 1941): 785–96; W. Lloyd Warner and W. Allison Davis, "A Comparative Study of American Caste," in *Race Relations and the Race Problem*, (Durham, N.C., 1939), ed. Edgar T. Thompson, pp. 219–40; W. Allison Davis and John Dollard, *Children of Bondage* (Washington, D.C., 1940); W. Lloyd Warner, Buford H. Junker, and Walter A. Adams, *Color and Human Nature* (Washington, D.C., 1941); W. Allison Davis et al., *Deep South* (Chicago, 1941); John Dollard, *Caste and Class in a Southern Town* (New Haven, 1937); Buell G. Gallagher, *American Caste and the Negro College* (New York, 1938); Donald Young, *Research Memoranda on Minority Peoples in the Depression* (New York, 1937); Robert Austin Warren, *New Haven Negroes* (New Haven, 1940); Kingsley Davis, "Intermarriage in Caste Societies," *American Anthropologist* 43 (September 1941): 376–95; Robert L. Sutherland, *Color, Class and Personality* (Washington, D.C., 1942); Edward A. Ross, *New-Age Sociology* (New York and London, 1940); William F. Ogburn and Meyer F. Nimkoff, *Sociology* (Boston, 1940); Robert L. Sutherland and Julian L. Woodward, *Introductory Sociology* (1940); Stuart A. Queen and Jennette R. Gruener, *Social Pathology* (New York, 1940); Alain Locke and Bernhard J. Stern, *When Peoples Meet* (New York, 1942); and others.

2. Warner, "American Caste and Class," p. 234.
3. Warner and Davis; "A Comparative Study of American Caste," pp. 230, 229.
4. Davis, "Intermarriage in Caste Societies," pp. 376–95.
5. Warner and Davis, "A Comparative Study of American Caste," p. 231.
6. *Race Relations and the Race Problem*, p. 232.
7. Hortense Powdermaker, *After Freedom* (New York, 1939), pp. 331 and 325.
8. W. E. B. DuBois, *Darkwater* (New York, 1921), p. 10.
9. Edwin Sapir, "Culture, Genuine and Spurious," *American Journal of Sociology* 29 (January 1924): 410. See also Albert Bushnell Hart, *Slavery and Abolition, 1831–1841* (New York-London, 1906), p. 321.
10. Adolf Hitler, *My Battle*, E. T. S. Dugdale, transl. (Cambridge, 1933), p. 182.
11. Professor Robert Redfield describes the evolution of a racial dichotomy into a class system. It is significant to note that no such process could be suggested as a means of liquidating the caste system: "It requires little special knowledge to assert that the contact of the Spanish with the Maya, as is generally the case with long-continuing interaction between diverse ethnic groups, began with the existence of two separate societies, each with its own racial and cultural characteristics, and moved toward the formation of a single society in which the original racial and cultural differences disappear. At the time of the Conquest there were two groups that looked across at each other both aware of the marked ethnic differences that attended their sense of distinctness one from the other. As the two groups came to participate in a common life and to interbreed, the ethnic differences became blurred, so that other criteria of difference, such as occupation,

costume, or place of residence, came to be relatively more significant signs of social distinctness than was race or general culture. . . . At first there were two societies, ethnically distinct. At last there is a single society with classes, ethnically indistinct." (*The Folk Culture of Yucatan* [Chicago, 1941], p. 58).

12. Robert E. Park, "Racial Assimilation of Secondary Groups," *Proceedings of the American Sociological Society*, 8: 77.

13. "The view that the relationships of whites and Negroes in the South are systematically ordered and maintained by a caste structure, and that the status of individuals within each of these groups is further determined by a system of social classes existing within each color-caste, was the creation of Warner" (Davis and Dollard, *Children of Bondage*, p. xvi). "The presence of caste and class structures in the society of the deep South was reported upon first by a member of our research group" (Davis, *Deep South*, p. 5). "An original interpretation of class and caste distinctions in the United States, providing a useful frame of reference for an appreciation of caste phenomena in this country" (Ogburn and Nimkoft, *Sociology*, p. 343).

14. Charles Sumner, *The Question of Caste*, (Boston, 1869).

15. Among the best of them are C. H. Cooley, *Social Process* (New York, 1922), p. 279; and *Social Organization* (New York, 1919), pp. 209–28; Park and Burgess, *Introduction to the Science of Sociology* (Chicago, 1924), pp. 722 and 205–6.

16. See, for example, Herbert Risley, *The Peoples of India* (Calcutta, 1908), p. 263; and *Census of India*, 1901.

17. E. B. Reuter, *The Mulatto in the United States* (Boston, 1918), p. 360; Charles S. Johnson, "Caste and Class in an American Industry," *American Journal of Sociology* 42 (July 1936): 55–65. See also Robert E. Park, "Racial Assimilation in Secondary Groups," *Proceedings of the American Sociological Society* 8 (1913): 73.

18. Davis et al., *Deep South*, pp. 7–8.

19. As a typical example of this, see Davis et al., *Deep South*, pp. 15–136 and 228–539. Consider the weighty significance with which the following commonplace is introduced. "The critical fact is that a much larger proportion of all *Negroes* are lower class than is the case with *whites. This is where caste comes to bear. It* puts the overwhelming majority of Negroes in the lowest class group, and keeps them there" (Davis and Dollard, *Children of Bondage*, p. 65; emphasis added). This quotation also illustrates the mystical way in which real problems have been explained away.

20. See Robert E. Park in the introduction to Bertram W. Doyle, *The Etiquette of Race Relations* (Chicago, 1937); and Charles S. Johnson, *Growing Up in the Black Belt* (Washington, D.C., 1941). However, this is not to say that either Park or Johnson fully appreciates the worth-lessness of the caste belief, for they are still toying with it.

2

An American Dilemma:
A Mystical Approach to the
Study of Race Relations

These two volumes, *An American Dilemma* by Dr. Gunnar Myrdal,[1] are perhaps the culminating achievement of classical scholarship on the subject of race relations. They bring to finest expression practically all the vacuous theories of race relations which are acceptable among the liberal intelligentsia and which explain race relations away from the social and economic order. The theories do this in spite of the verbal desire of the author to integrate his problem in the ongoing social system. In the end the social system is exculpated, and the burden of the dilemma is poetically left in the "hearts of the American people," the esoteric reaches of which, obviously, may be plumbed only by the guardians of morals in our society.

This critical examination, to be sure, is not intended to be a review of *An American Dilemma*. As a source of information and brilliant interpretation of information on race relations in the United States, it is unsurpassed. We are interested here only in the validity of the meaning [. . .] Myrdal derives from the broad movements of his data. The data are continually changing and becoming obsolescent; but if we understand their social determinants we can not only predict change but also influence it.

In his attempt to explain race relations in the United States Myrdal seems to have been confronted with two principal problems: (a) the problem of avoiding a political-class interpretation, and (b) the problem of finding an acceptable moral or religious interpretation.[2] In the first part of this discussion we shall attempt to show how the caste theory is employed and, in the second part, how a shying away from the obvious implications of his data is contrived as solutions for these problems. We shall not discuss the concept from which the book derives its title, for it seems quite obvious that none of the great imperialist democracies either can or intends to practice its democratic ideals among its subject peoples.[3] Myrdal does not bring to light the social determinants of this well-known dilemma; he merely recognizes it and rails against its existence. [. . .]

The Caste Hypothesis

The whole theoretical frame of reference of *An American Dilemma* is couched in a caste hypothesis. As Myrdal himself puts it: "Practically the entire factual content of . . . this book may be considered to define caste in the case of the American Negro."[4] Now it is evident that Myrdal—in spite of the lamentable use of such phrases as "in our view," "as we have defined it," and so on—does not intend to coin a new concept. In criticizing Charles S. Johnson's view of caste he declares, "We do not believe that such a caste system as he has defined ever existed."[5] Therefore, in his explanation of race relations in the United States, our author means to accept the known concept as a norm. Of some significance is the way in which the term is selected. This is the reasoning:

> The term "race" is . . . inappropriate in a scientific inquiry since it has biological and genetic connotations which . . . run parallel to widely spread false racial beliefs. The . . . term "class," is impractical and confusing . . . since it is generally used to refer to a non-rigid status group from which an individual member can rise or fall. . . . We need a term to distinguish the large and systematic type of social differentiation from the small and spotty type and have . . . used the term "caste."[6]

Obviously, in arriving at this decision to use the term "caste" in explaining race relations in the United States, Myrdal employs the method of successive elimination. . . .

. . . Myrdal has adopted not only the whole theory of the caste school of race relations in the United States but also its procedure. Like the leadership of this school, he appears to have taken some pride in regarding as worthless a study of Hindu society as a basis of making comparisons with Western society. Yet, as we should expect, he depends entirely on the Hindu system for his orientation. Thus, the reader is asked to accept generalizations about the caste system in America when no other reference is made to the cultural norm than the following:

It should be pointed out . . . that those societies to which the term "caste" is applied without controversy—notably the ante-bellum slavery society of the South and the Hindu society of India—do not have the "stable equilibrium" which American sociologists from their distance are often inclined to attribute to them. A Hindu acquaintance once told me that the situation in the United States is as much or more describable by the term "caste" as is the situation in India.[7]

From this, one thing is clear: Myrdal is very much in error in believing that it is recognized without controversy that slavery in the South constituted a caste system.[8] Moreover, it is difficult to see how one could avoid the conclusion that the author has descended to some vulgar means in referring to the hearsay of "a Hindu acquaintance" as authority for the sociology of caste.

The Biological Problem

Probably the crucial circumstance in attempts to use some term other than race in describing race relations is a desire to get around the biological implications in the term. Yet it has never been shown that there is a real necessity for this. In fact those who verbally eschew the biological connotation of the term proceed, nonetheless, to make physical differences the crux of their discussion. This is particularly true of Myrdal. Says he, "Negro features are so distinct that only in the Negro problem does [belief in the desirability of a light skin and 'good" features] become of great social importance."[9] And he proceeds, evidently without realizing it, to point out the relationship of skin color to caste:

> . . . the average Negro cannot effectively change his color and other physical features. If the dark Negro accept the white man's valuation of skin color, he must stamp himself an inferior. If the light Negro accepts this valuation, he places himself above the darker Negroes but below the whites, and he reduces his loyalty to his caste.[10]

Myrdal continues his biological interpretation of race relations with great clarity. "When we say that Negroes form a lower caste in America," he asserts, "we mean that they are subject to certain disabilities solely because they are 'Negroes.'"[11] Manifestly, that is to say, solely because they are colored or black. Moreover, although the writer did not elaborate this point, he refers to Asiatics, Indians, and Negroes as "the several subordinate castes."[12] It should be interesting to see how he fits these peoples into an American caste hierarchy. At any rate, with this conception of race relations, the author inevitably comes to the end of the blind alley: that the caste system remains intact so long as the Negro remains colored. [. . .]

Myrdal is so thoroughly preoccupied with the great significance of skin color that, although he realizes that in America Negroes of lighter complexion have greater social opportunities, he believes that they may as well be unmixed blacks as far as the "caste line" is concerned. Accordingly, he asserts:

> Without any doubt a Negro with light skin and other European features has in the North an advantage with white people when competing for jobs available for Negroes. . . . Perhaps of even greater importance is the fact that the Negro community itself has accepted this color preference."[13]

This, however has nothing to do with the rigidity of the caste line.

When Myrdal strays from his physical emphasis, he becomes confused. For instance, he concludes that "being a Negro means being subject to considerable disabilities in practically all spheres of life."[14] Evidently it must follow logically from this that to the extent to which these "disabilities" are removed, to that extent also a person ceases to remain a Negro. The confusion is further deepened by the combination of a cultural and biological view of caste.

> Caste . . . consists of such drastic restrictions to free competition in various spheres of life that the individual in a lower caste cannot, by any means, change his status except by a secret and illegitimate "passing" which is possible only to the few who have the physical appearance of members of the upper caste."[15]

In other words, caste consists in restrictions to free competition, but restrictions to free competition are entirely limited by a man's physical appearance. Now, we may ask, what is the nexus between physical appearance and caste?

Rigidity of the Caste System

We may reiterate that the caste school of race relations is laboring under the illusion of a simple but vicious truism. One man is white, another is black; the cultural opportunities of these two men may be the same, but, since the black man cannot become white, there will always be a white caste and a black caste. . . .

Closely related to this amorphous concept of the rigidity of caste is the meaning given to interracial endogamy. Myrdal uses it to identify the races in the United States as castes.

> The scientifically important difference between the terms "caste" and "class" is . . . a relatively large difference in freedom of movement between groups. This difference is foremost in marriage relations. . . . The ban on intermarriage is one expression of the still broader principle . . . that a man born a Negro or a white is not allowed to pass from the one status to the other as he can pass from one class to another.[16]

Now it could hardly be too much emphasized that endogamy of itself is no final criterion of caste. Endogamy is an isolater of social values deemed sacrosanct by social groups, and there are many kinds of social groups besides castes that are endogamous. The final test of caste is an identification of the social values and organization isolated by endogamy. To say that intercaste endogamy in India means the same thing as interracial endogamy in the United States is like saying that a lemon and a potato are the same things because they both have skins.

An illustration of Myrdal's complete disregard of the nature of caste organization is his discussion of "caste struggle." This concept of caste struggle, to be sure, is totally foreign to our norm, the Indian caste system. Moreover, this must be so because castes in Brahamanic India do not want to be anything other than castes. There is no effort or logical need to homogenate themselves. A caste is a status entity in an assimilated, peaceful, self-satisfied society. Regardless of his position in the society, a man's caste is sacred to him, and one caste does not dominate the other.[. . .]

Mysticism

[. . .] Myrdal seems to attribute magical powers to caste. Speaking of the cause of the economic position of Negroes in the United States he says: "Their caste position keeps them poor and ill-educated."[17] And, "Caste consigns the overwhelming majority of Negroes to the lower class."[18] Indeed, the whole meaning of racial exploitation in the United States is laid at the altar of caste. Thus it is observed: "The measures to keep the Negroes disfranchised and deprived of full civil rights and the whole structure of social and economic discrimination are to be viewed as attempts to enforce *the caste principle*."[19]

More immediately, this mysticism is due primarily to a misapprehension of the whole basis of race relations. Caste is vaguely conceived of as something, the preservation of which is valuable per se. "The caste system is upheld by its own inertia and by the superior caste's interests in upholding it."[20] It is no wonder, then, that Myrdal falls into the egregious error of thinking that the subordination of Negroes in the South is particularly the business of poor whites.[. . .] This, obviously, is a conception of race relations in terms of personal invidiousness.[. . .]

[. . .] The caste system lumps all white people and all Negroes into two antagonistic groups struggling in the interest of a mysterious god called caste. This is very much to the liking of the exploiters of labor, since it tends to confuse them in an emotional matrix with all the people. Observe in illustration how Myrdal directs our view: "All of these thousand and one precepts, etiquettes, taboos, and disabilities inflicted upon the Negro have a common purpose: to express the subordinate status of the Negro people and the exalted position of the whites. They have their meaning and chief function as symbols."[21]

It thus appears that if *white people* were not so wicked, if they would only cease wanting to "exalt" themselves and accept the "American Creed," race prejudice would vanish from America. "Why," asks Myrdal, "is race prejudice . . . not increasing but decreasing?" And he answers sanctimoniously: "This question is . . . only a special variant of the enigma of philosophers for several thousands of years: the problem of Good and Evil in the world."[22] The philosophers' enigma evidently leads him directly into the mystical play with imponderables. As he sees it, "white prejudice" is a primary determinant in race relations. "White prejudice and discrimination keep the Negro low in standards of living. . . . This, in turn, gives support to prejudice. White prejudice and Negro standards, thus mutually 'cause' each other."[23] Moreover, "the chief hindrance to improving the Negro is *the white man's firm belief in his inferiority*."[24]

Poor Whites

We should point out again that Myrdal not only closes his eyes to the material interests which support and maintain race prejudice but also labors the point that there is basic antagonism between poor whites and Negroes. Says he: "What a bitter, spiteful, and relentless feeling often prevails against the Negroes among lower class white people in America. . . . The Marxian solidarity between the toilers . . . have a long way to go as far as concerns solidarity of the poor white American with the toiling Negro."[25] In fact the author goes further to intimate that the poor whites may assume a dominant role in the oppression of Negroes in the South, since the interest of the poor whites is economic, while that of the ruling class is a feeling for superiority.[. . .]

The author hesitates to come to that obvious conclusion so much dreaded by the capitalist ruling class: that the observed overt competitive antagonism is a condition produced and carefully maintained by the exploiters of both the poor whites and the Negroes. Yet, he almost says this in so many words:

> Plantation owners and employers, who use Negro labor as cheaper and more docile, have at times been observed to tolerate, or cooperate in, the periodic aggression of poor whites against Negroes. It is a plausible thesis that they do so in the interest of upholding the caste system which is so effective in keeping the Negro docile.[26]

And even more strikingly he shows by what means white workers are exploited through the perpetuation of racial antagonism. Says he: "If those white workers were paid low wages and held in great dependence, they could at least be offered a consolation of being protected from Negro competition."[27]

At any rate, Myrdal refuses to be consistent. Accordingly, he asserts, attitudes against interracial marriage seem "generally to be inversely related to the economic and social status of the informant and his educational level. . . . To the poor and socially insecure, but struggling, white individual, a fixed opinion on this point seems an important matter of prestige and distinction."[28] It would not do, of course, to explain the situation realistically by concluding that if the revised black codes, written by the white exploiting class, against intermarriage, were abrogated, an increasing number of marriages between the white and the black proletariat would take place, the consequence of which would be a considerably reduced opportunity for labor exploitation by this class.[29]

The Ruling Class

Myrdal does not like to talk about the ruling class in the South; the term carries for him an odious "Marxist" connotation. Yet, inevitably, he describes the class as well as anyone:

The one-party system in the South . . . and the low political participation of even the white people favor a *de facto* oligarchic regime. . . . The oligarchy consists of the big landowners, the industrialists, the bankers, and the merchants. Northern corporate business with big investments in the region has been sharing in the political control by this oligarchy.[30]

And he stresses the ineffectiveness of the exploited masses. "The Southern masses do not generally organize either for advancing their ideals or for protecting their group interests. The immediate reason most often given by Southern liberals is the resistance from the political oligarchy which wants to keep the masses inarticulate."[31] Furthermore he indicates the desperate pressure endured by Southern workers when he says: "The poorest farmer in the Scandinavian countries or in England . . . would not take benevolent orders so meekly as Negroes and white sharecroppers do in the South."[32]

Sometimes Myrdal shakes off the whole burden of obfuscation spun about caste, creeds, and poor-white control to show, perhaps without intending to do so, the real interest of the ruling class and how it sets race against race to accomplish its exploitative purpose:

The conservative opponents of reform proposals (that is to say the ruling class in the South) can usually discredit them by pointing out that they will improve the status of the Negroes, and that they prepare for "social equality." This argument has been raised in the South against labor unions, child labor legislation and practically every other proposal for reform.

It has been argued to the white workers that the Wages and Hours Law was an attempt to legislative equality between the races by raising the wage level of Negro workers to that of whites. The South has never been seriously interested in instituting tenancy legislation to protect the tenants' rights . . . and the argument has again been that the Negro sharecropper should not be helped against the white man.[33]

It seems clear that in developing a theory of race relations in the South one must look to the economic policies of the ruling class, and not to mere abstract depravity among poor whites. Opposition to social equality has no meaning unless we can see its function in the service of the exploitative purpose of this class. "When the Negro rises socially," says Myrdal, "and is no longer a servant, he becomes a stranger to the white upper class. His ambition is suspected and he is disliked."[34] Again: "The ordinary white upper class people will 'have no use' for such Negros. They need cheap labor—faithful, obedient, unambitious labor."[35] And the author observes further: "In most Southern communities the ruling classes of whites want to keep Negroes from joining labor unions. Some are quite frank in wanting to keep Negroes from reading the Constitution or studying social subjects."[36]

In the South the ruling class stands effectively between the Negroes and the white proletariat. Every segregation barrier is a barrier put up between white and black people by their exploiters. Myrdal puts it this way: "On the local scene the accommodation motive by itself does not usually encourage Negro leaders to such adventures as trying to reach behind the white leaders to the white people."[37] Moreover, it is not the poor whites but the ruling class which uses its intelligence and its money to guard against any movement among Negroes to throw off their yoke of exploitation. "In many communities leading white citizens make no secret of the fact that they are carefully following . . . all signs of 'subversive propaganda' and unrest among the Negroes in the community, and that they interfere to stop even innocent beginnings of Negro group activity."[38]

The reasoning which we are now following, it may be well to state, is not Myrdal's; we are merely culling those conclusions which the data seem to compel the author to make, but which he ordinarily surrounds with some mysterious argument about caste.

During slavery the masters did not have so great a need for racial antagonism. Black workers could be exploited in comparative peace. As Myrdal observes: "Exploitation of Negro labor was, perhaps, a less embarrassing moral conflict to the ante-bellum planter than to his peer today. . . . Today the exploitation is, to a considerable degree, dependent upon the availability of extra-legal devices of various kinds."[39] Obviously, among these extralegal devices are race prejudice, discrimination, and violence—especially lynching and the threat of lynching. "Discrimination against Negroes is . . . rooted in this tradition of economic exploitation."[40]

Emphasis Upon Sex

In spite of this, however, Myrdal refuses to accept a realistic interpretation of race relations. Throughout these volumes he warns his readers not to put too much reliance on an economic explanation. [. . . He] thinks it is more revealing to take sex as our point of reference. In fact, Myrdal presents a scheme of social situations in which he ranks intermarriage and sexual intercourse involving white women as the highest motives for discrimination, while he ranks economic conditions sixth and last:

> (1) Highest in this order [of discrimination] stands the bar against intermarriage and sexual intercourse involving white women (2) . . . several etiquettes and discriminations . . . (3) . . . segregations and discriminations in use of public facilities such as schools . . . (4) political disfranchisement . . . (5) discriminations in the law courts . . . (6) . . . discriminations in securing land, credit, jobs.[41]

This rank order evidences the degree of importance which "white people" attach to certain social facts calculated to keep the Negro in his place; and it is "apparently determined by the factors of sex and social status."[42] The Negroes' estimate, however, is just the reverse of this: "The Negro's own rank order is just about parallel, but inverse, to that of the white man."[43] Here, then, is a perfect example of social illusion, an illusion that must inevitably come to all those who attempt to see race relations in the South as involving two castes.

In reality, however, both the Negroes and their white exploiters know that economic opportunity comes first and that the white woman comes second; indeed she is merely a significant instrument in limiting the first. If the white ruling class intends to keep the colored in their place, that is to say, freely exploitable, this class cannot permit them to marry white women; neither can it let white men marry Negro women. If this were allowed to happen, Negroes would soon become so whitened that the profit makers would be unable to direct mass hatred against them,[44] and would thus lose their principal weapon in facilitating their primary business of exploiting the black and white workers of the South.[45] If a Negro could become governor of Georgia, it would be of no particular social significance whether his wife is white or colored; or, at any rate, there would be no political power presuming to limit the color of his wife. But if, in a democracy, you could insist that his wife must be black, you could not only prevent his becoming governor of Georgia but you could also make him do most of your dirty and menial work at your wages.[46] Sexual obsession, then, functions in the fundamental interest of economic exploitation.

The Vicious Circle

Capitalist rationalizations of race relations have recently come face to face with a powerful theory of society and, in order to meet this, the classical theorists have become mystics. This evidently had to be so because it is exceedingly terrifying for these scientists to follow to its logical conclusion a realistic explanation of race relations; and yet they must either do this or stultify themselves. In illustration, Myrdal advises Negroes not to become too radical and to think of many causes as of equal significance with the economic factor. [. . .]

Although Myrdal overlays his discussion of race relations with a particularly alien caste belief, his controlling hypothesis has nothing whatever to do with caste. His "theory of the vicious circle"[47] is his controlling idea. This theory is essentially an abstract formulation, inspired by a largely inverted observation of "a vicious circle in caste" by Edwin R. Embree[48] and rendered "scientific" by the application of certain concepts which Myrdal seems to have used to his satisfaction in his study of *Monetary Equilibrium*.

As we have seen in a previous section, the vicious circle runs as follows: "white prejudice . . . keeps the Negro low in standards of living. . . . This, in turn, gives support to white prejudice. White prejudice and Negro standards thus mutually 'cause' each other." These two variables are interdependent but neither is consistently dependent; a change in either will affect the other inversely. If we initiate a change in Negro standards, say, by "giving the Negro youth more education," white prejudice will go down; if we change white prejudice, say, by "an increased general knowledge about biology, eradicating false beliefs concerning Negro racial inferiority," then Negro standards will go up.

It is this kind of mystical dance of imponderables which is at the basis of the system of social illusions marbled into Myrdal's discussion. In the first place Myrdal does not develop a careful definition of race prejudice. [. . . His] studied analysis would lead us rather to deduce the following definition of race prejudice: a feeling of bitterness, especially among poor whites, aroused particularly by a standing sexual threat of Negro men to white women.

If, according to Myrdal's "rank order of discrimination," the whites are most concerned with sex and Negroes with economic advancement, his fundamental equilibrium of social forces should be a correlation of white prejudice and Negro sexual aggression— not Negro standards, which are clearly basically economic. In this way white prejudice will tend to vanish as Negro men give up their interest in white women; Negro standards will also go up, but then only incidentally. If, for instance, Negro men would relinquish their desire to marry white women, "white people" would no longer be prejudiced against Negroes; the latter would be encouraged, say, to vote and campaign for political office, and to demand their share of jobs and public funds in the Deep South. To be sure, Myrdal does not demonstrate any such proposition. We may put it in still another way: If Negro standards go up and at the same time Negroes increase their interest in white women, then, to be consistent with Myrdal's sexual emphasis, white prejudice must increase. From this it follows that Negro standards is a nonsignificant variable.

The point which the author seems to have avoided is this: that both race prejudice and Negro standards are consistently dependent variables. They are both produced by the calculated economic interest of the southern oligarchy. Both prejudice and the Negro's status are dependent functions of the latter interest.

The assumption [by] Myrdal that racial beliefs are primary social forces leads him to conclude almost pathetically that the "white man's" beliefs are only a "mistake," which he would gladly correct if only he had truthful information. [. . .]

Evidently the misapprehension in this presentation inheres in Myrdal's moral approach. He does not recognize consistently that the propagators of the ruling ideas, those whose interest it is to replace debunked beliefs with new ones, are not mistaken at all, and that they should not be thought of merely as people or white people. They are, in fact, a special class of people who fiercely oppose interference with the established set of antagonistic racial beliefs. The racial beliefs have been intentionally built up through propaganda. They are mass psychological instruments facilitating a definite purpose; therefore, they can best be opposed by realistic, aggressive propaganda methods.[49]

Furthermore, the author's unstable equilibrium between race prejudice and Negro standards is evidently too simple. For instance, if Negro standards go up because of interference from some outside force, say the federal government, the cultivated race prejudice among the poor whites may tend to diminish, but, at the same time, the hostility of the ruling class whites may increase. The reason for this is that, because of the interference, the status and problems of Negroes and those of the poor whites may be made more nearly to coincide and thus enhance the possibility of an establishment of a community of interest between these two groups, a process diametrically opposed to the purpose and interests of the white ruling class. Therefore, it becomes incumbent upon the latter class to reaffirm its position by bringing into play those very well known means of effecting racial antipathy.

Although Myrdal never permits himself to accept a consistently realistic approach to the study of race relations, he recites as historical fact that which his theory confutes. For instance, the following historical passage says quite clearly that race prejudice is an attitude designedly built up among the masses by an exploiting class, using acceptable rationalizations derogatory to the Negro race, so that the exploitation of the latter's labor power might be justified:

> The historical literature of this early period . . . records that the imported Negroes—and the captured Indians—originally were kept in much the same status as the white indentured servants. *When later the Negroes gradually were pushed down into chattel slavery* while the white servants were allowed to work off their board, *the need was felt . . . for some kind of justification above mere economic expediency and the might of the strong.* The arguments called forth by this need . . . were broadly these: that the Negro was a heathen and a barbarian, an outcast among the peoples of the earth, a descendent of Noah's son Ham, cursed by God himself and doomed to be *a servant* forever on account of an ancient sin.[50]

Now there is no mysticism here—nothing about "sexual drives," "fears," "inhibitions," "labile balance," and so on—the historical process is clear. The exploitative act comes first; the prejudice follows. It explains unequivocally that a powerful white exploiting class, by "the might of the strong" and for "economic expediency," pushed the Negroes down into chattel slavery and then, as a justification and facilitation of this, utilized the means of propaganda, which are ordinarily in its control, to develop racial antagonism and hate in the white public for the Negroes.[51]

[. . .] A positive program [. . .] calls for an attack on the source of the beliefs, so that it might be divested of its prestige and power to produce and to substitute antiracial beliefs among the masses. In other words, the problem is that of teaching the white masses to understand and to recognize the ruling-class function of the beliefs and their effect as instruments in the exploitation of the white as well as of the black masses. Then, not only will the old beliefs lose their efficacy but also the new ones will die aborning.

A positive program calls for the winning of the white masses over to a different system of thinking. But the effectuation of such a program, the intent of which must be to alienate public support of the aristocracy, will undoubtedly evoke terrific opposition from this class. To be sure, this fact merely demonstrates further the basis of racial antagonism in the South and the correctness of the suggested positive program. At the same time, of course, Negroes must learn that their interest is primarily bound up with that of the white common people in a struggle for power and not essentially in a climb for social status.

At any rate, it is precisely this realization which Mydral constantly seeks to circumvent. Accordingly he argues inconsistently that the ruling class in the South is the Negroes' best friend:

> Our hypothesis is similar to the view taken by an older group of Negro writers and by most white writers who have touched this crucial question: that the Negroes' friend—or the one who is least unfriendly—is still rather the upper class of white people, the people with economic and social security who are *truly a "non-competing group."*[52]

The author, by one symptom or another, cannot help showing of what he is really apprehensive: the bringing into consciousness of the masses the identity of the interests of the white and the black workers. In accordance with this attitude he takes a superficial view of the economic order and asks Negroes to go to the labor market and see who is their real enemy. Thus he asserts:

> The aim of (the theory of labor solidarity) is to unify the whole Negro people, not with the white upper class, but with the white working class. . . . The theory of labor solidarity has been taken up as a last "solution" of the Negro problem, and as such is escapist in nature; its escape character becomes painfully obvious to every member of the school as soon as he leaves abstract reasoning and goes down to the labor market, because there he *meets caste* and has to talk race and even racial solidarity.[53]

[. . .] Myrdal says: "The philanthropist, the Negro educator, the Negro trade unionist . . . and, indeed, the average well-meaning citizen of both colors, pragmatically applies the same hypothesis."[54] In reality, however, this is not a confirmation of a sound theory of race relations; it is rather an apology for reformism. Within the existing system of power relationship, this is the most that is respectably allowed. Reformism never goes so far as to envisage the real involvement of the exploitative system with racial antagonism. Its extreme aspiration does not go beyond the attainment of freedom for certain black men to participate in the exploitation of the commonality regardless of the color of the latter. This aspiration is the prospect which the southern oligarchy with some degree of justification ordinarily refers to as "Negro domination."

Besides, with reformation as an end, the logical "friend" of the Negro leader must necessarily be this same white aristocracy; for he must ultimately become, like the aristocracy, the inevitable economic adversary of the exploited masses. Indeed, assuming burgeois proclivities, his very appeal to the masses for support in his struggle for "equality" is an unavoidable deception.

The reformer seeks to eliminate only the racial aspects of the exploitative system. In other words, he compromises with the system which produces the racial antagonism. But the white ruling class cannot willingly compromise, for it knows that the whole system [would be] doomed if Negroes were permitted to achieve unlimited status as participating exploiters. In such an event, there would be no racial scapegoat or red herring to brandish before the confused poor whites as a means of keeping them and the Negro masses from recognizing the full impact of political-class oppression.

Today, "conservative" theories of race relations are not merely denied: They are confronted with a counter theory, the theory that racial antagonism is in fact *political-class* antagonism and that race prejudice is initiated and maintained by labor exploiters. It is not, it would seem clear, that the aristocracy is less antagonistic to the Negroes but that this class uses more respectable weapons against them, which are also infinitely more powerful and effective. As a matter of fact, the poor whites themselves may be thought of as the primary instrument of the ruling class in subjugating the Negroes. The statement attributed to a great financier, "I can pay one-half of the working class to kill off the other half," is again in point.

As we have seen, Myrdal does not favor this explanation. He declares that all the Negro's troubles are due to the simple fact that "white people" want to be superior to colored people; or, indeed, merely to the fact that the Negro is colored. [. . .]

Throughout the study the author has found it sufficient simply to mention the name of Karl Marx in order to counter views upon economic determinism.[55] After a studied argument in favor of the futility of Negroes' adopting a Marxian view of society, he concludes: " 'Even after a revolution the country will be full of crackers' is a reflection I have often met when discussing communism in the Negro community."[56] The least we could say about this is that it is very crude. [. . .]

There will be no more "crackers" or "niggers" after a socialist revolution because the social necessity for those types will have been removed. But the vision which the capitalist theorist dreads most is this: that there will be no more capitalists and capitalistic exploitation. If we attempt to see race relations realistically, the meaning of the capitalist function is inescapable. At any rate, although Myrdal criticizes Sumner and Park for their inert and fatalistic views of social change, he himself contends that any revolutionary change in the interest of democracy will be futile:

> A national policy will never work by changing only one factor, least of all if attempted suddenly and with great force. In most cases that would either throw the system entirely out of gear or else prove to be a wasteful expenditure of effort which could reach much further by being spread strategically over various factors in the system and over a period of time.[57]

This is not the place to discuss the theory of revolution, but it must be obvious that the purpose of revolution is not to "throw the system out of gear." It is to overthrow the entire system, to overthrow a ruling class; and the cost of revolution did not frighten the capitalists when it became their lot to overthrow the feudalists.

This book, the most exhaustive *survey* of race relations ever undertaken in the United States, is a useful source of data. In detail it presents many brilliant analyses of the materials. But it develops no hypothesis or consistent theory of race relations; and, to the extent that it employs the caste belief in interpretations, it is misleading. Moreover, since we can hardly accuse Myrdal of being naive, and since he clearly goes out of his way to avoid the obvious implications of labor exploitation in the South, we cannot help concluding that the work is in many respects a powerful piece of propaganda in favor of the status quo. In this connection we are conscious of the author's recognition that "social science is essentially a 'political' science." One thing is certain, at any rate: the work contributes virtually nothing to a clarification of the many existing spurious social theories of race relations—indeed, on the latter score, Myrdal's contribution is decidedly negative. And for this reason, evidently, he has been able to suggest no solution for the dilemma; but like the fatalists whom he criticizes, the author relies finally upon time as the great corrector of all evil.

Notes

1. Gunnar Myrdal, *An American Dilemma* (New York and London, 1944). Although this is a work of considerable scholarly collaboration, we shall, in this discussion of it, assume that it is entirely by Dr. Myrdal.
2. Myrdal conceives of his problem, that is to say of race relations in the United States, as "primarily a moral issue of conflicting valuations" and of his "investigation" as "an analysis of morals" (Ibid., p. xlvi).
3. In a debate on the status of South African Indians General Smuts faces the dilemma in this way: "I do not think our Indian fellow-subjects in South Africa can complain of injustice. . . . They have prospered

exceedingly in South Africa. People who have come there as coolies, people who have come there as members of the depressed classes in India, have prospered. . . . They have been educated, and their children and grand-children today are many of them men of great wealth. They have all the rights, barring the rights of voting for parliament and the provincial councils, that any white citizen in South Africa has. . . . It is only political rights that are in question. There we are up against a stone wall and we cannot get over it" (quoted in P. S. Joshi, *The Tyranny of Colour* [Durban, 1942], p. 107).

4. Myrdal, *An American Dilemma*, p. 669.
5. Ibid., p. 1375.
6. Ibid., p. 667.
7. Ibid., p. 668. See also note c.
8. We cannot be certain, however, that Myrdal has a settled view on this point, for he says elsewhere: "After the (Civil) War and Emancipation, the race dogma was retained in the South as necessary to justify the caste system which succeeded slavery" (ibid., p. 88; see also pp. 221–24).
9. Ibid., p. 669.
10. Ibid.
11. Ibid.
12. Ibid., p. 670.
13. Ibid., p. 697.
14. Ibid., p. 668.
15. Ibid., p. 675
16. Ibid., p. 668.
17. Ibid., p. 669.
18. Ibid., p. 71.
19. Ibid., p. 690. Emphasis added.
20. Ibid., p. 669.
21. Ibid., p. 66.
22. Ibid., p. 79.
23. Ibid., p. 75.
24. Ibid., p. 101. Emphasis added.
25. Ibid., p. 69.
26. Ibid., p. 598. And in another context he recognizes that "there had been plenty of racial competition before the Civil War. White artisans had often vociferously protested against the use of Negroes for skilled work in the crafts. But as long as the politically most powerful group of whites had a vested interest in Negro mechanics, the protesting was of little avail" (ibid., p. 281).
27. Ibid., p. 286. In the South African situation Lord Oliver makes a similar observation: "When the capitalist employer comes on the scene, making discriminations as to the labor forces he must employ for particular work in order to make his profits, which is the law of his activity to do, then, and not till then, antagonism is introduced between the newly-created wage-working proletarian white and the

native—who, in regard to the qualifications which properly determine wage contracts, are on exactly the same footing" (*The Anatomy of African Misery* [London, 1927], p. 135).

28. Ibid., p. 57.
29. Hinton R. Helper, the renegade Southerner, who never bit his tongue in his criticism of the white ruling class of the South and who, however, never concealed his prejudices against the Negroes, spoke more than a grain of truth when he described the position of the poor whites. It is essentially applicable to present-day conditions: "Notwithstanding the fact that the white non-slaveholders of the South are in the majority as five to one, they have never yet had any part or lot in framing the laws under which they live. . . . The lords of the lash are not only absolute masters of the blacks . . . but they are also the oracles and arbiters of all the non-slaveholding whites, whose freedom is merely nominal and whose unparalleled illiteracy and degradation is purposely and fiendishly perpetuated. How little the 'poor white trash,' the great majority of the Southern people, know of the real conditions of the country is indeed sadly astonishing. . . . It is expected that the stupid and sequacious masses, the white victims of slavery, will believe and, as a general thing, they do believe, whatever the slave-holders tell them; and thus it is that they are cajoled into the notion that they are the freest, happiest, and most intelligent people in the world, and are taught to look with prejudice and disapprobation upon every new principle or progressive movement" (*The Impending Crisis* [New York, 1860], pp. 42–44, *passim*).
30. Myrdal, *An American Dilemma*, p. 453.
31. Ibid., p. 455.
32. Ibid., p. 466.
33. Ibid., p. 456.
34. Ibid., p. 593.
35. Ibid., p. 596.
36. Ibid., p. 721.
37. Ibid., p. 727.
38. Ibid., p. 459.
39. Ibid., p. 220.
40. Ibid., p. 208.
41. Ibid., p. 61. In similar vein he asserts: "It is surely significant that the white Southerner is much less willing to permit intermarriage or to grant 'social equality' than he is to allow equality in the political, judicial and economic spheres. The violence of the Southerner's reaction to equality in each of these spheres rises with the degree of its relation to the sexual and personal, which suggests that *his prejudice is based upon fundamental attitudes toward sex and personality*" (p. 61; emphasis added).
42. Ibid.
43. Ibid.
44. It should be made crystal clear that the motive of the ruling white

people is not primarily to keep the blood of the white race "pure," but to prevent race mixture; it is, therefore, definitely as frustrating to their purpose to infuse white blood into the Negro group. Their purpose can be accomplished only if the Negroes remain identifiably colored.

45. Decades ago George W. Cable observed: "The essence of offence, any and everywhere the race line is insisted upon, is the apparition of the colored man or woman as his or her own master; that masterhood is all that all this tyranny is intended to preserve . . . the moment the relation of master and servant is visably established between race and race there is a hush of peace. . . . The surrender of this one point by the colored man or woman buys more than peace—it buys amity" (*The Negro Question* [New York, 1903], pp. 22–23).

46. In order to support his specious argument, Myrdal relies pivotally upon such sour-grape expressions as the following by R. R. Moton: "As for amalgamation, very few expect it; still fewer want it; no one advocates it; and only a constantly diminishing minority practise it, and that surreptitiously. It is generally accepted on both sides of the color line that it is best for the two races to remain ethnologically distinct" (*An American Dilemma*, p. 62). This, from a Negro, is assumed to be evidence that Negroes do not want intermarriage. On its face, Myrdal might have asked: Why should something that is not wanted be practiced "surreptitiously"? Moreover, would the white ruling class be obsessed with the prevention of intermarriage if the natural likelihood of its occurring were exceedingly remote?

47. Ibid., pp. 75–78, 207–09, and Appendix 3.

48. Ibid., p. 1069, note.

49. This view also holds against certain popular conceptions of race prejudice as "superstition" or "myth."

50. Myrdal, *An American Dilemma*, p. 85. Emphasis added.

51. It is interesting to observe with what anonymity. Myrdal uses such key concepts as: "imported," "captured," "kept," "pushed down," and so on. One would think that the subject referred to by these terms of action would be of primary concern in the investigation. It is, however, highly impersonalized and the whole situation tends to remain as if it were an act of Nature.

52. *An American Dilemma*, p. 69. Emphasis added. It is interesting to observe how Dr. Myrdal has finally become almost reactionary in the sense of the incorrigible segregationist W. T. Couch, who also says: "Nothing is more needed in the South today than rebirth of [Booker Washington's] ideas, restoration of the great leadership that he was giving" (see Rayford Logan, ed., *What the Negro Wants* [Chapel Hill, 1944], p. xxiii).

53. Ibid., p. 793. Emphasis added.

54. Ibid., p. 1069.

55. And yet Myrdal has shown himself to be vitally wanting in an understanding of the difference between status rivalry and class struggle.

Observe, for instance, the following typical confusion: "Our hypothesis is that in a society where there are broad social classes, and in addition, more minute distinctions and splits in the lower strata, the lower class groups will to a great extent, take care of keeping each other subdued, thus relieving, to that extent, the higher classes of this otherwise painful task necessary to the monopolization of the power and the advantages.

"It will be observed that this hypothesis is contrary to the Marxian theory of class society. . . . The Marxian scheme assumes that there is an actual solidarity between the *several lower class groups* against the *higher classes,* or, in any case, a potential solidarity. . . . The inevitable result is a 'class struggle' where all poor and disadvantaged groups are united behind the barricades" (ibid., p. 68). Myrdal thinks that Marx thinks the *upper class* and the *lower class,* mere social illusions, are in conflict. No wonder he seems to conclude that Marx is rather foolish. And he does not trouble himself at all to explain how the "higher classes" exercise the "necessary painful task" of keeping the lower classes subdued when, per chance, the latter stop fighting among themselves and turn their attention to their common enemy. This is, to use the term so frequently employed by Myrdal, "escapism."

56. Ibid., p. 509.
57. Ibid., p. 77. Long before this, John Locke had said quite as much; (see *Essay Concerning Human Understanding* (London, 1690)).

3

Race and Caste: A Distinction

In recent theoretical explanations of race relations probably no concept has been used so consistently as that of "caste." The social scientists have popularized again a concept that was just about losing its popularity. Many early sociologists, including Robert E. Park, had struggled with the problem of identifying race relations with caste relations, but it took the engaging style of Professor W. Lloyd Warner to sell the idea to the generality of sociologists.[1] Perhaps nothing shows so well how thoroughly Warner has succeeded as Dr. Gunnar Myrdal's wholehearted and elaborated acceptance of his caste belief, admittedly the only theoretical explanation of race relations in *An American Dilemma*.

[. . .] In this article we shall hope to show that race relations are not caste relations; and, for this purpose, we shall assume that Brahmanic-Indian society represents the only developed caste system in the world.[2] Moreover, we shall refer mainly to Negro-white relations in the United States for our illustrations of race relations.

In attempting to differentiate race and caste relations it should be kept in mind that two major types of social organization are involved and not merely two institutions within the societies. Our comparison, however, will be concerned with certain distinguishing features. As distinguished from a bipartite interracial adjustment, the caste system is ancient, provincial, culturally oriented, hierarchical in structure, status conscious, nonconflictive, nonpathological, occupationally limited, lacking in aspiration and progressiveness, hypergamous, endogamous, and static.

Ancient and Modern Societies

In a study of race and caste relations our first realization should probably be that modern Western society is characteristically dif-

ferent from any other previously existing society. It is called "bourgeois society," which amounts to the same thing as "businessmen's
society." It is an aggressively exploitative, profit-making system as
compared with apparently all the ancient systems, which were
based mainly upon production for a "sufficiency of existence." In
Western civilization there is basically a limitless urge to exploit the
means of production. In the caste system this is not nearly so
pronounced. Production in the caste system is based on hereditary
monopoly rather on competitive opportunism.

There are other significant differences; our point here is, however, that "race relations" developed in modern times as our own
exploitative system developed.[3] Moreover, race relations or problems are variants of modern political class problems—that is to say,
the problems of exploitation of labor together with the exploitation
of the other factors of production. In the caste system there is no
proletariat, no class struggle—indeed, no need for the proletarianization of workers. We shall assume "judicial notice" of the
fact that the race problem in the United States arose, from its
inception in slavery, out of the need to keep Negroes proletarianized.

Occupation

Western society has been built about the market place, and the
freedoms of the latter institution have permeated the system. But
quite frequently in a "free economic system" the monopolist may
acquire certain advantages. In the caste society there is no such
dual system of economic forces; production is completely monopo-
lized. The slaveholder sees, or thinks he sees, an opportunity for
maximizing his profits by purchasing his labor like capital in a "free
market"; his extreme fear is the labor union, which seeks to control
the supply of labor. We should expect certain quite obvious types of
rationalization and religion to develop from the latter situation,
and the race problem is vitally enmeshed in it.

In the caste society there is no need to develop public antagonism
against a whole people for the purpose of exploiting its labor power
because each caste is a circumscribed productive unit. No group has
a right to change its work; yet, in the event that some occupation
becomes plethoric or unproductive, the caste may assume another
less respectable occupation. The latter provision is necessary to make
it as distasteful as possible for castes to change their occupations.

[. . .] Production in the caste economy, then, is carried out by hereditarily specialized producers' associations which have not only a right to peaceful enjoyment of their specialty but also a sacred duty to execute it faithfully and contentedly. Castes do not have the alternative opportunity of working in those industries which yield the largest returns. The significant point of difference here is that there is no "boss" employing castes at stipulated wages to produce commodities which belong to the entrepreneur and which he expects to sell at a profit. The material products of a caste belong to the caste; and it ordinarily disposes of them according to certain established rules of the community.

On the other hand, Negroes in the United States have a right to sell their labor in the best market. Competition of different varieties and especially open exploitation tend to keep Negroes out of many employments; so far as constitutional and religious *right* to any given occupation is concerned, however, both Negroes and whites are on equal footing. Thus, not only are the races not identified with any particular occupation, but there is also no accepted plan for the sharing of occupations. It should be observed that in Brahmanic India each caste is expected to have an occupation and not particularly that every occupation is supposed to have a caste.

If we should attempt to explain race relations in terms of caste relations, slavery and the Black Codes, peonage, and, indeed, the very concept of the Negro's "place" can have no meaning. In Brahmanic India there is no caste problem because the system of labor exploitation which produces the race problem in America is totally foreign to the caste system.

Race Relations Physical; Caste Cultural

"Just as a Sudra begets on a Brahman female a being excluded from the Aryan community, even so a person himself excluded procreates, with females of the four castes, sons more worthy of being excluded than himself."[4] This law from Manu reveals graphically a pattern of caste stratification that is the opposite of every known system of race relations. Thus, if we consider only the two castes mentioned, Brahman and Sudra, it is obvious that the lawgiver maintains that successive crosses between lower-caste men and pureblood Brahman women result in offspring of increasing inferiority. In other words, the mixed progeny of a Sudra man and a Brahman woman is very much superior to a man whose father is, say, one sixty-fourth Sudra along the male line, while his mother is pure Brahman. Yet, so far as physical difference is concerned, it is clear that the latter must be considered virtually pure Brahman. We are not, of course, assuming here that there was originally a recognized physical difference between the two castes; the point is that the meaning of "blood" in caste relations is not the same as that in race relations.

The crucial basis of race relations is physical identifiability. When we speak of Chinese, Indians, Europeans, Negroes, or Filipinos, we expect responses indicating consciousness of ocular evidence of physical differentiation. But when we refer to such groups as Chamars, Baniyas, Telis, Doms, Brahmans, Kayasthas, or Jolahas, no sense of physical distinction need be aroused. We see rather only East Indians. If we are familiar with these castes, one name might suggest filth and human degradation, while another might call to mind scrupulous cleanliness and superciliousness, or very likely a certain occupation, or any one of a composite of cultural traits.

The concept of biological amalgamation is not particularly applicable to caste. Never, so far as we know, has Brahmanic India had a "color problem." Physical rapprochement does not affect the distinction or stability of castes. Indeed, historically, caste rigidity in India has proceeded hand in hand with physical amalgamation. It cannot be assumed, however, that the one caused the other. On the contrary, when two races have amalgamated, all possible "race questions" will have been answered.

It is impossible for a person to become a member of any given race other than by birth; but, although the membership of castes is ordinarily limited by birth, it is quite possible for two or more castes to merge if they so will it—consequences notwithstanding.[5] An individual may be initiated into a caste but clearly not into a race. In the caste system the heritage which gives the person distinction is cultural, hence he may be dispossessed of it; the individual born of a given race, however, inherits physical marks which are not only inalienable but also beyond the discretion of the race itself. It is manifest, then, that, being born within a given race, there is no alternative but to die within it;[6] in the case of caste no such obdurate rule obtains. In fact, the individual may abandon his caste at will, while he cannot possibly give up his race.

In Brahmanic India there are no half-caste people. A person is either in a caste or out of a caste; but a person may be half-race or any other fraction of a race. And, since race relations are concerned with physical attributes, we should expect two modern races—whites and some people of color especially—in contact to develop different problems for persons with different degrees of admixture. [. . .] In the United States, for instance, a person with very little Negro blood is confronted with different problems from those which either the pure white or the black person must meet.

Structure of Caste and Race Relations

The structure[s] of race and of caste relationship are incommensurable. Caste has reference to the internal social order of a society; race suggests a whole people, wherever found about the globe. A people in actual world dispersion will not conceive of themselves as members of a caste. While there may be rivalry for position among castes, between races in opposition there will be struggle for power. Racial antagonism tends to divide the society vertically; the caste system tends to stratify it into a status hierarchy.

[. . .] Both racial and caste separation tend to inhibit social mobility, but this common characteristic should not be conceived of as identifying them. The mobility which racial antagonism abhors is movement across a color fence which surrounds each race regardless of the social position of the individual. The mobility which the caste system limits is movement from one corporate group into another within an *assimilated* society.

Race and Caste Consciousness

Race sentiment and interest tend to be universal, while caste sentiment and interest tend to be circumscribed and localized. If a part of the membership of a caste were to migrate to some area beyond easy reach of the other, the likelihood is that it would become a new caste. Not so, however, with a race. The Indian people are very much concerned about the relationship of Hindus with other races all over the world. Thus the East Indians in Africa and in the West Indies may be outcasts, because of their migration from India, but they are by no means given up by the race. Caste pride is based on intrasocietal group invidiousness, while race pride cuts across caste lines and reaches out to the whole people, commanding their loyalty in a body.

At this point it may be well to say a word about the phenomenon known as "passing." Given a common culture, passing may be thought of as a procedure by which a mixed-blood person—having the physical characteristics of the dominant race—assumes full membership in that race so that he may participate in the social advantages which the former has reserved to itself. One form of passing may be called "shuttling." Here the mixed-blood moves back and forth between the two races, leading a primary familial life in the one, and a secondary, industrial life in the other. Almost always the familial group is of the subordinate race. The shuttler, to be sure, is open to greater risk of detection than the passer who has decided once and for all to make a complete break with one race.

A caste man does not pass; neither is he preoccupied with passing into another caste. However, the foolhardy may shuttle in pursuit of some transient gain, such as sitting in at the feasts and celebrations of other castes. On the other hand, we should expect most, if not all, subjugated peoples to desire to pass. Clearly, it is possible only for marginal men to pass; yet the general attitude is socially significant. If, for instance, the following question were put to American Negroes: "Would you wish that you were white?" the answer would be obvious. It would not be so obvious, however, if the same question were put to Negroes who had not yet felt the full pressure of white exploitation. But if one were to ask East Indians whether they would all like to become Brahmans, the question would elicit the same sort of response as if Americans were asked whether they would all like to become priests, or judges, or congressmen.

Race Conflict Addressed to the System Itself

Race conflict is directed either against or toward the maintenance of the entire order of the races. On the other hand, caste rivalry never brings the caste system into question; its purview of opposition is circumscribed by identified castes. As a matter of fact, races are not status-bearing entities in the sense that castes are. For instance, Negroes and whites in the United States stand toward each other in the relationship of subordination and superordination—a relationship implying suspended conflict. Conversely, castes stand toward each other in the relationship of superiority and inferiority, a relationship implying *natural*, socially accepted, peaceful status-ordering of the society. In the first case we have a power relationship in which definite aims and ends of each group are opposed; the second is a situation of mutual emulation or symbiosis among little status-bearing groups.

Intercaste jealousy and invidiousness tend to strengthen the fabric of the caste system; interracial conflict, on the other hand, is usually a challenge to the pattern of interracial adjustments. Thus we might say that the greater the rivalry between caste and caste, the more stable the caste system; while the greater the conflict between race and race in one society, the greater the opportunity for settling interracial differences. It is only when the subordinate race has obtained a relatively advanced conception of itself that it will make a bid for "social equality." To be sure, failure or a definite achievement of further suppression by the superordinate race will obviously widen the breach between them.

[. . .] The world position of a race tends, moreover, to determine the attitude of its members in their relationship with other races. Thus Englishmen in India derive their dominant attitude not only from the might of the nation which they represent but also from the position which white people occupy all over the world. Mohammedans in India are humiliated by a military reverse of the Turks; and East Indians attained a new gratifying conception of themselves in the 1904–05 defeat of Russia by Japan (a colored people), while Marcus Garvey saw the hope of black men in great ships of war manned by Negroes. This principle of power and force, which seems to underlie race adjustments, gives it a peculiarly eruptive and unstable character.

Race Relations Pathological

We may call any system or intergroup adjustment "pathological" which harbors latent conflict attitudes directed toward its destruction. However, no form of seeming oppression of one group by another is of itself a conclusive index. In some cultures slavery is normal, in others extreme class subordination, and in still others, outcasting. A stable social adjustment may be thought of as one in which the beliefs of a people are in harmony with their practices and in which the social system itself never comes up for critical public discussion. The occasion for a defense of the social order does not arise, and this notwithstanding the possible adverse judgment of persons residing in other societies.

Now, in the United States, the racial system has been under extreme internal criticism and discussion. The basic ideological problem of whites in their relationship with Negroes has been that of reconciling two standards of morality. The powerful democratic, Christian beliefs, developing in Western society at an increasing rate, are on the side of the colored people. The racially articulate whites must shoulder the responsibility of demonstrating that these beliefs do not include Negroes, hence they strive to see democracy as implying equal opportunity among whites in their exploitation of Negroes. At any rate, such a position must be constantly reinforced, for it rests insecurely on a broader world view. It is frequently attacked from within the ranks of whites themselves, while virtually all Negroes are opposed to it. There are probably more words spent upon the race problem in the South than upon all other social problems combined.

We may think of the racial adjustment in the South as being in a state of great instability. The cultural pattern is unsatisfactory to both races—a serious problem to each—and it is antipathetic to the fundamental social norms of the country. Respect for law in a representative form of government must be relied upon for preserving the integrity of social institutions. But in America respect for the white race takes precedence—a condition which has resulted, especially in the South, in endemic social dysphoria. Thus we may conceive of the interracial accommodation as a persistent, malignant system which remains ominous of violent interracial strife. Anxiety, fear, mutual mistrust, and social stricture are typical mental states.

[. . .] The mob, nightriders, gangs, and ruling-class organizations such as the Ku Klux Klan; slugging, kidnapping, incendiarism, bombing, lynching, flogging, and blackmailing are among the principal reliances of the racially articulate whites for securing their position. The instability of this accommodation may be indicated by the fact that a goodly number of southern whites are ashamed of it.

In Brahmanic India, on the other hand, intercaste violence never takes such a pattern. In order to establish his superiority a Brahman does not have to resort to clandestine terrorization of lower-caste men, since undisputed public opinion gives him the right overtly to subdue disrespectful inferiors. Therefore, as a constituted form of punishment, a Brahman may direct the flogging of a low-caste man. The position of high-caste Hindus is guaranteed to them in Hindu society; but in America there is no such fundamental guaranty for whites. In the caste system there is social peace with the order; it is blessed in the most sacred books of the Hindus.

Aspiration a Factor

[. . .] In practically every instance of white-colored race contacts there has been a remarkable stimulation of ambition and aspiration among the colored people. In most instances the white dominant group has observed this attitude with apprehension. It is, however, exceedingly persistent, for it goes hand in hand with acculturation, and the internal dynamism of capitalism makes it inevitable.

Unlike caste in India, Negroes in America have been seeking to increase their participation and integration in the dominant culture. The absence of such striving is an inseparable feature of the caste system. Indeed, culturally speaking, the castes have arrived; the idea of progress is totally foreign to the system.

If, for instance, the Negro-white relationship were a caste relationship, Negroes would not be aspiring toward the social position occupied by whites; their concern, rather, would be almost entirely with the development of a socially sufficient internal organization. It is this centrifugal cultural drive among Negroes which produces fear and antagonism among the white ruling class. Indeed, the most potent weapon of racial aggression—segregation—has been devised to inhibit it. Thus, the scheme of race relationship in America centers about attempts of Negroes to reach new levels of participation and opposition to these attempts by whites. . . .

Hypergamy

. . . In India superior-caste males may marry inferior-caste women, and this does not result in consolidation of castes. . . .

The higher the caste, the greater the opportunity for "mixture of blood." Yet hypergamy has not resulted in a lessening of caste consciousness. "If caste was based on distinction of race," says R. V. Russell, "then apparently the practice of hypergamy would be objectionable, because it would destroy the different racial classes."[7] In the Punjab outcaste women, Chamars, are sold to Jats, Gujars, and Rajputs as wives.[8]

The taking of colored women by white men, at least in their early contact with a people of color, is also considered a form of hypergamy; in fact, some writers have found it possible to identify caste and race relations on this very point. But the significant difference between these two forms of hypergamy is that in the case of castes the identity of the groups are not affected by it; while in the case of race relations, the more frequent the intermarriages the less clear the racial distinctions. Women taken from lower castes may be a total loss to the latter—unless it be that the lower caste gains some spiritual gratification from a sense of one of its members' participating in a higher *dharma*—but the gain to the people of color

varies all the way from complete amalgamation to the establishment of a restless mixed-blood people who tend to become a
challenge to the pretensions of their fathers' race. Hypergamy can
never become a law in a biracial system, for the system will be
doomed from the moment of its enactment. Here again, then, we
have a social fact which seems common to two different situations,
yet whose social meanings are distinct.

Endogamy

Endogamy is self-imposed restriction on out-marriage by a social
group. Any group which explicitly limits marriage of its members
to persons within the group may be called endogamous. In Western
society there are negative sanctions against upper-class persons
marrying lower-class persons; yet we do not ordinarily think of the
upper class as being endogamous. In fact, a social class cannot be
endogamous because it has no consciousness of its limits.

With the exception of hypergamy, endogamy among castes in
India is a basic trait. A group cannot function within the
Brahmanic system if its social area of choice of partners in marriage is undefined. The caste is a truly endogamous social entity.
The prohibitions against out-marriage are not a reaction to similar
actions of some other castes; they are the most reliable means
available to the caste for protecting its heritage. Furthermore, the
social heritage of low castes is to them as important as that of high
castes is to the latter.

Some students of the caste system have concluded that endogamy
among castes is similar to endogamy as they observe it between race
and race in Western society. But if we return to our situation in the
United States, we shall see that neither Negroes nor whites belong
to groups that are endogamous in the caste sense. Their choice of
partners in marriage is limited only by matters of cultural compatibility or localized racial antagonisms. A caste is organized as a
caste not only with respect to some specified group but with reference to every other conceivable group or individual. White people
in the United States, on the contrary, may marry whites from any
other part of the world. Generally they are opposed to intermarriage with any people of color; but, unless racial antagonism becomes directed, a marriage here and there is not particularly
objectionable. When the social situation is favorable, as in Hawaii,
whites may intermarry even more readily than some other races.

Being themselves a colored people, Negroes have only a cultural inhibition. They will intermarry comparatively freely with every other race in the United States. Indeed, in some states, whites have found it contrary to their interest to permit marriage between Negroes and other people of color within the state. The opposition of Negroes to intermarriage with whites is a rather complex reaction. It varies in response to the attitudes of whites in different parts of the country.

We may conclude, then, that endogamy is of different significance in caste and race relations. The caste is socially and contentedly locked within its immediate marital circle; the race, on the other hand, is opportunistic and will intermarry or refuse to do so as its interest or cultural strategy demands.

Dynamics of Race Relations

The fundamental social force operating among Negroes is social assimilation and amalgamation. In America there has been a strain toward assimilation among most minority groups. This is particularly powerful among Negroes because their parent culture not only was designedly extirpated but also lost virtually all prestige on the American scene. Colored people, then, are oriented toward the broader culture of the country; only through social rebuffs are they turned back upon themselves. In this the attitude of whites and Negroes is not similar but opposed. The racially articulate whites feel that they must guard their exploitative advantage (not specifically their occupation) for exclusive enjoyment, while Negroes are seeking increasing cultural participation. The difference between the racial attitude of whites and the caste attitude, so far as the social ideals of each system are concerned, is that whites *wrongfully* take the position of excluding groups from participating freely in the common culture, while castes *rightfully* exclude outsiders from participating in their *dharma*.

The world view of the caste is turned inward, and its force is centripetal; that of Negroes is turned outward, and its force is centrifugal. Negroes, in America at least, are working toward the end that Negroes as such shall become nonexistent. However, the caste of either low or high status is devoted to the perpetuation of itself.[9] The solidarity of Negroes is admittedly temporary; it is a defense-offense technique. The ideal of Negroes is that they should not be identified; they evidently want to be workers, ministers, doctors, or teachers without the distinction of being *Negro* workers, *Negro* ministers, and so on. In short, they want to be known unqualifiedly as American citizens, which desire, in our capitalist society, means assimilation and amalgamation.

The Belief Not Useful

There are many reasons why the caste belief should not be used in scientific discussions of race relations. The following are some of them. In the first place, social scientists are theoretically as interested in the social attributes of the caste system as they are in those of any other system. Hence a simple, almost thoughtless, consideration of that system is definitely to be discouraged. The caste system of our own time is not very much different from what it was some three thousand years ago, being a very powerful form of cultural organization. The early Greek invasion left almost no imprint on it; and when the modern Europeans came upon it, Mohammedanism seemed just about to be swallowed. Evidently, however, Hinduism, like all other cultures, has met its match in Western culture. The caste system is not yet in its death throes, but it is squirming under the impact of capitalism. It should be more interesting to observe the social phenomena involved in the battle of these two great cultures than to make a hasty identification of them. It may be well to mention that the Vedic Indians could not possibly have known the phenomenon which we today call "race prejudice."

Then, too, the use of the concept "caste" in the study of race relations is a diseconomy. It involves a definition of race according to common usage and a substitution of the term "caste" for "race," then a definition of the term "caste," which must again be identified with the popular meaning of the concept "race"—a totally unwarranted neology.

Probably the most serious objection to the use of the caste belief is that it serves almost invariably to obfuscate the most significant aspects of race relations. At points where light is most needed, the caste school of race relations usually brings into service the mysticism of caste, and the result is frequently utterly misleading.

Moreover, the caste idea as used by them is neither a hypothesis, a theory, nor a description of some society; therefore it explains nothing. It is, in fact, a mystical concept, which has authority neither in the caste system of India nor in the dynamic social and political class system of Western society.

Notes

1. See my "The Modern Caste School of Race Relations," *Social Forces* (December 1942): 218–26.
2. We do not know of any sociologist who relies, for his criteria of caste relationship, on any other system.
3. For two good discussions emphasizing the recent development of the social attitude of race prejudice and antagonism see Frederick G. Detweiler, "The Rise of Modern Race Antagonisms," *American Journal of Sociology* (March 1932): 738–47; and Ina Corinne Brown, *National Survey of the Higher Education of Negroes,* "Publications of the U.S. Office of Education," misc. 6, vol. I (Washington, 1942), pp. 4–8. See also M. F. Ashley Montagu, *Man's Most Dangerous Myth* (New York, 1942), p. 10.
4. *The Laws of Manu,* "The Sacred Books of the East," ed. F. Max Müller, vol. XXV (Oxford, 1886), chap. x, p. 30.
5. "There is . . . apparently a tendency toward the consolidaton of groups at present separated by caste rules. The best instance of such a tendency to consolidate a number of castes into one group is to be found in the grazier castes which aim at combining under the term 'Yadava' Ahirs, Goalas, Gopis, Idaiyans, and perhaps some other castes of milkmen, a movement already effective in 1921. . . . The Census Superintendent of the Central Provinces quotes 'specific instances' . . . of marriage between members of different sub-castes of Brahmans, and between members of different sub-castes of Kalars, where the union would formerly have been condemned" (*Census of India, 1931,* I, pt. I, 431).
6. We are not unmindful here of the phenomenon of passing. However, only physically marginal men pass; hence, they may be said to have been born with the necessary physical characteristics.
7. R. V. Russell, *The Tribes and Castes of the Central Provinces of India* (London, 1916), vol. II, pp. 363–64.
8. George W. Briggs, *The Chamars* (Oxford, 1920), p. 42.
9. According to James Weldon Johnson, "We should by all means make our schools and institutions as excellent as we can possibly make them; and by that very act we reduce the certainty that they will forever remain schools and institutions for 'Negroes only.' . . . We should gather all the strength and experience we can from imposed segregation. But any good we are able to derive from the system we should consider as a means, not an end. The strength and experience we gain from it should be applied to the objective of *entering into,* not *staying out of,* the body politic" (*Negro Americans, What Now?* [New York, 1935], p. 17).

4

Race Relations:
Its Meaning, Beginning, and Progress

In a discussion of "the origin" of race relations it should be well to determine at the outset exactly what we are looking for. We shall proceed, therefore, by first eliminating certain concepts that are commonly confused with that of race relations. These are: ethnocentrism, intolerance, and "racism."

Ethnocentrism, as the sociologists conceive of it, is a social attitude which expresses a community of feeling in any group—the "we" feeling as over against the "others." This attitude seems to be a function of group solidarity, which is not necessarily a racial phenomenon. Neither is social intolerance . . . racial antagonism, for social intolerance is social displeasure or resentment against that group which refuses to conform to the established practices and beliefs of the society. Finally, the term "racism" as it has been recently employed in the literature seems to refer to a philosophy of racial antipathy. Studies on the origin of racism involve the study of the development of an ideology, an approach which usually results in the substitution of the history of a system of rationalization for that of a material social fact.[1] Indeed, it is likely to be an accumulation of an erratic pattern of verbalizations cut free from any ongoing social system.

What then is the phenomenon, the beginnings of which we seek to determine? It is the phenomenon of the capitalist exploitation of peoples and its complementary social attitude. Again, one should miss the point entirely if one were to think of racial antagonism as having its genesis in some "social instinct" of antipathy between peoples. Such an approach ordinarily leads to no end of confusion.[2]

The Beginning of Racial Antagonism

Probably a realization of no single fact is of such crucial significance for an understanding of racial antagonism as that the phenomenon had its rise only in modern times.[3] In other writings we have attempted to show that race conflict did not exist among the early Aryans in India, and we do not find it in other ancient civilizations. Our hypothesis is that racial exploitation and race prejudice developed among Europeans with the rise of capitalism and nationalism, and that because of the worldwide ramifications of capitalism, all racial antagonisms can be traced to the policies and attitudes of the leading capitalist people, the white people of Europe and North America.

By way of demonstrating this hypothesis we shall review briefly some well-known historical situations. In tracing the rise of the Anglo-Saxons to their position as the master race of the world[4] we shall omit consideration of the great Eastern civilization from which Greece took a significant cultural heritage. There seems to be no basis for imputing racial antagonism to the Egyptians, Babylonians, or Persians. At any rate, the Greeks were the first European people to enter the stream of eastern Mediterranean civilization, and the possibility of racial exploitation did not really occur until the Macedonian conquest. Our point here is, however, that we do not find race prejudice even in the great Hellenistic empire which extended deeper into the territories of colored people than any other European empire up to the end of the fifteenth century.

The Hellenic Greeks had a cultural, not a racial, standard of belonging, so that their basic division of the peoples of the world were Greeks and barbarians—the barbarians having been all those persons who did not possess the Greek culture, especially its language. This is not surprising, for the culture of peoples is always a matter of great moment to them. But the people of the Greek city-states, who founded colonies among the barbarians on the shores of the Black Sea and of the Mediterranean, welcomed those barbarians to the extent that they were able to participate in Greek culture, and intermarried freely with them. The Greeks knew that they had a superior culture to those of the barbarians, but they included Europeans, Africans, and Asiatics in the concept Hellas as these peoples acquired a working knowledge of the Greek culture.

The experience of the later Hellenistic empire of Alexander tended to be the direct contrary of modern racial antagonism. The narrow patriotism of the city-states was given up for a new cosmopolitanism. Every effort was made to assimilate the barbarians to Greek culture, and in the process a new Greco-Oriental culture with a Greco-Oriental ruling class came into being. Alexander himself took a Persian princess for his wife and encouraged his men to intermarry with the native population.[5] In this empire there was an estate, not a racial, distinction between the rulers and the un-Hellenized natives.

[. . .] The next great organization of peoples about the Mediterranean Sea—and insofar as European civilization is concerned this may be thought of as constituting the whole world—was the Roman Empire. In this civilization also we do not find racial antagonism, for the norm of superiority in the Roman system remained a cultural-class attribute. The basic distinction was Roman citizenship, and gradually this was extended to all freeborn persons in the municipalities of the empire. Slaves came from every province, and there was no racial distinction among them. Sometimes the slaves, especially the Greeks, were the teachers of their masters; indeed, very much of the cultural enlightenment of the Romans came through slaves from the East. Because slavery was not a racial stigma, educated freedmen, who were granted citizenship on emancipation, might rise to high positions in government or industry. There were no interracial laws governing the relationship of the great mass of obscure common people of different origin. Moreover, the aristocracy of the empire, the senators and *equites,* was constituted largely from responsible provincials in the imperial administration.

[. . .] If we have not discovered interracial antagonism in ancient Greece and Rome, the chances of discovering it in the system which succeeded the fall of the Roman Empire are even more remote. With the rise of the politico-religious system of Christianity, Western culture may be thought of as having entered its long period of gestation. Its first signs of parturition were the Crusades. But during all this time and even after the Renaissance the nature of the movement and of the social contact of peoples in this area precluded the possibility of the development of race prejudice.

[. . .] In Europe itself the policies of the Roman Catholic Church presented a bar to the development of racial antagonism. The church, which gradually attained more or less religious, economic, and ideological dominance, had a folk and personal—not a territorial or racial—norm of belonging. The fundamental division of human beings was Christian and non-Christian. Among the non-Christians the heathen, the infidel, and the heretic were recognized by differential negative attitudes; however, as a means of entering the Christian community, conversion or recantation was freely allowed and even sought after. There was in medieval Europe—indeed in the Christian world—an effective basis for the brotherhood of peoples. Although a man's economic, contractual relationship in his community determined his livelihood, to be excommunicated by the church almost had the effect of putting him beyond the purview of society itself. In the Middle Ages, then, we find no racial antagonism in Europe; in fact, Europeans were, at this time, more isolated and ignorant about foreign peoples and world geography than the Romans and Greeks were.

But gradually, under the commercial and religious impulse, Europe began to awaken and to journey toward strange lands. The First Crusade may be taken as the starting point which finally led to world dominance by Europeans. When after their travels in the last quarter of the thirteenth century the Polos returned from the court of the great Kublai Khan in China to tell Europeans a story of fabulous wealth and luxury, the astonished people could hardly believe what they heard. Yet Marco Polo's memoirs were a great stimulant to traders. It was not until the discovery of America and the circumnavigation of the globe, however, that in the movement assumed a decidedly irreversible trend. The people between the First Crusade and the discovery of America continued to be characterized by the religious view of world order; but it set a pattern of dealing with non-Christian peoples which was to be continued, minus only its religious characteristics, to this day. To the extent that the religious controls remained effective, racial antagonism did not develop; what really developed was a Jew-heathen-infidel antagonistic complex which was to color European thought for some centuries.

Up to the eleventh century Christian European was hemmed in from the North, East, and South by heathens and infidels; the Mediterranean was almost encircled by the Arabian Mohammedans, a people whose culture was superior to that of the northern Europeans. In the eleventh century, however, under the organizing influence of the popes, the holy warriors of Christendom began to carry conquering crusades into the territory of the heathen Slavic and infidel Asiatic peoples. As a general rule the church made the lands and even the peoples of the non-Christian world the property of the Crusaders, and the trader ordinarily followed the cross.

In fact, it was this need for trade with the East, especially by the Italian, Spanish, and Portuguese merchants, and its obstruction by the Mohammedans whose country lay across their path in the Near

East, which induced the Portuguese, in the fifteenth century, to feel their way down the African coast in the hope of sailing around this continent to the East Indies. Here began the great drama that was, in a few hundred years, to turn over the destiny of the world to the decisions of businessmen. But our concern at this point is to indicate that racial antagonism had not yet developed among the Europeans.

In the first place, the geography of the world was still a mystery, and some of the most fantastic tales about its peoples were believed. Stories of the splendor, luxury, and wisdom of the peoples of the East held all Europe in constant wonderment. No one would have been surprised if some traveler had returned from the heart of Africa to break the news that he had found a black monarch ruling over a kingdom surpassing in grandeur and power any that had then existed in Europe. In short, the white man had no conception of himself as a being capable of developing *the* superior culture of the world—the concept "white man" had not yet its significant social definition—the Anglo-Saxon, the modern master race, was then not even in the picture.

But when the Portuguese began to inch their way down the African coast they knew that the Moors and heathens whom they encountered were inferior to them both as fighters and as culture builders.[6] This, however, led to no conclusions about racial superiority. Henry the Navigator, himself, sought in those parts a Christian prince, Prester John, with whom he planned to form an alliance "against the enemies of the faith." All through the latter half of the fifteen century the Portuguese sailors and explorers kept up this search for the kingdom of the lost black prince.

Of more significance still is the fact that there was as yet no belief in any cultural incapacity of these colored people. Their conversion to Christianity was sought with enthusiasm, and this transformation was supposed to make the Africans the human equal of all other Christians. The Portuguese historian Gomes Eannes de Azurara, writing in the middle of the fifteenth century, gives us some idea of the religious motives for Prince Henry's exploits among the peoples on the West African coast. One reason for the Navigator's slave raids

> was his great desire to make increase in the faith of our lord Jesus Christ and to bring to him all souls that should be saved,—understanding that all the mystery of the Incarnation, Death, and Passion of our Lord Jesus Christ was for this sole end—namely the salvation of lost souls, whom the said Lord Infant [Henry] by his travail and

spending would fain bring into the true faith. For he perceived that no better offering could be made unto the Lord than this. For if God promised to return one hundred goods for one, we may justly believe that for such great benefits, that is to say, for so many souls as were saved by the efforts of this Lord, he will have so many hundreds of guerdons in the Kingdom of God, by which his spirit may be glorified after this life in the celestial realm. For I that wrote this history saw so many men and women of those parts turned to the holy faith, that even if the Infant had been a heathen, their prayers would have been enough to have obtained his salvation. And not only did I see the first captives, but their children and grandchildren as true Christians as if the Divine grace breathed in them and imparted to them a clear knowledge of itself.[7]

This matter of cultural conversion is crucial for our understanding of the development of racial antagonism. For the full profitable exploitation of a people, the dominant group must devise ways and means of limiting that people's cultural assimilation. So long as the Portuguese and Spaniards continued to accept the religious definition of human equality, so long also the development of race prejudice was inhibited. Although it is true that the forays on the African coast were exceedingly ruthless, the Portuguese did not rationalize the fact with a racial argument. To kill or to take into slavery the heathen or infidel was to serve the highest purpose of God. As Azurara pointed out, "though their bodies were now brought into subjection, that was a small matter in comparison to their souls, which would now possess true freedom for evermore."[8] In granting to Prince Henry a "plenary indulgence," Pope Eugenius IV gave "to each and all those who shall be engaged in the said war [slave raids], complete forgiveness of all their sins."[9]

The Portuguese people themselves had developed no racial hatred for the captives. Azurara relates how the townspeople at Lagos wept in sympathy for the suffering of the Moors as families were broken to be distributed among different masters. And, it seems, the captives were quite readily assimilated into the population:

... from this time forth [after their partition] they began to acquire some knowledge of our country, in which they found great abundance; and our men began to treat them with great favour. For as our people did not find them hardened in the belief [i.e., Islam] of the Moors, and saw how they came unto the law of Christ with a good will, they made no difference between them and their free [Portuguese] servants, born in our own country. But those whom they took [captured] while still young, they caused to be instructed in mechanical arts. And those whom they saw fitted for managing property, they set free and married to women who were natives of the land [of Portugal], making with them a division of their property as if it had been bestowed on those who married them by the will of their own fathers. . . . Yea, and some widows of good family who bought some of these female slaves, either adopted them or left them a portion of their estate by will, so that in the future they married right well, treating them as entirely free. Suffice it that I never saw one of these slaves put in irons like other captives, and scarcely any one who did not turn Christian and was not gently treated.

And I have been asked by their lords to the baptisms and marriages of such; at which they, whose slaves they were before, made no less solemnity than if they had been their children or relations.[10]

The Portuguese had no clear sense of racial antagonism because its economic and rationalistic basis had not yet developed among them. Indeed the Portuguese and Spaniards never became fully freed of the crusading spirit, which constantly held in check their attainment of a clear appreciation of the values of competitive labor exploitation.[11] The church received its share of African servants; as yet, however, it had no idea of the economic uses of segregation and "cultural parallelism"—of the techniques for perpetuating the servile status of the black workers. It had developed no rationalizations of inborn human inferiority in support of a basic need for labor exploitation. On the contrary, its obsession with the spiritual values of conversion left the Negroes free to be integrated into the general population. . . .

The next era in the history of race relations commenced with the discovery of America. . . . Modern society—Western civilization—began to take on its characteristics attributes when Columbus turned the eyes and interests of the world away from the Mediterranean toward the Atlantic. The mysticism of the East soon lost its grip on human thought, and the bourgeois world got under way. The socioeconomic matrix of racial antagonism involved the commercialization of human labor in the West Indies, the East Indies, and in America, the intense competition among businessmen of different western European cities for the capitalist exploitation of the resources of this area, the development of nationalism and the consolidation of European nations, and the decline of the influence of the Roman Catholic Church with its mystical inhibitions to the free exploitation of economic resources. Racial antagonism attained full maturity during the latter half of the nineteenth century, when the sun no longer set on British soil and the great nationalistic powers of Europe began to justify their economic designs on weaker European peoples with subtle theories of racial superiority and masterhood.

It should be observed that this view is not generally agreed upon. A popular belief among writers on modern race relations is that the phenomenon has always been known among most, if not all, peoples. This approach apparently tends to give theories of race relations a "scientific" aspect, but it contributes little to an understanding of the problem.

[. . .] When white scholars began their almost desperate search of the ancient archives for good reasons to explain the wonderful cultural accomplishments among the whites, European economic and military world dominance was already an actuality. Most of the discoveries which explain the racial superiority of the tall, long-headed blond may be called Hamite rationalizations; they are drawn from bits of isolated verbalizations or deductions from cultural situations which cannot be identified with those of modern race relations. Probably the most widely accepted of these has been the biblical story of the descendants of Ham as a people cursed forever to do the menial work of others.

When English, French, and German scholars discovered the Aryans in the Sanskrit literature of the Hindus, the Hindus themselves were unaware of the Aryans' racial potentialities. The concept "Arya" meant practically nothing to them. It remained for the nationalistic Germans to recognize that the term "Aryan" designated Germans particularly and that, because of this, the right of Germans to exploit all other peoples of the world, not excluding the Hindus, was confirmed.

In the study of race relations it is of major importance to realize that their significant manifestations could not possibly have been known among the ancients. If we had to put our finger upon the year which marked the beginning of modern race relations we should select 1493–94. This is the time when total disregard for the human rights and physical power of the non-Christian peoples of the world, the colored peoples, was officially assumed by the first two great colonizing European nations. Pope Alexander VI's bull of demarcation issued under Spanish pressure on May 3, 1493, and its revision by the Treaty of Tordesillas (June 7, 1494), arrived at through diplomatic negotiations between Spain and Portugal; put all the heathen peoples and their resources—that is to say, especially the colored peoples of the world—at the disposal of Spain and Portugal.[12]

Sometimes, probably because of its very obviousness, it is not realized that the slave trade was simply a way of recruiting labor for the purpose of exploiting the great natural resources of America.[13] This trade did not develop because Indians and Negroes were red and black, or because their cranial capacity averaged a certain number of cubic centimeters, but simply because they were the best workers to be found for the heavy labor in the mines and plantations across the Atlantic.[14] If white workers had been available in sufficient numbers they would have been substituted. As a matter of fact, part of the early demand for labor in the West Indies and on the mainland was filled by white servants, who were sometimes defined in exactly the same terms as those used to characterize the Africans. Although the recruitment of involuntary labor finally settled down to the African coasts, the earlier kidnappers did a brisk business in some of the most enlightened European cities. Moreover, in the process of exploiting the natural resources of the West Indies, the Spanish conquistadors literally consumed the native Indian population.

This, then, is the beginning of modern race relations. It was not an abstract, natural, immemorial feeling of mutual antipathy between groups, but rather a practical exploitative relationship with its socio-attitudinal facilitation—at that time only nascent race prejudice. Although this peculiar kind of exploitation was then in its incipiency, it had already achieved its significant characteristics.[15] As it developed and took definite capitalistic form, we could follow the white man around the world and see him repeat the process among practically every people of color. . . .

. . . The fact of crucial significance is that racial exploitation is merely one aspect of the problem of the proletarianization of labor, regardless of the color of the laborer. Hence racial antagonism is essentially political-class conflict. The capitalist exploiter, being opportunistic and practical, will utilize any convenience to keep his labor and other resources freely exploitable. He will devise and employ race prejudice when that becomes convenient.[16] As a matter of fact, the white proletariat of early capitalism had to endure burdens of exploitation quite similar to those which many colored peoples must bear today.

However, the capitalist spirit, the profit-making motive, among the sixteenth-century Spaniards and Portuguese was constantly inhibited by the philosophy and purpose of the Roman Catholic Church. A social theory supporting the capitalist drive for the impersonal exploitation of the workers never completely emerged. Conversion to Christianity and slavery among the Indians stood at cross-purposes; therefore, the vital problem presented to the exploiters of labor was that of circumventing the assimilative effects of conversion to Christianity. In the West Indies the celebrated priest, Las Casas, was touched by the destructive consequences of the ruthless enslavement of the Indians, and he opposed it on religious grounds. But work had to be done, and if not voluntarily, then some ideology had to be found to justify involuntary servitude. "The Indians were represented as lazy, filthy pagans, of bestial morals, no better than dogs, and fit only for slavery, in which state alone there might be some hope of instructing and converting them to Christianity."[19]

The capitalist exploitation of the colored workers, it should be observed, consigns them to employments and treatment that are humanly degrading. In order to justify this treatment the exploiters must argue that the workers are innately degraded and degenerate; consequently they naturally merit their condition. It may be mentioned incidentally that the ruling-class conception of degradation will tend to be that of all persons in the society, even that of the exploited person himself; and the work done by degraded persons will tend to degrade superior persons who attempt to do it.

In 1550, finally, the great capitalist interests produced a champion, Gaines de Sepulveda, brilliant theologian and debater, to confront Las Casas in open debate at Valladolid on the right of Spaniards to wage wars of conquest against the Indians. Sepulveda held that it was lawful to make war against (enslave) the Indians:

1. Because of the gravity of their sins. . . .
2. Because of the rudeness of their heathen and barbarous natures, which oblige them to serve those of more elevated natures, such as the Spaniards possess.
3. For the spread of the faith; for their subjection renders its preaching easier and more persuasive [and so on].[18]

It is not surprising that Sepulveda won the debate. His approach was consistent with the exploitative rationalizations of the time. He contrived a reasonably logical justification for the irrepressibly exploitative situation. This clearly was in answer to an urgent necessity for such an authoritative explanation; the whole world, so to speak, was calling for it. As a characteristic, it should be observed that no explanation at all need have been made to the exploited people themselves. The group sentiment and feeling of the exploited peoples were disregarded entirely.

Sepulveda, then, may be thought of as among the first great racists;[19] his argument was, in effect, that the Indians were inferior to the Spaniards, therefore they should be exploited. Yet the powerful religious interest among the Spaniards limited the establishment of a clear philosophy of racial exploitation. Some years earlier an attempt was made to show "that the Indians were incapable of conversion," but this was finally squelched by a threat to bring the advocate before the tribunal of the Inquisition.[20] It remained for later thinkers, mainly from northern European countries, to produce the evidence that "native peoples" have an inferior, animal-like capacity for culture.[21]

In the years to follow there will be unnumbered sermons preached and "scientific" books written to prove the incapacity for cultural conversion of exploitable peoples, and always with the implied or expressed presumption that this incapacity should stand as a bar to movements for the cultural assimilation of such peoples. (The ultimate purpose of all theories of white superiority is not a demonstration that whites are in fact superior to all other human beings but rather to insist that whites must be supreme. It involves primarily a power rather than a social-status relationship.) Assimilation diminishes the exploitative possibilities. This social situation is not especially a derivative of human idiosyncrasy or wickedness, but rather it is a function of a peculiar type of economic order which, to repeat, has been developed in the West among Europeans. The exploitation of native peoples, imperialism, is not a sin, not essentially a problem of morals or of vice; it is a problem of production and of competition for markets.[22] Here, then, are race relations; they are definitely not caste relations. They are labor-capital-profits relationships; therefore, race relations are proletarian bourgeois relations and hence political-class relations.

[. . .] Although both race relations and the struggle of the white proletariat with the bourgeoisie are parts of a single social phenomenon, race relations involve a significant variation. In the case of race relations the tendency of the bourgeoisie is to proletarianize a whole people—that is to say, the whole people is looked upon as a class—whereas white proletarianization involves only a section of the white people. The concepts "bourgeois" and "white people" sometimes seem to mean the same thing for, with respect to the colored peoples of the world, it is almost always through a white bourgeoisie that capitalism has been introduced. The early capitalist settlers among the colored peoples were disposed to look upon the latter and their natural resources as factors of production to be manipulated impersonally with "white capital" in the interest of profits. It is this need to impersonalize whole peoples which introduces into the class struggle the complicating factors known as race problems. If the colored people themselves are able to develop a significant bourgeoisie, as among the Japanese and East Indians, race relations are further complicated by the rise of conscious nationalism. [. . .]

[. . .] Caste prejudice is an aspect of culture prejudice, while race prejudice—as distinguished from culture prejudice—is color-and-physique prejudice. The latter is prejudice marked by visibility, physical distinguishability; it is not, however, caused by physical differences. We may repeat that precise anthropometrical definitions of race are not of crucial significance.[23] Racial attitudes are based upon simple obvious criteria, and the findings of anthropometry, whether genuine or spurious, may simply provide a basis for their rationalization. Color prejudice, as a psychological phenomenon, is a complex emotion manifested by a positive attitude of distance and a reaction; specifically it is an insistent attitude of white superiority and dominance and an accommodating reaction to persons of color. It is a cultural trait of Western society which took form during the era of explorations.

To achieve a simple understanding of the concept, it may be well for us to observe the problem from the point of view of the initiating factor; that is to say, the white factor in the relationship. As stated above, in the contact of color groups, whites have set the stage for the pattern which the racial adjustment will assume. It varies according to their needs and aspirations, while the colored groups attempt to meet the aggressor on whatever seem to them the most favorable grounds. Therefore, an understanding of modern race relations will be achieved only if we look at the situation from the point of view of the desires and methods of Europeans in their dealings with peoples of color. The caste hypothesis of race relations will hardly help us to understand why the white ruling classes in the West Indies contend with most exacting logic that the contact of East Indians and Negroes there is socially advantageous, while in Kenya they reason with equal verve that the contact of Indians and Negroes is socially insalubrious.[24] It would hardly give us a hint to the reason for the Portuguese's remarkable freedom from race prejudice in Brazil as compared with their scrupulousness about color in Hawaii. We should have no clue at all concerning the irreconcilable ways of the Dutch—their anticolor attitudes in South Africa as against their comparative liberality in Java. [. . .]

Notes

1. See Hannah Arendt, "Race-Thinking before Racism," *The Review of Politics* (January 1944): 36–73; and Frederick G. Detweiler, "The Rise of Modern Race Antagonisms," *American Journal of Sociology* 37 (March 1932): 738–47.

2. Consider, for instance, the following definitive statement by Professor Robert E. Park: "This [preudice against the Japanese] is due to the existence in the human mind of a mechanism by which we inevitably and automatically classify every individual human being we meet. When a race bears an external mark by which every individual member of it can infallibly be identified, that race is by that fact set apart and segregated. Japanese, Chinese, and Negroes cannot move among us with the same freedom as members of other races because they bear marks which identify them as members of their race. This fact isolates them. . . . Isolation is at once a cause and an effect of race prejudice. It is a vicious circle—isolation, prejudice; prejudice, isolation" (in Jesse F. Steiner, *The Japanese Invasion*, p. xvi).

   Since, however, we may assume that all races "bear marks which identify them as members of their race," it must follow, according to Park, that a certain human capacity for classification makes it impossible for races to come together without racial antagonism and prejudice. We shall attempt to show that this instinct hypothesis is too simple.

3. Cf. Ina Corine Brown, *National Survey of the Higher Education of Negroes*, U.S. Office of Education, Misc. no. 6, vol. I, pp. 4–8.

4. Professor G. A. Borgese makes an observation pertinent to this remark: "The English-speaking mind is not fully alive to the gravity of this issue. Unlike their German cousins and foes, the Anglo-Saxon stocks did not strive to *become* the master race of *Herrenvolk* holding sway over the world and mankind. . . . Yet, unlike their German cousins and rivals, they have succeeded in *being a Herrenvolk*, a race of masters" ("Europe Wants Freedom from Shame," *Life*, March 12, 1945, pp. 41–42: (emphasis in original).

   "The Germans needed all of Hitler's ranting and daily doses from the Goebbels propaganda machine to persuade them that they were better than other people. Englishmen simply take it for granted and rarely waste a syllable discussing it" (see John Scott, *Europe in Revolution*, [Boston, 1945], p. 216).

5. In describing the composition of Alexander's army invading India, E. R. Bevar says: "Mingled with Europeans were men of many nations. Here were troops of horsemen, representing the chivalry of Iran, which had followed Alexander from Bactria and beyond, Pashtus and men of the Hindu Kush with their highland-bred horses, Central-Asiatics who ride and shoot at the same time; and among the camp-followers one could find groups representing the older civiliza-

tions of the world, Phoenicians inheriting an immemorial tradition of shipcraft and trade, bronzed Egyptians able to confront the Indians with an antiquity still longer than their own" (*The Cambridge History of India* [Cambridge, 1922], vol. I, p. 351).

6. It should be noted that the Portuguese felt they were superior because they were Christians, not because they were white. In an address to his men just before they attacked an unsuspecting west-coast community, the captain of a caravel declared: "Although they are more in number than we by a third yet they are but Moors, and we are Christians one of whom ought to suffice for two of them. For God is He in whose power lieth victory, and He knoweth our good wills in His holy service" (Gomes Eannes de Azurara, *The Discovery and Conquest of Guinea*, [London, 1896–99], p. 138).

7. Ibid., p. 29.

8. Azurara, *Discovery and Conquest of Guinea*, p. 51.

9. Ibid., p. 53.

10. Ibid., p. 84.

11. Speaking of the activities of the Portuguese at Goa, India, soon after 1498, L. S. S. O'Malley says: "The Portuguese territories were intended to be outposts of their empire and their religion. . . . Colonization was effected not so much by immigration as by marriage with Indian women. There was no color bar, and the children of mixed marriages were under no stigma of inferiority. . . . Proselytization began soon after the capture of Goa. . . . At the same time the spread of Christianity was assisted by an appeal to material interests. Converts were to be provided with posts in the customs, exempted from impressment in the navy, and supported by the distribution of rice" (*Modern India and the West*, pp. 44–45).

12. As early as 1455 Pope Nicholas V had granted the Portuguese exclusive right to their discoveries on the African coast, but the commercial purpose here was still very much involved with the crusading spirit.

13. In a discussion of the arguments over slavery during the Constitutional Convention, Charles A. Beard observes: "South Carolina was particularly determined, and gave northern representatives to understand that if they wished to secure their commercial privileges, they must make concessions to the slave trade. And they were met half way. Ellsworth said: 'As slaves multiply so fast in Virginia and Maryland that it is cheaper to raise than import them, whilst in the sickly rice swamps foreign supplies are necessary, if we go no farther than is urged, we shall be unjust towards South Carolina and Georgia. Let us not intermeddle. As population increases, poor laborers will be so plenty as to render slaves useless'" (*An Economic Interpretation of the Constitution* [New York, 1943], p. 177; quote from Max Farrand, *Records*, vol. II, p. 371).

14. In a discussion of the labor situation among the early Spanish colonists

in America, Professor Bailey W. Diffie observes: "One Negro was reckoned as worth two, four, or even more Indians at work production" (*Latin American Civilization* [Harrisburg, 1945], p. 206).

15. Francis Augustus MacNutt describes the relationship in Hispaniola: "Columbus laid tribute upon the entire population of the island which required that each Indian above fourteen years of age who lived in the mining provinces was to pay a little bell filled with gold every three months; the natives of all other provinces were to pay one *arroba* of cotton. These amounts were so excessive that in 1496 it was found necessary to change the nature of the payments, and, instead of the gold and cotton required from the villages, labour was substituted, the Indians being required to lay out and work the plantations of the colonists in their vicinity" (*Bartholomew De Las Casas*, p. 25).

16. In our description of the uses of race prejudice in this essay we are likely to give the impression that race prejudice was always "manufactured" in full awareness by individuals or groups of entrepreneurs. This, however, is not quite the case. Race prejudice, from its inception, became part of the social heritage, and as such both exploiters and exploited for the most part are born heirs to it. It is possible that most of those who propagate and defend race prejudice are not conscious of its fundamental motivation. To paraphrase Adam Smith: They who teach and finance race prejudice are by no means such fools as the majority of those who believe and practice it.

17. Francis Augustus MacNutt, *Bartholomew De Las Casas* (New York and London, 1909), p. 83.

It should be kept clearly in view that this colonial movement was not a transference of the feudal manorial economy to America. It was the beginning of an entirely different economic enterprise—the dawn of colonial capitalism, the moving out of "white" capital into the lands of colored peoples who had to be exploited unsentimentally and with any degree of ruthlessness in the interest of profits.

18. Ibid., p. 288.

19. Among the Spanish writers of the time (about 1535 onward) who were in rather complete accord with the drastic methods of human exploitation in the New World was Gonzolo Fernandez de Oviedo, whose prolific works have been collected in the commentary *Historia General y Natural de las Indias*, 4 vols. It was Oviedo's opinion, even after visiting America on a royal commission, that the Indians were not far removed from the state of wild animals, and that coercive measures were necessary if they were to be Christianized and taught the uses of systmatic labor.

20. MacNutt, *Bartholomew De Las Casas*, pp. 94–95.

21. Beasts of burden do not have rights which human beings are bound to respect; they may be exploited at will. The latter convenience is a desideratum in the capitalist exploitation of labor, regardless of the color of the laborer. However, the fact of difference in color and culture makes available to the exploiters of colored workers a valuable

means of securing their dehumanization in the eyes of a certain public, that is to say, the public of the exploiting class. When a philosophy for the dehumanizing of the exploited people has been developed with sufficient cogency, the ruling class is ready to make its grand statement, sometimes implicitly, and to act in accordance with it: The colored people have no rights which the master race is bound to respect. The exploiting class has an economic investment in this conviction and it will defend it with the same vigor as it would an attack upon private property in land and capital.

22. Of course one should not be particularly disturbed about the fact that, although one never had the necessity or even the thought of exploiting colored people, yet an almost irresistible bitterness seems to well up as one finds himself in certain social situations with colored people. It is this very reaction which derogatory racial propaganda sets out to achieve and, knowing that even human nature itself is a social product, it would be surprising if the people did not hate whichever group the ruling class convinced them should be hated. Moreover, we naturally tend to dislike people who are degraded or brutalized. A degraded person is a contemptible person who should be despised and kept at a distance—the Christian Gospels notwithstanding.

   Such ambivalent conclusions as the following by Dr. Louis Wirth may be misleading: "Ethnic, linguistic, and religious differences will continue to divide people, and the prejudices that go with them cannot suddenly be wiped out by fiat. But whereas personal prejudices and antipathies can probably be expected to yield only to the tedious process of education and assimilation, collective programs and policies can be altered considerably in advance of the time when they have unanimous group consent. Law and public policy can go far toward minimizing the adverse effect even of personal prejudices" (in Ralph Linton, ed., *The Science of Man in the World Crisis*, p. 368).

23. We may illustrate this point. After delivering an invective against the assumed racial superiority of the whites in India, Krishnalal Shridharani declares: "An overwhelming majority of the Indian people belongs to the so-called white race, according to all anthropological and ethnological data. The tropical sun may have imparted pigmentation to the skin of the Indo-Aryan . . . but the ethnologist knows that the Indo-Aryan is of Caucasian origin" (*Warning to the West*, p. 191). The ethnologist may be equally convinced about the race of white American Negroes, but just as the British in India pays him no attention, so also white Americans turn to him a deaf ear. Says Robert Briffault, in his incisive review of the ways of the white sahibs in India, "The Hindus were treated, as they have been ever since, as 'niggers' " (*The Decline and Fall of the British Empire* [New York, 1938], p. 78).

24. See *Report of the Committee on Emigration from India to the Crown Colonies and Protectorates* (London, 1910).

   Warren S. Thompson comments upon the situation in Africa: "When all is said that can truly be said about the nefarious practices of the Indians in their dealings with the Negroes in East Africa, it seems more than probable that the chief objection to their economic relations with the natives is to be found in the fact that they render the white man's exploitation of the Negroes more difficult and less profitable than it would otherwise be. Naturally this is resented, and it certainly sounds better to object to the nefarious exploitation of the Negro by the Indian than to say that the Indian is not wanted because he makes white people work harder to maintain their profits, and renders their lives less pleasant than they would be if they did not have to compete with him. This is too frank an avowal of their own exploitative purposes" (*Danger Spots in World Population* [New York, 1930], p. 169; see also India, Central Bureau of Information, *India in 1930–31*, pp. 49ff.; and Maurice S. Evans, *Black and White in South East Africa* [London, 1911], p. 291).

In 1919 the Kenya Economic Commission reported: "Physically the Indian is not a wholesome influence because of his repugnance to sanitation and hygiene. In this respect the African is more civilized than the Indian, being naturally cleanly in his ways. . . . The moral depravity of the Indian is equally damaging to the African. . . . The presence of the Indian in this country is quite obviously inimical to the moral and physical welfare and the economic advancement of the native" (quoted by Raymond Leslie Buell, *The Native Problem in Africa*, vol. I, p. 291).

II

Contemporary Race Relations

Many of the selections included in this section are excerpted from Cox's last major work, *Race Relations: Elements and Social Dynamics,* published posthumously in 1976. The book was an attempt to present a comprehensive theory of race relations, but is disappointing in many respects, lacking coherence and failing to achieve its purpose. It is nevertheless important because it provides a view of Cox's thinking on race relations in the turbulent 1960s and 1970s, particularly his response to black nationalism and the black power movement, and his views on the black "underclass." While Cox continued to believe that racism was closely linked to the development of capitalism, he now argued that capitalism is a dynamic economic and cultural system with a formidable ability to assimilate diverse groups—and thus offers the possibility for black Americans to achieve full equality in the United States. Consequently, he was dissatisfied with any effort he believed would restrict the assimilation of blacks into the mainstream of U.S. society, either the ideology of black nationalism, which he firmly opposed, or misguided sociological conceptualizations that viewed black ghettos as internal colonies. Cox argued that the federal government and the business community were actively committed to a reformist program: eradicating racial discrimination, promoting equal opportunity, and improving the socioeconomic situation of the blacks. The problem that remained was the cultural legacy of segregation in the rural South, which endured in the subculture of the northern ghetto, as well as the lack of skills, education, and proper work habits that would make it possible for blacks to take advantage of opportunities that arose. Further, Cox thought that if blacks were to achieve their "place in the sun," it had to be in the mainstream of business and urban employment, and not as a separate group or nation. Nationalistic schemes that were aimed at "decolonizing" the

67

inner-city ghetto or teaching black English in the schools would only serve to relegate blacks to the status of cultural outsiders and weaken the competitive capacities of blacks as a group.

The first selection, "Significance of Rural Culture for Race Relations," describes the characteristic pattern of race relations in the southern Black Belt following slavery. Cox shows how, under a system of tenant farming and debt peonage, illiterate and unskilled black farmers were economically exploited and politically disenfranchised by an oligarchy of white planters, merchant-financiers, and lawyer-politicians. The culture of the plantation and the planter still dominated rural life while the legal rights of blacks were circumvented through the manipulation of state power. Furthermore, the weight of the total system relegated black tenant farmers and sharecroppers to a state of economic, physical, and psychological dependency. This in turn had resulted in some of the most injurious aspects of the southern political economy: family instability and the "slovenly state of its physical upkeep," a disruption of community life, and a lack of interest in education. Most important, the system of labor exploitation had "denied [blacks] access to the inherent individualism and competitiveness of the dominant American way of life." Thus when blacks migrated to the cities, their adjustment was in part affected by the racial pathologies of the rural South, as well as by the adverse conditions of urban life.

The second selection, "The Ghetto," is Cox's most scathing critique of the pathological nature of the black underclass—a point of view that, it should be pointed out, was prevalent among other black sociologists of his generation; the selection also underscores how strongly Cox held to his assimilationist views. The subculture of the ghetto, according to Cox, is inherently pathological and alien to the values of middle-class society. A product of racial oppression, the ghetto is also a constant source of fear, insecurity, and anguish. Its inhabitants are more likely to be segregated from the rest of society and to become the victims of crime perpetuated by other ghetto residents. On the other hand, because the ghetto is a "projected achievement of white power groups," its victims cannot be entirely to blame for their depressed social conditions and negative behavior. The life-style of the ghetto is tragic, particularly the widespread "dissipation of adult time and energy" and the "spectacle of men in the prime of life, in full daytime, sitting or lying or leaning about ghetto premises." Given this low level of cultural development, Cox recommends that the black ghetto be abandoned; or, to put it slightly differently, the abandonment of the ghetto would be a sure sign that blacks were being fully assimilated into the U.S. mainstream.

As the third selection, "Negro Protest and the Subculture," shows, Cox's attachment to the assimilation model influenced his perspective on the black protest movement of the 1960s. Here he presents contrasting images of the attitudes of the "Negro lower-class subculture" and that of the dominant middle class, which he contends sets the norms for the entire society. The attitudes of the former are incompatible with those of the latter: They are "largely negative, defensive, reactionary—with inherent processes such as 'getting by' and 'getting away with.'" The attitudes of the latter, on the other hand, stress "hard work, honestly, efficiency, sobriety, and upward cultural motivation, such as that which made possible the development and maintenance of the phenomenal American productive system." Cox writes approvingly of the "protest for assimilation," because it is led by the middle class, oriented toward middle-class values, and yet benefits the lower classes.

In the fourth selection, "The Question of Pluralism," Cox examines the conceptual weaknesses of various definitions of pluralism in order to demonstrate how different writers have interpreted this concept inconsistently. While the term purports "to define a specific state of intergroup relations," scientifically it is seriously limited because it "does not define a consistent pattern of social behavior." Further, the term "has been brought in as a shibboleth by groups ranging all the way from black and white separatists to black and white assimilationists." Some assimilationists, Cox notes, erroneously believe that pluralism may be a short-term solution in the face of the decline in support for the long-term goal of integration. In focusing attention on Nathan Glazer's article "Negroes and Jews: The New Challenge to Pluralism," Cox also argues that black demands for racial integration pose a threat to Jewish pluralism, since demands for integrated communities and education cannot be reconciled with the Jewish effort to maintain exclusivity over certain areas of opportunity. As Cox notes in another provocative paper, "Jewish Self-Interest in Black Pluralism" (1974; not included here), the desire of blacks for assimilation and the Jewish emphasis on ethnic pluralism create conflict and tension between the two groups. He argues that pluralism is not in the best interest of blacks because they, unlike Jews, have very little alien culture to protect.

The final selection, "The Road Ahead," sums up Cox's views on the extent of black progress in the 1970s. He argues that employment is a critical factor in the economic well-being of black Americans because work is very much tied to identity and a sense of self-worth. Responding to those writers who believe the race problem is not solvable because of the biological permanence of color, Cox points to the historical gains in federal legislation as evidence that race relations have not remained static, and argues that to the extent that barriers to black progress do persist, "immediate problems arise from questions of enforcement, and from the willingness or ability of Negroes to accept existing opportunities." Where white nationalism (i.e., racism) continues "in a 'free society' it is difficult to legalize this attitude." He also points to increasing black influence in the major urban centers, but notes that this can create problems as well as opportunities: where blacks have gained a hold over city politics, they have to deal not only with the opposition of whites, but with the "temptation of black ideologists to convert the city into a black nation." Yet if black politicians are to succeed, they must address the needs of all their constituents: economic prosperity must be their primary concern. Since this involves competing with their white counterparts in attracting businesses, economic interests must supersede concerns for racial solidarity or nation-building.

5

Significance of Rural Culture for Race Relations

We are interested here not so much in the particular study of the Negro American in agriculture as in identifying the focus and social situation which generated the characteristic pattern of race relations in the United States. The significance of relevant data does not change from census to census. The relationship of the Negro farm worker to the white, landlord class on the southern plantation tended to constitute the pivot of the inferiority-superiority definition of the groups for the entire nation. This relationship merits special attention because it became the generative seedbed of the racial tradition which spread not only to other parts of the country but also to Europe and Asia.

The pattern of discrimination can be consistently dealt with only as an inherent function of the major social system. We would dissipate the critical attributes of the relationship were we to generalize about the structurally alien caste system of India, thralldom in the ancient world, feudalism in different parts of the medieval world, or the intense in-group characteristics of African tribalism. As Woofter quite properly remarks: "The plantation system is bound up with the cash-crop system."[1]

Economic compulsions peculiar to the capitalist market drove illiterate, unskilled [Negro] freedmen into basic productive alliances with dispossessed whites and held them there in spite of the vexations of exploitation and the persistence of master class frustrations.[2] Although the relationship was an interactive one, we should not lose sight of the fact that the way of life of the colored people, and indeed of the South as a whole, remained largely dependent upon the dominant interests and leadership of the great planters:

> Plantation customs and ideology set the pattern for relationships in smaller farm units. This is true because of the dominance of the

71

plantation in southern rural life. Large planters persistently emerge as the political and economic leaders of the cotton areas. Even if there are only four or five large plantations in a county. The ownership of these considerable properties and the prestige of success on a large scale make it easy for the planters to assume prominence in community control if their personalities fit them for leadership. Add to this a sentimental attachment to land as a symbol of aristocracy and the consequent family ties to the land, and the plantation stands out as the basis for the hereditary oligarchy in southern community life.[3]

Besides the plantation oligarchy, the Black Belt merchant-financier and the lawyer-politician, "who knew how to make of little or no effect the Thirteenth, Fourteenth, and Fifteenth Amendments,"[4] converged into a structure of conservative authority which gradually enveloped and overwhelmed the freedmen.[5] The persistent influence of this force, plus dependence on the land for daily bread, brought the Negro farm operator close to total submission. Says Raper:

> Man-land relations, landlord-tenant patterns, the white primary, the expenditures for public schools, the location of the churches, the everyday doings of whites and Negroes all foster the sentiments and differentials which define and maintain the Black Belt's way of life. From the local point of view there are few problems: the tenant is improvident, dependent, and childlike and the planter furnishes him food and supervises his labor; mortal violence sometimes overtakes the Negro. . . . Lynching is resorted to . . . when the implied threat of it appears to be losing its efficacy.[6]

Conditions of Dependence

The social process of production perpetuated and demonstrated these attributes of the tenant. Although there are various types of tenancy, Negro tenancy has been especially characterized by landlord supervision, season subsistence credits, and provision of working capital for the operation of the farm and for housing. The tenant, on the other hand, worked in the field—sometimes under overseer direction—and received his means of subsistence, including shelter and fuel, as a charge against his annual income derived from the sale of his share of the cotton or tobacco produced on the farm. The primary opportunity for control and abuse of the tenant arose from the fact that traditionally the landlord not only kept and verified accounts of advances but also settled all conditions for sale and division of the crop. He was abetted by the subservience, intimidation, and illiteracy of the tenant.

According to the situation, the landlord could present to the tenant terms involving completed transactions regarding the price of provisions advanced to him, the amount of interest charged for the period of the loan, the final quantity and quality of the harvest, his income from its sale, or a face-to-face agreement concerning the size of his share. Ordinarily accounts were settled once a year at harvest time; but variations even in this could rebound to the advantage of the planter. It is also of importance to note that the landlord resisted any attempt by the tenant to hold him to formal written agreements. That would contravene the paternalistic, primary relations which define the tenant as a nonjuristic, dependent juvenile.[7] Thus, according to T. J. Woofter and associates:

> The relations between landlord and tenant are traditionally informal. Detailed agreements are not usually worked out and contracts are practically never written. Such records of advances and repayments as are kept are almost always in the hands of the landlord. This becomes a complicated account when debts from previous years are carried forward and added to current advances. This situation places the absolute control of relationships in the hands of the landlord and the fairness of settlements is largely dependent upon his sense of justice. The tenant's only recourse is to move, which of course does not adjust his past transactions but merely enables him to seek more satisfactory conditions.[8]

After having subsisted on a modicum of provision, however, the tenant could find himself not only in debt but also restricted in his attempt to transfer from farm to farm.[9] In periods of labor shortage especially, the landlord relied on state legislation to immobilize his workers. Laws were designed to prevent tenant families from moving until the crop was harvested in the fall or until all debts incurred as allowances were repaid. Since the books of the landlord were ordinarily the only record of the tenants' indebtedness, he could present them annually with end-of-year balances, including obligations to liquidate them at the next harvest. This well-known situation, called "peonage," achieved legal sanction in a number of states—Alabama, Florida, Georgia, Mississippi, North Carolina, South Carolina—and constituted traditional practice in others.[10]

Peonage lost favor during the great Depression, and has not resumed its earlier strategic role. During World War II, Gunnar Myrdal and his associates concluded: "We do not know whether the present shortage of farm labor has brought about any new increase in . . . debt-peonage. What we do know is that the whole legal system previously gave the tenants but little protection against such abuses and that, so far, there has been no fundamental change in this legal system. . . . It is certain, anyway, that there is some debt-peonage left."[11] The more recent advances in mechanization of farm production in the region and the Negro's newfound status in the law have doubtless reduced the practice to a minimum.

Intimidation

Nothing, perhaps, indicates so well the continuity of conditions of bondage as the planter's conception of himself as inheriting the prerogative to punish physically the tenant and members of his family, sometimes including females, for breaches of rules and practices. Informal physical punishment constitutes the ultimate source of coercion and intimidation directed against Negroes of the South. The worst manifestations occurred in rural plantation areas. The immediate causes of physical chastisement included charges of disrespect, stealing, refusal to work, and other forms of disobedience. Allison Davis and associates found stealing to be the most common reason for whippings. They explain: "The fact that stealing is the charge upon which most beatings are justified is the result both of the fact that the ownership of property is the basic principle of the society and of the fact that stealing is the most frequent offense of tenants."[12]

The most serious aspect of this form of intimidation, however, was that the formal judicial and police systems of the states condoned it. Colored people inevitably came to feel that, for them, the country was ruled by men, not by laws. The landlord or his agents administered floggings, even lynchings, with no fear of the consequences. "Threats are usually as effective as the use of violence because colored workers realize that the threats of white landlords are supported by the whole caste system."[13] The practice must be viewed as a basic form of social control in the South. And from there the tradition of assaulting Negroes with impunity spread over the rest of the nation.

Planter aggression has been expressed by such derogatory terms as "nigger," "Sambo," and "boy." In the Black Belt these epithets were commonly used by the sheriff and his deputies, sometimes almost as effectively as the whip. To call the adult person "nigger" was to assume accommodation to the forces of intimidation. Its implied challenge could be used as a test of the efficacy of more concrete racial controls. To address the Negro man as "boy," as the planter ordinarily did, was to strike at the very roots of his manhood, independence, and self-esteem. In the Deep south it was a constant reminder of his inferior status. Childlike personalities and behavior, according to Raper, could be viewed as a direct outcome of plantation organization and practices:

> The improvidence and dependence of the plantation workers rest primarily upon the demands of the plantation: they must be amenable to instructions, must live in the houses provided, must accept the merchant's and landlord's accounting, must remain landless. The very life of the plantation system is threatened when the tenants accumulate property, exhibit independence.[14]

Irresponsibility

Probably the most costly aspect of the system for its colored members has been its tendency to generate irresponsibility among them. Irresponsibility tended to become a trait of the Negro masses. It contributed to the instability of their family life and to the slovenly state of its physical upkeep. It has been doubtless accountable for the disreputable community existence that followed when the group moved into towns and cities, as well as for the relatively weak incentives toward formal education.

Myrdal recognizes this point when he says that the Negro tenant is "given to understand that his racial status provides an excuse for not being able to shift for himself, and that modest acceptance of a low position would rate a reward bigger than that offered for courageous attempts to reach a higher position."[15] Stupidity, as a cultural trait among Negroes, has had its value, particularly among slaves. It was nurtured by masters who looked on any initiative with suspicion. Slaves, on the other hand, tended to cultivate it as a means of avoiding all undirected or unsupervised work, and as an explanation for idleness. Even though it has now lost much of its original utility, the tendency to appear stupid still tends to persist, especially among the Negro lower classes. In another age, both white and Negro comedians—Bert Williams, Amos and Andy, Steppin Fetchit—simulated and exploited this situation, portraying stupidity as an elementary characteristic of the group.[16]

Manifestly, then, the primary purpose of labor exploitation on the plantation necessarily curtailed and perverted the existence of its black masses; it denied them access to the inherent individualism and competitiveness of the dominant American way of life. There has been, moreover, an abiding interest in maintaining these traditional traits of racial inferiority.

A Word on Migration

The continual movement of both whites and Negroes from the Deep South into other parts of the country tends to keep the nation alive to the culture of racism—the "seedbed" phenomenon. . . . On the whole, the "push" of the Negro population from the rural South has been greater than the inducements or "pull" of the cities. Both, of course, have operated to determine the extent and direction of the movement.[17] Factors contributing to the push include: relative severity of labor exploitation on southern farms, invasion of the boll weevil reaching disaster proportions from about 1910,[18] soil erosion and depletion, major transfers of cotton farming to western states, labor recruitment in the South during World War I, economic depressions of the early twenties and thirties, New Deal and subsequent limitations of farm acreage, and, most recently, mechanization of cotton and tobacco production.[19] The pull of the cities gained momentum as their colored population expanded and lines of communication between acquaintances multiplied. Contributing factors include: greater freedom from exploitation and social abuse, higher income and public relief, improved opportunities for economic and educational advancement, increased political recognition, and diversification of urban life.[20]

There seems to be nothing to indicate future reversal of the trek of Negroes from agricultural pursuits in the South. Reversal calls for success as a businessman on the farm under increasingly severe competition. The prospects, however, appear to support Beale's conclusion that "if the widespread and long entrenched disadvantages under which Negro farmers operate are not soon corrected, Negro farmers may well disappear as a significant group in American agriculture before the end of the twentieth century."[21]

The problems of race relations will continue to be associated with the American metropolis. The great cities are confronted with the heritage of racial pathologies from the rural South in addition to those inherent in the urban situation. The migrant, as L. V. Kennedy puts it, is involved in "a double adjustment from life in the South to life in the North and from rural conditions to those prevalent in a highly organized urban center."[22] In the urban milieu his immediate and abiding problem remains principally that of opportunity for employment.

Notes

1. William C. Holley, Ellen Winston, and T. J. Woofter, *The Plantation South, 1934–37* (Washington, 1940), p. xxiii.

2. Robert P. Brooks, "The Agrarian Revolution in Georgia, 1856–1912," *Bulletin of the University of Wisconsin* 639 (1914).

3. Holley, Winston, and Woofter, *The Plantation South*, p. xviii; also Robert L. Brandfon, *Cotton Kingdoms of the New South* (Cambridge, Mass., 1967), p. 135 *passim*.

4. Arthur F. Raper, *Preface to Peasantry* (Chapel Hill, 1936), p. 98.

5. Rembert W. Patrick, "The Deep South, Past and Present," in *The Deep South in Transformation*, ed. Robert B. Highsaw (Tuscaloosa, 1964), pp. 113–14.

6. Raper, *Preface to Peasantry*, pp. 22–23.

7. Charles Wesley, *Negro Labor in the U.S., 1850–1925* (New York, 1927), p. 286.

8. Holley, Winston, and Woofter, *The Plantation South*, p. 11.

9. Ibid., pp. xxvii-xxvii, for description of the habitat of the tenant.

10. In 1911 the Supreme Court declared peonage unconstitutional: *Bailey v. Alabama*, 219 U.S. 242. The tradition, however, tended to persist.

11. Gunnar Myrdal et al., *An American Dilemma* (New York, 1944), vol. 1, pp. 247–48.

12. Allison Davis, Burleigh B. Gardener, and Mary R. Gardener, *Deep South* (Chicago, 1941), p. 395.

13. Ibid., p. 400. Also, Oliver Cromwell Cox, "Lynching and the Status Quo," *Journal of Negro Education* 14 (1945): 576–88.

14. Raper, *Preface to Peasantry*, p. 171.

15. Myrdal, *An American Dilemma*, vol. 1, p. 240; Carter G. Woodson, *The Rural Negro* (Washington, 1931), p. 433.

16. Cf. Langston Hughes, "The Negro and American Entertainment," in *The American Negro Reference Book*, ed. John P. Davis (Englewood Cliffs, N.J., 1966), pp. 826–49; John Dollard, *Caste and Class in a Southern Town* (New York, 1957), chap. 12; John D. McCarthy and William L. Yancey, "Uncle Tom and Mr. Charlie," *American Sociological Review* 76 (1971): 648–72; Joseph Boskin, "Sambo, the National Jester in the Popular Culture," in *The Great Fear*, ed. G. B. Nash and R. Weiss (New York, 1970), pp. 165–85.

17. Cf. Rupert P. Vance, *All These People* (Chapel Hill, 1945), p. 247.

18. For the invasion of the beetle and the effects of its ravages on the lives of Negroes, see Calvin L. Beale, "The Negro in American Agriculture," in *The American Negro Reference Book*, ed. John P. Davis (Englewood Cliffs, N.J., 1966), p. 164.

19. Ibid., p. 166.

20. Raper, *Preface to Peasantry*, p. 6.

21. Beale, "The Negro in American Agriculture," p. 202.

22. Louise Venable Kennedy, *The Negro Peasant Turns Civilized* (New York, 1930), p. 40.

| 6 |

The Ghetto

Racial Ostracism as a Factor

The core of the Negro subculture in American metropolises constitutes an unassimilated way of life: the conjunction of black, southern plantation conditioning and the individualistic, highly motivated, racist spirit of modern urban society. Ecologically, the ghetto is the outcome of nationwide physical mobility and racial ostracism.

The "free air" of the American city attracts the ambitious underprivileged, but popular white exclusiveness enforces social disjunction and thus black concentration. The city, however, is the locus of commerce and industry: without these there can be no capitalist city. Labor here is auxiliary and residence supportive. The size of the urban population is a reflection of the magnitude of commercial and industrial processes. In other words, the great city is the product of businessmen acting individualistically but conforming nonetheless to a societal tradition conducive to a high degree of capitalist cultural achievement and progress. It is primarily from this tradition that ghetto blacks are largely alienated or excluded.

The growth of the Negro urban population does not, therefore, reflect a concomitant rise in the capacity of blacks to operate in the city. Negroes are free to organize their labor and thereby insist upon greater recognition as workers. This fact, however, does not necessarily involve them commensurably in the process of urban creativity and identity. For whites, on the other hand, such organization may be sufficient to relieve frustration because white labor tends, at least theoretically, to constitute business apprenticeship and thus a functional continuum with management. The ghetto is very much a product of the relative unavailability of this dynamic, associational cultural outlet.

Dependence upon political power has therefore been largely illusionary. Attempts to force political power already in the hands

of urban blacks to yield the economic base of central cities necessarily results in social confusion, even for the Negro community.

Ghetto culture is not critically lower-class despites its poverty,
substandard housing, family disrepute, static outlook, storefront
churches, slum conditions, and so on—it is lower-class culture
subject to implicitly planned degradation and repression. By and
large, the cultural failure and low reputation of Negroes may be
thought of as the desiderata of the white ruling elite especially in
the traditional homeland of the Negro, the plantation South.

"Deviant behavior" in Negroes confined to their communities
thus demonstrates arguments that Negroes are unfit for normal
cultural opportunities. Over the past one hundred years the Negro
masses have experienced forces of cultural repression such as, for
example, the unschooled European immigrant never had to face.
Toward the end of the Civil War, Frederick Douglass defined some
of these culturally repressive influences as follows:

> We cannot conceal from ourselves . . . the fact that there are many
> powerful influences, constantly operating, intended and calculated to
> defeat our just hopes, prolong the existence of the source of all our
> ills—the system of slavery—strengthen the slave power, darken the
> conscience of the North, intensify popular prejudice against color,
> multiply unequal and discriminating laws . . . consign to oblivion the
> needs of heroism which have distinguished the colored soliders, deny
> and despise his claims to the gratitude of his country, scout his
> pretensions to American citizenship, establish the selfish idea that this
> is exclusively the white man's country, pass unheeded all the lessons
> taught by these four years of fire and sword, undo all that has been
> done toward our freedom and elevation, take the musket from the
> shoulders of our brave black soldiers . . . exclude them from the
> ballot-box where they now possess that right . . . overawe free speech
> in and out of Congress, obstruct the right of peaceably assembling . . .
> revive the internal slave-trade . . . reverse the entire order and tend-
> ency of the events of the last three years.[. . .][1]

The cultural pathologies of the ghetto may thus be thought of as
a projected achievement of white power groups.[. . .]

[. . .] Except for [. . .] inherent societal pressure, there would be
no racial ghetto; and, let us not forget, the pattern is by no means
vanquished. There are powerful interests all over the nation continually devoted to its perpetuation. One could, for example, cite
the continuing popularity of the racist tactics of Governor George
C. Wallace of Alabama, in his quest for the presidency of the
United States, and the nature of his popularity to illustrate the
remarkable strength of anti-Negro sentiments. His almost gleeful

depiction of the pathologies of life in the ghetto seem to demonstrate their political value. And many agree with him that abrogation of the open housing laws would be an important means of remedying this situation.²

The Unwanted

Perhaps no phenomenon so profoundly characterizes the mentality of the core ghetto Negro as a sense of not being wanted, included, and accepted in the larger American society. He is not likely to feel encouraged to participate in the legitimate social order. The dominant society tends to speak over his head whereas a member of the Negro middle class is more likely to make this breakthrough.

The core ghetto tends to constitute an external society, racially identified. Thus, from the point of view of the dominant society, the behavior of ghettoites may seem illogical, erratic, or contradictory. If, for example, we study the life of Malcolm X, we observe three principal stages: his youthful ghetto behavior, which made him the prey of policemen and jails; his nationalistic transformation during the relative quiet of his incarceration; and, finally, his attempts at societal inclusion and identification with the larger community following his experience abroad.

This tendency to exclude Negroes from the dominant social processes goes back, of course, to pre–Civil War days. Frederick Douglass said of it: "The worst enemy of the nation could not cast upon its fair name a greater infamy than to admit that Negroes could be tolerated among them in a state of the most degrading slavery and oppression, and must be cast away, driven into exile, for no other cause than having been freed from their chains."³ Such difficulties are no doubt at the seat of the irresponsibility openly manifested among Negroes of the core ghetto.

After the 1954 Supreme Court school decision, it seemed to the leaders in many southern states that the time for legally enforcing the social assimilation of Negro Americans had arrived. To be sure, [all] means of traditional resistance to this purpose were brought into play.

Negroes were encouraged to leave the South. It was felt that if the North really knew the Negro, it too would be revolted by the thought of assimilating him. The following Associated Press report from South Carolina reveals that nature of this attitude:

Northern advocates of racial integration were challenged today by Gov. George Bell Timmerman, Jr. "to cast off their hypocrisy and accept the Negro into their communities, their institutions and their families." He called on "the integrationist to prove his sincerity" by supporting a program of voluntary migration of Negroes from the South to communities "where racial mixing is acceptable. A Federal program of financial aid to enable those who want to mix to move to other areas," he said, "would cost only a fraction" of the billions advocated for foreign aid.[4]

All over the Deep South there were similar acts of encouragement to those Negroes who were discontent with their status. In a number of [. . .] cities [in the Deep South] Negro families were actually put on buses for transportation to the North, their fares paid, and their debts cancelled on condition that they promise never to return. On March 1, 1956, the Alabama State Senate, "unanimously passed a resolution calling on Congress to appropriate funds to move southern Negroes to the North and Midwest, 'areas where they are wanted and needed and can be assimilated.' "[5]

Robbed of a normal sense of belonging, clothed with the anonymity and the physical freedom of the metropolist, the ghetto Negro develops a contrary, alienated subculture that is both isolated and self-isolating.[. . .]

The Ghetto and Social Classes: Crime as an Index

[. . .] Ghetto crime and delinquency rates are objective indices of the social situation. It is true that in the South especially, Negroes are more likely to be unjustly arrested and punished for some crimes, especially those affecting apparent interests of the white community.[6]

After all such allowances are made, however, the data probably underestimate actual conditions. Only about 25 percent or less of the crimes against property are cleared by arrests. Table 1 is a compilation of selected criminal acts in which Negro offenders rate inordinately high (over 50 percent of the total) and low (mainly white-collar). The abnormally high expectation of crimes of violence and robbery in the core ghetto tends to become a constant source of fear, insecurity, and anguish. Although the regular data show that crime and delinquency among ghetto Negroes are multiples of their incidence among whites, the figures frequently obscure the gravity of the situation. Again, as the U.S. Commission on Civil Disorders points out, "official statistics normally greatly understate actual crime rates because the vast majority of crimes are not reported to the police. For example, a study conducted for the President's Crime Commission in three Washington D.C. precincts shows that six times as many crimes were actually committed against persons and homes as were reported to the police."[7] Table 2 illustrates the situation by actual data for Chicago. The authors conclude in part: "Variations in the crime rate against persons within the city are extremely large. One very low-income Negro district had 35 times as many serious crimes against persons per 100,000 residents as did the high-income white district. . . . Low-income Negro areas have significantly higher rates than low-income white areas. This reflects the high degree of social disorganization in the Negro area."[8]

An important reason for relatively limited official records of criminal acts in the ghetto is that they are regarded as normal, a way of life. They involve techniques of defense and retaliation which may be in themselves unlawful, but are locally expected. Thus the incidence of deviant behavior falls most heavily upon typical inhabitants of the core ghetto. It has been shown, for instance, that almost nine-tenths of the crimes committed by Negroes in Chicago between September 1965 and March 1966 "involved Negro victims."[9]

The Ghetto Environment

Although most of the crimes in the ghetto are committed by a minority of its residents, the group as a whole is exposed to its consequences.[. . .] The pathologies tend thus to become an element of the subculture.[10] The physical environment of the community presents overt proof of the behavior that may be expected. Its very aspect alarms the middle class.

Our concern here, however, is mainly with certain recognized conditions. A list of these would include squalor, noise, physical deterioration, adult idleness, profanity, children unattended roaming the streets, vandalism, rape, theft, and robbery—all of which are likely to produce a sense of fear and insecurity; the critical point, however, is that core ghetto inhabitants tend to become inured to the situation. David R. Hunter states:

> The slum is more than any of its parts, more than you can see. It is more than the crowded buildings . . . more than the dirty streets, the lackluster people sitting on the steps, the shrieking children running

Table 1
Urban Arrests, Selected Offenses, by Race, 1970

Offense charged	Arrests*			
	Total White Negro and others	*White*	*Negro*	*Percent Negro*
Gambling	65,360	17,021	45,277	69
Murder and nonnegligent manslaughter	9,784	3,167	6,424	66
Robbery	66,436	19,790	45,321	68
Prostitution and commercialized vice	40,323	13,387	26,498	66
Forcible rape	11,237	4,869	6,171	55
Aggravated assault	93,079	44,137	47,147	51
Forgery and counterfeiting	31,043	19,919	10,842	35
Fraud	52,401	36,373	15,618	30
Embezzlement	6,501	4,658	1,808	28

*3,891 cities over 2,500; 1970 population 102,647,000.
Source: U.S. Department of Justice, *Uniform Crime Reports for the United States,* Washington, D.C., 1970, table 38.

Table 2
Number of Index Crimes and Patrolmen Assignments
per 100,000 Residents in Four Chicago Police Districts, 1965

Index crimes* and patrolmen	White district income		Negro district income	
	High	*Low-middle*	*Very low No. 1*	*Very low No. 2*
Against persons	80	440	1,615	2,820
Against property	1,038	1,750	2,508	2,630
Patrolmen assigned	93	133	243	291

*Index crimes: homicide, forcible rape, aggravated assault, robbery, burglary, grand larceny, and auto theft.
Source: Report of the National Advisory Commission on Civil Disorders, 1968, p. 267.

up and down, the sullen boys hanging on the corner, the stupefied addicts leaning against the wall, the cruising patrol car. It is a way of life, and it is a way of looking at the future, or perhaps looking away from it.[11]

Noise in core ghettos comes not so much from industrial operations as from the very process of living. The blare of soundmaking, amusement machines, the use of automobile horns as a means of social communication, and inconsiderate boisterousness are examples. The uproar which ordinarily goes with ghetto card-playing or drinking parties constitutes a particularly distracting form of noise.

Noisiness and loudness tend to follow the child and student into the school; and, as we should expect, they tend to engender culture conflict.

The way residential property is kept up is an indication of certain personality and cultural traits. The ghetto situation is no exception. Two principal forces lead to speedy deterioration of core ghetto property: neglect by landlords, and both neglect and destructiveness by occupants. At this point we are concerned not so much with landlord neglect as with tenant limitations—the immediate process of ghettoization.

As low-income Negroes move into housing vacated by whites or into subsidized apartments, a process of stripping its environs of articles of value is likely to begin. All movable decorative items including utilities may disappear: "even garbage cans . . . are sometimes stolen as fast as landlords can replace them."[12] This tendency to strip ghetto housing areas frequently gives them an appearance of ominous bareness.

One of the most tragic aspects of ghetto society is its obvious dissipation of adult time and energy. The spectacle of men in the prime of life, in full daytime, sitting or lying or leaning about ghetto premises is a stark example of the effects of societal isolation. These men seem not to be affected by the cultural spurs toward efficiency and achievement. To them, obviously, nothing seems worth doing. This, of course, may be easily explained as cultural lag, a continuation of work attitudes consistent with the historic culture of slavery. But the phenomenon persists.

One of the marks of the ghetto is the sight of children busily exploring the public community—running in and out of stores, crossing streets, climbing up trees, unattended. This manifestly is ideal preparation for the toughness and excitement of "street corner society." As one observer puts it: "With the father absent and the mother working, many ghetto children spend the bulk of their time on the streets—the streets of a crime-ridden, violence-prone and poverty-stricken world."[13] To these children regular school rooms would appear simply to be drab forms of punitive institutions. Moreover, granting the restrictive obligations of poor parents, questions about the nature of concern for their childrens' discipline still remain.

A continuing danger to peace and security in the ghetto is the existence of thievery and robbery. Indeed, burglary tends to be a settled preoccupation of residents. The thief is constantly inventing pretexts and physical devices for entering homes and businesses. By way of protection, windows and doors, especially those of stores, are frequently barricaded. Police officers tend increasingly to be stationed in self-service shops, in elevators, buses, subways, and lavatories. Handbag snatching and muggings are common. More and more, the firearm has been replacing the knife as the principal weapon of assault. Thievery may be regarded as justifiable behavior and sometimes even as a right. This sort of burglary sometimes leads the white retail merchant to withdraw in despair. Moreover, it limits the chances of Negro merchants in filling the void. The civil rights movement and recent protest riots seem to have augmented the boldness of the thief.

Explanations, of course, are not necessarily justifications. Negroes of the ghetto are the immediate sufferers from its social pathologies. It has been a socially limiting milieu for them. Their methods of solving its problems have been spontaneous and frequently self-defeating. It seems clear that the only lasting solution within the larger societal context is the abandonment of ghetto culture—elements of which tend to be consistently related to each other. And, since that culture has begun to overflow into the front room of the larger society, it has been increasingly recognized that its defects can no longer be tolerated.

Notes

1. Philip S. Foner, *The Life and Writings of Frederick Douglass* (New York, 1952), vol. 3, pp. 410–11.
2. *Washington Post*, 28 June 1968.
3. Douglass, in *The Life and Writings of Frederick Douglass*, vol. III, p. 392; John H. Franklin, *The Free Negro in North Carolina* (Chapel Hill, 1943), pp. 192–221, examines various aspects.
4. *New York Times*, 12 May 1956.
5. *New York Times*, 2 March 1956, 1 April 1956, 11 February 1963.
6. Cf. Gunnar Myrdal et al., *An American Dilemma* (New York, 1944), pp. 968 ff.

7. Ibid., pp. 267–68.
8. Ibid., p. 267.
9. *Report of the National Advisory Commission on Civil Disorders* (New York, 1968), p. 273.
10. The lower class can be divided into categories called "church centered," "respectable," "underworld," and "shady" groups: St. Clair Drake and Horace R. Cayton, *Black Metropolis: A Study of Negro Life in a Northern City* (New York, 1962), pp. 523–25; cf. Ulf Hannerz, *Soulside* (New York, 1969), pp. 34–58.
11. David R. Hunter, *The Slums* (New York, 1964), p. 10.
12. *Report of the National Advisory Commission on Civil Disorders*, p. 273.
13. Ibid., p. 262.

7

Negro Protest and the Subculture

The Negroes' protest is based fundamentally upon a conflict between economic interests peculiar to a type of social situation [. . .], cultural isolation, and opposition to their composite status. The material interests of the system demand their subservience, but the social ideals inherent in the system are morally inconsistent with the process of degradation. The history of their protest reaches back to their forebears' involuntary emigration from West Africa. Even then, their resistance to special interests was constantly manifest. It is not slavery per se—a condition known to both Europe and Africa during the precapitalist era—which generates protest but rather bondage under peculiar social circumstances. Slaves do not *protest* in all types of social organization. In some they accept the status with resignation.

Since this critical point has been frequently overlooked, we emphasize again that the movement which initiated the "age of discovery" was uniquely a development of the capitalist system that originated in the European medieval cities. "The conjunction in a single half-century of the discovery of an immense new labor supply and of a new and comparatively empty continent in which such a supply could be profitably utilized gave an importance and a permanence to" the slave trade which it could never have attained otherwise.[1]

Given this type of society, the only means of maintaining and utilizing the reluctant labor force was unremitting physical and psychological coercion. [. . .]

[. . .]As a group, however, the Negro people were never completely broken in. Their masters and the community organizations always had doubts about the reliability of their apparent contentedness. Herbert Aptheker has devoted a major part of his research career to demonstrating this fact. His definitive work on Negro slave revolts points to the ever-present concern of masters about latent unrest among the bondsmen.[2] [. . .]

But racial protest has its heritage not so much in the slaves' surreptitious uprisings [as] in the public, accusatory contentions of the abolitionists. The argument remains essentially that of an insistence upon complete inclusion of all men, Negroes specifically, in the American society. Frederick Douglass, an untiring abolitionist, who survived the Civil War to become the outstanding Negro assimilationist protest leader in the latter half of the nineteenth century, declared in an 1856 public address in Boston:

I have had but one idea for the last three years to present to the American people, and the phraseology in which I clothe it is the old abolition phraseology. I am for the "immediate, unconditional, and universal" enfranchisement of the black man, in every state of the Union. . . .

We may be asked . . . why we want it. I will tell you why we want it. We want it because it is our *right,* first of all. No class of men can, without insulting their own nature, be content with any deprivation of their rights. We want it, again, as a means of educating our race. Men are so constituted that they derive their conviction of their own possibilities largely from the estimate formed of them by others. If nothing is expected of a people, that people will find it difficult to contradict that expectation. . . .

Everybody has asked the question, and they learned to ask it early of the abolitionists, "What shall we do with the negro?" I have had but one answer from the beginning. Do nothing with us! Your doing with us has already played the mischief with us. . . . If the negro cannot stand on his own legs, let him fall. . . . All I ask is, give him a chance to stand on his own legs! . . . If you see him on his way to school, let him alone—don't disturb him! If you see him going to the dinner-table at a hotel, let him go! If you see him going to the ballot box, let him alone—don't disturb him. If you see him going into a workshop, just let him alone—your interference is doing him positive injury. . . . If you will only untie his hands, and give him a chance, I think he will live. He will work as readily for himself as for the white man.[3]

Since the Civil War, this is what protest has been essentially about; neither the NAACP [National Association for the Advancement of Colored People] nor the mid-twentieth-century Supreme Court has contravened its essence—indeed they have sought piecemeal to realize it. [. . .]

The Mainstream and the Subculture

Protest seeks to remove the status of outsider assigned to the Negro. Involved here, however, is the social structure of the dominant culture and its trailing, limited subculture. A critical objective of the southern ruling class has been to assure the integrity and continuity of the latter. It seems necessary, therefore, to refer briefly to the rise of this subculture.

At the time of emancipation, the Negro had retained very little if any of his original African culture.[4] He was dependent upon his master's tutelage for effective plantation labor. As Stanley M. Elkins observes:

> Much of his past had been annihilated; nearly every prior connection had been severed. Not that he had really "forgotten" all these things—his family and kinship arrangements, his language, the tribal religion, the taboos, the name he had once borne, and so on—but none of it any longer carried much meaning. The old values, the sanctions, the standards, already unreal, could no longer furnish him guides for conduct for adjusting to the expectations of a complete new life. Where then was he to look for new standards, new cues—who would furnish them now? He could now look to none but his master, the one man to whom the system had committed his entire being: the man upon whose will depended his food, his shelter, his sexual connections, whatever moral instruction he might be offered, whatever "success" was possible within the system, his very security—in short, everything.[5]

What the Negro acquired, however, was not a normal derivative of his master's culture. In 1865, 95 percent of the Negro population lived in the South and 90 percent of them were newly emancipated slaves. It was, therefore, the culture associated with American bondage that Negroes brought into freedom. And this, let it be noted, was not merely the culture of a lower class but of an extremely perverted lower-lower class.

The Negro *masses* became freedmen conditioned to a tradition of the most degraded form of family irresponsibility, with a distorted conception of the nature of property, with relatively little personal motivation for work, with the slave's orientation toward division of the day regarding rest, work, and relaxation; with feeble and restricted powers of reaching out toward the motivating forces of the larger culture. The Negro was almost entirely illiterate. He had a telltale drawl, servile rhetoric, and comparatively little use for quiet and cleanliness; he was trained for the crudest form of agricultural manual labor, and subject to the ambivalent control of his former master. All this was bound up in a cultural pattern that held him outside the normal structure of the American social status sytem. And yet, his was inherently an American culture with an American future.

What is more, the old, white power structure exerted itself to perpetuate this ineffective way of life. It isolated Negroes through segregation, put them in "their place" with formal and informal rules and violence, and thus contributed to the perpetuation of thralldom in the United States. [. . .]

Negro culture, then, is peculiarly of American origin and development. Urbanization has not effaced this fact: the Negro "went from the lowest status in the Southern countryside to the lowest status in the urban areas."[6] The immemorial past of this inherited culture must be sought largely in Europe, not in Africa.

"Equality" has meant not physical identity but the acquisition of ability so to behave in the larger American culture that the handicap of Negro culture would appear to have completely lost its restrictive conditioning effects. It is the latter achievement which the white detractors of Negroes in the South have sought most assiduously to forestall. We need hardly cite in illustration their determined resistance to prevent the simultaneous education of white and Negro children.

Many Negroes are so thoroughly submerged in their pattern of lower-class culture that they seem to think of it as inherently Negro and thus worth conserving. "This world of the lower class," observe Drake and Cayton in their Chicago study, "is, to lower-class people, the normal and familiar context of daily life."[7] Since the culture is the result of Americanization under singular social restraints and limitations, the normal avenues of escape for anger and aggressiveness have been largely blocked. A characteristic of the culture, therefore, has been in-group irrationality, conflict, and violence, with the constant threat of external explosion.

We may assume that all viable cultures have their built-in norms of social control. The operation of these norms tends to be accepted voluntarily. Persons belonging to the culture, therefore, "know how to behave," and corrections for any deviation are ordinarily supported by the group. But one of the great problems of Negroes—the Negro masses especially—has been the feeble operation, in their subculture, of the norms of the dominant society.

Since they do not have fully effective cultural controls of their own, and are more or less excluded from the purview of the dominant culture, their behavior tends to become erratic, frequently criminal, without compunction in terms of the dominant norms. Observe, for example, with what equanimity H. Rap Brown, who was reared on the streets of a Negro community, describes his behavior during an audience with President Lyndon Johnson at the White House in 1965: "I stole some stuff out of the

White House. . . . I was trying to figure how to get a painting off the wall and put it under my coat. I figured it belonged to me anyway."[8] Brown, incidentally, employs the scatological vernacular of the lower levels of ghetto culture.

Culture Conflict and Protest

The social variation that characterizes the lower class of the Negro subculture tends to be irreversibly incompatible with the dominant culture. What is more, the Negro subculture had to be largely negative, defensive, reactionary—with inherent processes such as "getting by" and "getting away with." In situations calling for positive, creative living it is, therefore, a culture which must be deliberately unlearned.

An important current definition of Negro self-respect is total American respect for the Negro lower-class subculture. The size of this class is relatively so large that its ethos, rather than that of the Negro middle class, has been frequently assumed to be the dominant orientation of all Negroes. American culture and society, of course, is middle-class oriented. Its educational system is devoted largely to middle-class motivation and American cultural dynamics. It seems, therefore, that to be successfully included in the larger culture, the ambition of Negroes, like that of whites, must be middle-class directed. Indeed it should now be clear that the whole world, including the socialist countries, has to develop in its people attitudes for hard work, honesty, efficiency, sobriety, and upward cultural motivation such as that which made possible the development and maintenance of the phenomenal American productive system. Both modern Russia and China agree on this point. There is no alternative if progressive maximization of the peoples' welfare is the objective.

Indecision about this notion among certain Negro leaders has involved race relations in a conflict of cultures. Some leaders seem to be asking that black, lower-class recognition constitutes a stable form of social organization in contradistinction to the larger middle-class socioeconomic system. Accordingly, the subculture has been thought of not in dynamic terms—not as progressively entering into the continuum of American social mobility—but rather in static, self-sufficient terms. The Negro's peculiar "language," food, plan of production and government, and complement of obscenities are all considered worth preserving against incursions of influences from the larger society. Nationalism normally calls for group solidarity, and this solidarity can be most conveniently developed by pointing to the enemy at the gates.

Black English

Since a people's language tends to constitute their primary mark of cultural distinction, attempts have been made to conceive of "black English" as a "separate language." The Center for Applied Linguistics in Washington, D.C., has made special efforts to study characteristics of the Negro dialect and to suggest that it should be taught in schools to all Negro children. Teaching standard English is not, it is assumed, like teaching standard mathematics. "English teachers," the argument runs, "try to wipe out all traces of a kid's right to continue speaking the dialect of his home."[9] According to this logic, red English, hillbilly English, Yoruba English—all should be taught respectively along with standard English.

In order to give prestige and national significance to black English, its origin has been sought in Africa, the West Indies, the ghetto—indeed everywhere but in its proper place: the southern slave plantation. One official from the center asserts: "A sentence such as 'He be at work' is a well-known stereotyped characteristic of black English . . . [meaning] 'he is at work all the time.'"[10] Ordinarily the black-English advocates cite no vestigial use of African languages among American Negroes, but rather concentrate on the latter's allegedly peculiar conjugation of certain defective English verbs. The derived structures are then said to have been determined by the Negroes' African origins.

Leaving aside the question of whether all Negro lower-class persons employ identical usage—and whether Negro schoolteachers speak the language in their informal gatherings—it seems clear that the slave who attempted to use standard English on the plantation would be a marked man. The dialect and idiom may well be studied for its servile characteristics. What is being sought as a nationalized language is a devious cultural development and, perhaps, a subtle means of perpetuating the Sambo image.[11] [. . .]

What is not always realized by those who propose to organize Negro lower-class culture as a counterpoise to the larger American culture is that its material base is, in a sense, more completely dependent on operations in the larger social system than that of any other social group. Its problem is that of the particularly disadvantaged poor. As the discriminatory laws which formerly

limited cultural participation are removed, the handicap and im-
permanence of Negro lower-class culture will become the more
glaringly manifest.

Attempts to "Africanize," standardize, and applaud these cultural
handicaps will only magnify them and thus aggravate the general
cultural gap.[12] That, no doubt, is precisely what the most determined white detractors of the Negro people would do if they had a
clear opportunity. The Negro is thus merely committing himself to
the status of a cultural outsider in his own country—apparently
something no other group of Americans has found profitable. The
traditional social strategy of Jews, on the other hand, has been
devotion to mastery of the dominant culture and achievement of
societal inclusion on their own terms.

Structure of Negro Protest

Now that we have reviewed the cultural bias of interracial conflict
in the United States, it seems appropriate to consider the ways in
which protest has been expressed and the nature of its opposition.

Historically, protest has taken different forms but these forms
have not always been mutually exclusive. We will attempt to bring
them together under the following headings: aims, methods, and
leadership. We shall consider the consequences of protest as
characterized mainly by assimilation, nationalism, and anarchy.
Emigration from the United States as a solution was realistically
abandoned with the Emancipation Proclamation and the Thirteenth Amendment to the Constitution. Table 1 is a suggestive
outline.

The Protest for Assimilation

The protest for assimilation has been oriented toward the federal
government and its courts, as the power capable of producing
positive results, and toward the South and its leadership as the
germinal force in the United States devoted to the suppression of
the Negro race.[13] Moreover, the Negro people were generally
known to be southerners, hence there could be no effective liberation until the hand of the southern oligarchy was restrained. It was
in the South particularly that the Negro was driven back into his
limited subculture. And it was normally to be expected that southern representatives in Congress and among the great leaders of

Table 1
Characteristics of Negro Protest

Aims	Methods	Leadership and ideology
(1) *Assimilation:* abolition, suffrage, civil rights, social rights, economic opportunity	(1) Action directed to specific ends: appeals to federal and state governments, to courts, and to private influential groups—boycott and picketing, sit-ins, freedom rides, marches and mass demonstrations, civil disobedience, "demands," voter registration	(1) The abolitionists, Frederick Douglass and members of Congress, William M. Trotter, the NAACP, W. E. B. DuBois, Roy Wilkins, M. L. King, Jr., the original SCLC, SNCC, CORE
(2) *Emigration:* colonization, Garveyism's "back to Africa"	(2) Personal enterprise; settlement in Liberia and Sierra Leone by free Negroes and manumitted slaves with Western governmental assistance	(2) Paul Cuffe, Martin Delany, the American Colonization Society, state colonization societies, Abraham Lincoln, Marcus Garvey
(3) *Nationalism:* Garveyite, Muslimite, separatism, self-determination	(3) Nationalistic propaganda, racial pride, black racism, exotic religion, Garvey's UNIA, regalia and uniforms, patriotic business enterprise, ghettoization, strategic violence	(3) Marcus Garvey, Elijah Muhammad, Malcolm X, more recently SNCC, CORE
(4) *Anarchy:* liberation, revolt and rebellion, chaos, induced fear and destruction (ends and means tend to converge)	(4) Conspiracy, police confrontation, rioting, looting, arson, shooting, bombing—utilizing cover of darkness and escape	(4) Malcolm X, mobs, gangs, Black Panthers, Marx-Lenin, Frantz Fanon, Che Guevara, Mao Tse-tung's Red Book

business in the North would watch for any evidence of action leading to the social integration of Negroes and strike it down.

The first great battle after the Civil War, fought in the tradition of the abolitionists, resulted in amendments to the Constitution defining Negroes as citizens, and in federal civil rights laws designed to grant citizenship status. At this point, Negroes theoretically became assimilated Americans; the forces of public alienation were *legally* removed, and they now had to find their places competitively in the social status system. We have seen, however, the way in which nullifying devices and federal court decisions in a post-Reconstruction set of reactions virtually nullified the Reconstruction gains. Protest, therefore, tended to be spontaneously initiated against these obvious deprivations.

From the beginning—from the writing of the Constitution itself—the situation of the Negro has involved the federal government. At the turn of the century, there was no place to look for help save the national government. In 1909 the NAACP organized for active protest, and the federal courts seemed to be the only avenue open to action. Appeals to the courts regarding removal of the obstacles to political participation [and] to equality in public accommodations and in education gradually brought positive results. It was, of course, in 1954 that the Warren court, upon the petition of the NAACP, handed down its historic decision on desegregation in public education.

The decision implicated the federal government directly. The Court, moreover, obligated itself to supervise the desegregation of public schools in the United States and especially in the South; and it implicitly bound the administration to use force in the process. Thus, race relations suddenly became headline news; the public was awakened, and protest leaders became champions of the national morality. The decision involved so wide an area of racial discrimination that the NAACP seemed to have its hands full merely in helping to support the mandate of the Supreme Court. For the first time resolution of the "Negro problem" had become an obligation of the United States. And blame for the social conditions of Negroes became increasingly centered upon "American institutions."

[. . .] One of the most effective types of mass behavior is certain forms of boycott. It is difficult to locate and punish. By peacefully withholding patronage, it may compel concessions. An opportunity arose in 1955 to test this strategy against racial segregation in public transportation in Montgomery, Alabama, the "cradle of the Confederacy." The movement gradually gained momentum, affecting more and more of the southern power structure and gaining the attention of the nation.

As a form of protest, the boycott had already become traditional among Negroes. It started in Chicago in April 1929 when James H. Porter, a public-spirited individual, wrote the president of the Metropolitan Life Insurance Company complaining that no Negroes were employed by the corporation either in its offices or as agents. He received a long answer, which read in part: "You ask why we do not employ colored people to look after the large amount of business which we have in force in colored lives. The reason is that we know from experience that better service is given our colored policy-holders by white people than would be given by colored agents."[14] Porter took the letter to the editors of the Chicago *Whip,* Joseph D. Bibb and A. C. McNeal, who published it in full with an editorial denouncing the Metropolitan and calling for a boycott. They said: "After you read the letter below you will understand why colored people are poverty-stricken, in need of the necessities of life, and unable to do the great things they have in mind."

The campaign continued with increasing intensity from May 1929 to December 1930. Although the company did not capitulate, Negro insurance companies in the area admitted that they used the argument and publicity in sales talks and thus experienced some transfer of business to their own establishments.

During the drive against Metropolitan, almost all other businesses in the area were also brought under attack and most of them agreed to employ Negroes. The F. W. Woolworth five-and-ten-cent stores held out stubbornly, but they too eventually gave in and began to employ Negroes as clerks. The motto was "Don't spend your money where you can't work"; and the pickets carried signs reading "this store unfair to colored labor." Discrimination against black labor by the public utilities and labor unions was also challenged as never before but with only partial success. This, let us recall, was during the nadir of the Great Depression.

The boycott and picketing spread rapidly among Negroes in other cities—New York, Cleveland, Baltimore, Detroit, Washington. It did not openly penetrate the South. Here and there *businessmen* resorted to legal injunctions. In 1938, however, the U.S. Supreme Court held that the boycott was a proper instrument in the Negro's struggle against discrimination in employment. Both the NAACP and the Urban League actively supported the movement although they did not assume leadership in organizing a national campaign. The movement hardly received attention in the metropolitan dailies.

When, therefore, early in December 1955, Mrs. Rosa Parks was arrested in Montgomery because she refused to give up her seat on a city bus to a white passenger, E. D. Nixon, a Pullman porter, who had had public experience as an officer of the local NAACP, was able confidently to announce to the Negro ministers of the community: "I feel that the time has come to boycott the buses. Only through a boycott can we make it clear to white folks that we will not accept this type of treatment any longer."[15] Over 90 percent of the habitual Negro bus riders devised other means of transportation, and many buses cruised almost empty at rush hours.

On first consideration it may appear that this act constituted nothing more than the precedent-making desertion of Woolworth stores by colored shoppers in Chicago. On closer examination, however, it is clear that the Montgomery development represented a distinct phase in the rise of Negro protest. First, it involved the use of the boycott in the Deep South, and second, it directed the instrument against both the policies of business and the laws of the state. It is the latter aspect especially that distinguishes the Montgomery episode from the northern buying-power boycott. Before the leaders had fully developed their line of action, they became aware that their major antagonist was not merely a private business but rather the government of a state and its laws. Martin Luther King, Jr., relates that at one of their first meetings the strategists became almost "crippled by fear."

Without originally intending it, therefore, the boycott constituted a form of civil disobedience. Indeed, the boycott had hardly begun when a sympathetic white librarian, Juliette Morgan, in a letter to the *Montgomery Advertiser*, compared the act of Negroes walking rather than using the buses to Gandhi's salt march to the sea. From then on the leadership, especially that of Martin Luther King, Jr., progressively defined its program in terms of Gandhian nonviolent ideology.

As the campaign developed, public officials became almost the sole adversaries. They kept all the leaders under continuous surveillance and eventually summoned them into court to answer not only the charge of creating a public nuisance by the operation of a "car pool," but also a plea for damages accruing from alleged loss of tax revenue to the city as a result of the reduction of earnings by the bus company.

Adoption of Gandhian principles—which are altogether compatible with the teachings of Christianity—provided a foundation for the group's discipline as it confronted the political power of a Deep South state. For the first time since the Civil War Negroes en masse were defying legalized racism in the South. The struggle gained nationwide and international publicity. Sympathetic whites encouraged and supported it liberally. By November 13, 1956, when the U.S. Supreme Court handed down its decision invalidating the bus segregation laws of Alabama, a new form of protest, nonviolent direct action, had been devised and tried in the South. The leadership, in January 1957, formed the Southern Christian Leadership Conference (SCLC) to propagate and encourage the practice. In speech after speech, King spread the following doctrine:

> If the Negro is to achieve the goal of integration, he must organize himself into a militant and nonviolent mass movement. . . . We will take direct action against injustice without waiting for other agencies to act. We will not obey unjust laws or submit to unjust practices. We will do this peacefully, openly, cheerfully because our aim is to persuade. . . . The way to nonviolence may mean going to jail.
>
> If such is the case the resister must be willing to fill the jail houses of the South. It may mean physical death. But if physical death is the price that a man must pay to free his children and his white brethren from a permanent death of the spirit, then nothing could be more redemptive. . . . This then, must be our present program: nonviolent resistance to all forms of racial injustice, including state and local laws and practices, even when this means going to jail.[16]

Up to 1960, however, the movement had not increased sufficiently to test the capacity of the region's prisons. Clearly, to do so would require Negroes to act en masse, something more difficult than would appear at first sight. The movement called not only for a repetition of the negative action taken in the bus boycott—although this type of withdrawal was then being imitated in other cities of the South—but also for open resistance to racial exclusion. For this further step, King needed, at least initially, a special kind of Negro group: one selected for its ability to assume a dignified posture, for its ability to understand the subtleties of nonviolence, for its interest in sustaining an attack on segregated facilities that are chiefly of middle-class concern, and for its physical stamina and courage in the face of public violence and formal punishment.

An indiscriminate mass of Negroes—the larger the better— would no doubt have served the purpose of a typical Gandhian, nationalistic struggle; but not one designed to achieve the more limited goals of desegregating, say, the public facilities of a southern airport, of a library, or a restaurant. It was not clear that SCLC had evolved a plan of action to meet this problem.

By February 1960, however, the problem seemed to have solved itself. On the first of the month, at Greensboro, North Carolina, four Negro freshmen students, seventeen to eighteen years of age, from North Carolina Agricultural and Technical College, quietly took seats at the lunch counter of a Woolworth variety store and waited for service. They were not served, but they held their places for about an hour until the store closed, as usual, at 5:30 P.M. On the following day, accompanied by some twenty other students, they returned to occupy seats and read textbooks while they waited at the counter, but with no better results. The strategy, however, gained instant national publicity, and it quickly spread to other parts of the city and beyond. Students from white and Negro colleges in the area joined in the campaign. In April 1960, a group of students meeting at Shaw University in North Carolina organized the Student Nonviolent Coordinating Committee (SNCC) under sponsorship of Martin Luther King, Jr., and SCLC.

The force of the sit-in inheres in the public embarrassment and inconvenience it occasions. The Greensboro incident was of critical importance because it sparked the contagion which directly activated other groups in the South. It should be observed, however, that this was not the first sit-in. Probably the first deliberate, nonviolent attack upon racial segregation in public places was that which the newly formed biracial Congress of Racial Equality (CORE) successfully leveled against a Chicago Loop restaurant in October 1942. From that time on, the organization continually employed the method of small-group, biracial pressure against the segregation in border states. The leadership of CORE, with its home base in New York, was therefore already accustomed to this form of nonviolent action. But it had not challenged the Deep South.

The most common reaction to sit-in requests for service was the closing of lunch counters. In a few cities, such as Charlotte and Raleigh, proprietors of variety stores removed their counter seats and the public was served standing. In a few instances Negro customers were forced to pay exorbitant prices. Almost everywhere the protestors were subjected to harassment by white persons or groups. Some were dragged from their seats and beaten, as in Nashville and Jackson. There were hundreds of arrests for trespass, vagrancy, loitering, disorderly conduct, or, as in Nashville, "conspiracy to disrupt trade and commerce," and, in Baton Rouge, "criminal anarchy."

Sit-ins of various types assert civil rights that are either implied or clearly expressed in statutory law. The Civil Rights Act of 1964 produced widespread desegregation in the South; in many places, however, resistance to Negro pressure took the form of severe violence. White leadership, especially in rural areas and small towns, expected Negroes to abide by custom, not to assert rights based on legal mandates. The sit-in protest was used to oppose such attitudes.

Freedom Rides were started by CORE in March 1961, and followed by others, in the Deep South to test desegregation in interstate traveling facilities.[17] The activities of the Mississippi Freedom Democratic Party (MFDP), sponsored by SNCC, may be thought of as forms of sit-ins. At the 1964 Democratic National Convention in Atlantic City, for example, the latter sat in the seats of the Mississippi delegation. The march and demonstration, however, embody special characteristics.

The March-Demonstration

Unlike the sit-in, which ordinarily addresses itself to specific discriminations, the march-demonstration attempts to appeal to the public over the heads of racists and their officials or to sympathetic but apathetic whites. It also seeks to uplift and encourage Negroes, thus relieving them of the pressures of social isolation and a sense of hopelessness. When it is peaceful, it may find Negro communities sympathetic; in the South especially, it has been generally regarded as a challenge, an open answer, and an act of resistance to the entire structure of white racial superiority. In racist communities, therefore, the march-demonstration either drives whites away from the scene or arouses them to violent opposition.

The execution of the march-demonstration must necessarily be nonviolent and nonretaliatory or it will almost certainly be transformed at its inception into a riot or a fight against superior forces. When, during World War I, President Wilson proclaimed his purpose of making the "world safe for democracy" and Negroes were being lynched in the South and violently molested in the North, W. E. B. DuBois led the first protest march (1917) in New York.[. . .]

The march did not become generally popular, however, until around 1960. Since then they have numbered in the thousands. Between August and December 1967, for instance, in Milwaukee alone, more than one hundred marches were led by Father Groppi, a white Roman Catholic priest, in support of demands for racial reforms in that city. They survived violent opposition and imprisonments. The march-demonstrations that draw national and international attention have been few but they have served as bellwethers. Perhaps the following are the most significant: the Birmingham sit-ins and march-demonstrations, beginning in the spring of 1963; the March on Washington, August 28, 1963; the Selma-Montgomery marches in March 1965; and the James H. Meredith Memphis-to-Jackson march in June 1966.

Each of these events publicly exposed and emphasized different aspects of racial conflict. In Birmingham it was the dramatic exposure of southern police brutality in their dealings with Negroes. The Washington demonstration, 200,000 strong, including many leading Americans, emphasized interracial concern over discrimination in the United States. It was climaxed by King's memorable "I have a dream" speech. The Selma-to-Montgomery march showed most clearly how nonviolence, strategically employed in protest demonstrations, could arouse the nation to help carry the contest to the very doorstep of the capital of southern racism. And James Meredith's almost fatal individual attempt to march into Jackson against "fear and for the right to vote" made clear to the nation and the world that extreme hazards confront Negroes in their struggle to exercise civil rights in the South.

As we should expect, scores have been injured, thousands jailed, and many murdered in these march-demonstrations. On April 4, 1968, Martin Luther King, Jr., himself was cut down by the sniper's bullet while preparing for such a march in Memphis. The murderers are usually aware of the tacit approval of white officials in high places. When, to illustrate, on Sunday, March 7, 1965, state troopers, on orders from Governor George C. Wallace, violently turned back the first attempt to march from Selma to Montgomery, the governor said to reporters: "We saved their lives by stopping their march. If they had gone on they could have been attacked by angry whites along the highway."[18] At least two persons lost their lives by engaging in that march: the Reverend James J. Reeb and Mrs. Viola Liuzzo; the former beaten to death and the latter run down and shot in her car while driving on the Montgomery-Selma highway. Violence resulting in death was even more atrocious in Birgmingham.

And yet, this violence must be reckoned as small compared to the unrequited injury and death which Negroes continually suffered in the Deep South at the hands of whites and which the demonstrations were intended to expose and change.

No other form of protest could have created so much concern and positive action on the part of the news media, the Congress, the presidency, the Supreme Court, and religious organizations. It was, no doubt, the Birmingham police severity and the worldwide publicity it received that led President John F. Kennedy, in 1963, to take effective steps in the promotion of a civil rights law which finally became the basic Civil Rights Act of 1964. "Moved by that emotional crisis, and seizing that sympathetic moment to go to Congress, the President [on June 19, 1963] proposed the broadest civil rights legislation ever seriously suggested."[19] In admittedly the most persuasive speech of his career, President Lyndon B. Johnson on the evening of March 15, 1965, during the crisis period of the Selma-Montgomery march-demonstration, addressed the Congress and the nation in support of the Civil Rights Act of 1965. Said he in part:

> I speak tonight for the dignity of man and destiny of democracy. I urge members of both parties, Americans of all religions and colors, from every section to join me in that cause. . . .
> The real hero of this struggle is the American Negro. His actions and protests—his courage to risk safety and even life—have awakened the conscience of the nation. His demonstrations have been designed to call attention to injustice, to provoke change and stir reform. . . . At the heart of battle for equality is a belief in the democratic process. . . . Their cause must be our cause, too. It is not just the Negro but all of us who must overcome the crippling legacy of bigotry and injustice. And we shall overcome.

One remarkable fact about assimilationist protest is that it is middle-class oriented and led. This does not mean that the lower class does not benefit directly. In the United States lower-class individuals can benefit permanently only by the provision of such means as would reduce its numbers. The availability of the ballot is of elementary assistance; the opening up of skilled labor to Negroes relieves economic pressure on the lower class; and the wider availability of education should attract the more energetic of the lower class. But protest can only help the permanently lower class by seeking for them equitable poor relief. According to American standards, if the poor are helped, they will no longer be poor.

It was no doubt the criticism that his concerns were for the middle class that led Martin Luther King, Jr., to plan, before his death, a Poor People's March to Washington. During the summer of 1968, "A-frame" shelters near the Reflecting Pool in the heart of Washington were set up to form "Resurrection City" under the leadership of the Reverend Ralph Abernathy and SCLC. The project collapsed late in June because of fragmented leadership and an absence of concrete purpose. And yet, it called attention to the problems of the poor—easpecially among Negroes in the South. The Department of Health, Education, and Welfare was repeatedly brought into the spotlight. At the final cleanup of the fast-decaying "city," an editorial in the *Washington Post* took the attitude of good riddance; but in the same issue Jean M. White in her article, "Resurrection City: Symbol that Soured," concluded: "The question now is whether the poor people's leaders can move on from Resurrection City to . . . 'creating a sensitive enough country to deal with the problem of poverty.'"[20] Since then the problem of poverty has loomed ever larger. It commands the attention of the nation.

Notes

1. Elizabeth Donnan, *Documents Illustrative of the History of the Slave Trade to America* (Washington, 1930), p. 1; cf. Gilbert Osafsky, ed., *The Burden of Race* (New York, 1967), pp. 6–23.
2. Herbert Aptheker, *American Negro Slave Revolts* (New York, 1963).
3. Frederick Douglass, *The Equality of All Men Before the Law Claimed and Defended* (Boston, 1865), pp. 36–39.
4. The question has been repeatedly raised. See Frazier's debate with Herskovits in E. Franklin Frazier, *The Negro in the United States* (New York, 1957), pp. 3–21.
5. Stanley M. Elkins, *Slavery* (Chicago, 1959), pp. 101–102.
6. Michael Harrington, "The Economics of Protest," in *Employment, Race and Poverty,* ed. A. M. Ross and H. Hill (New York, 1967), p. 239.
7. St. Clair Drake and Horace R. Cayton, *Black Metropolis: A Study of Negro Life in a Northern City* (New York, 1962), p. 602.
8. H. Rap Brown, *Die, Nigger, Die!* (New York, 1969), p. 53.
9. Larry Bryant, "Black English: A Separate Language," *St. Louis Post-Dispatch,* 7 November 1969.
10. Ibid.
11. Langston Hughes, "The Negro and American Entertainment," in *The American Negro Reference Book,* ed. John P. Davis (Englewood Cliffs, N.J., 1966), p. 873.
12. Tom Mboya, "The American Negro Cannot Look to Africa for Escape," *New York Times Magazine,* 13 July 1969, pp. 30 ff.
13. For discussion of the distinction between integration and assimilation, see W. D. Borrie, *The Cultural Integration of Immigrants* (UNESCO, 1959), pp. 89 ff.
14. From Cox, unpublished ms. on the Chicago boycott movement.
15. Martin Luther King, Jr., *Stride Toward Freedom* (New York, 1958), p. 45.
16. Ibid., pp. 214–23.

17. A. Meier and Elliott Rudwick, "The First Freedom Ride," *Phylon* 30 (1969): 213–22.
18. *New York Times*, 14 March 1965.
19. Anthony Lewis, "Civil Rights: Decade of Progress," *New York Times*, 20 December 1964.
20. *Washington Post*, 25 June 1968.

8

The Question of Pluralism

Pluralism is one of the most widely discussed terms among sociologists and yet it still remains far from conceptualization. The expression is currently being used even in the streets by radical militants. The question thus arises: Of what value is it as a general sociological concept and, more specifically, to what extent may it be employed as an instrument in the study of race relations?

The problem, it seems, begins with the nature of the term itself. Pluralism is an abstract substantive purporting to define a specific state of intergroup relations. There is no such thing as a "plural" or a "dual"; ordinarily referents are to ethnics, minorities, subcultures, associations, dominant groups, and so on. It is intended to identify a peculiar relationship between or among such groups or cultures. Thus the modifier "plural" implies a societal condition of pluralism. The term "subcultural pluralism" has also been used.

Perhaps it may be well, at the outset, to raise further questions about our subject: Is pluralism situationally spontaneous hence normally characteristic of a type of social system? Does pluralism involve socially planned situations in the face of group resistance? As illustrations of pluralism, is the European minority group situation—where cultures are essentially similar—identifiable with the European–non-European colonial situation? What are the culturally differentiating limits of pluralism? Is pluralism peculiar to capitalism or is it historically and anthropologically unrestricted? Is there any characteristic way in which pluralistic societies change? What do we mean by more or less pluralistic or more or less homogeneous societies? Is pluralism merely a means of classifying societies? Should pluralism be regarded as a favorable social phenomenon? We shall not, of course, proceed with attempts at direct answers.

Let us, however, observe actual usage. We shall start with the following three: *the political, the legalistic,* and *the societal.*[1] *The political* use of the term pluralism refers essentially to ideas and doctrines of political theorists about concentration or dispersal of power in society. It is, in other words, largely concerned with decentralization of state sovereignty. To illustrate, according to one source:

> The English pluralist doctrine . . . is a plea for the rights and interests of groups which form no part of the official government of the community. Since man's social nature finds expression in numerous forms of association—vocational, economic, religious, political—no one of which is supreme in moral significance or practical force over the others, the state cannot properly be said to be a sovereign organization.[2]

The state should thus recognize the value of functioning decentrally through its spontaneous organizations. Indeed, theorists debate whether the United States, for example, constitutes a "pluralist" power structure—a "congeries" of interest groups each exercising its peculiar power component—or a monopolistic system with only a few major organizations and classes inherently concentrating national power.[3]

The legalistic conception of the term has been directed toward the rights of minorities in national states. This is the way in which Louis Wirth uses it. Here pluralism refers to the aim of a minority group with respect to its political and civil rights while maintaining its cultural identity. "A pluralistic minority," he explains, "is one which seeks toleration for its differences on the part of the dominant group."[4] Europe has been the traditional arena of minority-group problems of this type. It is thus to this area that Wirth refers when he writes:

> Ever since the revolutionary epoch of the late eighteenth century the economic and political enfranchisement of minorities has been regarded not merely as inherent in the "rights of man" but as the necessary instrument in the struggle for cultural emancipation. Freedom of choice in occupations, rights of land ownership . . . these and other full privileges of citizenship are the foundations upon which cultural freedom rests.[5]

Although minority groups are themselves the normal champions of their rights, the process has had all sorts of international repercussions. Critically, these range from expressions of sympathy abroad for the disadvantaged group to use of the situation as a pretext for war—all of which, of course, disturbs world peace.

It was a recognition of this fact which led the League of Nations in 1919 and 1920 to conclude a series of treaties on minority rights between the Allied and Associated Powers and various European States.[6] In some ten such treaties states with large minority populations obligated themselves to the League as final arbiter in assuring certain explicit rights to these minorities. The treaties generally stipulated that, without regard to differences in race, language, or religion, minorities shall be free to follow any creed, "enjoy the same civil and political privileges," and exercise rights of maintaining their own schools and other private institutions.[7]

The treaties thus became legalistic devices which sometimes raised questions calling for decision of the Permanent Court of International Justice.* Minorities ranged all the way from weak "pluralistic" pockets of Jews striving to maintain their cultural identity to communities of militant Germans insisting upon being a law unto themselves.[8] As Harris concluded in the late thirties: "Minorities are just as often unreasonable as the dominant State is arbitrary in its treatment; and the League accordingly has as often to restrain the one party as to remonstrate with the other."[9]

This process, then, constitutes pluralism as Wirth uses the term. The League of Nations was able to get along without a similar usage. The phenomenon, moreover, is necessarily limited to the culture of modern Western society. The caste system of India, or feudalism, for example, has no place for a grant of *rights* such as these—they are indeed *urban* privileges of special citizens. Bewton Berry observes in point: "Pluralism is a delicate form of accommodation, difficult to achieve, applicable only in rare circum-

---

*League of Nations Secretariat, *Essential Facts about the League of Nations* (1938), pp. 105–6. It is not our purpose here to analyze or to explain historically the relationship of the League of Nations with minority groups and parent nations but merely to identify the content with which this definition of pluralism is concerned. The legalistic tenor of these treaties may be further gauged by the opening and closing words of the Albanian declaration made in October 1921: "The stipulations of this Declaration are recognised as fundamental laws of Albania. . . . Full and complete protection of life and liberty will be assured to all the inhabitants of Albania, without distinction of birth, nationality, language, race or religion. . . . The stipulations in the foregoing Articles . . . are declared to constitute obligations of international concern, and will be placed under the guarantee of the of the League of Nations" (League of Nations, *Protection of Linguistic, Racial and Religious Minorities by the League of Nations* [Geneva, 1927], pp. 4–5).

Article 26 of the U.N. Draft Covenant on Civil and Political Rights states: "Any advocacy of national, racial or religious hostility that constitutes an incitement to hatred and violence shall be prohibited by the law of the state." As Inis L. Claude, Jr., shows, however, by the time of the Second World War "there was a strong tendency to abandon the assumption that national minorities and national states could be reconciled." Three substitute movements developed. "Transfer, human rights, and assimilation form a conceptual combination which undercuts the status of national minorities in national states" (*National Minorities* [Boston, 1955], pp. 208 and 211).

stances, and demanding a high degree of mutual tolerance and sympathy."[10]

At about this time also, during and after the First World War, a reaction among social philosophers to the Americanization movement, directed toward immigrants in the United States, began to be heard. It was, perhaps, not by mere chance that its protagonist, Horace Kallen, was a Jew. Jews were likely to be among those most directly affected by both the advocacy and the fact of the American melting-pot.[11]

To put it briefly, Profesor Kallen pleaded for respect, protection and encouragement of national cultures. The goal of the United States, he maintained, should be "cultural pluralism" rather than "cultural monism."[12] The American idea "is an orchestration of . . . diversities—regional, local, religious, ethnic, esthetic, industrial, sporting and political—each developing freely and characteristically its own enclave, and somehow so intertwined with the others, as to suggest . . . the dynamic whole.'[13]

Kallen's work has been very much criticized especially for its imprecision and for its intermixture of fact and advocacy. Professor Milton Gordon summarizes the position of the group, saying "the presumed goal of the cultural pluralist" is the maintenance of separte subsocietal primary relations, excluding intermarriage, "while cooperating with other groups and individuals in secondary relations."[14] He himself observes that this situation actually obtains among Protestants, Catholics, Jews, and Negroes in the United States, and that it should be termed "*structural pluralism* rather than cultural pluralism."[15] The question, however, whether the concepts "structural" and "cultural" are commensurate seems to remain.

As Gordon puts it axiomatically: "It is not possible for cultural pluralism to exist without the existence of separate subsocieties" but it is possible for separate subsocieties to exist without cultural pluralism.[16] It will be recalled that, years ago, Booker T. Washington, in an attempt to placate Southern racists, declared: "In all things that are purely social we can be separate as the fingers, yet one as the hand in all things essential to mutual progress."[17] Could Negroes develop distinct societal organizations and still expect to participate comparably in the dominant culture? Would Gordon's proposition hold for Jews but not for Negroes? Defining the social has not been so simple as it probably appeared at the time of that Atlanta address.

Boeke and Furnivall

The conception of pluralism as a societal process is, of course, the principal concern of sociologists. This approach has been directed not simply by some group seeking protection for its social heritage and guarantees of political rights within a larger societal context but rather to a peculiar form of social organization. As members of this society, the behavior of all groups is ordinarily designated pluralistic; and pluralism, it is assumed, defines the total social process. It ordinarily develops spontaneously. Two Dutch social scientists, John S. Furnivall and Julius H. Boeke, had devoted themselves consistently to the study of this pattern of social and economic relationships. We shall attempt to review here what seems to be essentially their assumptions and conclusions. They have been frequently cited by other students of the subject but generally with considerable imprecision.

To Furnivall and Boeke, pluralistic society derived from the disintegration of native cultures under the impact of capitalism. Their principal problem was thus to explain how the native cultures of the world, all nonwhite and living mainly in the tropics, contrived to deal with capitalist culture during the period of colonization. Furnivall wrote his basic essay on this topic as early as 1910[18] when colonialism was in full flower. Their preoccupation was intriguing because they were conscious of their dealing with the most widespread cultural revolution known to mankind. "This is a modern invention," says Furnivall, "because only in modern times have economic forces been set free to remould the social order."[19] Boeke identifies the plural society as follows:

It is not necessary that a society be exclusively dominated by one social system. Where this is the case or where, at least, one social style prevails, the society in question may be called homogeneous; where, on the contrary, simultaneously two or more social systems appear, clearly distinct the one from the other, and each dominate[s] a part of the society, there we have to do with a dual or plural society. It is, however, advisable to qualify the term dual society by reserving it for societies showing a distinct cleavage of two synchronic and full grown social styles which, in the normal, historical evolution of homogeneous societies, are separated from each other by transitional forms, as for instance, precapitalism and high capitalism by early capitalism, and therefore which do not coincide as contemporary dominating features. Without this qualification it would be impossible to distinguish between homogeneous and dual societies, because every society, in its progression, will show, beside the prevailing social system, the remains of the preceding and the beginnings of its future social style.[20]

The essence of pluralism, Boeke observes further, "is the clashing of an imported social system with an indigenous social system of another style." All "colonies of exploitation" would thus tend to constitute plural societies. He limits the incoming system, significantly, to either capitalism or socialism.[21] The situation arises when the Europeans have been able neither to "oust nor to assimilate" the natives; and the force of the new culture lies in its peculiar economic determinism. As Furnivall puts it: "Whether the method of development be through native enterprise working for the market or through western enterprise employing native labour, the disintegration of social life is an almost inevitable result of the contact of primitive peoples with European civilization."[22] And, to repeat, the critical aspect of this civilization is its economic organization.

One permanent form of disruption of native life is thus the substitution of the capitalist physical structure of existence—the introduction of *the city* as the center of productive life—for the system of villages serving largely self-sufficient agricultural communities. It is, indeed, the strain toward this centralization in colonialism which brings pluralism into being. What Boeke has to say regarding the entrance of capitalism into Southeast Asia may be applied to the whole non-European world with relevant historical modifications.

> To the purely eastern social organism, *left to grow along its own lines*, the city is alien. . . . That which . . . is indicated by the term "city" is simply the court, the royal center, the religious center, or the military center—merely a consumer living . . . on the village economy. Only on the fringes, along the open rivers and on the coast . . . do we find the beginnings of real capitalistic centers, trading cities. . . . These coastal cities impose tribute in kind and in labor on the interior. . . . Even now, the city in these dualistic countries is a capitalistic enclave . . . and we do find those small and middle-sized centers scattered over the country, those country towns that are so characteristic of western Europe.[23]

The modern cities, then, are a capitalistic development. They ordinarily do not struggle directly for the land of the old, native leadership but rather make its usefulness dependent on urban production, which, in turn, relates to the great metropolises of the world. Land becomes commercialized, a process which, of course, might exclude natives from title:

These people, in South East Asia at least, have been absorbed by, and have become dependent on, the fully developed western capitalism; they have become off-shoots of this social economic system. Their independent handicraft industries have turned into units of whole-sale enterprises; their independent local traders have become agents for importers and exporters. They have lost the typical characteristics of the early-capitalistic handicraftsman, since they draw their raw materials from abroad and since each is free to promote his individual economic interests with no guild regulations or city by-laws to hamper him. They must be regarded as organs of western capitalism, the only role in which their function becomes comprehensible. These early-capitalistic elements accentuate the economic dualism, they have to bridge the chasm that yawns between precapitalism and high-capitalism.[24]

Thus the critical characteristic of plural society, according to Furnivall and Boeke, is the distinct pattern of economic behavior inherent to colonialists and natives, and the collapse of "corporate and village life" resulting from the impact of capitalist individualism and social "atomization."[25] The plural society represents a stage, peculiar to these cultures, in their progress toward "high capitalism." The self-interested, political force in the situation is the colonial government.[26]

With the disruption of native economy, the new urban areas became the loci of intergroup relations defined as pluralistic. One elementary reason for emphasizing "production," says Furnivall, "rather than . . . social life, which is characteristic of plural society" is that labour becomes sectionalized. "Although the primary distinction between the groups may be race, creed or colour, each section comes to have its own functions in production, and there is a tendency toward the grouping of the several elements into distinct economic castes."[27] The author also makes the following remarkable point on the structure of the society: "In a plural society the sections are not segregated; the members of the several units are intermingled and meet as individuals; the union is not voluntary but is imposed by the colonial power and by the force of economic circumstances; and the union cannot be dissolved without the whole society relapsing into anarchy."[28]

Two facts obviously led to this conclusion. The new society, built by European foreigners, had effectively liquidated both the native economic order and its system of authority. There could be no return to that. And, secondly, it is assumed, no native group had become sufficiently integrated into the capitalist order to run it dependably. The natives of Indonesia had not gone through the experience of nationalism. Perhaps the situation of Haiti and the Congo might be taken as examples of colonies winning sovereignty without sufficient colonial tutelage; India and the Philippines, on the other hand, may be thought of as having had greater opportunity to master the socioeconomic bases of the new system.

This characteristic is further elaborated in Furnivall's assertion that "in a plural society there is no common social will."[29] Basic interest is not in national welfare. The European, who sets social standards, is concerned mainly with the most successful exploitation of the situation. He "works in the tropics but does not live there. His life in the tropics centers round his business, and he looks at social problems, political or economic, not as a citizen but as a capitalist or an employer of labour."[30] In such places as Burma and Java, therefore, each "section"—native, Chinese, Indian, or European—looked after its own economic interests: "they mixed but did not combine." Social ethos was thus enfeebled. "There may be apathy even on such a vital point as defence against aggression."[31] Immigration was left to the play of economic forces. Indeed, "the plural society arises where economic forces are exempt from control by social will."[32] The society remains together because of sectional dependence upon the dominant colonial organization.

In capitalist society the critical force producing group solidarity and "social will" is nationalism—the psychological basis of the struggle for independence or for international position. But in a plural society, according to Furnivall, nationalism stimulates internal counter-nationalism. It "sets one community against the other so as to emphasize the plural character of the society and aggravate its instability."[33] Perhaps the postcolonial antagonism between Hindus and Moslems in India and the intertribal eruptions in Nigeria may be taken as striking illustrations of this. The tendency of postcolonial "democratic" politics may be to upset the system of social stratification developed under colonialism.

Thus far, the idea of pluralism, as defined by Furnivall and Boeke, seems clear. If they wished to consider this term as applicable to the economic process by which non-European countries of the world were brought into the universal capitalist matrix,* they

---

*I think that the following position of Professor Boeke, rejected by some classical economists, is essentially sound: "Every social system has its own economic history. A social economic theory is always the theory of a special social system. Even if it announces itself as a general theory, still it is historically determined. Therefore, the economic theory of a dualistic, heterogeneous, society is itself dualistic. It has to describe and to explain the economic interactions of two clashing social systems. . . .

would have had to take the chance of all neologists regarding its academic acceptance. Subsequently, however, the authors, especially Furnivall, moved away from this relatively secure base to give the concept almost unlimited applicability. Perhaps we may best illustrate this by citing the following two positions—the first is the earlier statement.

> Outside the tropics society may have plural features, notably in South Africa, Canada and the United States, and also in lands where the Jew has not been fully assimilated into social life; in other countries also there are mixed populations with particularist tendencies. But in general these mixed populations have at least a common tradition of western culture, and, despite a different racial origin, they meet on equal terms and their relations are not confined solely to the economic sphere. There is a society with plural features, but not a plural society.[34]

Then the later, more generalized view conceives of virtually any cultural difference in social groups as a basis of pluralism. This, to repeat, disregards—with considerable contradiction—his limited, detailed, colonial analysis:

> In this matter Netherlands India is typical of tropical dependencies where the rulers and the ruled are of different races; but one finds a plural society also in independent states, such as Siam, where Natives, Chinese and Europeans have distinct economic functions, and live apart as separate social orders. Nor is the plural society confined to the tropics; it may be found also in temperate regions where, as in South Africa and the United States, there are both white and coloured populations. Again, one finds a plural society in the French provinces of Canada, where two people are separated by race, language and religion, and an English lad, brought up in an English school, has no contact with French life; and in countries such as Ireland where, with little or no difference of race or language, the people are sharply divided in their religious allegiance. Even where there is no difference of creed or colour, a community may still have a

---

It . . . will have to be three economic theories combined into one: the economic theory of a precapitalistic society, usually called primitive economics, the economic theory of a developed capitalistic or socialistic society, usually termed general economic theory, and the economic theory of the interactions of two distinct social systems within the borders of one society, which might be called dualistic economics" (Boeke, *Economics and Economic Policies of Dual Societies*, pp. 4–5). See, for example, the *jajmani economic system* described by Gerald D. Berreman in "Caste and Economy in the Himalayas," *Economic Development and Cultural Change* (July 1962): 386–94, where socio-situational factors rather than the open market tend to determine economic exchange.

plural character, as in Western Canada, where people of different
racial origin tend to live in distinct settlements and, for example, a
Northern European cannot find work on the railway, because this is
reserved for "Dagoes" or "Wops." And in lands where a strong Jewish
element is regarded as alien, there is to that extent a plural society.
Thus Netherlands India is merely an extreme type of a large class of
political organizations.[35]

It is perhaps obvious that pluralism cannot now be accepted as a
scientific concept. It does not define a consistent pattern of social
behavior. Europeans, for example, assume different positions in
the pre- and postcolonial situations—as whites in Kenya and in
Northern Rhodesia well understand. In the postcolonial situation
the old economic laissez-faire of the colonies tends largely to be
abolished and there is greater insistence by the government on
domestic national identity for all groups. A national "will" or "we-
feeling" tends to be established, and all groups must respect it: the
drive here is antipluralist in favor of national solidarity. Not pluralism, it seems, but rather mainly the size and international position of the former colony determines the pattern of intergroup
behavior.

Other Approaches

Let us move now to consider certain attempts by modern sociologists to conceptualize this term. Perhaps the symposium on
pluralism in the Caribbean, held in New York and reported in 1960
as an issue of the *Annals of the New York Academy of Sciences*, constitutes, thus far, the most searching investigation of the subject.[36]
Even so, however, results were inconclusive and perhaps disappointing. The leading paper, "Social and Cultural Pluralism," was
submitted by Professor M. G. Smith, who is especially familiar with
the culture of the West Indies.[37]

In attempting to ferret out Smith's explanation one seems to be
involved initially with imprecision. He begins by relying explicitly
upon Furnivall, saying the latter "saw clearly that . . . *economic* pluralism was simply an aspect of the *social pluralism* of these colonies."[38] Furnivall, of course, did basically just the opposite. In his
original formulation, the latter saw social organization as a direct
function of the economics of colonialism. We are concerned here,
however, with the variety of uses of the term "pluralism" without a
systematic definition of each. Thus "cultural pluralism [refers to]
diversity of the basic institutional system. . . . The United States

and Brazil . . . contain *plural communities* and evince pluralism without themselves being plural societies."[39]

Professor Smith defines pluralism as "that condition in which there is a formal diversity in the basis system of compulsory institutions. This basic institutional system embraces kinship, education, religion, property and economy, recreation, and certain sodalities."[40] Given this difference in institutional affiliation, pluralism requires further that there be a monopoly of power by one group. As Smith puts it: "The dominant social section of these culturally split societies is simply the section that controls the apparatus of power and force, and this is the basis of the status hierarchies that characterize pluralism."[41] This definition would also exclude a country like Switzerland. The Canadian situation further illustrates the author's point:

> In Canada the French dominate Quebec, while Anglo-Saxons control the other provinces. Even if the French and British Canadians practiced different institutional systems, their provincial separateness would mean that the Canadian Federation is an association of groups differentiated territorially and institutionally. If this unit were dominated by a distinct cultural minority, it would then present a special form of plural society.[42]

This description of the place and the role of the dominant power would be particularly true of the colonial situation. But Smith generalizes the concept, as Furnivall ultimately did, to include almost any time and place—"the Norman conquest, Roman conquests," and so on—so that "the most general answer to the question of the origin [of pluralism] is migration."[43]

We are led to inquire of what value is the term "pluralism" to the study of modern race relations? It is, according to Professor Smith, of basic importance. "The function of racism," he explains, "is merely to justify and perpetuate a pluralistic social order. This being the case, the rigorous analysis of race relations presupposes analyses of their context based on the theory of pluralism."[44] Thus far, as we have seen, pluralism, if it is a legitimate sociological concept, appears to be the identification of a condition or state rather than an analytical theory. Consider, for example, the following proposition, which clearly remains to be tested:

> In certain parts of the United States it is possible that the Negro population practices a distinct institutional system in my sense of the term. There is evidence that certain Negro communities in the South differ sharply in their social, religious, and *economic organization* from those of the adjoining whites. Assuming this to be the case, we must

regard such Negro-white populations as plural communities. They are communities, but not societies, even if they embrace entire member states of the Union.[45]

Would it not be more meaningful to say that according to the influence of the white power structure of the Deep South, Negroes and whites constitute socially segregated communities—a form of apartheid? Is pluralism—we may inquire again—based upon enforced social separation?

As a member of the New York symposium, Professor Leonard Broom, maintained: "A society is not a plural society just because it contains populations from more than one racial or cultural origin. . . . Not all, and perhaps not most, nations made up of differing populations are plural societies."[46] Pluralism presupposes separate identities, but

> in order to maintain the society as a going concern, the several populations are taken into account as such. In the extreme case this takes explicit political form, the ideal type of which is probably federalism. In other words, in a plural society the problem of diversity has been resolved by adjustments that presume the continued separate identity of significant population elements and a specification of limited spheres of contact, especially in the market place and in politics.[47]

Canada, Broom points out—as Smith does not—"is a good case of a plural society. . . . The two major populations are distinguished by almost everything but race. . . . As a consequence, constitutional adjustments have been made to accommodate government to reality."[48] Perhaps the American North and South, according to this point of view, could also be considered exemplary of pluralism. From the beginning, constitutional adjustments have been made to accommodate basic cultural differences. The North, however, has never "presumed continued separate identity."

Probably an elementary question would be: Suppose one school of pluralists agrees that the existing differentiation does indeed define the nation as "plural," what theoretical advancement would it make to our understanding of the country's social life? Professor Broom, at any rate, thinks that the United States "will remain plural" because of the "durable and institutionalized cleavage between Negroes and whites."[49] Negro separatists, at least, should be surprised at this conclusion. One may ask at random: Does the durability of social relations between feudal estates define all feudal society as pluralistic?

The city, Broom recognizes further, is the traditional locus of pluralism; it normally attracts a relatively great variety of people. The author makes a distinction, however, between the effects of "preindustrial and industrial cities." "Ethnic subgroups may survive longer in preindustrial cities than in industrial ones"; and most Caribbean cities are preindustrial.[50] If, however, the industrial cities are "melting pots," it must be, apparently, the preindustrial cities that are most highly "pluralistic."

Let us now cite some of the basic conclusions arrived at from the use of "social and cultural pluralism" as an instrument of analysis by two writers who put expressed reliance upon the terms. The following may be considered representative of Professor Pierre L. van den Berghe's findings:

> Cultural pluralism between ethnic groups cannot exist without institutional duplication and hence without social pluralism; that is, any form of cultural pluralism has a structural facet which can be treated as social pluralism.
>
> Racial segregation represents, together with other types of caste divisions (such as the . . . Hindu caste system), one of the most extreme and rigid forms of social pluralism.
>
> In South Africa a high degree of social pluralism (exhibited through a rigid system of four main racial castes) exists in conjunction with continued cultural pluralism. However, as a result of considerable westernization, the racial and cultural lines of cleavage no longer coincide.
>
> Over the years [in the United States], as a result of the color line, the Negro working class and peasantry have developed a subculture that differs in some respects (dialect, family composition, and values) from the dominant white culture, even if one controls for social class.
>
> Segregation and discrimination are the foremost mechanisms for the preservation of racial pluralism in the presence of cultural assimilation and other integrative pressures. Thus a competitive situation is one in which the ruling group deliberately maintains social pluralism by force in order to protect its privileged position.[51]

The commonplaces of race relations together with their distortions are thus couched in the abstract, imprecise terminology of "pluralism," Professor Schermerhorn follows van den Berghe rather closely in his extensive application of the term in his own work. We submit a brief illustration of the nature of his conclusions:

> Since race is an independent factor, it apparently has the special power to produce its own form of social pluralism which is a high degree of *enforced* enclosure typified by the segregated status of Negro life in the United States. Considering that the American Negro has only minor differences in culture when compared with other

Americans, it makes sense to say that we have "a nearly pure case of deep structural pluralism with little cultural pluralism.[52]

Recently, in race relations discussions, the term "pluralism" has been brought in as a shibboleth by groups ranging all the way from black and white separatists to black and white assimilationists. Whitney M. Young, Jr., Executive Director of the National Urban League—to cite at random—uses it in this way: "It may be that a period of self-development and ghetto rehabilitation will coincide with a temporary decline in efforts at integration, but such a period should be seen not as a retreat, but as a strength-gathering preliminary to build a *pluralistic society.*"[53]

It is not clear whether Dr. Young has considered the logic of the realtionship between integration and pluralism. It seems that Negroes cannot consciously pull out without suffering isolation.* No doubt, the ghetto will deteriorate if taken over noncompetitively. The Negro community has never been the principal

---

*Very much of Dr. Young's argument for "community control" seems utopian. Consider the following in illustration. "Community control is not a scheme to get whites out of the ghetto; if anything, it is designed to attract the talents and skills of white people. . . . White teachers, policemen, businessmen, and others should be welcomed, for we need what they can contribute. The only difference is that, with community control, their presence will be welcomed by a community that sees them as helpers, not occupiers" (Young, *Beyond Racism*, p. 161). The old concept of *parallelism*, advocated by Southern racists for Negroes, may be achieved by Negroes themselves in their quest for *pluralism*. Few Negro separatists have stated it more cogently than Edgar Gardner Murphy in 1904: "The clue to racial integrity for the negro is thus to be found . . . not in race suppression but in race sufficiency. For the very reason that a race, in the apartness of its social life, is to work out its destiny as a separate member of a larger group, it must be accorded its own leaders and thinkers, its own scholars artists prophets; and while the development of the higher life may come slowly, even blunderingly, it is distinctly to be welcomed. As the race comes to have within itself . . . a world that is worth living for, it will gain that individual foothold among the families of men which will check the despairing passion of its self-obliteration . . . It will begin to claim its own name and its own life. That is the only . . . permanent security of race integrity for the negro" (*Problems of the Present South* [New York, 1905], p. 274).

In 1949, Maurice R. Davie wrote: "With regard to social relations, the national policy and practice, with regional modifications, is that of separateness and parallelism. By this dual term is meant that there is no basic cultural difference between Negroes and whites—they both have the same language, religion, political views, and other customs and values—but they operate separately along parallel lines of the basic national pattern. . . . In the South separatism is not accompanied by parallelism; the line between the two groups as they participate in the national culture is not the vertical line of a biracial society; it is still near the horizontal line of a caste society" (*Negroes in American Society* [New York, 1949], pp. 476 and 478).

source of the Negroes' income. They can thus have no decisive power to *build* any type of American society. They are part of the total economic process, which they can never hope, as a group, to direct or lead. The more securely they enter into that process as participant workers, the better for the ghetto. The author seems to say there will be integration after "pluralism."

In a very studied article, "Negroes and Jews: The New Challenge to Pluralism," Professor Nathan Glazer shows how the Jews advocate 'pluralism' to the probable disadvantage of Negroes.[54] Jews, of course, have been historical "pluralists," as Louis Wirth defines the term. They have both suffered and profited materially from their cultural separation.[55] They have been traditionally a part of the urban West where, as Glazer emphasizes, they have been able to specialize in money-getting and scholarship. Unlike the tradition of Negroes, then, their subculture concentrates on sharpening them for competition in those fields.

Glazer's critical point is that the integrity of the "pluralistic institutions," the institutions of the white society, which facilitate the success of Jews—the schools (including their own private schools) and the system of grading, the free market, the right to religious and social exclusiveness—are threatened by the demands of Negro integration.

> There were certainly delicate moments when it looked as if the strongly pressed and effectively supported Jewish demand for formal equality, combined with Jewish wealth and grades, would challenge the rights of vacation resorts, social clubs, and private schools of the old established Protestant community. . . . But after a time the . . . Protestant community realized there were limits to the demands of the Jews. . . . They realized that Jews . . . could not demand the complete abolition of lines between communities because they too wanted to maintain communities of their own.[56]

It should be observed, however, that Negroes have been primarily distressed by the pseudo-private, the "all whites allowed" or the "no Negro need apply" situations, and not by the truly exclusive.

But Glazer is chiefly concerned with Negroes' challenge to the norms which tend to make *equality* of little or no consequence to them. "Here we come to the crux of the Negro anger and the Jewish discomfort. The Negro anger is based on the fact that the system of formal equality produces little for them. The Jewish discomfort is based on the fact that Jews discover they can no longer support the newest Negro demands . . . which are designed to break down this pattern of communities."[57] If the peculiar demands of Negroes were met, Glazer thinks, the social system would be negatively reoriented. These demands do not contemplate equality of opportunity to the equally qualified, but rather equality of the *results* of education and economic effort.[58] His illustration of this emphasizes the threat to Jewish "pluralism:"

> Suppose one's capacity to gain from education depends on going to school with less than a majority of one's own group? Or suppose it depends on one's home background? Then how do we achieve equality of results? . . . The deprived group must be inserted into the community of the advantaged. For otherwise there will be no equality of outcome. The force of present-day Negro demands is that the subcommunity, because it either protects privileges or creates inequality, *has no right to exist.* That is why these demands pose a quite new challenge to the Jewish community.[59]

The author is also concerned about a possible Negro invasion of "the true seats of Jewish exclusiveness—the Jewish business . . . the Jewish union, or the Jewish (or largely Jewish) neighborhood and school."[60] The answer of the Jews, especially to Negroes' entry into their neighborhood or even their favorite public schools, has been to withdraw. In New York City this problem has been especially acute.

On December 7, 1969, for example, the *New York Times* reported an address on the subject by Dr. Nathan Brown, Acting Superintendent of Schools, in which he called on Jewish leaders "to help keep middle-class youngsters in the school system by deemphasizing and, in some instances, discouraging enrollment in Jewish day schools." Speaking directly to the point, he said "I deplore any action on the part of Jewish parents who escape the city school system for the sole purpose of avoiding racially integrated schools." Of the 1.1 million students in the city system, there are about 600,000 Negroes and Puerto Ricans.

Perhaps Professor Glazer's critical difficulty lies in his suggestion that Negroes ought to "proceed in such a way as to respect the group pattern of American life," and that the Negroes' demand "for equality of results" will "create communities very different from the kinds in which most of us . . . now live." The communities in which most of us now live are partly based upon a severe perversion of the spirit of American democratic organization. Perhaps with the social inclusion of Negroes, even at some expense to Jewish "pluralism," a restoration of this pristine virtue may be achieved.

Conclusion

It seems to me, in conclusion, that the value of the term "pluralism" for the study of race relations is quite limited. It has been given no consistent meaning or interpretation. It has been applied to distinct or even opposite types of social organization and, in the process, frequently redefined.[61] Occasionally, it has been limited historically and ecologically, but mostly not. It has been sometimes aplied to Negroes as a "national minority" and sometimes as an American group having only a definable subculture. Its difficulty, therefore, seems to remain that of conceptual definition. Its appearance frequently has a distracting effect; but it is popular and scientifically resonant, hence I have no illusions about its future career.

Notes

1. A similar division but somewhat different analysis, especially regarding "legal pluralism" is that of Arend Lijphart, *The Politics of Accommodation* (Berkeley and Los Angeles, 1968), p. 2. For philosophical discussions of pluralism, see Joseph W. Evans, "Jacques Maritain and the Problem of Pluralism in Political Life," *The Review of Politics*, July 1960; pp. 307–23; and Frederick A. Olafson, "Two Views of Pluralism," *The Yale Review*, Summer 1962, pp. 309–31.

2. Francis W. Coker, "Pluralism," *Encyclopedia of the Social Sciences* (New York, 1937), pp. 170–73.

3. Andrew S. McFarland, *Power and Leadership in Pluralist Systems* (Stanford, Calif., 1969), chs. 2–5. Robert A. Dahl in his *Pluralist Democracy in the United States* (Chicago, 1967) says quite simply: "The fundamental axiom in the theory and practice of American pluralism is . . . this: Instead of a single center of sovereign power there must be multiple centers of power, none of which is or can be wholly sovereign . . . even the people ought never to be an absolute sovereign" (pp. 22–24).

4. Louis Wirth, "The Problem of Minority Groups," in *The Science of Man in the World Crisis*, ed. Ralph Linton (New York, 1945), p. 354.

5. Ibid., p. 356. Wirth sees minorities as constituting four types: pluralistic, assimilationist, secessionist, and militant.

6. H. Wilson Harris, *What the League of Nations Is* (London, 1933), p. 139. As Harris puts it: "Most of the States of Continental Europe have always included within their borders a certain number of persons whose race, religion, or language, or all three, differed from that of the State in which they lived. The Peace Settlement of 1919, with its extensive rearrangement of political frontiers, created new Minority

problems throughout Central Europe and many of them became the more acute in that a race which had been dominant, and as such had acted with severity toward the Minority within its borders, itself became in its turn a Minority. . . . The bottom dog . . . had become the top dog. . . . Minorities in Europe . . . total certainly not less, and probably much more, than 30,000,000" (ibid., p. 139).

7. Ibid., pp. 140–41. For an enumeration of these rights, see League of Nations Secretariat, *Essential Facts about the League of Nations,* 9th ed. (Geneva, 1938), p. 202.

8. For a discussion of the "militant minority," see Wirth, "The Problem of Minority Groups," pp. 354ff.

9. Harris, *What the League of Nations Is,* p. 143. The following Assembly resolution on September 21, 1922, was a warning to the domineering minority: "While the Assembly recognizes the primary right of minorities to be protected by the League from oppression, it also emphasizes the duty incumbent' upon persons belonging to racial, religious or linguistic minorities to cooperate as loyal fellow citizens with the nations to which they now belong."

10. B. Berry, *Race and Ethnic Relations* (Boston, 1958), p. 364.

11. Cf. Milton M. Gordon, *Assimilation in American Life* (New York, 1964), p. 141.

12. Horace M. Kallen, *Cultural Pluralism and the American Idea* (Philadelphia, 1956), p. 97. As one conclusion of a UNESCO Conference held in Havana in April 1956, "cultural pluralism" is considered a "right" of immigrants. This position, say the authors, "rests upon a belief in the importance of cultural differentiation within a 'framework of social unity'" (W. D. Borrie et al., *The Cultural Integration of Immigrants* [UNESCO, 1959], p. 97). To the same effect, see Brinley Thomas in ibid., p. 114.

13. Kallen, *Cultural Pluralism,* p. 98.

14. Gordon, *Assimilation,* p. 158.

15. Ibid., p. 159. Emphasis in original.

16. Ibid., p. 158.

17. Booker T. Washington, *Up from Slavery* (New York, 1901), pp. 160ff.

18. John S. Furnivall, "Organization of Consumption," *Economic Journal* 20 (1910): 23–30. He was concerned here, however, mainly with the impact of "Western civilization" on the economic behavior of the "natives." See also for a similar emphasis his *Progress and Welfare in Southeast Asia* (New York, 1941), p. 6.

19. John S. Furnivall, *Colonial Policy and Practice* (New York, 1956; first published in 1948), p. 306.

20. Julius H. Boeke, *Economics and Economic Policies of Dual Societies* (New York, 1953), p. 3. Boeke is understandably concerned about the historic connotations of the term "capitalism." It is, no doubt, a costly limitation. He defines capitalism in terms of its spirit: "I do not hesitate to answer the question in this sense that the only true and really cogent antithesis is represented by the words *capitalistic and non- or pre-*

capitalistic. These terms have not as yet been generally adopted; and, besides, the word capitalistic in the Marxian terminology has acquired a critical and polemical connotation which is not easily got rid of—more's the pity. Nevertheless, it is worth our while to use it in a literal and neutral sense. What, then, do we wish to express by these words—capitalism and capitalistic? In the first place, we must endeavor to apply them non-materially: capitalism is a philosophy of life, an attitude toward life; it is not a complex of outer phenomena but the mental urge that has given rise to these phenomena" (p. 12; emphasis in original).

21. Ibid., p. 4. Furnivall makes the same point as follows: "All tropical dependencies, and indeed all tropical countries, so far as they have been brought within the modern world, have in common certain distinctive characters in their social structure. In Dutch colonial literature they are often said to present a dual economy, comprising two distinct economic systems, capitalist and pre-capitalist, with a western superstructure of business and administration rising above the native world in which the people, so far as they are left alone, lead their own life in their own way according to a traditional scale of values in which economic values rank so low as to be negligible" (*Colonial Policy and Practice*, pp. 303–04).

22. Furnivall, *Colonial Policy and Practice*, p. 303.

23. Boeke, *Economics and Economic Policies of Dual Societies*, p. 16; emphasis added. "We Westerners" no longer have any villages in the pre-capitalistic sense. . . . In the Occident, during the middle ages, cities arose as products of early capitalism and, in the course of their further development, they gradually carried the rural districts with them, absorbed their population surplus, opened markets to them, commercialized agriculture—and destroyed village economy" (p. 16).

24. Ibid., p. 15.

25. Furnivall, *Colonial Policy and Practice*, p. 307. "The mutual relations of the elements of a plural society tend to be governed solely by the economic process, with the production of material goods as the prime end of social life" (Furnivall, *Netherlands India* [New York, 1944], p. 450).

26. But Boeke holds that "economic dualism" and "colonialism" are not necessarily associated—that economic dualism will tend to remain even with the introduction of national sovereignty (*Economics and Economic Policy in Dual Societies, p. 20*). Nationalism need not exclude the impact of capitalist culture.

27. Furnivall, *Netherlands India*, p. 450. Cf. Burton Benedict, "Stratification in Plural Society," *American Anthropologist* (1962): 1235–46. It is the colonial definition of pluralism which Benedict selects for his identification of the situation in Mauritius.

28. Furnivall, *Colonial Policy and Practice*, p. 307.

29. Furnivall, *Netherlands India*, p. 447.

30. Furnivall, *Colonial Policy and Practice*, p. 306.

31. Ibid., p. 308. "The society as a whole comprises separate racial sections; each section is an aggregate of individuals rather than a corporate or organic whole; and as individuals their social life is complete" (p. 306).
32. Ibid. This, obviously, would not be true of a country like Switzerland.
33. Furnivall, *Netherlands India,* p. 459.
34. Furnivall, *Colonial Policy and Practice,* p. 305.
35. Furnivall, *Netherlands India,* p. 446. I am conscious of the fact that what I call here the earlier statement appeared in Furnivall's *Colonial Policy and Practice;* and that which I refer to as the later statement is taken from *Netherlands India.* Although I cannot enter into an exegesis of the author's writings, it seems clear that the *Colonial Policy* statement is the earlier approach. A note to the very title of the section, "The Plural Society," refers the reader to the author's 1910 thinking; and the section itself appears to be an unintegrated addition. In *Netherlands India,* on the other hand, a full chapter, "Plural Economy," considers the concept from a wider point of view, giving some attention to the position of other writers on the subject. It seems to me that Furnivall could not have written the second explanation first without suffering great mental perturbation.
36. Vera Rubin, ed., "Social and Cultural Pluralism in the Caribbean," *Annals of the New York Academy of Sciences* 83 (January 20, 1960): 761–916.
37. M. G. Smith reproduced the study in his book *The Plural Society in the British West Indies* (Berkeley and Los Angeles, 1965).
38. Ibid., p. 75.
39. Ibid., p. 85. Emphasis added.
40. Ibid., p. 82.
41. Ibid., p. 86. In one answer to a question at the symposium, Smith said: "A plural society exists only when there is a small dominant group that is preoccupied with maintaining power over culturally discrete sections of a society. If there are many groups that share in the government and power, then a *simple plurality* exists" (p. 915; emphasis added). See *Annals of the New York Academy of Sciences* 83 (Januray 20, 1960): 915. With the coming of independence, however, even Trinidad and British Guiana would lose their "small dominant" group.
42. Smith, *The Plural Society in the British West Indies,* p. 87.
43. Ibid., pp. 88–89.
44. Ibid., p. 89.
45. Ibid., p. 84 Emphasis added.
46. Leonard Broom, "Urbanization and the Plural Society," *Annals of the New York Academy of Sciences* 83 (January 20, 1960): p. 880.
47. Ibid., p. 881.
48. Ibid.
49. Ibid., p. 880.
50. Ibid., p. 886. It should be observed that this use of the term "prein-

dustrial city" is not the same as that of Julius H. Boeke referred to above.

51. Pierre L. van den Berghe, *Race and Racism* (New York, 1967), pp. 133–43; the quote is from an unpublished 1967 van den Berghe manuscript.

52. R. A. Schermerhorn, *Comparative Ethnic Relations* (New York, 1970). Emphasis in original. Compare this point as Milton Gordon puts it above.

53. Whitney M. Young, Jr., *Beyond Racism* (New York, 1969), p. 241. Emphasis added.

54. Nathan Glazer, "Negroes and Jews: The New Challenge to Pluralism," *Commentary*, December 1964, pp. 29–34.

55. For a discussion of the forces which continue to drive Jews together as a subgroup, see George E. Simpson and J. Milton Yinger, *Racial and Cultural Minorities*, 3d ed. (New York, 1965), pp. 230–33.

56. Glazer, "Negroes and Jews," p. 33.

57. Ibid., pp. 32–3.

58. Ibid., p. 34.

59. Ibid., p. 34. Emphasis in original.

60. Ibid.

61. For another listing and explanation of some of the different uses of the term, see Schermerhorn, *Comparative Ethnic Relations*, pp. 122–25.

9

The Road Ahead

The Place of Economics

If our study and analysis of race relations are valid, the on-going, day-to-day social process should be consistent with them. The student does not create social situations; he seeks rather to arrive at verifiable explanations of them. Different investigators of this subject have chosen different points of reference: moral, psychological, political, religious, economic, "cultural," and so on; or a combination of these with similar emphases. We have chosen the socioeconomic approach and attempted to arrive at a specific meaning of the term "economic."

The term economic is, per se, indefinite, and thus likely to be misleading. The concept, in its present usage, is necessarily always modified by the relevant social system. It is in context, therefore, that we employ it. The economics of the mercantile-industrial city, for example, is by no means identical with the economics of the feudal manor, of the Hindu village, or of the tribal village of Africa. Historically, convergence of these systems has resulted in revolutionary clashes.

As race relations increasingly become the direct concern of the American government, we should normally expect socially therapeutic measures to be mainly economically structured. Let us then observe the place given to economics. [. . .]

At the head of the list of remedies [. . .] is full employment. This is assumed to be the critical means by which the Negro might enter the mainstream. The "job gap" showing an unemployment rate consistently twice that of whites must be closed, an undertaking calling for a faster rate of economic advancement for Negroes than for whites. As Vivian Henderson puts it:

> Basically, the question facing the nation, the South, and Negroes today is whether Negroes are narrowing the gaps in their economic status. The issue is not whether Negroes have been making progress,

but whether it has been rapid enough to enable them to adjust to an economy whose rate of change is cumulative and intense. The issue is whether the momentum of change is great enough, to generate an economic base among Negroes which will guarantee their continued movement up the economic ladder.[1]

[. . .] [E]mployment, then, [is] a primary concern of Negroes and of those engaged with programs for their social adjustment. Incidentally, Frederick Douglass recalled an experience of his which suggests the engrossing place of employment in the Negro's conception of himself. He refers to Negro clerks working in the Freedmen's Bank in Washington, D.C., during the Reconstruction period.

> The magnificent dimensions of the building bore testimony to its flourishing condition. In passing it on the street I often peeped into its spacious windows and looked down the row of its gentlemanly and elegantly dressed colored clerks, with their pens behind their ears and button-hole bouquets in their coat-fronts, and felt my very eyes enriched. It was a sight I had never expected to see. I was amazed by the facility with which they counted the money; they threw off the thousands with dexterity, if not the accuracy, of old and experienced clerks. The whole thing was beautiful.[2]

This reaction might have been expected; a man tends to be what he does; and unemployment, of course, means that he does nothing. Incidentally, the record of even such a small movement in economic status among Negroes should put militants on guard with respect to assertions that there has been no consequential change in the social and economic status of Negroes since 1860.

The Mainstream

We have used the "mainstream" view to define the traditional tendency among Negro Americans. There have been, however, persistent nationalist episodes all through the history of race relations. Sometimes, as in the pre-Civil War era, they have been fostered directly by whites as panaceas for the racial situation. Nationalism, as an intermittent movement, has been led by militant Negroes frequently supported by conservative whites. It has been characterized by black nativism, separatism, and racism. It tends to have greater mass appeal among Negroes than assimilationism. The chances, however, of a black nation arising within the larger American society seem illogical and unrealistic.

If we rule out utopias, we may assume, on reliable grounds, that there are only two types of viable societies presently available to mankind: capitalism and socialism. Modern socialism is a direct outgrowth of capitalism, and the process of its evolution continues universally with increasing determination. This development does not apply to Negroes as a group in the United States any more than to, say, American Indians. And yet, unlike the future of the peoples of the "Third World," the future of Negroes is inevitably involved in the change.

Some years ago there was a popular school of race relations which defined blacks and whites in the United States as constituting two castes. The groups thus conceived were compared in detail and identified with relationships among Hindu castes. There is currently an opposite, rapidly developing tendency to regard American race relations as essentially a form of colonialism. Negroes, it is said, are colonials seeking "liberation." This, obviously, provides a theoretical base for the advocacy of "guerrilla warfare," which in reality constitutes a diversionary, dead-end recourse.[. . .]

Solution to the Problem

To some students of race relations there can be no solution to the race problem in the United States. To them analytical answers are but evidence of desperation and escapism. According to Lewis M. Killian, for instance, "There may be social ills for which there is no cure. . . . Reluctantly the author must state his honest conclusion: there is no way out." In support of this decision he cites what seems to be the irreducible obstacle. "Above all [the Negro] is still visibly a Negro, and he can change that identity only if he is able to 'pass.' The United States is ceasing to be a Protestant, rural nation, but it still remains a white man's country."[3] Impeccable though this reasoning may seem, it is nevertheless illusory.

In the study of race relations the critical data are not to be sought in the biological stability of color but rather in its changing cultural definition. Between 1860 and 1870, for example, there was a radical shift in the significance of color without, of course, any modification of complexion itself and, since then, there has been a consistent trend that changes the meaning of color, in spite of the fact that, in the foreseeable future, the United States will remain demographically a "white man's country."

National political power will theoretically remain in the hands of whites. And yet the circumstances of the Civil War should disabuse us of any notion that, in American race relations, whites are always solidly arrayed on one side and blacks on the other. The ecology of the races, moreover, significantly contradicts the assertion. This society, therefore, is inevitably also a "black man's country."

Indeed, the nation is *inherently* "color-blind." If it were not, there could be no logic in the insistence that it demonstrate this trait. Actual power increasingly becomes an attribute of citizens regardless of race. And yet, at this stage, color remains an empirical fact.[. . .]

In a sense, there is no alternative to the integration of the American Negro population. The very cultural forces have absorbed millions of white immigrants, abolished slavery, produced the Thirteenth, Fourteenth, and Fifteenth Amendments to the constitution, endured Reconstruction, brought pressure on the courts to concretize those amendments, and have recently motivated Congress and the chief executive to act positively. As one federal agency puts its, "since 1957 [Congress] has passed five civil rights laws, including the landmark Civil Rights Act of 1964, the Voting Rights Act of 1965, and the Federal Fair Housing Act of 1968." Furthermore, this source continues,

> the various laws, Executive orders, and judicial decisions constitute a formidable array of civil rights guarantees providing broad protections against discrimination in virtually every aspect of life—in education, employment, housing, voting, administration of justice, access to places of public accommodation, and participation in the benefits of federally assisted programs.[4]

Thus the direction of the major effort in race relations has been staked out. Immediate problems arise from questions of enforcement, and from the willingness or ability to Negroes to accept existing opportunities. But the road to integration now seems clearly indicated, and the federal government has recognized its obligation to keep it open.

For Negroes, then, the very process of living in America as citizens implicates them in an interminable struggle for social equality. The major civil rights organizations—the [National Association for the Advancement of Colored People] NAACP, the Urban League—are working with the government for the realization of such available values. The immediate source of Negro inequality has been private and governmental discrimination especially in economic life. Equality—freedom of access to mainstream culture—is thus being approached at different rates in different areas of life. Our preoccupation has not been with the question of whether there is a solution to the race problem, but rather with the process by which it is being and must inevitably be resolved.

The Problem as White Nationalism

In spite of all we have said, the primary instrument in American race relations might still seem to be obscured. Even though it remains brutal, violent, and fiercely intimidating, the driving force of race relations seems to remain hidden. Lower-class Negroes especially seem to think that every white person is capable only of self-interest. This self-interest was emotionally solidified in the white southern nation as that country prepared for civil war. It has never been completely vanquished.

The South is still at war—implicitly at least—over its position regarding the place of blacks in the United States. The Confederate flag, Confederate songs and hymns, are still flaunted in the face of Negroes as warnings lest they forget their subordination and humiliation. It is this threat of oppression which when tapped by counter-nationalistic Negro orators, can provoke Negro crowds to mass hysteria.

It has taken actual armed force by the federal government to confront elements of the white ruling class in attempts to secure the increments of citizenship rights for blacks in specific situations. At the end of every military engagement, some leaders of the white ruling class have pulled away, regrouped, and taken another life-or-death stand on racial subordination.

To some Negroes, therefore, white nationalism and racism represent the source of a problem that the achievement of civil rights has not solved. Society, they feel, ought to devise means of attacking this attitude directly as well as the acts which it generates. Racism, in other words, should be labeled [. . .] morally wrong and thus opposed independently by the northern liberal government.[. . .]

Place of Negroes in the City

In the foreseeable future, Negro Americans will continue to concentrate in the central cities and whites will gravitate toward the suburbs. Conceivably, great cities like Newark and Detroit may become 100 percent black by the year 2000. And yet the city cannot be essentially abandoned by mainstream society; whites cannot forsake it altogether. Negroes, moreover, cannot take it over completely. Capitalist enterprise produced the modern city as its indispensable milieu, and its survival apparently will be critically affected by the fate of its metropolises. We may be sure that the city will not be allowed to wither away without a frantic struggle to maintain it, and in the process the concept of the Negro will be changed.

The city, in other words, is the locus of capitalist entrepreneurial production; it did not evolve as a vehicle of endogenous consumer demand. The tendency to identify mere numbers of Negroes in the city with the extent of their contribution to the city's wealth and with its productive characteristics has been grossly misleading. Left to Negroes alone, the city would probably crumble and vanish; indeed, left to white labor alone, the city would also quickly perish. There is, however a peculiar functional continuum between white labor and white entrepreneuriship in the city, a phenomenon still largely missing in the Negro relationship. The distorted, temporary reaction to this limitation has been ghettoization, or development of a black community on the periphery of mainstream culture.[5] The ghetto is anything but self-sufficient.

Ghettoization polarizes whites and blacks in the central cities. As the weight of numbers increasingly emphasizes the presence of blacks, city government tends to become their responsibility. The city is thus faced with the paradox of having a possibly alienated group in control of its political destiny. One perceptive journalist suggests the outlook for the rest of metropolitan America as follows:

> There is a white-dominated, business-oriented Newark, and there are the densely populated sections where blacks and Puerto Ricans live. Business Newark looks almost as prosperous as ever. . . . But out of the west and south, in the Central and the South wards is a different story. "It is a jungle," says one cab driver, and another adds: "This city is dead." The juxtaposition of white authority and the jungle strikes one with forcible impact. . . . Shattered, gaping, sightless windows stare out at the county buildings, and only a short jog away . . . one comes upon still ghastly rubble of a war-ravaged [riot] Newark.[6]

This state of cultural incongruity cannot be resolved merely by improving employment conditions among blacks. The problem is not essentially a moral one. To enter the mainstream of urban life, Negroes would have to become in practice and in attitude, part of the imperialistic tradition of American capitalism. Jews, for example, have always participated in it. The Negroes' solidarity could be creatively centered in the characteristic patriotism derived from competition and conflict with other nations for the resources and markets of the globe. That is the psychological matrix in which the great cities have arisen and prospered.

What then? Are Negroes to be forever excluded from the core of American patriotism? Three considerations seem to modify the negative implications of this question: (1) Negroes are not currently being deprived of market positions previously held by them—these positions are indeed recognizably improving; (2) the center of creativity in the system seems to be moving gradually from rampant competitiveness for economic dominance abroad toward reliance on technological progress and efficiency in domestic production; and (3) all signs seem to indicate that social inclusion will be increasingly a matter of education and absence of racial discrimination in the distribution of jobs. These trends are not entirely new; they may be considered projections on an upward-turning curve.

Although better education and greater access to jobs would not provide all the ultimate answers, they would provide escape from the depressing conceptions Negroes have of themselves as "the unwanted." Fortunately, the capacity of society itself to include Negroes has been expanding.

The Negro as a Problem to Negroes

[. . .] The internal problem for Negroes arose mainly from the basic position of the Black Muslims. The Negro middle class was disparaged and denounced for its identification with mainstream culture, and the life of the lower class was, willy-nilly, extolled. Values of the ghetto, almost without lower limits, now attained prestige even among some of the Negro middle class. The whole attack was couched in the fiery emotions of black nationalism. The mainstream middle class seemed to be cornered and intimidated.

This anticultural tendency wormed its way among militants of various stripes, and some whites seemed to condone it. The hearing accorded it in the mass media proved to be an invaluable stimulus. For example, in his study of the change in attitude among white liberals, Gene Roberts of the *New York Times* observed: "A growing number are saying that integration is impossible for the foreseeable future, that the nation should concentrate instead on building up Negro institutions, and that only then—perhaps in a generation or two—can it talk about integration."[7] The separatist philosophy tended to converge with the attitude of extreme white racists.

Nothing seems more elusive than the recurrent belief that Negroes in the central cities of the metropolitan areas live by some unitary culture comparable and equivalent to that of the larger society; and that it may be stabilized for future parallel growth with the culture of the dominant society. This messianic version, no doubt, has been mainly responsible for widespread personal frustrations and destructive behavior.

Normally, mainstream culture resists the typical Negro way of life. Where Negroes hold numerical majorities as, for example, in college dormitories on black campuses—not to mention places of amusement in the ghettoes—whites tend to be repulsed. It is a tendency toward stabilization of this self-isolating subculture that separatism inevitably imposes. Its elements are almost totally lower class, and must, therefore, be abandoned through reeducation. That indeed was precisely what slave masters attempted to do for those Negroes who, in the mid-nineteenth century, faced independence through emigration.

There should be no hesitancy or doubt in the minds of social scientists about the nature of cultural maturity in the modern world. There is no harking back nor lateral approaches to cultural advancement. Everywhere in the modern world social maturity inevitably means mastery of Western culture. Socialism seeks essentially to modify and render capitalist culture more effective in the service of its people.

The Negroes' cultural problem is not similar to that of religious groups such as the Jews.[8] It is, rather, inevitably a dependent offshoot of the larger culture. *Development* can thus have no other realistic meaning than incremental inclusion of the group with its generative society. Essentially, the effective Negroes' social posture entails infighting—not separatism.

Education

Since abolition, and indeed even during slavery, the question of education for Negroes has been at the very forefront in considerations of their status. In order to repress the race, its education had to be limited and controlled. Even in the North, the education of Negroes was restricted and sometimes barred altogether. Improvement in the social status of Negroes, therefore, has been marked by their enlarging educational opportunities.

The decisions of the Supreme Court in the fifties revolutionized the nation's attitude toward education for blacks. The Court declared, in effect, that education is a civil right which should not be racially restricted by law. Of particular significance for an understanding of the future of race relations is that this doctrine fell upon relatively fertile ground. Not even the white conservatives of the Deep South have been able fully to withstand it.

The vicissitudes normally associated with its realization and the schemes devised to escape its effects have indeed been staggering. But the country as a whole has apparently become reconciled. This, no doubt, is the stand from which the future of Negro education may be judged.

Since the drive for equality in education is consistent with larger social trends, we should expect such contrary forces as resegregation in the metropolises, black-studies campaigns,[9] the politics of devotion to neighborhood schools, the white private-school movement, the self-serving aversion to busing of school children, to take only temporary root. [. . .]

Freedom of education for Negroes will probably produce a new breed of people. We should expect no significant regression of the group.

New Dependence on Politics

[. . .] Population movements in the metropolitan areas are entrusting political leadership, in an ever larger number of central cities, to the hands of blacks. A sobering datum, frequently cited, is the estimate of the National Advisory Commission on Civil Disorders that, by 1984, thirteen central cities including Chicago, St. Louis, Philadelphia, Los Angeles, Detroit, Atlanta, and Baltimore will be over 50 percent Negro. The U.S. Census shows that "among the 30 places in the Nation with the highest proportion of Negroes in 1970, there has been a dramatic increase since 1960 in the number that have at least as many Negroes as whites. The count is now 16, compared to 3 in 1960."[10]

In 1970, to illustrate at random, Gary, Indiana, was included among the thirty *places* in the nation with highest proportion of Negroes. In 1960 about 39 percent of Gary's population [was] Negro; but, in 1970, 53 percent [was] Negro. That city is therefore one of the sixteen places referred to that have at least as many Negroes as whites. The trend is upward. Negroes, moreover, may become mayors of important cities before their black population reaches 50 percent.

Sometimes the mayoralty and membership in city councils have been regarded merely as economic plums to be exploited by victors at the polls. The cities, however, are the fundamental loci of capitalist organization. They embody the ultimate in the cultural achievements of the system: the perfection of its economic institutions, its art and architecture, its societal order, its science and education, and the nuclei of its global communications. It is ironic that Negroes, who have been traditionally regarded as subcitizens incapable of comprehending this complex cultural matrix, are now likely to find themselves in positions of political authority calling for initiative in its development and guidance.

The central city, manifestly, cannot be suburbanized. Unless our basic political structure is radically to be transformed, we should expect the nation's future sense of responsibility for the Negro's education and cultural participation to be given new self-interested consideration. In any event, black leadership in these strategic urban positions will, no doubt, have very much to learn. The obligations of this function should give Negroes a greater sense of identification with their country and its prevailing culture. There is apparently no alternative; the Rubicon has been crossed.

Although the Negro executive might have won the highest political office in the state or the city because of the size of the Negro vote, he cannot logically regard that office as an institution primarily in the service of the special interests of Negroes. At most he has gained only a means of enlarging opportunities for blacks without killing the goose in the process. This theory has not always been accepted, however. [. . .]

[I] think [. . .] the success of the city under white leadership depends upon its economic prosperity. That indeed is the source of attraction of both Negro and white migrants. Under a black governor or mayor, economic prosperity must continue to be the primary concern. The black urban executive is structurally in competition with leaders of other cities for all legitimate business. Manifestly, then, he must make his city as attractive as possible to businessmen.

It is indeed through devotion to the welfare of the state or city that he, like the white executive, can most effectively show his devotion to the citizens, black or white. If he reveals himself, to the black people who mainly elected him, as hostile to and alienated from the fundamental political structure and major economic processes of the city, he will fail in his task.

It was the operation of mainstream politics, in Gary, Indiana, which Edward Greer saw as socially unfortunate. As he put it:

Richard G. Hatcher's insurgency was contained within the existing national political system. Or, to express it somewhat differently, the attempt by black forces to use the electoral process to further their national liberation was aborted by a countervailing process of neo-colonialism carried out by the federal government. Bluntly speaking, the piecemeal achievement of power through parliamentary means is a fraud—at least as far as black Americans are concerned.[11]

The situation in Gary illustrates two aspects of the political situation with which the Negro who attains the mayoralty becomes involved: severe white opposition, and temptation of black ideologists to convert the city into a black nation. Let us observe the Gary model briefly. Mayor Hatcher became involved with both these forces in his campaign for office in January 1968.

Hatcher did what he could to resist fraud and corruption by local Democratic and Republican factions, equalize economic and welfare opportunities for Negroes, and counter the overwhelming control by the great corporations in the city. When, in May 1973, Thomas Bradley was made mayor of Los Angeles, a city of only about 16 percent black voters, he was the first Negro to hold that position. He "promised to make the city safe from violence, build a rapid transit system, trim waste in government, and cut taxes from those most heavily burdened."[12] Other black mayors—Kenneth Gibson of Newark, Carl Stokes of Cleveland, Charles Evers of Fayette, Mississippi—faced their problems in a similar way.

Hatcher, on the contrary, engaged in a bold attempt to lead an "independent" black political movement. In March 1972, he delivered the keynote address at a three-day convention (March 10–12) assembled in Gary for this purpose. He declared before the National Black Political Convention: "We must emerge from this convention with an independent national black political agenda: a dynamic program for black liberation that, in the process, will liberate all America from its current decadence." And the mayor issued the following challenge:

> Democrats or Republicans . . . how much difference has it really made to black people? . . . Hereafter, we shall rely on the power of our own black unity. . . . Every political party must make up its mind. It cannot represent both the corporations and the people. . . . The 70's will be the decade of an independent black political thrust.[13]

The convention was constituted by Negro representatives from all over the United States; present, besides Hatcher, were Congressman Charles C. Diggs, Jr., Roy Innis, and Imamu Baraka (the former LeRoi Jones). The National Black Political Agenda which emerged was amended and eventually published on May 6, 1972. This agenda, a fifty-five-page program, is even more explicit:

> [The agenda] . . . is an attempt to define essential changes which must take place in this land as we move to self-determination and true

independence. . . . A new Black Politics must come to birth . . . the Black Politics of Gary must accept major responsibility for creating both the atmosphere and program for fundamental, far-reaching change in America. . . . The society we seek cannot come unless Black people organize to advance its coming. . . . So, Brothers and Sisters of our developing Black nation, we now stand at Gary as people whose time has come. . . . We begin here and now in Gary . . . an independent Black political movement . . . an independent Black spirit. . . . An incalculable social indebtedness has been generated, a debt owed to Black people by the general American society. So we must not rest until American society has recognized our . . . right to reparations, to a massive claim on the financial assets of the American economy.[14]

This then is the nature of black separatism with which the mayor of a great American city identified himself. It is obviously elusive but it returns like a refrain, interspersed with demands for something for practically every Negro group. It is consistent with the vaguely expressed moral philosophy at the base of Negro criminality in the cities. And indeed Gary has become known as one of the worst such spots. For example the mayor seems to be perplexed by the following report:

An apparent gang war for control of drug traffic here that has left 17 [black] bodies dumped in alleys, streets, and parked cars has prompted an intensive effort by local and Federal officials to stem the Gary area's heroin supply. . . . Mayor Richard G. Hatcher was so concerned . . . that he flew to Washington . . . to stress the situation's gravity to Senator George McGovern, the Democratic Presidential nominee. . . . Mr. Hatcher said that the initial attitude . . . was to "let the pushers kill each other off." But then you realize innocent bystanders are caught in the crossfire. And if a gang can organize to take over drug traffic, what's to stop them from taking over businesses in the same fashion?[15]

Perhaps a different attitude among the political leaders might have brought about different results. Negroes could have been given a sense of belonging—a sense of being Americans. Without taking our point of view, Edward Greer recognized "the erosion of popular support after the successful mobilization of energies involved in the campaign. . . . [Moreover, the black people's] political experiences are not enlarged, their understanding of the larger society and how it functions has not improved, and they are not being trained to better organize for their own interests. . . . After the inauguration, old supporters found themselves on the outside looking in."[16]

The immediate difficulty here, of course, resides in the irreconcilability of black nationalism and Americanism. On this point delegates to the Gary Convention were split—some walked out. The NAACP did not attend at all; nor did Congresswoman Shirley Chisholm. However, influential politicians like Congressman Charles Diggs, Jr., and indeed Mayor Hatcher himself were manipulated by such seasoned nationalists as Imamu Baraka and Roy Innis.

It was mainly the artful influence of the latter group which led many to characterize the proceedings as "irresponsible and separatist."[17] It should be said that the Negro politician who attains a position of power and responsibility through the operation of the American political system and then uses the opportunity to serve the purposes of black nationalists inevitably betrays the Negro people.

We may consider the following as characterizations and projections of the Negro's political position in the United States:

1. Negroes now vote all over the United States as normal citizens. The federal government stands ready to assume responsiblity for removal of sporadic racial limitations.

2. Currently, it is expected that Negroes will vote solidly as a group for black candidates and thus automatically against white opposing contestants.

3. The deeper South the political contest, the more racial considerations tend to determine the ballot count.

4. In the North and West particularly, Negro politicians may win office in places with smaller percentages of black voters than white politicians with higher percentages of white voters.

5. Negro candidates have a better chance to win office in areas of less than 50 percent black voters than white candidates backed by white voters.

6. Ordinarily, in the larger cities, Negro politicians may count on votes from the solid Negro bloc, the habitual white Democrats, and the freewheeling white voters attracted to the black candidate because of his personality or his position on issues.

7. The winning of office by Senator Edward Brooke of Massachusetts and Thomas Bradley of Los Angeles suggests that in the long run we may expect Negroes to run for office more and more because of their qualifications and less and less because of their race.

8. When white candidates running for elective office win in black majority communities over black candidates for reasons of merit, then the race issue will have become an inconsequential factor in American politics.

Notes

1. Vivian W. Henderson, *The Economic Status of Negroes*, Southern Regional Council pamphlet (1965), p. 5.
2. Frederick Douglass, *Life and Times of Frederick Douglass* (Hartford, 1881), pp. 409–410.
3. Lewis H. Killian, *The Impossible Revolution* (New York, 1968), pp. xv, 25.
4. U.S. Commission on Civil Rights, *The Federal Civil Rights Enforcement Effort* (1970), p. 2.
5. H.J. Simons and R.E. Simons, *Class and Colour in South Africa* (Baltimore, 1969), p. 616.
6. F.J. Cook, "Mayor Kenneth Gibson Says: 'Wherever the Central Cities Are Going, Newark Is Going to Get There First,'" *New York Times Magazine*, 25 July 1971, pp. 7 ff.
7. "A White Liberal Shift on Integration," *New York Times*, 17 December 1967.
8. For distinction of the social position of Jews and Negroes, see Nathan Glazer, "Race Relations: New York in 1969," in *Agenda for a City*, ed. L.C. Fitch and A.H. Walsh (Beverly Hills, 1970), pp. 545–46.
9. For a review of the rise and progress of black studies, see Theodore Draper, *The Rediscovery of Black Nationalism* (New York, 1970), chap. 10.
10. U.S. Department of Commerce, *The Social and Economic Status of Negroes in the United States* (1970), table 13, p. 9.
11. Edward Greer, "The 'Liberation' of Gary, Indiana," in *Cities in Change*, ed. J. Walton and D.E. Carns (Boston, 1973), p. 501.
12. *Detroit News*, 30 May 1973.
13. *New Courier*, 25 March 1972.
14. National Black Political Convention, Inc., *The National Black Political Agenda* (Washington, D.C., 1972).
15. A.H. Malcolm, "17 Slayings Spur a Drive on Heroin Traffic in Gary," *New York Times*, 13 August 1972.
16. Greer, "The 'Liberation' of Gary, Indiana," p. 499.
17. *Detroit News*, 13 March 1972.

| III |

Class Struggle in Capitalist Society

The selections included in this section reveal Cox's lifelong concern with the issues of social class, inequality, and the dynamics of the capitalist system. With the exception of the first article, which is another example of Cox's skill in clarifying loosely defined concepts, the other selections are from *Caste, Class, and Race* (1948) and represent Cox's most penetrating analysis of the role of the class struggle in capitalist society. This writing is part of the reason many of Cox's academic contemporaries stigmatized him as a disgruntled Marxist polemicist, whose vision of the scientific enterprise and of democracy was very different from their own. Thus Cox squarely confronted the issues of class and democracy by presenting conceptual refinements of his own and by mounting a critical appraisal that was largely ignored by establishment social scientists—his explication of the analytical differences between social and political classes is a case in point. In this endeavor, Cox attempted to clarify what he perceived as problems with both mainstream and Marxist definitions of class, arguing that existing conceptualizations have confused social and political class (in ways that will be discussed below), in the process obscuring the real meaning of class struggle. The amount of attention Cox paid to explaining the concept of political class struggle shows how important he felt this phenomenon was to the understanding of the dynamics of modern capitalist society. He also questioned the limits of democracy in a society where the productive resources are controlled by a small minority—a discussion that is particularly timely today.

In the first selection included here, "Estates, Social Classes, and Political Classes," Cox briefly examines the literature on social stratification to show how ambiguously the term "class" has been used by social scientists. Estates, found in precapitalist societies, are strata in static and hierarchical social-status systems where rank is determined by either custom or law. Social classes, unique to modern urbanized societies, do not necessarily constitute a hierarchy, but are aggregated heuristic constructs that comprise a system of social status, have overlapping and changing boundaries, and are devoid of class consciousness. In contrast, political classes, found throughout history, have discrete boundaries: a political class is "normally weighted with persons from a special sector of the social-status pyramid [but] may include persons from every position" who have a common interest and a common purpose, but not necessarily a common status (or social class). Unlike social classes, political classes are "organizations arrayed face to face against each other" and can attract members from diverse strata. Cox thus argues that much of the confusion about the term "class" stems from the use of the same term to refer to both the ranking of individuals on various dimensions of social inequality *and* to power groups that are functioning, conscious entities, organized for specific purposes. Cox's approach to social class clearly sets him apart from both established sociological thinking *and* Marxist thinking on the subject. In many ways, his analysis predates the line of thinking made popular by such sociologists as Ralf Dahrendorf, Anthony Giddens, and Erik Olin Wright, and, among European Marxists, by Nicos Poulantzas. His work on class distinctions also resembles such recent distinctions as those between "realist" and "nominalist" definitions of class.

The second selection, "The Political Class," is a more elaborate theoretical analysis of the main characteristics of political classes. Here Cox argues that control of the state apparatus is one crucial characteristic of political-class behavior, and that political and social classes differ in this regard. Cox cautions the reader not to confuse conflicts between self-interested "intraclass institutional groups"—"pluralistic" interest groups that engage in conflict but do not seek to perpetuate their rule and win control of the state—and political classes, which, once they have been organized for conflict into dominant and subordinate power groups, do seek either to perpetuate their rule or to overthrow the existing economic order—and with it the state. Cox then adopts the Marxian distinction between a "class-in-itself" and a "class-for-itself," noting that "as a function of the economic order, the [political] class has potential existence, but as the result of agitation it becomes organized for conflict." He concludes by arguing that the resistance of a dominant political class to change, and its control over the means of force, makes violence an inevitable outcome of class struggle.

In the third selection, "Facets of the Modern Political-Class Struggle," and the fourth selection, "Modern Democracy and the Class Struggle," Cox provides a theoretical discussion of specific political-class situations that further illustrate how he employed the political-class concept in his work. His aim was to demonstrate the substantive differences between capitalism and socialism—two major social systems representing the interests of two major political-class groups—and he incorporated into his analysis data on events that had happened during his lifetime.

"Facets of the Modern Political-Class Struggle" is a broad sketch of the key characteristics of the modern political-class struggle in Western society. Here Cox argues that the ruling class in capitalist society is mainly composed of businessmen and "has only recently achieved its power through bitter and bloody struggle with another ruling class." The bourgeoisie, a despised subordinate class during feudalism, rose to power on the basis of controlling economic production and by shaping the laws of the society to suit its interests. The result has been an exploitative social system based on free enterprise and a state apparatus that serves the narrow interests of the capitalist class while appearing to benefit all members of the society. Because of this, "capitalism is supported not only by the owners of capital goods, who produce for a profit, but also by a distinct class of free workers" whose labor has become proletarianized.

Revolutionary change, however, is always possible. Like the bourgeoisie's ascendancy from feudalism, a revolutionary proletarian movement will emerge, not because of absolute misery, but through relative deprivation and the economic disorder generated by the profit system. Cox then connects other aspects of the political class struggle to fascism and capitalism—in particular, the role of the church and of nationalism in promoting fascism in capitalist society—and makes a brief excursus into the labor movement of the 1930s in order to explain some of the reasons for the weak proletarian movement in the United States and to try to dispel some misconceptions about socialism and communism.

In "Modern Democracy and the Class Struggle," Cox explains why he believes democracy is unattainable in capitalist society. He argues that electoral politics and the form of government created by the bourgeoisie during its rise to power were instrumental in advancing the democratic movement (and thus the movement toward socialism), but did not result in the achievement of a mature democratic society. Democracy can be achieved only when the great mass of the people obtain control over the economic resources of the society and are empowered to make decisions about their social destiny. "Modern democracy, therefore, is antagonistic to capitalism": the greater the development of democracy, the greater the limitations on the capitalists' freedom and the stronger the proletariat. To oppose socialism is to fear democracy and lend support to an oligopolistic social system. For Cox, the political-class struggle between capital and labor is therefore intrinsically linked to the struggle for democracy.

10

Estates, Social Classes, and Political Classes

There are few subjects of such paramount significance to the social scientist that have remained in so ill-defined a condition as that of class. We cannot, for instance, comprehend clearly what is meant by the concepts "social stratification," imperialism, ruling class, race conflict, fascism, communism, and so on unless we know what classes are and how they function. At any rate, the literature on this subject is extremely confused.

There seem to be two principal reasons for this confusion: (a) a nonrealization that different writers may refer to quite distinct social phenomena under the same designation "class," and (b) a tendency to disregard one of these phenomena altogether. In this article we shall hope to distinguish two primary meanings of the concept class and to characterize them briefly. To one of these meanings we shall apply the term "social class" and to the other "political class." A brief reference to social estates is intended to clarify our discussion.

The Literature

First, however, it may be well to take a running view of the literature. The two published volumes of the "Yankee City Series" are the most elaborate attempts to study social classes in the United States.[1] Here the authors accumulated a considerable quantity of data which are supposed to characterize "six social classes and seven different kinds of social structures." In an earlier study by A. M. Carr-Saunders and D. Caradog Jones of "the social structure of England and Wales"[2] no social classes could be discovered. The authors inquire: "Do social classes exist? We hear less than formerly of the 'upper,' 'middle,' and 'lower' social classes. We do, however,

145

hear much about 'class consciousness' and 'class warfare.' If class warfare is a fact, it should be possible for the statistician to estimate the strength of the battalions ranged against each other."

In a critical discussion of Warner and Lunt's book *The Social Life of a Modern Community*, C. Wright Mills suggested that the authors might have been saved many a serious error had they consulted the theoretical work of Max Weber on social classes.[3] Mills himself, however, seems to have been lost in the detailed characteristics of social classes, and the fundamental question as to whether social classes should have been found at all by the authors is never broached.

R. M. MacIver also admits his reliance on Max Weber for his discussion of the subject. Says he:

> We shall . . . mean by a social class any portion of a community which is marked off from the rest . . . primarily by social status. . . . It is the sense of status, sustained by economic, political, or ecclesiastical power and by the distinctive modes of life and cultural expressions corresponding to them, which draws class apart from class, gives cohesion to each, and stratifies the whole society.[4]

In illustrating this concept Professor MacIver asserts "the owner-farmer and the tenant-farmer (in North America) . . . form a social class as we have defined it," and says further:

> A broader class distinction may be asserted in the name of the pride of race, such as that between the West European stocks and the "new immigrant," between Gentile and the Jew. But these barriers do not create clearly defined social classes, and some of them seem to be transitional lines, becoming less determinative in the degree in which cultural differences between groups are merged in the new environment. Only the racial barrier of color completely resists the triumphant claim of wealth to be at length the chief determinant of class, and this defeat is less decisive because of the general poverty of the colored people.[5]

In a way typical of the majority of American and English social scientists, MacIver questions the position of writers on the class struggle. "It should be observed," he emphasizes, "that we have not defined social class in purely economic terms. This alternative mode of definition, generally maintained by the followers of Karl Marx, stresses a very important factor that commonly underlies class distinctions, but it is inadequate sociologically."[6] More specifically he declares: "Certainly in countries of western civilization the Marxist dichotomy is too sweeping to fit the facts of the class system. So broad a division and so sharp a cleavage are more applicable to a feudal order, such as that of pre-revolutionary Russia, than a complex industrialized society."[7]

Indeed, Karl Marx and Friedrich Engels are extremely provocative. Although they gave no clear definition of class, the authors never changed significantly from the following position taken during the middle of the last century:

> The history of all hitherto existing society is the history of class struggle. Freemen and slave, patrician and plebeian, lord and serf, guild-master and journeyman, oppressor and oppressed, stood in constant opposition to one another, carried on an uninterrupted, now hidden, now open fight, a fight that each time ended either in a revolution, reconstitution of society at large, or in common ruin of the contending classes. . . . The modern bourgeois society that has sprouted from the ruins of feudal society has not done away with class antagonisms. It has but established new classes, new conditions of oppression, new forms of struggle in place of old ones. Our epoch, the epoch of the bourgeoisie, possesses, however, this distinctive feature: it has simplified the class antagonisms. Society as a whole is more and more splitting up into two great battle camps, into two great classes directly facing each other: Bourgeoisie and Proletariat.[8]

This is the kind of thinking that probably most social scientists refuse to digest; it has prejudiced them against the Marxists. At any rate, H. H. Gerth and C. Wright Mills think that Max Weber has completed Karl Marx's unfinished definition of class.[9] Marx had begun a definitive statement in the last pages of *Capital*. The fact seems to be, however, that Weber's work itself is unfinished.[10]

Weber gives no clear definition of class.[11] He recognizes many types of class: "possessing or property class," "earning or income class," and subdivisions of these, but here class becomes a classification rather than a sociological concept. Moreover, such passages as the following call for basic clarification:

> The organization of classes purely on the basis of property is not dynamic, i.e., it does not necessarily lead to class struggle and class revolution. The decidedly positively privileged property class of slave owners often exists side by side with the much less positively privileged class of peasants, even with the "declassé," frequently without any feeling of class antagonism. . . . A classical example of the lack of class antagonism was the relation of the "poor white trash" to the planters in the Southern States. The "poor white trash" was far more hostile to the Negroes.[12]

Probably no writer has stated this subject so intelligibly as Werner Sombart. He distinguishes between estates *(Stände)*, "social classes," and (in our meaning) "political classes." To him "estates are large

unions based upon a community of living, and organically integrated in a community; classes [political classes], on the other hand,
are large individualistic unions held together externally by common interests in an economic system and mechanically integrated
in a community."[13] Estates develop naturally as a function of community life, but they are essentially legal entities. "To this inner
nature the estate owes its political significance: it becomes almost
everywhere a *legal community* and is integrated as such, with certain
tasks, in the whole of the state. . . . The estate feels itself as being a
part of a great organism, to whose aims it subordinates its own
aims."[14] Quite different from the estate is the social class (political
class):

> The class does not arise in a natural way, but it is created artificially.
> To be sure, certain communities of destinies of life are present, but
> not that easy living together in a natural community. The class pre-
> sents a consciously developed conviction of belonging together;
> therefore, class cohesion is brought in from the outside, so to speak,
> by way of a reflective process of consciousness. So long as a com-
> munity of interest has not been impressed on the consciousness of the
> individuals, the class will not come into being. Therefore, a class has
> class consciousness, but we consider it to be nonsense to speak of *class-
> honour,* to which some conscious process of class-solidarity corre-
> sponds.[15]

Sombart definitely recognizes class (political class) as a conflict
group, but he thinks "the social class [political class] is an entirely
modern formation. Antiquity knows only germs of social classes.
The latter emerged as an offspring of capitalism in recent European history." Accordingly he conceives of "class action" as essentially a bourgeoisie-proletariat struggle;[16] in our view this
constitutes only one situation of political class struggle.

Finally Sombart holds that there are no social strata in our
society. The social phenomena which Professor Warner, for instance, claims to have isolated are in fact not there at all. Thus he
says—and we shall quote him fully:

> Besides these fairly clearly definable large groups, estate and class,
> we distinguish in addition a social structure, whose limits, however,
> disappear in a fog. We designate these also in German by the term
> "Stand," or "ordre" in French, and "class" in English, but only with
> some prefix such as "middle," e.g., the *Mittelstand,* the *moyen ordre,* or
> the middle class. These groups obviously have nothing to do with an
> estate or a class in the previously designated meaning, for they really
> exist as a unity only in the conception (in der Vorstellung) of statisti-
> cians, social theoreticians, social pedagogues and other third persons.

This social structure is conceived of by dividing the members of a community into (mostly) three parts or strata according to their income: an upper, a middle, and a lower stratum.[17]

The foregoing discussion is intended to indicate the state of the literature on this subject. We shall now attempt a brief characterization of estates, social classes, and political classes.

Estates

There are no estates in modern, capitalist society. Estates are social-status strata which ordinarily develop in relatively static social orders. To be sure, the term "estate" in the English language, like *Stände* in the German and *état* in the French, has a variety of meanings. It may be correctly employed to mean status, degree of rank, position in the world, state, public, property, profession, social class, and so on. But the meaning with which we shall be concerned is that of a social order or stratum of society; and we shall mean by an estate system a society divided into estates. From a political point of view, an estate may be thought of as one of the orders of a body politic, having expressed or implied legal claim to some degree of importance in the government. From the point of view of social structure an estate may be thought of as one of the generally recognized social divisions of society, standing in relation to other divisions as socially superior or inferior. In other words, in any society, a number of persons forming a social-status stratum more or less clearly delimited from other strata in customary or statutory law constitutes a social estate.

In agricultural societies where land is the basic economic resource and where it may be held by individuals as transmissible property, social status ordinarily correlates directly with the extent of land ownership. In Western society, feudalism, and indeed feudalism wherever it is found, represents this form of estate society. A feudal system may be thought of as a society living on "frozen capital"; its status structure is consequently static.

Social Classes

The term "social class" has been frequently applied to the status system of modern urban society. In this sense it appears that its use should be restricted, for no other society, not even that of ancient Rome and Greece, is exactly like ours. Modern society started in the town economy of the later Middle Ages and, for the most part, it has superseded feudalism. The remarkable fact is that it has eliminated all interstitial social forces among status groups, so that the status system is no longer stratified. In other words there are, in capitalist society, no social classes amenable to objective circumscription.[18] The status system does not constitute a hierarchy but rather a continuum; status is atomized, and the atoms are exceedingly labile. There is, moreover, no class consciousness among social classes, for social classes are merely heuristic constructs.

Political Class

The term "political class" is used here for want of a more suitable one to distinguish the social phenomenon usually called "class" or "social class" from that which we have previously described as social class. Instead of the term "political class," the designation "economic class" might have been used, but economic determinants are evidently at the base of social classes also.[19] At any rate, the designation may be of less significance than its meaning.

The political class is a power group which tends to be organized for conflict; the social class is never organized for it is a concept only. The organized political class is always class conscious. Those persons in whose interest the economic order is mainly functioning are ordinarily called the ruling class. The political class which is organized for the overthrow of the economic system is commonly called the "revolutionary class." Although the political class is normally weighted with persons from a special sector of the social-status pyramid, it may include persons from every position. Hence we do not speak of a political class as forming a status pyramid.[20]

In other words, members of a political class ordinarily have a common interest and a common purpose but not necessarily a common status. Therefore these classes are not thought of as social-class strata, but as organizations arrayed face to face against each other. Furthermore, unlike the social class, the political class seeks to attract members to itself, and group solidarity is highly valued. Social solidarity, of course, is not a characteristic of social classes.

One test of a political class lies in its expressed or implied purpose. If by its actions it challenges the social system, it is a political class. However the Vandals who pillaged Rome are not a political class; neither are the Spanish adventurers, who destroyed the social system of the Indians in the West Indies, a political class. The political class is not only nurtured within the social system itself but also struggles for the institution of a new, more or less well-defined system. A peasant or slave revolt, for instance, may be only a reaction to social pressure without any positive designs on the social order.

Political classes seem to become a challenge to the existing system not from increasing misery of its members but from increasing economic power and influence. In modern times the colonial-American bourgeoisie, the merchants and manufacturers, instigated and financed the American Revolution. The French Revolution, of course, is the great classic of bourgeois revolutions in which the feudal ruling classes were virtually liquidated. The current cycle of class struggles puts the social system of the bourgeoisie on trial, and the proletariat constitutes the revolutionary class.

Conclusion

From this point of view we can now review some of the literature presented. Carr-Saunders and Jones were apparently correct in their conclusion that there are no social criteria for segregating social classes in modern urban society, but they err in identifying social classes with political classes. To be sure, the statistician may not be able to count the members of political classes, yet no one can mistake the seriousness of their purpose at Petrograd, Madrid, and Athens. Warner and Lunt do not really show that they have isolated social classes, while MacIver seems to have confused estates, social classes, political classes, race relations, and divisions within political classes.

Marx and Engels's celebrated statement also needs considerable clarification. It is intended to be a historical description of class struggle, but "freeman and slave," "patrician and plebeian," and "lord and serf" may all refer to social estates, "guild-master and journeyman" are occupational groups; "oppressor and oppressed" do not refer particularly to political classes. The only true political classes mentioned are "bourgeoisie and proletariat."

The bourgeois order developed on the periphery of feudal society and, like a great octopus, it gradually stangled the agricultural system; but the proletariat may be thought of as developing within the "womb" of the bourgeois system and it is evidently proceeding to slough off. It should be mentioned that the term "middle class," applied to the business community in Europe since the later Middle Ages, designates a political class in an estate society. It does not have the same meaning as middle class in a bourgeois society, which represents the middle status group of the status continuum.

Notes

1. W. Lloyd Warner and Paul S. Lunt, *The Social Life of a Modern Community* and *The Status System of a Modern Community* (New Haven, 1941, 1942 respectively).
2. A. M. Carr-Sunders and D. Caradog Jones, *A Survey of the Social Structure of England and Wales* (London, 1927).
3. See *The American Sociological Review* (April 1942): 262.
4. Max Weber, *Society* (New York, 1937), p. 167.
5. Ibid., pp. 170–71.
6. Ibid., p. 167.
7. Ibid., p. 177.
8. Karl Marx and Friedrich Engels, *Communist Manifesto* pp. 12–13.
9. See *Politics*, October 1944, pp. 271–78.
10. See especially Max Weber, *Wirtschaft und Gesellschaft* (Tübingen, 1922), vol. I, ch. II, "Stände und Klassen," and vol. II, pp. 631–40, "Klasse, Stand, Parteien." For some discussion of Weber see Othmar Spann in the *Handwöterbuch Der Staatswissenschaften*, "Klasse und Stand."
11. For instance, Weber concludes: "In our terminology 'classes' are not communities; they merely represent possible, and frequent, bases for communal action. We may speak of a 'class' when (1) a number of people have in common a specific causal component of their life chances, insofar as (2) this component is represented exclusively by economic interests in the possession of goods and opportunities for income, and (3) is represented under the conditions of the commodity or labor markets. These points refer to 'class situation,' which we may express more briefly as the typical chance for a supply of goods, an 'external' life fate, and an internal life fate, insofar as this chance is determined by the amount and kind of power, or lack of such, to dispose of goods or services in a market situation. The term 'class' refers to any group of people that is found in the same class situation" (*Wirtschaft und Gesellschaft*, 3, ch. IV, trans Gerth and Mills, in *Politics*, October 1944, p. 272).
12. *Wirtschaft und Gesellschaft*, vol. I, p. 178.
13. Werner Sombart, *Der Modern Kapitalismus* (Munich and Leipzig, 1928), vol. II, p. 1091.
14. Ibid., p. 1092.
15. Ibid., p. 1093.
16. Ibid., p. 1094.
17. Ibid.
18. For a more detailed discussion of social class see my "Class and Caste," *The Journal of Negro Education*, Spring 1944, pp. 139–49.

19. In his speech in Naples, August 11, 1922, Mussolini called the Fascists "a new political class."
20. The status system of any society, whether estate, caste, or social class, always prsumes the inclusion of every individual; but, although the outcome of political-class struggle invariably affects the social condition of every individual in the society, the immediate contending political classes may include only a minority of the population. In other words, the political classes may have a "phantom public" larger in number than themselves. This is not to say, however, that its public is of no importance. It seldom remains apathetic; it may shift its weight of sentiment toward one side or another—it is always watched by the contending classes.

| 11 |

The Political Class

[. . .] The term "political class" is used here, for want of a more suitable one, to distinguish a social phenomenon usually called "class" or "social class" from that which we have previously described as "social class." Instead of the term "political class," the designation "economic class"[1] might have been used, but economic determinants are evidently at the base of social classes also. On the other hand, to substitute the German word *Stände* for "social class" is to introduce a concept that is already confused in the literature. At any rate, the designation may be of less significance than its meaning.[2]

Meaning of Political Class

[. . .] We could [cite] conclusions about class struggle almost indefinitely, but they would all tend to be divided into two main groups: those before, and those after, Karl Marx. Marx himself says:

> The history of all hitherto existing society is the history of class struggle. Freeman and slave, patrician and plebeian, lord and serf, guild-master and journeyman, in a word, oppressor and oppressed, stood in constant opposition to one another, carried on an uninterrupted, now hidden, now open fight, a fight that each time ended either in a revolutionary reconstitution of society at large, or in the common ruin of the contending classes. . . . The modern bourgeois society that has sprouted from the ruins of feudal society has not done away with class antagonisms. It has but established new classes, new conditions of oppression, new forms of struggle in place of the old ones. Our epoch of the bourgeoisie, possesses, however, this distinctive feature; it has simplified the class antagonisms. Society as a whole is more and more splitting up into two great battle camps, into two great classes directly facing each other: Bourgeoisie and Proletariat.[3]

In all the voluminous works of Marx, however, there is no definition of class, and, naturally, no clear distinction between the idea of these "two great classes directly facing each other" and that of the social-class system. These are both products of bourgeois economy, and in the literature following Marx both are usually referred to as "social classes." At the outset it should be made clear that political-class action may be found in all organized society, and certainly it is not necessarily limited to the period of the rise of urbanism in Europe. Bourgeoisie-proletariat struggle is one type of political-class action; it is a product of modern capitalistic society. But we may repeat that fully developed social-class systems are also unknown to ancient society; they came into their own only after 1789.

It must be already obvious that political and social classes are distinct phenomena. Social classes form a system of cooperating conceptual status entities; political classes, on the other hand, do not constitute a system at all, for they are antagonistic.[4] The political class is a power group which tends to be organized for conflict; the social class is never organized, for it is a concept only. Although the political class is ordinarily weighted with persons from a special sector of the social-status gradient, it may include persons from every position.[5] Hence we do not speak of political classes as forming a hierarchy; they may conceivably split the social hierarchy vertically; therefore, there is here no primary conception of social stratification. In other words, members of the political class ordinarily do not have a common social status. These classes, therefore, are not thought of as social-class strata but as organizations arrayed face to face against each other. Furthermore, unlike the social class, the political class seeks to attract members to itself, and group solidarity is highly valued. Social solidarity is not a characteristic of social classes, for it is expected that persons are constantly attracted upward and away from their social position, while those who fall may be allowed to sink even farther.

Control of the State—A Goal

As a power group, the political class is preoccupied with devices for controlling the state. In emphasizing this point, Lewis L. Lorwin says: "Since the power of the ruling class is always concentrated in the organization of the state, the oppressed class must aim directly against the mechanism of the state. Every class struggle is thus *a political struggle,* which in its objectives aims at the abolition of the existing social order and at the establishment of a new social system."[6] However, political-class action may not be identified with that of political factions, for the faction may have as its purpose nothing more than the acquisition of the spoils of office. Thus different political factions may represent the same political class. Political factions may come into being, disappear, or regroup, "but the fundamental interests of the classes remain. That party [faction] conquers which is able to feel out and satisfy the fundamental demands of a class."[7]

Furthermore, in class-conflict situations the object on trial is not an administration but rather a political system; the whole institutional order may be marked for weeding out. Says Paul M. Sweezy: "Any particular state is the child of the class or classes in society which benefit from the particular set of property relations which it is the state's obligation to enforce."[8] It is this pattern of property relationships which political-class conflict threatens. Hence the goal of a political class is always control of the state. As an instance of this, Frederick L. Schuman, commenting on the seizure of power by the German Nazis, declares: "The first step in the evolution of the judicial system of the Third Reich was the identification of the [Nazi] Party with the State and the punishment of offences against the Party as crimes against the State."[9]

Method and Procedure

Class struggle is not only a course of action but also a process of winning new adherents to some political ideal or of maintaining old convictions. The political class usually has a policy and a propaganda machine. The ideal of the attacking political class is neither utopian nor merely conflictive; it involves a rational plan for displacing the existing government. "An effective revolutionary ideology," says Alfred Meusel, "must reveal to the rising social class that it is and why it is a class distinct from the society into which it was born; it must offer a critique of the existing order and draw the general outline of the ideal substitute."[10]

[. . .] A political class develops naturally—that is to say, new political classes come into being inevitably with significant changes in the method of economic production and economic distribution. On the other hand, class conflict is consciously developed between the classes. Werner Sombart gives the following stages in the development of class struggle: ". . . first a difference of class, then class interests [consciousness], then class opposition, finally class strife."[11] A political class beomes conscious of itself only through successful propaganda; the objective position of the class and its aims must be focused by its leaders. We may put it in this way: As a function of the economic order, the class has potential existence, but as the result of agitation it becomes organized for conflict. The dominant political class becomes class conscious—and sometimes with overwhelming vehemence—in response, or as a counteraction, to the developing class consciousness of the subordinate class.

[. . .] In all social movements the masses are taken into consideration; both the ruling class and the attacking class appeal to the people. Yet the outcome of the struggle may affect the interest of the people only indirectly. Some of the most violent class conflicts in history, fought in the interest of one privileged class against another, have utilized the exploited masses on both sides. Even though the real purpose of the class is antagonistic to the interest of the common people, it will always seek to convert them.[12] [. . .]

Leadership

Ordinarily it is not possible to delimit definitely a political class by observing actual personal characteristics such as occupation, wealth, religious affiliation, or social-class position. The idealism of political classes may override individual differences. Indeed the leadership of the aggressor class may arise from the ruling class itself. Robert Michels emphasizes this in concluding that "every great class movement in history has arisen upon the instigation, with the co-operation, and under the leadership of men sprung from the very class against which the movement was directed."[13]

Marx and Engels had already said: "In times when the class-struggle nears the decisive hour, the process of dissolution going on within the ruling class, in fact, within the whole range of the old society, assumes such a violent, glaring character that a small section of the ruling class cuts itself adrift and joins the revolutionary class."[14] The particular disadvantaged group, then, may not produce its own leadership. It is obvious, however, that no great part of one class will desert and enter the ranks of the other; the desertion, though significant, occurs only in isolated cases.

The Purpose and Composition of Classes

The political class is probably always motivated by some socioeconomic interest.[. . .] The class aims primarily at controlling the policies of production and distribution of wealth. Sometimes this interest may be couched in a religious, racial, or even a nationalistic rationale, in which case some analysis will be necessary to determine the purpose of the class. A political-class movement will develop when, because of new methods of production or maturation of old methods, economic power has been shifted to some section of the population without at the same time shifting the political power. This is the basis of political-class discontent.

[. . .] There are many group skirmishes which result from local group friction. In their adjustments, however, the social order remains entirely out of view; furthermore, there may be international wars between ruling classes which do not contemplate a rearrangement of the political-class alignment in any nation. A peasant revolt may be simply a defense of certain customary rights.

A gang, sect, denomination, social club, or lodge need not represent a political class. These are intraclass institutional groups, and they may have problems [. . .] they seek to solve politically; yet their end is ordinarily the fostering of their own limited interests rather than the controlling of the state for the purpose of reorganizing the economic order. Institutional groups of this kind may be called special-purpose groups; their outlook is circumscribed, specialized, and exclusive. They may, however, be altruistic. Within the ongoing social order they propose to work for their own welfare or for that of certain limited groups in the society.

Their limits of possible social activity are those of political and social reform; they are, at most, interested in a more propitious operation of the status quo. As an illustration, ordinary opportunistic labor unionism is not politically class-minded, though it is always interested in seeing its friends in office as an assurance of its own welfare. Labor unionism begins to have a political-class appeal when it becomes explicitly revolutionary—that is to say, with reference to a capitalistic society, when it becomes socialistic, syndicalistic, communistic, or anarchistic.[15]

Ordinarily only those persons who take the side of a political class will be included in that class, and this must be so because it is a conflict group. It is, therefore, practically impossible to define the membership of a political class in terms of objective criteria only. The correlation between the material position of a person and his social attitudes may not be perfect. Thus in attempting to delimit a political class, to differentiate proletariat from bourgeoisie, Goetz A. Briefs concludes:

> A proletarian is a propertyless wage earner . . . who regards himself and his kind as constituting a distinct class, who lives and forms

his ideas in the light of this class consciousness according to class ideals, and who on the basis of this class consciousness rejects the prevailing social and economic order. . . . To be a proletarian . . . is, therefore, not to have a certain occupation or a certain economic and social status, but to have a characteristic mental set, a predisposition to react to one's given environment in ways no better to be described than by the term proletarian.[16]

Recognizing this inevitable characteristic of the political class will enable us to explain what Professor Sorokin thinks is a contradiction. According to this writer, "the theoretical conceptions of the Communists are vaguely different and contradictory, [because] in their practice . . . a proletarian has been regarded as anyone who has supported the Communists although he occupied the position of a capitalist or was a privileged and wealthy man. The non-proletarians have been regarded as all who have not supported the Communist government, though they were the common laboring men in factories."[17] This, obviously, is not an inconsistency of political-class action. One may put it briefly that a political-class member is one who believes in and is willing to follow the ideals of that class. This, at any rate, is a decisive characterization in open political-class conflict.

Relationship of Political and Social Classes

Sometimes a confusion of the meaning of social and political class has caused many writers to question the proposition that it is possible for an advanced society to be a "classless" society. They will argue that men are born unequal, both in physique and aptitude, that society will always contrive to distribute its favors among its members according to their contributions to the social welfare, and that this principle holds even though the range of social emoluments is narrower in some societies than in others. Clearly, however, this constitutes a social-class reference, which the advocates of a classless society could not have in mind. The latter are thinking about large groups with fundamentally divergent economic interests—about antagonistic groups—and not particularly of the cooperative status system.[. . .]

A political-classless society, then, need not imply a statusless society.[18] In other words, there seems to be no necessary functional relationship between political and social classes. It may not be even true . . . that the greater the rigidity of the status system, the greater the likelihood of the formation of political classes. The stable caste system of India, for instance, has not been particularly disposed to political-class conflict. At any rate, the absence of political classes does not imply an absence of social classes.[19] But reference to one political class always implies the existence of one or more counterclasses. If there is only one unopposed political class, the society may be said to be politically classless.

Thus, in the days of rampant capitalism in the United States, there was probably only one organized political class; there is probably only one active political class in Russia today. Yet there have always been social classes in these countries. There is always latent or open class struggle in a society in which there is more than one political class; but social classes, to reiterate, are not in conflict. They supplement and support each other.

The political class may become "class conscious"; social classes, on the other hand, cannot be. Class consciousness is a political-class attribute;[20] however, with reference to a social-class system, persons may be status-conscious.[21] Although a significant number of persons in a society may be characterized by some common economic or other social interests, they do not become an active political class until they develop class consciousness. Thus, the search for and conversion of potential class members are major functions of political-class leaders.

The Economic Man and the Class Struggle

Political classes have almost never been able to attain their ends without violence. This, of course, is due to the fact that the ruling class does not yield without it, and because this class holds its position by virtue of its monopoly of power. The Machiavellian postulate that a man's property—his economic interest—is as good and sometimes better than his life clearly obtains in interclass relationships. Political classes are never convinced merely by arguments at the round table.[. . .]

Ordinarily, the greater the apparent cogency of the logic of the one side, the greater the intransigence of the other. Conviction by argument and reasoning comes only when these are backed up by a show of overwhelming physical might. To put the matter otherwise, the ruling class knows well on which side its bread is buttered and it will not be hoodwinked, or argued, or cajoled out of its position. Moreover, the ascendant class cannot be eased down gently with a *Satyagraha* or a sit-down strike,[22] it will accept no substitute for an

open matching of physical power.[23] "Attempts at persuasion fail
miserably," says Robert Michels, "when they are addressed to the
privileged classes, in order to induce these to abandon, to their own
disadvantage, as a class and as individuals, the leading positions
they occupy in society."[24] To expect a ruling class to commit suicide
for the mere asking is clearly too colossal a presumption. As Leon
Trotsky put it: "One can talk over petty details with an enemy, but
not matters of life and death." Werner Sombart presents the com-
monsense logic of the position of the ruling class when he asserts:

> The utopists fail to see, in their optimism, that a part of the society
> looks upon the *status quo* as thoroughly satisfactory and desires no
> change, that this part also has an interest in sustaining it, and that a
> specific condition of society always obtains because those persons, who
> are interested in it, have the power to sustain it. . . . Now judge for
> yourself what a mistaken estimate of the true world, what boundless
> underestimate of opposing forces, lie in the belief that those who have
> power can be moved to surrender their position through preaching
> and promise.[25]

This discussion, to be sure, must rest partly upon historical
proof, or at least the absence of it, for it cannot be shown that in the
past any political class has yielded without a conflict. Indeed, the
position has been taken that a major change in the social order
necessarily involves drastic measures, because "no political system is
so flexible as to be susceptible to fundamental change by 'legal'
means; and illegality implies resort to force by the revolutionist as
well as by the state which he attacks."[26]

As a matter of fact, the law itself is the instrument of the ruling
class; hence it is a logical impossibility for another class to assume
power legally.[. . .] The political postulates of the opposing classes
are inevitably antagonistic; as a consequence there can be no common judicial procedure. "The law is not an abstraction. It cannot be
understood independently of the political foundation on which it
rests and the political interest which it serves."[27]

The ideology of the ruling class and the established social order
will be defended obstinately, not only because it ensures the interest
of that class, but also because it will inevitably seem that its defense
is "indispensable to the preservation of society."[28] The suppression
of one political class by another, then, is seldom, if ever, a windfall.
When the vested interests of the ruling class are threatened, its
members will deal mercilessly with the challenging class, at the
same time readily putting even their own lives in jeopardy. Thus,
the exercise of violence is the constant and inevitable prerogative of

the ruling class; the revolutionaries can assume power only after they have limited or relieved this class of its freedom to control the decisive instruments of violence.

[. . . We] must hasten to add that the potentialities of violence exercised by the different classes may not be the same. In a real political-class struggle—that is to say, a struggle for the recognition of a social system economically rooted in the society itself—violence is particularly the effective instrument of the attacking class. The leadership of the attacking class can seldom be killed off; it is a sort of sporiferous social phenomenon, regenerating increasingly under violence. Therefore, at a certain state of intensity in the struggle, the use of violence by the ruling class may serve only to crystallize antityrannical sentiment against itself, thus expediting its own doom. On the other hand, the destruction of the leadership of the senescent ruling class will necessarily mean its consumption, because with this event not only is the old leadership supplanted, but also a new and more vigorous social system emerges.

An example of a common type of fearful, hopeful thinking on this subject, a position ordinarily taken by revisionist and Fabian socialists, is the following argument by Professor John Dewey. This authority advocates a "dependence upon socially organized intelligence" as a humane substitute for class conflict:

> The curious fact is that while it is generally admitted . . . that a particular social problem, say of the family, or railroads or banking must be solved, if at all, by the method of intelligence, yet there is supposed to be some one all-exclusive social problem which can be solved only by violence. This fact would be inexplicable were it not for a conclusion from dogma as its premise. . . . There is an undoubted objective clash of interests between finance capitalism . . . and idle workers and hungry customers. But what generates violent strife is failure to bring the conflict into the light of intelligence where the conflicting interests can be adjudicated in behalf of the interest of the great majority.[29]

It is evident that [. . .] Dewey, in his analogy between a "particular social problem" such as "banking" or the "family" and a political-class-conflict situation, completely misunderstands his subject. In other words, he has confused intraclass problems with interclass conflict. Ordinarily problems of banking, or the family, or education, or Coolidge versus Davis, are political-party, faction problems; they do not involve a challenge to the political order. In political-class struggle intelligence is used to maneuver the opponent for a destructive blow. Indeed, political-class antagonisms are too highly pitched to achieve solution at the round table.[30] The attacking class is treasonous and blasphemous from the beginning. It is un-American, un-German, or un-English, and ungodly. It is necessarily against "law and order," against "our form of government," and against "our way of life"; consequently, it cannot be free to speak its mind.[31]

The aim of the attacking class is not cooperation; it does not want law and order, since law and order means perpetuation of the old order. It does not want to discuss or to negotiate problems in a conciliatory manner with the old rulers, for such a procedure tends to continue the latter's prestige. Indeed, the two groups do not have the same but contrary problems. The end of the attacking class is the vanquishing not only of the old leaders but also of the old system itself—a problem [. . .] the ruling class cannot be expected to discuss. Therefore, the struggle for power tends to be involved with a succession of conspiracies, imprisonments, and summatory conflicts, while compromise and appeasement may postpone but not settle the basic antagonism. Moreover, very much of the sanctimonious abhorrence displayed by the ruling class and its apologists against the use of violence in the class struggle is rooted in the desire to maintain the integrity of its class monopoly of violence.

[. . .] The irreconcilability of political-class antagonism is a consideration of primary significance for an understanding of the history of revolution. Those who believe in the possibility of peaceful settlement of all political problems will not understand, for instance, the passion which moved the royalist Convention Parliament to unearth the putrefied bodies of Cromwell, Bradshaw, and Ireton and hang them in public on the gallows of Tyburn; they will not be struck by the summatory, vitriolic clashes of interest groups which before the Civil War, rendered the American Congress totally impotent as an institution for averting political violence; they could not explain the mission of the armies of Great Britain, France, Japan, and the United States in Russia at the end of World War I;[32] they will be unable to read meaning into the action of the Dies Committee in prosecuting Americans who had fought the Nazis and Fascists in Spain; they will not see why it is very necessary that Harry Bridges be either deported from the United States or silenced in jail; and they will not know that an assurance by the Allies to "respect the right of all people to choose the form of government under which they will live" is in fact an extremely involved political matter.[33]

[. . .] In all significant social revolutions, organized religion will necessarily be involved. The church and other forms of organized priestcraft thrive in harmony with and, on the whole, sanction the status quo; in other words, the church is normally rightist; it is the most lethargic and inert of the institutions confronting the revolutionists, partly because it is essentially traditional.[34] In fact, the church has a vested interest in the status quo and it will fight in the protection of this. Therefore, the social system cannot be changed radically unless the church is either overthrown or forcibly brought into line with the movement. [. . .]

Organized religion is never a private matter; it is inevitably political. In this regard, ever since the early Christians began to find their first converts among the slaves and common laborers of the Roman Empire, Christianity became an intensely political institution in the West. The established religion represents the ruling class, and it is "used in their interests." Frequently the state, God, and society are associated in the minds of the people, and a blow at the state may be shifted, more or less, to either or both of the other two.

The ascendant political class will invariably take advantage of the coincident struggle to stigmatize the radicals as God-haters.[35] In actuality, however, religion as such need not be seriously involved. Historically the Christian Church has labored in the interests of feudalism; it has defended slavery; it is at the service of capitalism; and we should expect it to accommodate to any succeeding system. [. . .] Religion evidently fills an indispensable need of mankind, and society will always contrive to institutionalize it. The church may be crushed beneath the grinding wheels of revolution, but there need be no fear that religion is likewise mangled in the process.

The dominant political class will also be disposed to take advantage of another basic confusion, that between the state and society. Society in this sense will seldom be defined, but as an amorphous concept it will be made to include especially many deep-seated loyalties of the group. Love of one's country, devotion to one's family as one has come to know it in its social setting, and a passion for "all the things one has learned to love and enjoy"—these are some of the values which may appeal for protection when "society" is threatened by an overthrow of the government. However, it need hardly be said that one may love his country and hate his government with equal intensity at the same time.

The political class in power, which is apprehensive of attack, will countenance only one political party and one political faction. Political classes that are firmly entrenched may encourage a system of parties and party factions, for the latter never bring the economic order seriously into question. Neither the Democrats in the southern United States nor the Fascists in Spain, for example, could harbor two strong political parties; the same, of course, is true for Russia—Russia is still open to political-class conflict, especially that initiated from without. And their methods must necessarily be ruthless. The vanquished must be broken in spirit as well.

Notes

1. In this study we shall not discuss economic classes as functional groups. Farmers, bankers, investors, teachers, and so on, are occupational groups that may be classified into economic classes according to the immediate interest of the taxonomist. These groups cannot be equated with either social or political classes.
2. In this speech in Naples, August 11, 1922, Mussolini called the Fascists "a new political class."
3. Karl Marx and Friedrich Engels, *Communist Manifesto* pp. 12–13.
4. Cf. Joseph A. Schumpeter, *Capitalism, Socialism, and Democracy* (New York and London, 1942), pp. 53–54.
5. The status system of any society, whether estate, caste, or social class, always presumes the inclusion of every individual; but, although the outcome of political-class struggle invariably affects the social condition of every individual in the society, the immediate contending political classes may include only a minority of the population. In other words, the political classes may have a "phantom public" larger in numbers than themselves. Of course, we do not mean to say that this public is of no importance. It may remain apathetic or it may shift its weight of sentiment toward one side or the other—it is always watched by the contending classes.
6. Lewis L. Lorwin, see "Class Struggle," in *Encyclopedia of the Social Sciences*.
7. See Leon Trotsky, *The History of the Russian Revolution*, vol. III, p. 338. In the United States there is only one effective political party, with two factions: Republicans and Democrats. There is no effective Socialist party, the organized leadership of the opposite political class.

   The following is a political-faction, and thus quite misleading, analysis of the modern class struggle: "The important long-run consideration is not what political philosophy or what ideology the present ruling class now holds, but rather to what extent the economic powers, and hence the livelihood of all the people in those countries [Germany, Italy, and Russia], are in the hands of the government. How governments use such important powers will change from time to time depending on what groups of politicians temporarily are in power. And what these groups will be is, in *totalitarian* states as in other countries, to a large extent accidental, and certainly unpredictable"

(James Harvey Rogers, *Capitalism in Crisis* [New Haven, 1938], pp. 6–7; emphasis added).

8. Paul M. Sweezy, *The Theory of Capitalist Development* (New York, 1942) p. 242.

9. Frederick L. Schuman, *The Nazi Dictatorship* (New York, 1935), p. 301. Dr. Goebbels had already said: "If in our struggle against a corrupt system, we are today forced to be a 'party' . . . the instant the system crumbles we will become the State" (quoted by Daniel Guerin, *Fascism and Big Business* [New York, 1939], p. 134). And another revolutionist, Leon Trotsky, declares: "A class struggle carried to its conclusion is a struggle for state power."

10. Alfred Meusel, "Revolution and Counter-Revolution," in *Encyclopedia of the Social Sciences*. Werner Sombart sees the activities of the aggressive political class definitively: "By a social movement we understand the aggregate of all those endeavors of a social class which are directed to a rational overturning of an existing social order to suit the interests of this class" (*Socialism and the Social Movement in the 19th Century,* [New York, 1898], p. 3).

11. Sombart, *Socialism and Social Movement,* p. 110.

12. Louis Adamic quotes the financier Jay Gould as remarking symbolically: "I can hire one half the working class to kill the other half" (*Dynamite: The Story of Class Violence in America* [New York, 1931], p. 23).

13. Robert Michels, *Political Parties,* trans. Eden Paul and Cedar Paul (New York, 1915), pp. 238–39.

14. Marx and Engels, *Communist Manifesto,* p. 26. Quite frequently in discussions of contemporary political-class action charges are made that the aggressor class is planning an overthrow of democracy. This, however, is misleading. The attack is really against the bourgeois economic system, and a supplanting of the latter need not necessarily involve an abandonment of all possible forms of democratic method.

15. The term "political class" in our meaning is not synonymous with Gaetano Mosca's ruling class, which seems to be limited to the administrative head of a government. See *The Ruling Class* (New York 1939).

16. Goetz A. Briefs, *The Proletariat* (New York, 1937), pp. 50–51.

17. *Contemporary Sociological Theories,* p. 543, note.

18. It seems that R. H. Tawney has been forced to stretch his logic extremely in order to achieve some meaning of a classless society. He declares: "A society marked by sharp disparities of wealth and power might properly, nevertheless, be described as classless, since it was open to each man to become wealthy and powerful" (*Equality* [New York, 1929], p. 123).

19. See on this point Sidney Webb and Beatrice Webb, *Soviet Communism: A New Civilisation?* [New York, 1936], pp. 1021–24.

20. It is to political-class consciousness that Robert Briffault refers when he says: "There will . . . be a type of mind, an ideology, corresponding to the economic situation of a ruling land-owning aristocracy; another

type determined by the economic situation of a trading middle class, or a bourgeoisie; another corresponding to the situation of a servile proletarian class. The specific characters of those types of mind and of their contents will vary according to their respective relations. Thus, the character of the aristocrat mind will be modified according as its power is unchallenged, or as it is involved in conflict with rival class interests. The middle class, or bourgeois mind, will assume a slightly different form according as it is contending for emancipation from feudal domination or its own power is challenged by the proletarians. The proletarian mind will differ according as the servile class is completely crushed or is content and resigned, or acquires hopes of emancipation and becomes 'class-conscious.' . . . The class mentality is thus not only determined by a fixed tradition, but is constantly active and undergoing adjustment in relation to changing conditions" (*Reasons for Anger* [New York, 1936], pp. 52–53).

21. We are assuming here that social classes are conceptual entities. Persons of given statuses occupying a certain span of the social-status continuum constitute an entity only in the minds of individuals.

22. To be sure, "passive resistance" is ordinarily the only way to fight when one is empty-handed. Little children sometimes fight their parents in that way. Certain groups may make a virtue of this necessity and exploit it religiously. Even so, we should remember that not all fights are political-class struggles.

23. Again Hitler is in point: "In the last analysis, the decisive question is always this: what is to be done if passive resistance finally gets on the opponent's nerves and he launches a fight against it with brute force? Is one determined to offer further resistance? If so, bear, for better or worse, the most violent, bloodiest hounding. In that case one faces what one faces in active resistance, namely, struggle. Hence every so-called passive resistance has real significance only if backed up by a determination, if need be, to continue resistance by open struggle or by means of clandestine warfare" (*Mein Kampf*, pp. 989–90).

24. Michels, *Political Parties*, pp. 244–45. The author declares further: "A class considered as a whole never spontaneously surrenders its position of advantage. It never recognizes any moral reason sufficiently powerful to compel it to abdicate in favor of its 'poorer brethren.' Such action is prevented, if by nothing else, by class egoism." Thomas Jefferson realized this clearly when he wrote to John Quincy Adams in 1823 concerning the European class struggle between the bourgeoisie and the nobility, saying: "To obtain all this [liberty in European countries], rivers of blood must yet flow, and years of desolation pass over; yet the object is worth rivers of blood and years of desolation" (*Democracy*, p. 239).

25. Sombart, p. 33.

26. Meusel, "Revolution and Counter-Revolution."

27. E. H. Carr, *The Twenty Years' Crisis* (London, 1939), p. 229.

28. See Henri Pirenne, *Economic and Social History of Medieval Europe*, p. 51.

Already Marx and Engels had said: "Just as to the bourgeois, the disappearance of class property is the disappearance of production itself, so the disappearance of class culture is to him identical with the disappearance of all culture" (*Communist Manifesto*, p. 35). For a naïve construction of this see W. H. V. Reade, *The Revolt of Labor Against Civilization* (Oxford, 1919).

29. John Dewey, *Liberalism and Social Action*, pp. 78–79. Sombart is outspoken in his analysis of this attitude. "It is assumed," he says, "that it is only ignorance on the part of the opponent that keeps him from accepting openly and freely this good, from divesting himself of his possessions and exchanging the old order for the new. The classic example of this childish way of viewing things is the well-known fact that Charles Fourier daily waited at his home, between the hours of twelve and one, to receive the millionaire who should bring him money for the erection of the first phalanstery. No one came" (*Socialism and the Social Movement*, pp. 33–34).

30. Robert Briffault cites an incident in point: "At a meeting of the General Council of Trades Unions in 1925, Mr. F. Bramley, criticizing the attitude of the meeting, remarked: 'It appears to me you can discuss any other subject under the sun without getting into that panicky state of trembling fear and excitement and almost savage ferocity you get into when you are discussing Russian affairs. . . . You can discuss calmly and without excitement the operations of the Fascists in Italy; you can discuss with great calm the suppression of trade-unions organizations in other countries; you can discuss the activities of capitalist governments and their destruction of the trade-union movement in one country after another without this unnecessary epidemic of excitement. But when you begin to discuss Russia, you begin to suffer from some malignant disease" (*The Decline and Fall of the British Empire*, p. 175).

   In this connection Harold F. Laski observes: "Whenever privilege is in danger, it flies into that panic which is the mortal enemy of reason; and it is a waste of time to ask its consideration of arguments that, in another mental climate, it is capable of understanding" (*Where Do We Go from Here?* [New York, 1940], p. 164).

31. It is only by a recognition of this fact, for example, that we can explain the frantic efforts of the ruling class in the United States to silence Henry A. Wallace—to say nothing about thousands of lesser men. Thus, the Associated Press reported on June 11, 1947, that United States Representative Meyer (Rep. Kans.) declared before the House that the Attorney General should indict Mr. Wallace for treason. And he implicated President Roosevelt as he would a foreign enemy: "Let it not be forgotten that this Henry Wallace is one of the heritages left us by the late Franklin Roosevelt."

32. For a discussion of the nature of the "war of intervention" in Russia see Michael Sayers and Albert E. Kahn, *The Great Conspiracy* (Boston, 1946), chap. VI.

33. On the diplomacy involved in the question of post-World War II political freedom for smaller nations one may read the story of its progress all over his daily newspapers. The following news item is taken at random from this source. Says the United Press, May 17, 1946: "The United States has served notice on Soviet Russia it will fight developments of communism in Japan just as vigorously as it does at home. It promised not to suppress communist parties in Japan, but left unsaid the plain warning that it will do everything short of that to discourage them. This political challenge to the only communist state in the world was first made by George R. Acheson, Jr., top American diplomat in Tokyo. . . . This conflict, underlying all Big Three troubles for several years, has led many top Allied leaders to ask: 'Are the two systems reconcilable?' "

34. Professor William Oscar Brown puts it in this way: "Religion, always and at all times, tends to sanction the current mores, values, ideals, practices, attitudes, and relationships—provided, of course, they have been established in a culture for a sufficient period of time" ("Race Prejudice," Ph.D. diss., University of Chicago, 1930, p. 294).

35. Probably Edmund Burke's stricture on the French Revolutionists illustrates this type of religio-political involvement as well as any. Instead of "the Religion and the Law," he declares, "by which they were in a great political communion with the Christian world, they have constructed their Republic on three bases. . . . Its foundation is laid in Regicide, in Jacobinism and in Atheism. . . . I call it Atheism by establishment when any State . . . shall not acknowledge the existence of God as a moral Governor of the world; when it shall offer to Him no religious or moral worship; when it shall abolish the Christian religion by a regular decree; when it shall persecute with a cold, unrelenting steady cruelty, by every mode of confiscation, imprisonment, exile, and death, all its ministers; when it shall generally shut up, or pull down, churches; when the few buildings which remain of this kind, shall be open only for the purpose of making an apotheosis of monsters whose vices and crimes have no parallel amongst men, and whom all other men consider as objects of general detestation, and the severest animadversion of law. When in the place of that religion of social benevolence, and of individual self-denial in mockery of all religion, they institute impious, blasphemous, indecent theatric rites, in honor of their vitiated, perverted reason, and erect altars to the personification of their own corrupted and bloody Republic; when schools and seminaries are founded at publick expense to poison mankind; from generation to generation with the horrible maxims of this impiety; when wearied out with incessant martyrdoms, and the cries of a people hungering and thirsting for religion, they permit it, only as a tolerated evil—I call this *atheism by establishment*" (*Burke Selected Works*, vol. II., ed E. J. Payne [Oxford, 1926], pp. 70–72).

12

Facets of the Modern Political-Class Struggle

The Problem

Although the modern class struggle presents a problem of preeminent social significance, social scientists have given it very little attention. . . . The fact that most orthodox social scientists have avoided this subject is itself a social trait of political-class behavior. The mere recognition of the existence of political-class conflict tends to arouse the displeasure of the ruling class. "The position of the scientist in both endowed and state tax-supported institutions depends not only in the long but also in the short run on the existing social order. His membership-character is in the bourgeois region, and consequently he usually does not even so much as mention the class struggle."[1] Some writers who see the problem more or less clearly prefer to take the road of Erasmus, of whom it has been said: "For no idea in the world, for no conviction, could he be induced to place his head upon the block, and suffer for what he at heart knew to be true and right."

It has been as serious as this, then, that the scholar's bread and butter ordinarily depends upon his avoiding the study of contemporary class conflict. To be sure, if he happens to be convinced that the status quo is right, he could speak freely.[2] At any rate, the social scientist is being constantly criticized for closing his eyes to the tremendous human drama unfolding before him. For instance, Robert S. Lynd says: "It is no accident that . . . a world of scientists who comb their fields for important problems for research have left the problem of the power organization and politics of big business so largely unexplored."[3] Even Hitler, that past master in the art of manipulating ideas for a purpose, warns the scholar:

> One should guard . . . against refuting things which actually exist. The fact that the class question is not at all one of spiritual problems as

one would like to make us believe, especially before elections, cannot be denied. The class pride of a great part of our people, just like the low esteem of the hand laborer, is, above all, a symptom which does not come from the imagination of one who is moon-struck.

But apart from this, it shows the inferior thinking ability of our so-called intelligentsia when just in those circles one does not understand that a condition which was not able to prevent the rise of . . . Marxism will far less be able to regain that which is lost.

The bourgeois parties . . . will never be able to draw the proletarian masses to their camp, as here two worlds face each other. . . and their attitude towards each other can only be a fighting one.[4]

Probably not one in a hundred American college graduates majoring in the social sciences is equipped to understand the foregoing passage, far less to argue about it. To the ruling class such conditioning of the young is desirable; yet the powerful forces of social change move on.[5] And, as Werner Sombart well says: "We [need], above all, to see that the [social] movement springs not out of the whim, the choice, the malevolence of individuals; that it is not made, but becomes."[6] Our approach to this problem, then, is from the view that it is real and worthy of the best efforts of students of social problems. Moreover, the social determinism which seems to inhere in the social processes under consideration renders it fascinating. Thus Sombart declares impressively:

It seems to me that the first impression to be made upon anyone by quiet observation of the social movement must be that it is necessary and unavoidable. As a mountain torrent, after a thunder storm, must dash down into the valley according to "iron unchangeable law," so must the stream of social agitation pour itself onward. This is the first thing for us to understand, that something of great and historic importance is developing before our eyes. . . . Probably there are some who believe that the social movement is merely the malicious work of a few agitators . . . probably there are some who naturally are forced to the false idea that some medicine or charm can drive away this fatal poison out of the social body. What a delusion! What lack of intelligence and insight as to the nature of all social history![7]

The Ruling Class

There are few social concepts more elusive than that of a ruling political class, and in capitalist society this is particularly so. The concept is likely to be identified with the idea of military power, with that of political office, or with that of mere wealth. Alexis de Tocqueville, in a sort of doctrinal echo of Aristotle, even thinks that in a "democracy" the government is controlled by the poor.[8] In locating the ruling class, however, it is necessary to rely on two criteria: material interest and conscious political sympathy. The material interest of the individual in the system of production gives him his potential class affiliation, and his conscious sympathies born of class antagonism complete him as an active affiliate. In a capitalist society, the economic system, as is well known, is run by businessmen principally for their benefit; free workers are exploited for profit.

Roughly, then, businessmen constitute our ruling class.[9] Yet, obvious as it might seem, it is not ordinarily recognized that this ruling class has only recently achieved its power through bitter and bloody struggle with another ruling class. The present ruling class, which is so eager to identify its pattern of society with God, was at one time held in little respect by the landed ruling class. Members of our current ruling class were called "common," "ignoble," "ungentle," "bourgeois." Indeed, its members themselves had a low estimate of their position. The richest of them frequently married into the nobility and tried to forget their past in the city, and at one time the priests, at a price, listened to their dying confessions of mortal sin for their taking interest and making profits after the fashion of good businessmen. "No one would have dreamed in the Middle Ages that the despised creed of the trader and the money lender—a creed of selfishness and worship of the then lowest material values—should rise to be a compendium of everything most respectable in temporal affairs."[10]

However, economic power gradually shifted into the hands of the businessmen.[11] And as the dominant ways of trade and production continued to change, these capitalists began to recognize that they were being exploited or, more particularly, inhibited by the social system of the landlord ruling class. The laws were against them; the church was against them; they had inferior social prestige; and yet they were becoming richer and more influential. To be sure, they realized the futility of merely asking the landed ruling class to reorganize the society so that businessmen in the city, who had come to control economic production, could take the helm and run the system in their own interest. Consequently, as a way out and sometimes unconsciously, they encouraged the development of a number of philosophers, writers, journalists, and propagandists, who undermined the morale of the people who supported the ruling class; and finally, in open battle, they chopped the leaders of the feudal order to pieces.

Then the business people, the bourgeoisie, freely fashioned laws and otherwise adjusted the society to suit their convenience. It would be a very great mistake to think that these revolutions, of which the French Revolution is the classic, were fought in the interest of the working people, either skilled or unskilled. As John Strachey puts it: "The liberty which had been established in eighteenth-century England was a liberty for the big merchants, the great land owners, and the trading aristocrats. They and they alone possessed the freedom of the market."[12]

An illusion concerning the rule of this capitalist class lies in the fact that its laws are literally objective; power has been apparently given to things instead of to men. "The sacredness of private property" is the key concept. The bourgeois state is "first and foremost the protector of private property"; therefore, the owners of property, "accumulated on their own initiative," have power to set the machinery of the state in motion. The working class does not govern; it merely supports a form of government that has been already established in the interest of a ruling political class. The ultimate power in this system is in the hands of the great capitalist financiers.[13]

Capitalist Production and the Proletariat

Capitalism is a social system based on free enterprise and on production, by means of large quantities of capital goods, for private profit. The state is set up to administer and to defend this system.[14] The capitalist state is not a spiritual product; its function, from its inception in the medieval town, has always been primarily to secure the interest of a certain class. The intimate relationship of this interest and the state is readily apparent, for the laws, the customs, the way of life of the society will ordinarily be thought of in its totality as a product of all members of society. Indeed, the individual is so much a part of his society that he is seldom able to conceive of any other system in terms other than variants of his own. At any rate, capitalism is supported not only by the owners of capital goods, who produce for a profit, but also by a distinct class of free workers.

Before capitalism can take root workers must be proletarianized. The proletarianization of workers may be thought of as the "commoditization" of their capacity to labor, that is to say, the transformation of the major human element in production into a mass of persons mainly dependent for their means of subsistence on the vicissitudes of a labor market. In this way labor is freed—indeed, as mercilessly freed as an inanimate commodity.

This working class should not be thought of simply as poor people or as miserable people; they are a class of people peculiar to a capitalist system of production. Their plane of living is, on the whole, very much higher than that of the hand workers under feudalism.[. . .] The proletariat, to mention again the well-known fact, is a class of freed workers, freed from the land and freed from the ownership of the means of production. It sells its services in a "free" market to entrepreneurs, and its product becomes a commodity. The largest possible human interest which profit makers can have in workers is interest in their efficiency. As Alfred P. Sloan, Jr., chairman of General Motors, says, "Increased efficiency means lower costs, lower selling prices, and expanded production";[15] and, we may add, especially greater profits.

The capitalist system "has as a necessary presumption the rending of all society into two classes: the owners of the means of production, and the personal factors in production. Thus the existence of capitalism is the necessary preliminary condition of the proletariat.[16] Capitalism tends to objectify the productive capacity of both the capitalists and the workers. The human element in production, as we have seen, is divided essentially into two camps: that of "entrepreneurship" and that of labor, and the divergence in interests of these two positions increases as labor refuses to be freely manipulated in the interests of entrepreneurship.

On the surface it might seem that these two classes in modern society have been selected from a complex system of classes in order to gain a point. Certainly, one is likely to think, there are other possible groupings besides those of workers and capitalists. But here again one must distinguish carefully between functional classes and political classes.[17] There were many functional classes in western Europe in the middle of the eighteenth century, but only two significant political classes; the capitalists and the feudalists. Today the proletariat has become pivotal in the production system, but the latter functions mainly in the interest of the capitalists—and therein lies source of dissatisfaction. The professional groups in the system do not form a political class; they tend to unite themselves by birth or position to one or another of the two primary political classes. The functional classes constitute a part of the "public" of the two political classes.[. . .]

Causes of Proletarian Unrest

A very common approach to the study of modern class conflict is that, based on the assumption that since the masses are economically better off today than they ever were in history, class antagonism is mostly fictional. This approach inevitably leads to an argument centered about what has been called indelicately the "full-belly hypothesis" of socialism, and of course it can seldom attain the view that dissatisfaction with the social system itself may arise. The leaders of the proletariat look ahead to a better form of social organization, while the ruling class and its sympathizers tend to look backward and to compare instances of worse conditions of workers.[18] [. . .]

[. . .] We may state broadly that social misery of itself never breeds revolution; in fact, it is not improbable that the greater the misery of a social class the less the likelihood of its revolting. In Brahmanic India, for instance, we should expect that the outcastes will be the last to entertain revolutionary ideas. The serfs and slaves of feudalism never planned a revolution—a movement directed toward the institution of a new social system. "In reality," says Leon Trotsky with respect to proletarian revolutions, "the mere existence of privations is not enough to cause an insurrection; if it were, the masses would be always in revolt. It is necessary that the bankruptcy of the social regime, being conclusively revealed, should make these privations intolerable, and that new conditions and new ideas should open the prospect of a revolutionary way out. Then in the cause of the great aims conceived by them, those same masses will prove capable of enduring doubled and tripled privations."[19] Thus it is only when a class comes to feel that it has power to insist on superior rights that it thinks of revolt.[. . .]

The bourgeoisie who instigated and fought the capitalist revolutions were clearly not the most degraded and miserable part of the population; they were simply the most dissatisfied and the most powerful subordinate class. Their wails of misery, oppression, tyranny, and suffering were largely a function of their own inflated conception of themselves.[. . .]

In some measure it is not the misery of poverty but rather the misery of invidious comparison which renders the workers dissatisfied.[. . .]

A more tangible source of proletariat discontent, however, is the economic uncertainty of the profit system—its anarchy. Basically, the system has little regard for human beings as such; it is practical and mechanistic. So far as the proletariat is concerned, the system is interested in the productivity of its labor and not in its welfare. In capitalistic production labor is included in the same impersonal accounting as natural resources and capital, a fact which ordinarily brings home to the worker a fearful sense of being cut adrift in a sea of anonymity to eat and especially to be eaten as opportunity arises. Moreover, in the very nature of good business practice the profit maker cannot be satisifed.

Unemployment has become endemic in the capitalist system. Yet it is not so much the fact of unemployment as a recognition that unemployment is a function of the profit motive which has the potentiality of galling the worker. This is especially true in times of business-cycle troughs. The hard times of old, the famines, were recognized to be acts of God. Beyond a probable magical interpretation no one could be held blamable for them. But the great modern economic debacles, the business depressions, are recognized as inevitable consequences of capitalism. These cannot be prevented while private profit remains the supreme goal of the economic order.[. . .]

Thus there is a double cause for irritation among the workers. They suffer privation and degeneracy at a time when the markets are glutted with goods. A depression is the opposite of a famine. During a famine there are practically no goods, but during a depression there is a plethora of goods. It is the abundance of goods which jams the profit system and causes the entrepreneur to shut down his machinery and turn out the workers to starve.[. . .]

The system, of course, having been organized in the interest of profit makers, cannot be particularly concerned with the workers' plight. The workers must wait until the large stocks of goods work themselves down either by gradual consumption, decay, and waste, or by their purposeful destruction. Then and only then can the owners of the means of production again give the word to rehire labor and start producing. Thus the process of building up stocks to another glut is on its way. Under capitalism, the more economic goods we have, the greater the likelihood of a famine among the masses.

[. . .] One point of confusion to the worker is the inevitable definition which capitalism gives to his services—that of a commodity. "When once a labor market has been established, the ability of men to work is also turned into a commodity. For it is the distinguishing characteristic of a labor market that in it people's power to work is bought and sold by the hour, day, or week."[20] Paul M. Sweezy points out the likelihood of workers' misunderstanding freedom of the market for personal freedom: "The world of commodities appears as a world of equals. The labor power of the worker is alienated from the worker and stands opposed to him as any commodity to its owner."[21]

But the shortcomings of capitalism are only one aspect of the development of proletariat discontent. The other two are the proletariat's acquisition of increasing power and its increasing recognition that an economic order which admits of planning in the interest of the people is an immediate possibility. Capitalism abhors planning; to attempt to introduce it is to precipitate conflict.

Never before in history has a cultural situation developed wherein the burden of producing a social revolution devolves on the base of the population. In overthrowing feudalism, for instance, the bourgeoisie, a rival ruling class, fought for themselves in the name of the masses, but until capitalism created the opportunity the masses had never fought for themselves in their own interest.[22]

The current class struggle is an inherent attribute of capitalism,[23] and this makes it characteristically different from all previous class conflicts. In Brahmanic India the priests wrested power from the military class, but there is no necessary conflict between priests and warriors in society. Whenever a bourgeois people gain a foothold in a feudalistic or prefeudalistic society, there will be class conflict; yet feudalism of itself does not produce a bourgeois class. On the other hand, the proletariat is not only a potential or active political class; it is also an inevitable product of capitalism. Indeed, the capitalists and the proletariat are twin-born of the same economic matrix, capitalism; therefore, the challenging proletariat is not the offspring of a distinct change in the mode of production as was the case with the rise of the European "middle class."

To put it in other words, feudal systems do not evolve "naturally" into capitalism; feudalism contains no necessary internal social antagonisms; it may persist indefinitely without necessarily transforming itself into anything else. But capitalism, especially industrial capitalism, because of its inevitable dialectical development, its internal contradictions, is unstable and will sooner or later resolve itself into a more permanent system. The bourgeois class had a sort of exterior, parasitic growth which finally strangled feudalism, but the proletariat has developed within the very heart of capitalism, which it now threatens, at least in its ideological leadership, to slough off.

Moreover, the greater the advancement of capitalism, the

greater the relative potential power of the proletariat. Hence capitalist society nurtures the very political class that is necessarily devoted to the destruction of capitalism. This is the idea of social determinism in modern political-class conflict.

Fascism

There is considerable difference of opinion even among scholars concerning the characteristics of the fascists as the organization of a political class. Sometimes the conflict of views is purposely induced by the ruling class itself. Ordinarily, in the capitalist democracies, the people are made to believe that the fascists are a foreign tribe, while in the fascist countries the people are taught to believe that fascism is developed in the interest of the masses. At any rate, the first error to guard against appears to be that of thinking of fascists and potential fascists as unsocial, degenerate people—gangsters, indeed, the very opposite of this is nearer the truth.

Those persons in a capitalist society who finally organize in an active fascist party are mainly the most respectable and respected people. They are the undeniably 100-percent German, or English, or American, or Spanish citizens. The fascist party and its sympathizers would ordinarily include the majority of men who have achieved great business success, of politicians of upper chambers, professional men of the highest order, distinguished scholars, eminent bishops and cardinals, the most powerful newspaper owners and editors, learned judges, the valiant upper crust of the military forces, and so on.[24] And this is quite natural since fascism is a rightist, conservative, capitalist reaction. The fascists constitute essentially the cream of a capitalist society. Adolf Hitler,[25] the great leader and spokesman of the fascists in all capitalist countries, expressed their conviction: "A view of life which, by rejecting the democratic mass idea, endeavors to give the world to the best people . . . to the most superior men, has logically to obey the same aristocratic principle also within this people."[26] Therefore, to locate this group that is now attempting to stabilize its inheritance of the earth we must look about the pinnacle of capitalism.

The fascists are the capitalists and their sympathizers who have achieved political-class consciousness; they have become organized for action against the proletariat, and especially for defense against the normal disintegration of the capitalist system. They despise the masses, conceding them neither capacity to think nor to develop their own leadership.[. . .]

Fascism is outspokenly antidemocratic; its reactionary nature makes this inevitable. Although capitalist democracy never meant that the masses should run the government, the idea of political democracy itself increasingly opened the way for some obstruction to the dominant purpose of the capitalists. Business may endure political democracy but not economic democracy. Robert S. Lynd has this to say on the point:

> Liberal democracy has never dared face the fact that industrial capitalism is an intensely coercive form of organization of society that cumulatively constrains men and all of their institutions to work the will of the minority who hold and wield economic power; and that this relentless warping of men's lives and forms of association becomes less and less the result of voluntary decisions by "bad" or "good" men and more and more an impersonal web of coercions dictated by the need to keep "the system" running.[27]

The purpose of capitalist democracy is to provide a favorable situation for the exercise of free enterprise and not for the planning of a society that will make business a social service. If the commonality attempts to take the latter view of democracy and to implement it, the capitalist will quickly scrap the institution.[. . .]

It should be [also] emphasized that the distinguishing fact about fascist governments is not that they are dictatorships. There is a popular belief, sometimes purposedly indoctrinated, that all dictatorships subsume an identity of economic organization.[28] Nothing, however, is further from the truth. When a people is at war, a degree of dictatorship becomes imperative, and the greater the intensity of the conflict, the more complete the dictatorship is likely to become. "Fighting groups cannot be tolerant, nor can they harbor cynics."[29] Hence the presence of a dictatorship does not necessarily indicate the form of social organization. The proletarian government of Russia, for instance, is a dictatorship; all fascist governments are also dictatorships, but these two types of economic organization lie at opposite extremes of modern social systems.

Furthermore, they differ even in the durability of their dictatorships. The proletarian dictatorship has no basis for continuance after capitalist aggression, especially from without, has ceased; but since the fascist dictatorship can never expect a cessation of either internal or external aggression, it must endure. The social condition which produced fascism is not removed by fascism itself. Fascism is born of and perpetuated by irreducible conflict; hence its dictatorship must be permanent. It is an attempt to halt and to turn back a democratic trend.[. . .]

The Ways of Fascism

The fascists [. . .] cannot themselves fight their counterrevolution; they must have even the masses, their potential antagonists, to support them.[. . .]

It is this high-powered appeal to the masses [. . .] which brings about confusion in some and conviction in others. Indeed the people may be consciously prepared for the fascist counterrevolution. Thus Lynd points out: "Organized business is extending this anti-democratic web of power in the name of the people's own values, with billboards proclaiming 'What's Good for Industry Is Good for Your Family,' and deftly selling itself to a harassed people as 'trustees,' 'guardians,' 'the people's managers' of public interest."[30]

In any fascist movement emphasis on race superiority and racial antagonism or intolerance helps to confuse the masses and to develop a degree of racial egocentrism. As an example of this technique, consider Hitler's artistry in the following: "In Russian bolshevism we must see Jewry's twentieth-century effort to take world domination to itself."[31]

Fascism and the established religion, or rather the modern church, are on the whole closely associated, and naturally so. The church as a whole, as we have seen, is always reactionary; it upholds and stabilizes the social norms and values of the status quo, hence its natural sympathy must be with the counterrevolutionary class. In their revolutions the capitalists had to reckon with the church, and today, in like manner, the church confronts the proletariat.[. . .]

Indeed the function of the church as a prime deflator of social movements has been repeatedly recognized. After the Napoleonic revolutions in Europe the reactionary nobility entrenched themselves with the support of a reinvigorated Catholic Church. Professor Geoffrey Bruun, in describing the backwash of a later upsurge of liberalism and democracy, asserts: "The propertied classes had . . . been so gravely alarmed by the socialist and communist menace in 1848 and 1849 that they cast about for measures to combat it, and in several states (France, Austria, Prussia) the government and the middle class repented the curbs which they had imposed upon the Roman Catholic Church and welcomed it again as a useful ally in combating socialist heresies."[32] It should also be recalled that the "infallible" leadership of the Catholic Church has consistently defined practically every revolutionary development in science or social ideology as a direct attack upon its vested interests.

The involvement of the fifteenth-century astronomers with the selfish policies of the church was no less serious than that of the nineteenth-century biologists and paleontologists.

However, the church has now been accommodated to capitalism; hence it is, as we should expect, up in arms on its own initiative against any threat to the status quo. In an editorial in the English *Catholic Times,* the duty of the Catholic Church is thus clarified: "Our mission of salvation to Europe is to establish a united anti-communist Front. We must restore friendly relations with Italy and Germany, even at a great sacrifice, and then induce France, which will not be difficult, to fall into line with us on grounds of political safety."[33]

Probably no sect of the Christian religion is so thoroughly opposed to the proletarian movement as the Roman Catholics. The established authority of tradition in the Catholic Church makes it fundamentally antipathetic to social change. "The papal court," says Briffault, "viewed England in Elizabethan days in much the same manner as it views Bolshevik Russia today."[34] The Roman Catholic Church has never wholly given up its medievalism, and proletarianism is even further removed from its hierarchical formalism than capitalism. Moreover, it has been well recognized that "the Roman Catholic Church is the richest single land and property-owning 'corporation' in Europe. Its policies were and are always in defense of its metaphysical and physical property."[35]

Recently the pope reached a rather complete accord with the aims and methods of fascism. The papacy evidently lent financial support to the fascist venture in Abyssinia, and "in the Spanish Civil War it allied itself openly with Il Duce." Says Robert A. Brady in his revealing study of the development of solidarity between the Roman Catholic Church and fascism: "In the Lateran Accord of 1929 Fascism adopted the papacy on condition that the papacy concede popular allegiance to the objectives of Fascism and the State and Empire in which those objectives were embodied."[36]

[. . .] It may be pointed out again that religion in a capitalist society must be revolutionized if the economic order is to be revolutionized. The religion of capitalism is not the religion of feudalism. Capitalism could not reach maturity before medieval Catholicism had been revamped and brought into working consistency with the ends of capitalism; therefore, modern institutionalized religion is to a very large extent bourgeois-made. Indeed, Max Weber even thinks that the Protestant religion embodies the vital spirit of capitalism, the essence which made capitalism possible, so that the distinguishing social fact of bourgeois society is its characteristic religious ethics. A radical capitalist revolution, then, must inevitably involve a radical reformation of its religious basis. Proletarian society can be built only upon a fundamentally different system of ethics—that is to say, proletarian ethics. Thus, as antiproletarian reaction sets in, we should expect the ruling class in both England and the United States especially to develop an increasingly intimate diplomatic and propagandistic affiliation with the Vatican, the time-honored hotbed of worldwide reaction.[37]

Another significant feature of fascism is nationalism. Nationalism is essential to fascism because mature capitalism is not only concerned with internal political-class struggle but also with international struggle for world markets. Again Brady is in point; says he: "If we can draw any certain lesson from events in the recent past it is surely this, that organized business in one national system will show no mercy to organized business in another national system, once conflicts of interest have forced matters to the arbitrament of war."[38]

Extreme nationalism makes it possible for the capitalist state to muster its full strength in international conflict.[. . .] But nationalism breeds counternationalism; hence fascism merely clears the way for unending struggle "between mighty antagonists each of whom can enlist the power of whole states." Sweezy puts it thus: "Capitalism, by its very nature, cannot settle down but must keep expanding, and since the various sectors of the world capitalist economy expand at different rates, it follows that the balance of forces is bound to upset in such a way that one or more countries will find it both possible and advantageous to challenge the *status quo* with respect to territorial boundaries."[39]

No one can give a meaningful interpretation to certain paradoxes in World War II without understanding the internal and external conflict necessity of capitalism. Insofar as the aim of the fascists is the destruction of the proletarian movement, they are the allies of the ruling class in all the capitalist countries; but insofar as their aim is the redivision of world markets and territories, they face head-on collision and war with the capitalists of other states. Thus the basis of many of the seeming inconsistencies in the politics of World War II lies in the fact that the capitalist alliance was interested in destroying the fascists as competitors for world markets and natural resources but in saving them as bulwarks against the proletariat.[40]

Although it has been frequently asserted by such authorities as the former secretary of state of the United States, the Honorable Cordell Hull, that the purpose of World War II was to destroy fascism wherever it was found, the fact remains that fascism cannot be destroyed by war between capitalist nations. Since a fascist state is a capitalist state in a certain stage of degeneration, the most that brother capitalist nations can hope to accomplish for a defeated fascist nation is the artificial setting up of a "capitalist democracy" which, if left to itself, will move rapidly back to its former position. Fascism, as a political-class phenomenon, can apparently be liquidated only by intranational action, revolutionary action, of the opposite political class. However, an international imperialist war may so weaken the military power of a fascist government as to present the opportunity for its overthrow. But since capitalism itself is an international system, any attempt by the common people to liquidate fascism in favor of economic democracy will tend to arouse the violent reactions of the great capitalist nations. It is the latter situation which, after the fall of Adolf Hitler, produced Winston Churchill as the outstanding champion of fascist governments all over Europe.[41]

Nature of the Revolution

[. . .] It appears that capitalism cannot be transformed into socialism by means of the institutions and values of capitalism; the socialist state may arise only upon the ashes of these institutions. The proletariat cannot vote for socialism in a bourgeois parliament because the capitalists will not permit themselves to be destroyed by their own instrument. The machinery of the capitalist state has been fashioned by the bourgeoisie to suit the needs of their class; therefore, in the achievement of its ends, the working class must contrive its own institutions. Indeed, even though it were possible to take over the capitalist state ready-made, this state organization will not be adapted to the new proletarian society.

As we have already intimated, socialism cannot be instituted on the system of ethics developed by capitalism; consequently, a labor party seeking to gain the power must be prepared to ignore bourgeois concepts of right and wrong and to *force* the bourgeoisie to accept a new system of ethics as a mandate of the people. We may illustrate this: Suppose a labor government decides to "socialize" industry—that is, the means of production—by a "just and fair compensation" to the private owners of them—a sort of extension of the idea of eminent domain; very little may probably be thereby accomplished. In fact, such a procedure may be not only highly uneconomical but also disastrous to the government itself.

In the first place, it must at least tacitly accept capitalism, and there is no reason to believe that a labor government will be a better capitalist entrepreneur than the bought-out businessmen: the likelihood is that it will be worse. Then, too, it will not make sense to have the people pay for the industries of their country. They clearly could not do so completely. We need no Keynesian equation to show that if the government taxes the people to pay gradually for the industries, businessmen will first seek other industries at home for their investments; and, when opportunity for home investments becomes scarce, they will export their capital, thus leaving the country and the people heavily obligated to foreigners. The great capitalists may even follow their investments, since the home country will continue to become less and less favorable to "free enterprise."[42]

Socialism, it seems, begins with the conviction that capitalism is presently wrong; it begins with the realization that between itself and capitalism two mortally incompatible systems of ethics are involved. The capitalists believe that, in accordance with their sacred principle of freedom of contract, they have the right to exploit human beings in their own private interest. On the contrary, the socialists believe that production and the income of industry belong to the workers, to be disposed of by them in the interest of their own welfare. These two views are unalterably opposed; they involve two distinct forms of social organization.

Therefore, the function of a labor party which is in "control of the government" would seem to be (a) to get control of the military power by making sure that it is in the hands of convinced socialist officers, and (b) to dispossess without compensation the bourgeois masters of industry. This will clearly be justice in a democracy, for in a democracy the great mass of people must inevitably believe that none of their members should have the private right of control over the livelihood of others. In this situation, moreover, the very act of capitalist exploitation naturally becomes criminal. The leaders of the workers, then, are concerned with educating the workers to the point where they come to realize the nature of the opposition which confronts them and the probable human cost of reducing it.[. . .]

The Struggle in the United States

The explanation usually suggested for the quietude of the workers in the United States is that their solidarity is constantly disrupted by the relatively easy movement of individuals into upper social classes.[. . .]

[. . .] Does this mean that there is a concomitant increase in social mobility? Does it mean that opportunities for workers to become capitalists are increasing? Evidently not.[43]

The principal reason for the weak proletarian movement in the United States seems to lie in the strategy of a small but powerful group of workers themselves. Before the achievement of dominance of business unionism in American labor, the workers were repeatedly coming into conflict with the ruling class. Their natural condition of struggle was everywhere evident. In commenting upon the temper of organized workers in this period, Selig Perlman writes:

> The movement bore in every way the aspect of a social war. A frenzied hatred of labor for capital was shown in every important strike. . . . Extreme bitterness towards capital manifested itself in all the actions of the Knights of Labor, and wherever the leaders undertook to hold it within bounds they were generally discarded by their followers, and others who would lead as directed were placed in charge. The feeling of "give no quarter" is illustrated in the refusal to submit grievances to arbitration when the employees felt that they had the upper hand over their employers. . . . No warning from a leader, however high, was capable of restraining the combative rank and file.[44]

In a similar vein, Corey sums up the militancy of the labor movement of the period:

> The great strikes of 1877 assumed the character of mass insurrections, and were followed by strikes of an equally militant character, culminating in the 8-hour strikes of 1886 and ending with the great Pullman strike of 1894 (the Debs Rebellion). The militancy of American labor in this stage is indisputable, comparable with the militance of any labor movement anywhere.[45]

[. . .] Gradually, however, labor was to be tamed by some of its old leaders into a highly individualistic form of organization. The great revolutionary labor struggles of the last quarter of the nineteenth century tended to degenerate into the sporadic, individualistic racketeering and petty violence of interbusiness rivalry. In 1886 the American Federation of Labor defeated a true workers' organization, the Knights of Labor, in a jurisdictional strife and began a policy which clearly bears a greater share of the responsibility for the peaceful exploitation of the masses of workers than the activities of the employers themselves. This policy has also been adopted by the great railroad brotherhoods, and its apparent success has been a source of envy among unorganized workers.

We call the Knights of Labor a true workers' organization because it was interested in all workers. Business unionism is not interested in all workers, but only in those whose organization pays. The guiding principle of Samuel Gompers, who held the presidency of the [American Federation of Labor] AFL and its parent organization almost continuously from 1882 to 1924, centered about the watchword: "If it doesn't square with your due book, have none of it."[46]

The AFL organizes those workers in positions of greatest strategy in the labor market, the skilled workers, the so-called labor aristocrats. Its federated nationals charge high dues, pay good benefits, and depend for their strength on the consciousness of a brotherhood of skill and of mutual if exclusive interests. They act as a monopoly of labor to the degree that it is possible.[47]

At this point we should mention that the unorganized worker is practically helpless as a bargaining or political force. Outside of a labor union he could hardly become conscious of his proletarian interests; therefore, other things being equal, the smaller the organization of the workers, the less the likelihood of radicalism among the proletariat. The business unionism of the AFL cannot and does not have an interest in the organization of all workers; on the other hand, an organizing policy which includes and has for its end the incorporation of the great mass of workers must inevitably be radical.

Every indiscriminate organization of workers will be revolutionary. Conservative unionism is the inevitable result of discrimination among workers on the basis of their capacity for organization cooperatively with business. But the great mass of unskilled and semiskilled proletariat cannot be thus organized, for it is upon the opportunity for coincident exploitation of this mass by the selected workers that the conservatism of the latter mainly depends.

[. . .] Labor leaders, who do not understand the ultimate antagonism between the working class and the bourgeoisie, are always frightened by the extremes to which worker-conscious unions go when they clash with the employers. These leaders ordinarily mistake immediate demands for higher wages and better conditions of work for the real destiny of the working class. At any rate, it took years of selection of workers and ruthless suppression by rank-and-file organization by capitalistically minded labor leaders before conservative unionism came to characterize the American labor scene.

The remarkable fact of the role assumed by the AFL is not that it does not organize the masses of workers but that it stands directly in opposition to the organization of these workers. The AFL stands as an impregnable barrier, a formidable wall of ice, against the development of a working-class consciousness in the United States. Though its membership ordinarily amounts to only about one-tenth or less of the organizable workers, it always speaks in the name of the underprivileged masses in its own interest. It collaborates whenever possible with employers, because, to put it in Gompers's rationalization: "I knew that the cause of labor was so just and our methods *so practical* that a hearing before employers must necessarily result in better relations."[48]

This, of course, is business diplomacy adopted by a privileged clique of workers. As a business they pit themselves against other businesses, and their greatest enemy is not infrequently the out-group workers, organized or unorganized, which they conceive to be their immediate competitors. What they are really asking for is a share of the lucre, which, when obtained by a "hearing," ordinarily means collaboration in the further exploitation of the mass of unorganized workers—a secondary exploitation of weak workers by the leadership of workers in strategic positions. This trait of business unionism may justly be called labor cannibalism.[. . .]

The most effective and consistent method used by the AFL to keep the masses of workers unorganized and docilely exploitable is the refusal to organize the strong with the weak workers. The insistence on picking out the skilled workers in an industry and disregarding all others has destroyed many opportunities for wider labor organization. On this score Gompers states in smooth diplomatic language: "The Federation having no power of compulsion, could not enforce practices contrary to the wishes or rules of affiliated unions. The Federation does not instruct unions as to the structure of their organization. Unions may select the industrial form if they so desire.[49]

As an illustration of what this means, when in 1935 the auto workers offered themselves to the AFL as an industrial union, the "affiliated unions," assembled in convention, rejected them. "The auto workers could not vote for what they wanted; the votes were in the hands of the national crafts. The cards were stacked in advance."[50] As practical business people, the crafts wanted to siphon off the skilled workers at a "hearing" with the employers and to leave the masses totally unprotected and helplessly exploitable. It would then be perfectly good business practice of the few organized skilled workers to have their wage increase offset by a reduction in the wages of the unorganized masses.

[. . . Additionally,] nothing shows up the character of business unionism so well as the history of the AFL's struggle with the CIO [Congress of Industrial Organizations]. The eight international unions which separated from the AFL constituted the original CIO and organized a number of major industries. One would think that the AFL, having this great job of organization finished, would consider it a windfall to give charters to the great new unions. Not so, however. The condition of accepting these workers into the federation is that they allow their unions to be raided and shattered by the international craft unions according as the latter's business profits indicate.

The AFL and other business unions, therefore, have been a real barrier to the formation of a true proletarian movement in the United States. Their methods of struggle with the worker's movement have been exactly that of the businessman.[. . .]

The State and the Class Struggle

Probably one of the most difficult aspects of socialist thought to digest, even among socialists themselves, has been the idea of the vanishing proletariat state,[51] and yet it is based upon a simple truism. By definition, according to the socialists, the state is an instrument of class exploitation. If, in a proletarian society, there will be no political classes, then there will necessarily be no state. In commenting upon the taking over of power by the proletariat, Engels says:

> As soon as there is no longer any social class to be held in subjection, as soon as class rule . . . [is] removed, nothing more remains to be repressed, and a special repressive force, a State, is no longer necessary. The first act by virtue of which the State really constitutes itself the representative of the whole of society—the taking possession of the means of production in the name of society—this is, at the same time, its last independent act as a State. State interference in *social relations* (relations between classes) becomes in one domain after another, superfluous, and then *dies out of itself;* the government of persons is replaced by the administration of things, and by the conduct of processes of production. The State is not "abolished." It withers away.[52]

This is the central idea of the vanishing socialist state. It is clear that the socialists intend to do nothing to "abolish" the state. Their preoccupation is with the abolishment of political classes; this end achieved, the state merely atrophies from disuse. "The proletariat seizes political power and turns the means of production into state property. But, in doing this, it abolishes itself as proletariat."[53] Herein lies the crucial difference between the design of the anarchists and that of the socialists. The anarchists see the state, rather than the social forces which produce the state, as their primary concern.

The anarchists have no clear idea as to what the proletariat will put in place of the state, nor how it will use its revolutionary power.[54] This is utopianism. The socialists, however, do not seek to destroy the state directly. Their end, to repeat, is the liquidation of the exploiting capitalist class and consequently of all political classes. They insist on using the machinery of a state to accomplish this. Having eliminated the exploiters from within and from without, the state naturally becomes obsolete. It should be observed that, of the known types of advanced societies, only a socialist system can hope to achieve statelessness.

The socialists do not confuse the idea of a state as a power organization serving the exploitative purpose of a ruling class with administrative institutions devoted only to the accomplishment of increasing well-being among the whole people. Indeed, Engels's statement, "The government of persons is replaced by the administration of things," may be paraphrased: The exploitation of persons is replaced by the exploitation of things.

Moreover, it is likely that, with a hasty consideration of the idea of the vanishing socialist state, one may think of the socialist community as being finally in chaos. However, planning and social control are particularly the business of the proletariat. Clearly, a stateless society need not be a planless society. Whereas in the capitalist society the social scientist is likely to be looked on with suspicion, in the socialist society his function will be most desirable. In the latter system the unlimited application of science to the problem of human welfare will not constantly run afoul of the businessman's profits.[. . .]

Views of the Social Movement

Finally, a word should be said about certain popular views of the social movement. A common practice of capitalist economists is to criticize mercilessly some one or a number of points in Karl Marx's theory of value, price, and distribution. Having ripped through the Marxian conclusion, they dust off their hands and retire in the assurance that they have disposed of the social movement. This performance may be likened to that of a socialist economist who successfully refutes some arguments of David Ricardo's and on that ground concludes that capitalism has only a mythical existence.

Marx's writings have value only insofar as they help as to understand the actualities of the social movement; detailed negative criticism of them does not appear to have value per se.[55] As Edward Heimann puts it:

> What [Marx] did was to study the newly formed proletarian men to comprehend their blind instincts, and to express them in a coherent objective program of society that the workers could recognize for themselves. . . . He revealed to them the goal to be attained at the end of the road along which they were being driven by the inner necessity of their communal work; he showed them the meaning of their existence.[56]

Another rather vulgar view of the movement is that evinced in the argument that "the personal expenditures of the rich amount to very little, and [that] if their 'wealth' and incomes were evenly distributed, this would materially affect only the large body of incapables, derelicts, and mentally deficient survivals of neolithic population out of which modern civilization has arisen."[57] Some intelligent social scientists have actually computed the number of dollars each person in the United States would receive if the wealth of the rich were divided among them and, finding this amount to be only a small sum, come to the conclusion that socialism is a fallacy. Of course this is ridiculous, for it must be clear that the new social order contemplated by the proletariat—by democracy—does not mean a mere sharing of dollars while still retaining capitalism. "The distinguishing fact," says John Strachey, "is that in a communist society no incomes shall be derived by virtue of the possession of the instruments of production."[58] Moreover, production by use of large quantities of capital goods is a primary motive of socialism; that is to say, capitalistic production without capitalism.

"The distinguishing feature of Communism is not the abolition of property generally, but the abolition of bourgeois property." Any view of socialism that does not assume a logical social order developing out of a senescent capitalism is utopian. Such vacuous statements as "There will be no family under socialism," or "God will be abolished under socialism" or "Socialism means dictatorship" are typical of utopian thinking. We can know what will necessarily characterize a socialist society only by reasoning within the frame of reference of a capitalistic economic order without capitalists, an order determined by and devoted to the welfare of the whole people. The detailed features of such a system will depend on the dgree of resistance of capitalists during the period of "transvaluation of values" and the social history peculiar to the people.

A variant of what may be called the share-the-wealth view of socialism is the argument that, with the rise of the modern corporation, so large a number of persons have come to own shares of stock that it may be said profits have become socialized. To the great majority of small stockholders however, dividends are of the nature of interest; these small stockholders have none of the functions of entrepreneurship. Here, too, the significance of capitalism as a social system based upon a peculiar method of production is reduced to the simple idea of distribution of profits. The question of class conflict inherent in the system is translated into a question of status relationship between the rich and the poor. It is assumed that the only aim of the proletariat is to have more money regardless of the system in which it is produced. Suppose, for instance, the activities of gangsters were to be judged antisocial; would their decision to share their income among certain interest groups be sufficient to liquidate the source of antagonism against them? The difficulty with capitalism inheres not so much in the way profits are distributed as in the social pathology developing out of the system of profit making per se.[. . .]

Notes

1. J. F. Brown, *Psychology and the Social Order* (New York, 1936), p. 169.
2. Cf. *In Fact*, October 29, 1945, where the whole issue is given over to the review "U.S. College Professors in the Service of Fascism."

    "It is often profitable," says Professor E. B. Reuter, "in terms of salary and security of tenure and academic honors and advancement, to defend exploitation and human exploiters and to justify class as well as racial discrimination and abuse. And in doing so, one has nothing to lose, except his self-respect and the respect of decent men" ("Southern Scholars and Race Relations," *Phylon* VII [1946]: 234). And yet this is not quite so, for the scholar who challenges the exploitative system may lose not only his position but also the "the respect of decent men."
3. Quoted in Robert A. Brady, *Business as a System of Power* (New York, 1943), p. xvi. For a discussion of the ways of the ruling class in

America with social scientists who go against the grain of the status quo see Ferdinand Lundberg, *America's 60 Families* (New York, 1937), pp. 388ff. Says Lundberg: "While the University presidents may meddle in public affairs to their trustees' content, and while the professors may also do likewise provided only that they support the *status quo*, especially in its more evil phases, it goes hard . . . with any faculty member who espouses an unorthdox point of view. . . . The instructors in the social sciences are taught circumspection by the mishaps of outspoken colleagues. Those who remain often become, to all intents and purposes, social as well as academic eunuchs" (pp. 393–94).

4. In Brady, *Business as a System of Power*, p. 225. Pope Pius XI, in his plan for reconstruction of the social order, wrote in 1931: "Society today still remains in a strained and therefore unstable and uncertain state, being founded on classes with contradictory interests and hence opposed to each other, and consequently prone to enmity and strife. . . . The demand and supply of labor divides men on the labor market into two classes, as into two camps, and the bargaining between these parties transforms the labor market into an arena where the two armies are engaged in combat. . . . It is patent that in our days not alone is wealth accumulated, but immense power and despotic economic domination are concentrated in the hands of a few, and that those few are frequently found not [to be] the owners, but only the trustees and directors, of invested funds, who administer them at their good pleasure. . . . Free competition is dead, economic dictatorship has taken its place . . . the whole economic life has become hard, cruel and restless in a ghastly measure" ("Quadragesimo Anno—Encyclical Letter of His Holiness Pius XI," quoted in Walter C. Langsam, *Documents and Readings in the History of Europe since 1918* [Philadelphia, 1939], pp. 567–72).

5. Even when young Americans are called upon to give their lives for a cause that fundamentally involves the class struggle, they must ordinarily do so without understanding its nature. Roy A. Grinker and John P. Spiegel, psychiatrists of considerable experience with the Army Air Forces, observe: "The average soldier is not well informed as to the final causes for the War or its ultimate necessity. . . . When the combat soldier overseas is asked what he is fighting for, the usual answer is short and pointed: 'So I can go home!'" (*Men under Stress* [Philadelphia, 1945], p. 181).

6. Werner Sombart, *Socialism and the Social Movement in the 19th Century*, trans. Anson P. Atterbury (New York, 1898), p. 5.

7. Ibid., pp. 169–70.

8. Thus he writes: "Whenever universal suffrage has been established, the majority of the community unquestionably exercises the legislative authority; and if it be proved that the poor always constitute a majority, it may be added with perfect truth, that in the countries in which they possess the elective franchise, they possess the sole power of making laws. But it is certain that in all the nations of the world the

greater number has always consisted of those persons who hold no property, or of those whose property is insufficient to exempt them from the necessity of working. . . . Universal suffrage does therefore in point of fact invest the poor with the government of society" (Alexis de Tocqueville, *Democracy in America* [3d ed., London, 1838], vol. II, p. 23). It is the same kind of conclusion that Aristotle draws for another democratic situation: "In a democracy the poor ought to have more power than the rich, as being the greater number" (*Politics,* trans William Ellis, p. 185).

9. For a most convincing study of the determining role of big businessmen in the government and political life of the United States, see Lundberg, *America's 60 Families.*

10. Thurman W. Arnold, *The Folklore of Capitalism* (New Haven, 1937), p. 38.

11. Speaking of the growth of classes in urban centers of the fifteenth century, Prosper Boissonnade concludes: "At the top appeared a growing minority of bourgeois capitalists; in the middle developed the small or medium bourgeoisie of masters, who formed the free crafts and corporations; below were the workmen, who were slowly becoming separated from the class of small masters; and at the bottom of all came the hired wage-earners of the great industry, reinforced by casual elements, who formed the new urban proletariat" (Boissonade, *Life and Work in Medieval Cities* [London, 1927], p. 299).

12. John Strachey, *Socialism Looks Forward* (New York, 1945), p. 26. Strachey continues: "The members of the middle class, having destroyed the feudal monopolists, became themselves of the exclusive owners of the means of production: they became, in fact, the capitalist class as we know it today" (p. 49).

Sombart dilates upon this point: "Those historic occurrences in which the proletariat played a role, although they were not proletarian movements, are the well-known revolutions which we connect with the years 1789, 1793, 1839, 1832, 1842. . . . We have here movements which are essentially middle-class. In them political liberties are sought, and, so far as the proletarian elements are concerned, the masses fight the battles of the middle classes, like the common soldiers who fought in feudal armies. . . . The revolution of 1789 was purely a middle-class movement, and indeed carried on by the higher part of the middle class. It was a struggle of the upper middle class for the recognition of its rights, and for relief from the privileges of the ruling class of society—from the fetters in which it had been held by feudal powers. It expressed this struggle in demands for equality and freedom, but it really meant from the very start a limited equality and freedom" (Sombart, *Socialism,* pp. 38–39).

Henri Pirenne is also explicit on this point. "Everywhere," he writes, "it was the merchants who took the initiative and directed events. . . . They were the most active, the richest, the most influential element in the city population and they endured with so much the more impatience a situation which clashed with their interest and belittled their confidence in themselves. The role they then played . . . may fittingly be compared with that which the capitalistic middle class assumed after the end of the eighteenth century in the political revolution which put an end to the old order of things. In the one case as in the other, the social group which was the most directly interested in the change assumed the leadership of the opposition, and was followed by the masses. Democracy in the middle ages, as in modern times, got its start under the guidance of a select few who foisted their program upon the confused aspirations of the people" (*Medieval Cities*, trans. Frank D. Halsey [Princeton, 1925], p. 178).

13. For a good discussion of this, see Brady, *Business as a System of Power*. We should guard against the illusion in which advocates of the status quo frequently become involved. In illustration, William Graham Sumner declares: "Modern society is ruled by the middle class. In honor of the bourgeoisie it must be said that they . . . have not . . . made a state for themselves alone or chiefly, and their state is the only one in which no class has had to fear oppressive use of political power" (*Folkways* [Boston, 1906], p. 169). Clearly, Sumner confuses the medieval idea of the bourgeoisie as a middle class in feudal society with the concept of the bourgeoisie as a ruling class in bourgeois society. Furthermore, the illusion of the social effects of overwhelming power has evidently blinded him to the means by which the bourgeoisie rule.

14. Of course, the greater the advancement of democracy, the less will the system operate exclusively in the interest of the ruling capitalist class.

15. Alfred P. Sloan, Jr., "Post-War Jobs," an address at the opening Fall Session of the Economic Club of Detroit, October 11, 1943.

16. Werner Sombart, *The Quintessence of Capitalism*, trans. M. Epstein (New York, 1915), p. 9. On this point also Strachey says: "The very idea that it might be impossible to establish industry and commerce, not because of any technical reasons, but because no workers would respond to the offers of wages, does not occur to people. . . . Two essential conditions had to be secured before any such class of people, both able and ready to sell their power to labor, can exist. In the first place, all forms of slavery, serfdom, peonage, and villeinage must be abolished. For if the mass of the population belongs to certain overlords and landlords as their exclusive private property, it is no use for the enterprising entrepreneur to offer them wages in order to induce them to come and work for him. . . . Such condition of legal dependence must therefore be broken down. The establishment of the labor market . . . requires not only that the workers should be free—that they should not be possessed by any overlord or master—but also that they should neither possess nor have free access to the means of production. In other words, when the middle class freed the workers from the landlords they had to, and did, take very good care to free them from the land as well" (*Quintessence of Capitalism*, pp. 40–41). See

also Charles Gide, *Principles of Political Economy*, trans. Edward P. Jacobsen (Boston and New York, 1913), p. 146.

In discussing the ways of the capitalists as they operate today on the outer rim of Western society, Professor Mary E. Townsend says: "Most of the colonial powers have ruthlessly deprived the native of his land, and then, ironically enough, forced him to work upon it by making it impossible for him to live otherwise" (*European Colonial Expansion since 1871* [Philadelphia, 1941], p. 194).

17. Alfred M. Bingham evinces some misunderstanding of the nature of political classes. He says: "There are in fact many class struggles, for there are many classes. One may define classes arbitrarily as one will. One may classify as to sex, nationality, occupation, intelligence, or attitude. If, as the Marxists do, one chooses to classify as to general, economic status in relation to means of production—that is, workers and owners—one must accept the limitations of such a classification. It is rough, vague, and bears no necessary relation to mental attitudes or political effectiveness. There may, under certain conditions, be as bitter conflict between groups of capitalists, over world markets, for instance, or between groups of workers . . . as ever between employers and workers" (*Insurgent America* [New York and London, 1935], p. 16). To Bingham, apparently, a political class is one item of a promiscuous social classification.

18. See a recent propagandistic work taking this position: Carl Snyder, *Capitalism the Creator* (New York, 1940), p. 11.

19. Trotsky, *History of the Russian Revolution* (New York, 1922), vol. II, p. xi. It may not be inaccurate to assert that most of the desperate effort of Great Britain and the United States especially to "feed the hungry" in post-World War Europe is prompted not by merciful charity but rather by the frightful consciousness that the people, left to themselves, may rise, overthrow the capitalist ruling class, and establish a welfare economy. It is in this sense that American food has been used as a counterrevolutionary weapon. It is not so much the "feeding of the hungry millions" as it is a strategy of food distribution that serves the political purpose. For an indication of this as practiced after World War I, see Sayers and Kahn, *The Great Conspiracy* (Boston, 1946), pp. 86–87.

20. Strachey, *Socialism Looks Forward*, p. 39.

21. Paul M. Sweezy, *The Theory of Capitalist Development* (New York, 1942), p. 39. For a broad discussion of similar sources of discontent, see Erich Fromm, *Escape from Freedom* (New York, 1941), pp. 123–35.

22. See Boissonnade, *Life and Work in Medieval Cities* pp. 299–315, for a review of early proletarian unrest. A slave uprising, of course, should not be thought of as a revolutionary struggle.

23. On this point what N. S. B. Gras has to say seems to be pertinent: "So long as the handicraftsman was free to sell to any merchant, and so long as he was the owner of his raw materials and tools and com-

manded a profit (rather than a wage) from his enterprise, little could be said against the new system. But when in the early modern period industrial entrepreneurs arose who reduced the handicraftman to economic dependence, the new system stood condemned first by the sufferers and later by the general public. For industry, the change from retail to wholesale handicraft meant specialization in function, the separation of industrial from commercial capital, a larger supply of goods, and greater skill. It also was the beginning of the subordination of the workers and their exploitation. Revolts and civil turmoil in the larger industrial towns of the Middle Ages were signs of the slowly developing system of wholesale handicraft" ("The Economic Activity of Towns," in *The Legacy of the Middle Ages,* ed. C. G. Crump and E. F. Jacob, p. 438).

24. Robert A. Brady lists the following as the principal groups constituting the European fascists: "The die-hard landed aristocracy; the industrial, commercial, and financial barony; the old privileged and caste-like military hierarchy; the professional and imperial-minded upper reaches of the civil service bureaucracy, and the ruling cliques of the fanatical and cynical party demagoguery which has been ambidextrous enough to conjure—out of the witness frustrations of the still leaderless unemployed and growing ranks of the declassed rural and urban lumpenbourgeoisie a mass following." See his book review in *Science and Society* 7, no. 2 (Spring 1943): 175. See also George Seldes, *Facts and Fascism* (New York, 1943).

In the modern class struggle, as we have alluded to in a previous section, the fascists always seek the allegiance of the "middle class." This is the "public" for whose well-being the capitalists always seem to have an inordinate solicitude. In *The New Party Politics* (New York, 1933), A. N. Holcombe develops the thesis that the bourgeoisie can stabilize their position by winning and maintaining the good will of these adjuvant functionaries of capitalism. In practice fascism has been able to appeal with considerable success to the "middle class."

25. For a discussion of the use of demagogues by the ruling class, see Daniel Guerin, *Fascism and Big Business* (New York, 1939), chap. VI, "The Rise and Fall of the Fascist Plebeians."

26. Adolph Hitler, *Mein Kampf* (New York, 1940), p. 661.

27. In *Business as a System of Power,* p. xii.

28. This kind of thinking recurs in similar social situations. On February 9, 1790, Charles J. Fox, in an attempt to clear himself from a charge by Edmund Burke of sympathy with the French Revolution, declared before the British House of Commons that what he had said should not be taken to mean that he was a friend of democracy. "He declared himself equally the enemy of all absolute forms of government, whether an absolute monarchy, an absolute aristocracy, or an absolute democracy" (see William Cobbett, *The Parliamentary History of England,* 1789–91, [London, 1820], vol. XXVIII, p. 363).

By attempting a timeless, universalistic analysis of dictatorship, J. A. Hobson falls into this error. See his *Democracy and a Changing Civilization* (London, 1934).

29. George E. Vincent, "The Rivalry of Social Groups," *American Journal of Sociology* 16 (1910–11): 471ff.

30. Cited in Brady, *Business as a System of Power*, pp. xiii–xiv.

31. Hitler, *Mein Kampf*, p. 960. See also Robert A. Brady, *The Spirit and Structure of German Fascism* (New York, 1937), pp. 53–63.

32. Wallace K. Ferguson and Geoffrey Bruun, *A Survey of European Civilization* (Boston, 1942), p. 870.

33. Quoted by F. A. Ridley, *The Papacy and Fascism* (London, 1937), p. 208. Some of the most militant fascist movements in the United States—to say nothing of Europe—such as the Youth for Christ and the Christian Youth of America, are disguised as religious organizations.

34. Briffault, *The Decline and Fall of the British Empire* (New York, 1938), p. 147. Pope Pius XI sets up clearly the opposition of the Catholic Church to the social movement. Thus he declares: " 'Religious Socialism' or 'Christian Socialism' are expressions implying a contradiction in terms. No one can be at the same time a sincere Catholic and a true socialist" (see Langsam, *Documents and Readings*, p. 572). For a discussion of the place of the Catholic Church in the modern class struggle, see George Seldes, *The Catholic Crisis* (New York, 1939), especially chap. X, "The Vatican and the World." See also William Howard Melish, "Religious Developments in the Soviet Union," *American Sociological Review*, June 1944, pp. 279–86; "The Western Catholic Bloc," *The Nation*, 162 (June 29, 1946), pp. 775–77; J. Milton Yinger, *Religion in the Struggle for Power* (Durham, 1946), pp. 142–52.

35. See Robert Bek-Gran "5 Keys to Europe," *Politics* (November 1944): 317. The medieval church, of course, was a very much more formidable political institution; it owned probably more than one third of all the land in western Europe.

36. Brady, *Business as a System of Power*, p. 64. See also, for a discussion of democracy and the masses, Pope Pius XII, "The Dignity of Liberty of Man," Christmas address, Vatican City, December 24, 1944, reported in *Vital Speeches*, II (January 1, 1945). According to Pope Pius, "Democracy . . . can be realized in monarchies as well as in republics. . . . The masses are the capital enemy of true democracy and of its ideal of liberty and equality."

37. On June 6, 1946, a number of Protestant church leaders urged President Truman to sever "all diplomatic relations with the Vatican." These leaders expressed solicitude for the increasing political involvement between the government of the United States and the reactionary politics of the Vatican, and through their representative, Dr. Samuel Cavert, general secretary of the Federal Council of Churches of Christ in America, asked that Myron C. Taylor be recalled from the Vatican.

38. Brady, *Business as a System of Power,* pp. 4–5.

39. Paul M. Sweezy, *The Theory of Capitalist Development* (New York, 1942), p. 320.

40. The following is an Associated Press report of Dec. 3, 1944: "The Left Wing Commonwealth National Committee, meeting in London today, issued a statement condemning British policy in Europe as reactionary. 'In Belgium,' the statement said, 'an unpopular government has been maintained by British bayonets, and in Italy and Greece British influence and British armored forces are used on the side of reaction. Those who fought against Nazis are disarmed, and those who collaborated with the Nazis are often protected.'"

41. See Michael Sayers and Albert E. Kahn, *The Great Conspiracy,* for a discussion of Churchill's attitude toward socialism before Nazi Germany became a threat to the British Empire.

42. Cf. Strachey, *Socialism Looks Forward,* pp. 132–33; and A. C. Pigou, *Socialism versus Capitalism* (London, 1938), pp. 25–30.

43. It is interesting to observe how our practice looks when viewed from Europe. Thus Ramsay MacDonald said in 1912: "The brutal force which money exerts in America in the workshop, the corrupt force it can exert on the bench and in the capital of every state, make it the most natural thing imaginable for labor to contemplate a resort to such force as it can command—dynamite, sabotage, bad work, the revolutionary strike" (in the London *Daily Chronicle,* quoted by Louis Adamic, *Dynamite: The Story of Class Violence in America* [New York, 1931], p. 99).

44. John R. Commons and associates, *History of Labor in the United States,* vol. II (New York, 1926), pp. 374–75. See also John Swinton, *A Momentous Question: The Respective Attitudes of Labor and Capital* (Philadelphia, 1895) and Samuel Yellen, *American Labor Struggles* (New York, 1936).

45. Lewis Corey, *The Decline of American Capitalism* (New York, 1934), p. 556.

46. Samuel Gompers, *Seventy Years of Life and Labor* (New York, 1925), vol. I, p. 287.

47. See J. Raymond Walsh, *C.I.O.* (New York, 1937), p. 19.

48. Gompers, *Seventy Years of Life and Labor,* p. 400. Emphasis added.

49. Ibid, pp. 406–07.

50. J. Raymond Walsh, *C.I.O.,* p. 36.

51. Frederick Engels and V. I. Lenin are the leading exponents of the socialist theory of the state; see Lenin, *The State and Revolution* (New York, 1929), and Sherman H. M. Chang, *The Marxian Theory of the State* (Philadelphia, 1931).

52. Engels, *Socialism, Utopian and Scientific* (New York, 1935), pp. 129–30. Emphasis added.

53. Ibid., p. 69.

54. See Lenin, *State and Revolution,* p. 216.

55. A remarkable illustration of the uses of Marxian criticism is that

presented in one of Werner Sombart's later publications. Under the influence of the rise of Nazism, this distinguished author who had written realistically as a social scientist has, in his convenient criticism of Marx and laudation of the "divine" plan of National Socialism, speedily degenerated into a puerile scholastic dialecticism. One is literally astonished to observe the former scholar weaving his way into compatibility with "German Socialism", and all this in "the spirit which finds its expression in the words: 'all for the country'" (see *A New Social Philosophy,* trans. Karl G. Geiser; and cf. Talcott Parsons, "Capitalism in Recent German Literature: Sombart and Weber," *The Journal of Political Economy* 36: 658–61).

56. Edward Heimann, *Communism, Fascism or Democracy* (New York, 1938), p. 95.
57. Carl Snyder, *Capitalism the Creator* (New York, 1940), p. 411.
58. Strachey, *Socialism Looks Forward* p. 344.

13

Modern Democracy and the Class Struggle

Meaning of Modern Democracy

In present-day Western civilization "democracy" has become a war cry—a war cry of both the capitalists and the proletariat in their struggle for power. And yet quite frequently the public is at a loss about the meaning of democracy. It has been often said, for instance, that democracy has different meanings: neither the British, the Americans, nor the Russians mean the same thing when they refer to democracy. In reality, however, they do mean the same thing; they only conceive of it in different stages of development. If we view the phenomenon in its historical context we shall be able easily to observe that modern democracy has not yet fully emerged in any part of the world.[1]

Ordinarily the British and the Americans, among others, call their form of government and social system democracy, but, strictly speaking, this is a misnomer. The fact is that these social systems have been continually becoming something else; modern democracy is still in its fetal stage.[2] In the United States, Thomas Jefferson, Andrew Jackson, Abraham Lincoln, and Franklin Roosevelt are all symbols of democratic progress. In England the Cromwellian revolution and the Levelers, the Reform Bill of 1832 and the Chartist movement, and the rise to political ascendancy of labor mark great episodes in the development of democracy. Ever since the rise of towns in the later Middle Ages, Western society has been moving away from a definable, nondemocratic society toward a still unattained democracy.

To be accurate, then, the British and American systems should be called governments with democratic tendencies. They are oligarchic-democratic or capitalist democratic hybrids.[3] Therefore, the question of crucial significance must logically be: How far has the particular system advanced toward its apparent goal of an accomplished democracy? Moreover, the criteria here involved will be obviously based upon the extent to which capitalist practices and ideals give way to those of democracy. It is in this sense that it has been said democracy should be "respected rather more for its potentialities than for its achievements." .[. . .]

From the standpoint of degrees of development of democracy in the three great nations of the world—the United States, England, and Russia—the United States is probably most backward and Russia farthest advanced.[4] England (disregarding her colonial imperialism for the moment) is far more worker-conscious than the United States, while Russia has already successfully fought her proletarian revolution. As fear of internal and external counterrevolution diminishes, the problem of abolishing the Russian proletarian dictatorship should be a relatively simple matter. In that country a clear democratic foundation has been established. On this point Dr. Frederick L. Schuman makes the following lively assertion:

> Only those observers who are invincibly ignorant, or blinded by irrational fear and hatred, will deny that the Soviet system of business and power has, for all its abuses and crudities, promoted the liberation of men from impoverishment, exploitation, illiteracy, and prejudice and served the cause of human dignity and self-respect on an immense scale. These purposes are of the essence of the democratic dream. In this sense the USSR is a democratic polity.[5]

Meaning and Significance of Modern Democracy

If we are to be consistent in the use of the concept democracy, it is necessary to define it. Democracy may be thought of either as a form of government or as a social system including the government. As a form of government—a political system in which "the people" participate in deciding matters of public interest—democracy has been common among primitive peoples and in ancient Greece and Rome. In this sense the Hindu village panchayat is a democracy.[6] In modern democracy, however, the form of government is not the crucial fact; it is rather the dependent instrument of a determinable democratic system.

Democracy as a social system is a modern phenomenon; it is significantly different from the ancient or primitive social systems. Moreover, it did not grow out of or develop as a higher *stage* of ancient democracy. In other words, modern democracy does not have its origin in Grecian democracy any more than does the modern factory system. Above all, we would be misled by thinking of the democratic movement as primarily a developing system of ideologies or, as it is sometimes believed, a system of "foreign ideologies." The democratic movement is the most practical and insistent social force in Western society. Democracy as a social system is the direct outcome of the rise of capitalism, and it is essentially a system of economic and social organization; the form of government is being fashioned to facilitate this system. Within this context it has had three well-recognized periods of growth: that of "(1) the elimination of the vestiges of the old régime—the heritage of the middle ages; (2) the establishment of the liberal regime of the 'benevolent bourgeoisie'; and (3) the attack upon the supremacy of the bourgeoisie by the proletariat, beginning about the middle of the 19th century."[7]

Democracy, then, was made possible of achievement by the bourgeoisie, but it cannot be achieved by the bourgeoisie. In fact, the bourgeoisie is unalterably opposed to democracy.[8] The task of establishing a democracy necessarily devolves upon the proletariat, and its final accomplishment must inevitably mean its supersession of capitalism. We may put it in still another way: Capitalism not only destroyed the old land economy but also gave birth to a new type of society which gains in relative strength and influence with the advancement of capitalism.

Modern democracy, therefore, is antagonistic to capitalism; the greater the development of democracy, the greater the limitations on capitalist freedom and the stronger the proletariat. Thus, as history shows clearly, whatever fraction of democracy we possess today has been achieved in increments by and for the masses against the more or less violent opposition of bourgeois and even of remnant feudal classes. The great source of strength of the proletariat inheres not only in its indispensability to capitalist production, but also in its inevitable improvement in strategic position as capitalism develops. Moreover, the proletariat has been able to make certain periodic, democratic gains as a consequence of the military involvement of the bourgeoisie. Usually the bourgeoisie has had to make democratic concessions as a reward for the services of the proletariat both in the former's conflict with feudalism and among themselves internationally.

In its struggle for democracy, the first great aim of the proletariat everywhere has been the extension of the suffrage. Ordinarily, when a capitalist nation has conceded universal manhood suffrage, it is said to be a "political democracy."[9] The mere fact of universal suffrage and representative institutions, however, need not indicate the exact extent to which democracy has attained maturity. To the extent that the questions put to the people concern the welfare of capitalism, to that extent also the ballot is not in the service of the proletariat. For here "the people are a sovereign whose vocabulary is limited to two words, 'Yes' and 'No.' This sovereign, moreover, can speak only when spoken to."[10] The focus of interest of democracy is in the well-being of the masses, and this interest cannot be made dependent upon the success or pleasure of businessmen.[11] As Harold Laski observes: "Capitalist democracy was a compromise . . . approved by the capitalist so long as its democratic aspect did not threaten the foundations of capitalism."[12] [. . .]

[. . .] Clearly, then, accomplished democracy—democracy with its substance residing in the people—will be finally attained only when the democratic form has been fully impregnated with power to control the state and its economic resources. When the economic power of the state has been completely won from the bourgeois plutocracy by the great mass of people, the bourgeoisie will have, of course, been liquidated and capitalism will have come to an end. It is a realization such as this which prompted Rosa Luxemburg to say: "He who would strengthen democracy should want to strengthen and not weaken the socialist movement."[13]

In reality the essential of socialism is a fear of democracy, for socialism merely puts the government of the people into their own hands. To argue against socialism is not to argue against any known practice, existing or contemplated, but it is, rather, to argue against the capacity of a people to devise a system of practices most suitable to the utilization of their human and natural resources. The fear of socialism is a fear of the postulated ideals of the so-called democracies; it is a fear based upon the belief that the people cannot in fact run their society according to their best interest—in fine, the struggle for and against democracy is the struggle between the two great social systems of modern civilization.[14] [. . .]

Freedom and Democracy

One of the most persistent arguments of the capitalists and their apologists against democracy is that [socialism] destroys "freedom." Indeed, for most people in Western society the word "freedom" has acquired a certain rapturous stereotype on which the advocates of the status quo seldom fail to capitalize. This, of course, is not surprising, for the social trait is as old as capitalism itself—it is elemental in bourgeois civilization. And long before the rise of capitalism Christianity had associated freedom, spiritual freedom, with earthly peace and bliss—witness the power of the Gospels: "Ye shall know the truth, and the truth shall make you free." Occasionally even the proletariat may be so conditioned by this pervasive idea of "freedom" that it will yield to many an antidemocratic contention when confronted with the suggested possibility of interference with the integrity of freedom.[15] Sometimes the public is designedly made to think of freedom as the opposite of confinement, as the opposite of imprisonment—a glad state of liberation. As a matter of fact, everybody wants freedom; and yet, no society will ever be able to secure unlimited, abstract freedom for its members. Every social system has definite potentialities for social freedom, and we can know what these are only by a study of the social system itself. Professor Harry D. Gideonse points out that "freedom always meant 'freedom' within a given framework of social institutions, legal standards and regulatory practices."[16]

Sometimes it is argued that capitalism has abolished the "slavery" of feudalism and has given the individual his freedom, the end toward which all civilization has been tending. To be sure, the fact that no one wanted individualism in a feudal society is seldom if ever brought out. As Erich Fromm observes: "Medieval society did not deprive the individual of his freedom, because the 'individual' did not yet exist."[17] Sometimes, indeed, there is a further implication that the modern trend toward democracy is a return to feudalism—"the road to serfdom," "the assault upon freedom," "the return to slavery."

As a form of social organization, however, socialism is the very antithesis of feudalism. If we can conceive of any similitude in the development of these two systems, it is this: Just as at the dawn of feudalism the smaller landowners gave up their holdings to the great landlords and became his men in lieu of his protecting them against the lawless, raiding gangs who roamed over the country, so also the common people of modern times have increasingly become willing to give up their empty individualism in favor of concerted action against the powerful financial lords who exploit them and the resources of their country objectively, that is to say, in their own individual interest, without mercy.[18] In liquidating the feudal ruling class the bourgeoisie substituted themselves as masters of the common people.

But is it really true that freedom is lost in a democracy—that we cannot have democracy and freedom too? Is bourgeois freedom the only human freedom? As a matter of fact, it may be shown that the social history of Western society from feudalism to socialism has been the history of a continually widening base of freedom— movement from a social situation in which the masses were totally nonpolitical objects to one in which they may become full-fledged determiners of their social destiny. Feudalism, to be sure, had its freedom and its power. The nobility, which possessed freedom and power, was quite willing to die for their perpetuation. Under feudalism the possession of land gave the individual power and freedom, just as under capitalism the possession of great wealth gives the individual power and freedom. Now, for the first time in history, the masses have become ready to capture the source of freedom. Democracy will turn power and freedom over to the people. The bourgeoisie destroyed the freedom of the feudal nobility so that they themselves might be free, and the common people, the proletariat, are now seeking to destroy bourgeois freedom so that they themselves may be free. The latter is a struggle for the positive freedom of all the people.[19] In addition, the proletariat will gain a negative freedom: *freedom from exploitation.*

[. . .] In reality, it is not freedom that is in question but rather two distinct brands of freedom struggling for ascendancy: freedom of the few as over against freedom of the masses. These two kinds of freedom, capitalist and democratic, are inversely correlated. . . . Charles A. Beard observes in his study of early bourgeois tendencies in the United States: "The crowning counterweight to 'an interested and overbearing majority,' as Madison phrased it, was secured in the peculiar position assigned to the judiciary, and the use of the sanctity and mystery of the law as a foil to democratic attacks."[20] Capitalism constricts the freedom of the people, so that they are more or less impotent to act in accordance with their own welfare. The people are not free when a relatively few masters of industry could deny them the control of their resources. Under capitalist freedom the people may not eat or shelter themselves unless, in the production of food and shelter, some individual makes a profit. On the contrary, democratic freedom aims to put power—economic power—into the hands of the people themselves. With the achievement of democracy they will, as never before, be able to decide how and when their resources should be spent.

It is interesting to observe the way in which Professor Friedrich A. Hayek states the conditions of capitalist freedom:

It is only because the control of the means of production is divided among many people acting independently that nobody has complete power over us, that we as individuals can decide what to do with ourselves. If all the means of production were vested in a single hand, whether it be nominally that of "society" as a whole or that of a dictator, whoever exercises this control has complete power over us.[21]

In this passage Hayek does not put the question fairly; yet it indicates very clearly the great fear: the fear of democracy. If the resources, the means of production, are vested in "society," the people will not have "complete power over us," but rather *complete power over themselves.*[22] In a "democracy the State will be the political organization of all citizens, who are subjects only as instruments of or as obedient to the regulations made by themselves."[23] Under capitalism the people cannot have complete power over themselves for, in their attempts to achieve this, they are continually frustrated by private masters. To get this power they must first get it over the capitalists and their private officials. Moreover, compared with the total population, the individuals who control the means of production are not "many" but few.[24] In the United States in 1944, 60 percent of the industrial workers were employed by 2 percent of the manufacturing concerns.[. . .]

[. . .] Indeed, to the extent that these "independent" few control the national resources they control our lives—literally our very existence. Here a major freedom is sacrificed in the interest of individualism. But the unmistakable tendency of the masses is toward the recapture of that major freedom which will give them the right to control themselves through the purposeful control of their resources. Even so, however, the crux of the matter is not merely the fact of numbers in control; it is rather the question of social motivation and economic interests.[. . .]

It is significant that although the reactionary, capitalist economists can assure the high bourgeoisie tremendous material values in the continuance of capitalism, they have virtually nothing except freedom to offer the great masses of people. They contend that a hungry man with bourgeois freedom is better off than an economically secure worker with democratic freedom. Consider in illustration the reasoning of Professor Walter E. Spahr as he opposes a bill to assure employment to the workers of the United States:

> Continuing full employment cannot be assured in a *free* society [that is to say, under capitalism]. If this bill should become law, the probable effect would be to discourage rather than to encourage private enterprise. . . . The Federal Government will have assumed an explicit responsibility for "full" employment, and for unemployment in this country. . . . A basic question presented to the people of

the United States by the Full Employment Bill is whether their think-ing and activities are to continue in the direction of *preserving and enlarging the freedom of the individual* or whether they are to follow those of Socialist-Communist-Authoritarian Europe.[25]

The name calling at the end of the last sentence is a common propagandistic device. At any rate, the Full Employment Bill is simply another attempt of the workers and their leaders to push democracy another step forward, and, to be sure, it runs head on into a clash with the interests behind "free enterprise." It is, indeed, a bold and tragic irony that the most determined antagonist of the common people should submit to them the very essence of its privilege and power, bourgeois freedom, as a basis of arguments intended to confuse and distract them.

Professor Hayek does the same thing in this way. Says he: "Even though some workmen will perhaps be better fed, and all will no doubt be more uniformly dressed in that new order, it is permissi-ble to doubt whether the majority of English workmen will in the end thank the intellectuals among their leaders who have pre-sented them with a socialist doctrine which endangers their per-sonal freedom.[26]

Here the worker is asked to look on democracy with apprehen-sion. The people themselves, it is intimated, will be unable to fashion anything better than this demi-paradise of bourgeois free-dom; they will regiment themselves, to their own dissatisfaction and disgust. Thus the trend toward democracy becomes "the road to serfdom." In fact, one corroding fear of modern democracy is that it will reduce all persons in the society to the level of the "degener-ate masses."[27] This, however, could never be an end of democracy, for it does not drag down but lifts up the civilization. In a democ-racy there will be no need for a "multitude of ignorant poor." Here progress can have but one meaning: continual advancement in enlightenment and physical welfare of all the people.[28]

The argument, however, is almost beside the point, for it is not particularly that the ruling class fears that the masses lack the ability to govern themselves, since it has never taken the initiative in the preparation of the people for self-government. Rather it is a self-interested objection to any relinquishment of its power to control the social system, power [. . .] this class conceives to be naturally beyond the constitutional right of the people. Democracy is thus thought of as an unjust, irrational usurpation—an unconscionable dishonesty—which the leaders of the people seek to impose upon the rightful and traditional owners of the business system. From this point of view democracy is wrong, disorderly, and larcenous—a movement which should be and ordinarily is put down by the organized might of the capitalist state.

Individualism and Democracy Incompatible

Quite frequently, even among persons who call themselves socialists, it is not clearly seen that, the greater the advancement of democracy, the greater also will be the limitations upon individualism.[29] Yet the process of democratic development may be defined as a continually increasing limitation of individual freedom (i.e., individualism) in favor of greater social equality and freedom for the masses. Although his pupose is to condemn democracy, Hayek is essentially right in saying: "There can be no doubt that most socialists . . . still believe profoundly in the liberal ideal of freedom and that they would recoil if they became convinced that the realization of their program would mean the destruction of freedom.[30]

It must be admitted that the opportunities which bourgeois freedom presents, the remote chances of the worker's becoming economically powerful and of his ruling over the lives of others privately and individualistically, are precious values of capitalism. Yet nothing should be clearer than that we cannot have freedom, as Professor Hayek conceives of it—that is the laissez faire individualism of capitalism—and have democracy also.[31] In this regard J. A. Hobson states, "Excessive stress on individual liberty becomes an obstacle to the true growth of democracy."[32] Thus, democracy and competitive individualism are incompatible; and the trend of modern civilization is inevitably against this sort of freedom. As Henry Pratt Fairchild observes: "What is of importance to the modern man is not freedom to do as he likes as an individual, but freedom to decide the kind of society he wishes to live in. Social liberty is the twentieth-century desideratum. . . . Only through social liberty can there be attained that form of personal freedom which is harmonious with the conditions of modern life."[33]

If the resources of a people are to be controlled by that people in the interest of its own welfare, the economic interest of the individual cannot be allowed to stand in the way. And, conversely, if the profit-making interest of the entrepreneur is to be served, the welfare of the people cannot be allowed to stand in the way; here the people's welfare could never become a primary purpose of production.

Under capitalism a profit maker is free to exploit the human and natural resources of the people in his own interest; a slum dweller is free to live and die in filth. The new freedom of democracy is the freedom of the people so to govern themselves that they may be able to make judgments which can limit these minor freedoms. The people in a democracy may decide without hindrance both that slums should be cleared and that the individual who makes a profit from slums should give up that right. There is a loss of one kind of freedom and a gain of another; we cannot have them both. A labor union, the core of proletarian action, tends to destroy the freedom of the employer to develop and to patronize the cheapest labor market; it also destroys the freedom of the worker to sell his labor in such a market. If "freedom from want" is not just another euphonious cliché of "the democracies," it must necessarily mean some substitution of proletarian freedom for capitalist freedom.[. . .]

Sometimes it is intimated that capitalism is basically interested in "the fundamental value and dignity" of the individual. This conclusion is seldom if ever demonstrated, but it is ordinarily associated with individualism. As a matter of fact, however, democracy is the supreme champion of individual worth and personal value because it reaches down irresistibly and facilitates the political upthrust of that major group of persons known as the masses; it concerns itself with the personalization of the least privileged individuals. Democracy tends to confer upon every individual a priceless sense of wantedness in the society—a sense of being a recognized part of a supremely vital organization. By this means alone the individual is able to form a positive conception of himself as a responsible social object. On the other hand, individualism champions the cause of the successful few and of the ablest; it despises the weak and jealously withholds its privileges and recognition from the common people.

As we have seen, the social system in which individualism functions typically is deaf and icy toward the welfare of individuals who cannot compel the attention of the oligarchy. In this system the individual is ordinarily presumed to be worthless until he is able to prove his worth. Therefore, paradoxically, the greater the measure of capitalist individual liberty, the greater the tendency to define the individual as having no intrinsic social worth. Capitalism seeks to atomize and segregate the individuals who constitute the masses of common people, not because of an inherent solicitude and respect for the rights and political influence of these individuals but because by means of their atomization their political influence and economic power may be nullified. Thus, the same ideal of individualism, which augments the dignity and power of the members of the ruling class, serves, when applied to the masses, as a powerful weapon of oppression and abasement. The value which individualism recognizes in the common people is a "use value."

There seems to be no theoretical reason for believing that in a society which abhors individualism the people will feel any need for it. Socialism, the system of democracy, is not simply capitalism without individualism; it is rather a distinct social system in which bourgeois individualism does not function. In a democracy one cannot "spend" his individualism because it is not one of the values of democracy. In a democracy one derives his life satisfactions through the welfare of his fellows and not by "objectively" seeking to wring as much as he can out of them for his private enjoyment. Democracy will probably give social reality to Christianity, a perennial desideratum of Western society. Those highly atomized conflicts and rivalries among individuals under capitalism will be quieted, so that the power of the group will be pooled and augmented for the task of mastering its environment expeditiously and economically. When individualism has lost its claim to indispensability in the social system, it may be viewed critically; and the likelihood is that it will then seem so absurd that only its disadvantages, which certainly are many, will be emphasized. For it cannot be gainsaid that individualism, in its negative aspects, is a separative, indifferent, unbrotherly, selfish, gloating, antagonistic, predatory, asocial attitude.[32] Those who desire individualism with the abolishment of capitalism are not socialists but anarchists, and consequently unpredictable utopians.[35]

Capitalism and the Fear of Democracy

Bourgeois society tends increasingly to become *amoral,* and consequently more fearful and militaristic. The morality to which the present-day capitalists ordinarily pay lip service is the morality of democracy; notwithstanding this, however, their practice and interest must be sternly antidemocratic. Thus it becomes exceedingly urgent for capitalist social scientists to attack the social structure of democracy.

Sometimes it is argued that democratic institutions themselves will not work; a democracy may be ruled by the ignorant. Accordingly, Hayek stresses the ineffectiveness of democratic assemblies: "The inability of democratic assemblies to carry out what seems to be a clear mandate of the people will inevitably cause dissatisfaction with democratic institutions."[36] And he points out further that a people organized democratically will have no means of controlling their own resources: "For such a task [direction of the resources of the nation] the system of majority decision is . . . not suited. . . . A democratic assembly voting and amending a comprehensive economic plan clause by clause . . . makes nonsense. . . . Even if a parliament could, proceeding step by step, agree on some scheme, it would certainly in the end satisfy nobody."[37]

In fact, according to Hayek, a democracy will destroy itself in the very act of attempting to make plans for the utilization of its resources:

> Agreement that planning is necessary, together with the inability of democratic assemblies to produce a plan, will evoke stronger and stronger demands that the government or some single individual should be given powers to act on their own responsibility. The belief is becoming more and more widespread that, if things are to get done, the responsible authorities must be freed from the fetters of democratic procedure.[38]

Probably as good an illustration as any of the place of democracy, or socialism, in the class struggle is the subtle way in which it is sometimes identified even with fascism. It should be remembered that it has been convenient, during and after World War II, for certain fascists who live in "the democracies" to criticize fascism. This practice may have a double value: (a) it is likely to divert the attention of the reader from the fascist character of the arguments, and (b) it may give the advocate an opportunity to transfer any developed antagonism against fascism to socialism by identifying socialism with fascism and then directing public hate against both of them under some such dissimulative caption as "totalitarianism." Observe, for instance, the way in which Professor Hayek accomplishes the latter end. First he cites Peter Drucker as "justly" expressive of his views:

> The complete collapse of the belief in the attainability of freedom and equality through Marxism has forced Russia to travel the same road toward totalitarianism, purely negative non-economic society of unfreedom and inequality, which Germany has been following. Not that communism and fascism are essentially the same. Fascism is the stage reached after communism has proved an illusion and it has proved as much an illusion in Stalinist Russia as in pre-Hitler Germany.[39]

To be sure, it cannot be shown that Hitler overthrew a communist society in Germany; it is true, however, that he was instrumental in overthrowing the democratic efforts of the Spanish people in favor of fascism. This is not a "stage"; it is a counterrevolution. Indeed, but for the wisdom of the Russian leadership, Germany, with the help of the capitalist nations, would have done to Russia what she did to Spain. The conflict situation here is consistent with the theory of the class struggle.[40] At any rate, after preparing his readers with the stereotyped concept "totalitarism," Hayek proceeds to show "how closely related" communism and fascism are:

> It is true that in Germany before 1933, and in Italy before 1922, communists and Nazis or Fascists clashed more frequently with each other than with other parties. They competed for the support of the same type of mind and reserved for each other the hatred of the heretic. But their practice shows how closely they are related. To both, the real enemy, the man with whom they had nothing in common and whom they could not hope to convince, is *the liberal of the old type*. While to the Nazi the communist, and to the communist the Nazi, and to both the socialist, the potential recruits ... they both know that there can be no compromise between them and *those who really believe in individual freedom*.[41]

The counterrevolutionary practices of the fascists, the defenders of a decadent capitalist society, and the revolutionary practices of the democratic forces within capitalism may evince certain traits which are common to them as conflict groups; it would be sheer nonsense, however, to assume that these revolutionary traits identify them as social systems. We should emphasize that capitalist reactionaries ordinarily do not admire fascism; they accept it only as a last resort in the face of a serious threat from democracy. Yet they do not always see clearly that fascism is the only retrogressive system available to them at this stage in the transformation of capitalism.

This, then, is what the modern social revolution amounts to. It involves the taking over of the businessman's society, fashioned by him in his own interest, by the masses of the people who at one time lived in it and had value only by sufferance—lived in it and had value only insofar as the traders and manufacturers were able to use them in the furtherance of business interests. From one point of view it may seem presumptuous that the masses of people should now declare that "democracy" demands that the material and productive wealth of the nation should be taken out of the hands of its traditional heirs, the business oligarchs, and utilized in the interest and welfare of all the people—that within the same urban, capitalist milieu the descendants of the totally nonpolitical common people should today ask that their voice be given equal weight in the control of available economic resources. This, however, is exactly what modern democracy means; and it is with reference to its achievement that we logically use the phrase "the coming new world."

Democracy, therefore, is the great social movement against which the bourgeoisie have been constantly struggling, and in doing so they have sought alliance even with the anachronistic feudal ruling class and the medieval church. The achievement of the goal of this movement, as we have attempted to show, must necessarily mean the end of capitalism. But with the coming of democracy the people of the world will, for the first time, possess a social morality sufficient to cope with their advancement in technology. They will then not find it necessary, as they now do, to pervert their social scientists in the interest of human exploitation; but rather there will be every reason for encouraging the development of a science of human welfare with normal potentialities to make contributions to human happiness equal [to] or even greater than those of the physical sciences.[. . . .]

Notes

1. Cf. C. D. Burns, *Political Ideals* (London, 1936), p. 276; and Jean-Jacques Rousseau, *The Social Contract,* trans. Rose M. Harrington, 2nd ed., pp. 102, 104.
2. The fundamental error of William E. H. Lecky in his critique of democracy appears to be the belief that democracy has been already achieved in modern Western society. Says he: "Democracy has completely triumphed in two forms—the American and the French—and we see it fully working before us. Men may like it or dislike it, but only rare and very peculiarly moulded minds can find in the government of either republic a subject for real enthusiasm" (*Democracy and Liberty* [New York, 1899], p. 43). For an earlier discussion with a similar assumption, see Sir Henry Sumner Maine, *Popular Government* (New York, 1886), p. 337; and for a review, Benjamin Evans Lippincott, *Victorian Critics of Democracy* (Minneapolis, 1938).
3. Cf. Henry J. Ford, *The Rise and Growth of American Politics* (New York, 1898), pp. 61ff.

   It may be mentioned, incidentally, that for this very reason it becomes very difficult for either England or the United States to impose their oligarchic-democratic system on conquered nations. The hybrid systems not only limit specific definition but also present a major problem to the British and American mentors in determining where to establish the balance of power. The tacit assumption appears to be that the balance existing at home will be transferred to the foreign country, but even at home it is always under a potential threat of disruption.

It should be expected also that these very promoters of "democracy" abroad, because of their origin in the hybrid states, may have quite different conceptions of their mission according as they lean toward the oligarchic or the democratic side of the parent system. In this enterprise of indoctrinating foreign peoples in the theory and practice of democracy, Russia may be the most decided, and specific, because, although that country has not yet fully achieved democracy, it is very much less divided by the ideologies of two major conflicting systems.

4. Concerning the democratic movement, Professor Carl L. Becker remarks: "It will be said that in Russia the ideals of Communism are not in fact lived up to. That is true. It is also true that the ideals of democracy are not lived up to in the United States, England, or any other democratic country. . . . But the ideal forms are not to be despised or lost sight of for all that. . . . The worst thing that can be said about the Americans or the English or the Russians is that they do not live up to their ideal aims" (*Freedom and Responsibility* [New York, 1945], p. 105). See also Woodrow Wilson, *Constitutional Government of the United States* (New York, 1918), p. 203.

The United States may be thought of as the "last great stronghold of capitalism." But for the financial and military aid of the United States, to say nothing of moral approbation, British imperialism would speedily come to an end. It is likely that there is greater antagonism in the United States to the democratic reforms in England than there is in England itself. Of some significance is the appearance of the British Prime Minister, Clement Attlee, in the winter of 1945, before the Congress of the United States in order to explain by various arts of oratory that the reforms of the British Labor Government are not really anticapitalist. It should also be noted that this government was elected by vote of the British people.

5. Frederick L. Schuman, *Soviet Politics* (New York, 1946), pp. 585–86. C. D. Burns observes: "This ideal of democracy, which has set Russia ablaze, burns as well if less fiercely in other lands" (*Political Ideals*, p. 284). See also E. H. Carr, *The Soviet Impact on the Western World* (London, 1947), p. 11.

6. It was possible, by conceiving of "the word democracy" as a "formula and practice of suffrage—a mechanism of rule," for James Burnham (*The Machiavellians* [New York, 1943], pp. 236–54) to show that almost any form of social system can exist under democracy; or indeed to show, to his own satisfaction at any rate, that democracy is not possible at all. This kind of thinking, however, tends to be a sort of historical game played with abstract definitions. It led Burnham to say that Henry A. Wallace's election "was not a voluntary expression of the will of the people at large" because Wallace is a "Bonapartist *mystique*" who tells the people particularly that "the new democracy, the democracy of the common man," included "economic democracy, ethnic democ-

racy, educational democracy, and democracy in the treatment of the sexes." In a play with the logic of a definition of the word, Jean-Jacques Rousseau wrote: "To use the term in its rigorous acceptation, a true democracy has never existed, and will never exist. It is against the natural order of things that the majority should govern and the minority be governed. . . . If there were a people of gods its government would be democratic. So perfect a government is not suitable for men" (*The Social Contract*).

7. Harry E. Barnes, "Democracy," in *The Encyclopedia Americana*, 1940; see also by the same author, *The History of Western Civilization*, vol. II (New York, 1935), p. 489.

8. Lord Acton makes this observation: "The deepest cause which made the French Revolution so disastrous to *liberty* was the theory of equality. Liberty was the watchword of the middle class [the bourgeoisie], equality of the lower [the proletariat]. It was the lower class that won the battles of the third estate; that took the Bastille, and made France a constitutional monarchy; that took the Tuileries, and made France a Republic. They claimed their reward. The middle class, having cast down the upper orders with the aid of the lower, instituted a new inequality and a privilege for itself" (*The History of Freedom and Other Essays* [London, 1909], p. 88).

9. "The British constitution . . . is the expression of a politically democratic government; it is not the expression of a democratic society. . . . Our society is, overwhelmingly, what Mr. Tawney has called an acquisitive society, and its main governmental apparatus is in the hands of those who have been themselves successful in acquisition" (Harold J. Laski, *Parliamentary Government in England* [New York, 1938], pp. 24–25, 27).

10. E. E. Schattschneider, *Party Government*, p. 52. See also William B. Munro, *The Government of European Cities*, p. 258.

11. President Calvin Coolidge put the capitalist conception of the people's welfare as follows: "We justify the greater and greater accumulation of capital because we believe that therefrom flows the support of all science, art, learning, and the charities which minister to the humanities of life, all carrying their beneficent effects to the people as a whole" (speech at Amherst College alumni dinner, New York, November 27, 1920).

12. Harold Laski, *Where Do We Go From Here?* (New York, 1940), p. 30.

13. Rosa Luxemburg, *Reform or Revolution* (2nd ed., New York, 1937), p. 41. Cf. Hans Kohn, *The Idea of Nationalism* (New York, 1944), pp. 345–63.

14. In his discussion of the economic basis of the Constitution of the United States, Charles A. Beard observes: "In turning over the hundreds of pages of writings left by eighteenth century thinkers one cannot help being impressed with the fact that the existence and special problems of a working-class, then already sufficiently numerous to form a considerable portion of society, were outside the realm

of politics, except in so far as the future power of the proletariat was foreseen and feared" (*An Economic Interpretation of the Constitution of the United States* [New York, 1930], p. 25).

15. For a discussion of the meaning of bourgeois liberty, see John Strachey, *Socialism Looks Forward* (New York, 1945), pp. 58–64; and for a summary of definitions of liberty see Arthur N. Holcomb, *The Foundations of the Modern Commonwealth*, pp. 253–94.

16. Harry D. Gideonse, "Freedom and Planning in International Economic Relations," in *Planned Society*, ed. Findley Mackenzie (New York, 1937), p. 679.

17. Erich Fromm, *Escape from Freedom* (New York, 1941), p. 43.

18. In discussing the development of individualism Erich Fromm concludes: "The individual became more alone, isolated, became an instrument in the hands of overwhelmingly strong forces outside of himself; he became an 'individual,' but a bewildered and insecure individual" *Escape from Freedom*, p. 120.

Freedom, as a social trait of capitalist society, means individualism; in caste or feudal societies there is neither necessity nor desire for individualism. In the caste system the nearest approach to individualism is that social condition of isolation achieved by outcastes, a state which has been termed "living death." Freedom, in the sense of absence of restraint upon the individual, is a rather nonsignificant concept for the study of social systems. Only God is free from and independent of physical and social restraints. But for this very reason the discussion of freedom in the latter sense is valuable for propaganda purposes. There is surely an elemental human desire for freedom in the sense of absence of "restraints." An infant of tender age could be put into violent rage by simply pinning down his legs and arms. This, however, is not the idea of bourgeois freedom. Once upon a time a Northern banker stopped to joke with a janitor of his bank. Said he, "I am disgusted with all these wartime bureaus and red tape; they show just what one will have to go through in a communist system. Here it is almost a week since my doctor advised me to go to Florida for my health, and I still haven't my allowance of gas for the trip. Give me a free society any time." To this the janitor replied: "Well, sir, ever since I was born I have never been free nor ever shall be free to go to Florida for my health. Your freedom has been restrained for a week—mine for a lifetime." As Sidney Webb and Beatrice Webb point out: "There is no freedom where there is no opportunity of taking advantage of it" (*Soviet Communism: A New Civilization* [New York, 1936], p. 1034).

19. Speaking of the rise of capitalism, J. L. Hammond and Barbara Hammond observe: "For the working classes the most important fact about that wealth was that it was wealth in dangerous disorder, for unless these new forces could be brought under control of the common will, the power that was flooding the world with its lavish gifts was destined

to become a fresh menace to the freedom and happiness of men" (*The Town Labourer, 1760–1832* [London, 1917], p. 16).

20. Beard, *An Economic Interpretation of the Constitution,* p. 161. Sometimes even political thinkers of the stature of former Vice President Henry A. Wallace may confuse hopelessly the meaning of freedom and democracy as they developed and function in modern society. Says Wallace in his great speech, "The Price of Free World Victory" (May 8, 1942): "The idea of freedom—the freedom that we in the United States know and love so well—is derived from the Bible with its extraordinary emphasis on the dignity of the individual. Democracy is the only true political expression of Christianity."

21. Friedrich A. Hayek, *The Road to Serfdom* (Chicago, 1944), p. 104. We shall quote rather extensively from this work because it expresses the anti-democratic attitude of the capitalist class quite effectively. On the question in point Hayek repeatedly makes a spurious analogy between a monopolist, as we have come to know this fearful creature, and a democratic society: "Our freedom of choice in a competitive society rests on the fact that, if one person refuses to satisfy our wishes, we can turn to another. But if we face a monopolist we are at his mercy. And an authority directing the whole economic system would be the most powerful monopolist conceivable" (p. 93). Here the purpose appears to be to frighten people with the prospect that they will create a Frankenstein if they are permitted to control their resources.

   For a rather normative discussion of freedom with an obvious inclination to identify capitalist individualism with social freedom, see Frank H. Knight, "The Meaning of Freedom" and "The Ideal of Freedom," in *The Philosophy of American Democracy,* ed. Charner M. Perry (Chicago, 1943). With a similar purpose but more artificial approach, see Gerard de Gre, "Freedom and Social Structure," *American Sociological Review* 21 (October 1946): 529–36.

22. Sidney Webb and Beatrice Webb, in their discussion of attempts to establish a democracy in the USSR, observe: "What is being built up in the USSR is not a government apart from the mass of the people, exercising authority over them. What they believe themselves to be constructing is a new type of social organization in which the people themselves, in their threefold capacity of citizens, producers and consumers, unite to realize the good life. This is in fact not a state in the old sense of the word, but an organized plan of living which the people as a whole adopt" (*Soviet Communism: A New Civilization,* p. 1072). For a time, no doubt, that political class—numerically a small minority of the total population—in whose interest Professor Hayek is speaking will surely feel that it is being ruled over. But as other vanquished classes have accommodated themselves to new systems, so also we should expect this one to become reconciled to democracy.

23. Burns, *Political Ideals,* p. 283.

24. "If democracy was to live," as Professor Avery Craven sees it histor-

ically, "the emphasis had to shift from [bourgeois] freedom to equality. If men were to be equal, however, they could no longer achieve equality for themselves. Government would have to become more active. Democracy would be a choice from then on. It would have to be planned if it were to continue to exist. And all this in the face of strong men . . . who had no interest or desire for either freedom or equality for anyone except themselves" (*Democracy in American Life*, p. 143).

25. Walter E. Spahr, "Full Employment in Exchange for What?" *The Commercial and Financial Chronicle*, September 27, 1945 (emphasis added). In a two-volume work written in collaboration by twenty-one "top-flight economists and businessmen" as a commission of the National Association of Manufacturers, the conclusion is reached "that the authors and contributors base their whole approach on the dignity, indeed on the sanctity, of the individual as individual" (*The American Individual Enterprise System*, by Commission of National Association of Manufacturers [New York and London, 1946], p. xi. It is not, it seems, that we do not like socialism, for we have been inevitably going in its direction. Strachey agrees with Spahr in this way: "It is perfectly possible to do away with mass unemployment, even before the present economic system has been fully abolished; but it can only be done by measures which will seriously modify the system, and take an appreciable step toward socialism" (*Socialism Looks Forward*, p. 99).

26. Hayek, *Road to Serfdom*, pp. 199–200. For a just, though merciless, criticism of Hayek, see Herman Finer, *Road to Reaction* (Boston, 1945). Finer's own position, however, is weak; he seems to have no sense of the economic potentialities of social systems and of social movements.

27. Lecky put this argument characteristically: "One of the great divisions of politics in our day is coming to be whether . . . the world should be governed by its ignorance or by its intelligence. According to one party, the preponderating power should be with education and property. According to the other, the ultimate source of power, the supreme right of appeal and control, belongs legitimately to the majority of the nation—or, in other words, to the poorest, the most ignorant, the most incapable, who are necessarily the most numerous.

It is a theory which assuredly reverses all the past experience of mankind. In every field of human enterprise, in all the competitions of life, by the inexorable law of Nature, superiority lies with the few and not with the many, and success can only be attained by placing the guiding and controlling power mainly in their hands. . . . Surely nothing in ancient alchemy was more irrational than the notion that increased ignorance in the elective body will be converted into increased capacity for good government in the representative body. . . . The day will come when it will appear one of the strangest facts . . . that such a theory was regarded as liberal and progressive" (*Democracy and Liberty*, pp. 25–26).

Guido de Ruggiero puts the same idea in this way: "The evil of democracy is not the triumph of quantity, but the triumph of *bad quality,* which is revealed by numbers no less clearly than by every other manifestation of the democratic spirit (*The History of European Liberalism,* trans. R. C. Collingwood [Magnolia, Mass., 1971], p. 376, emphasis in original).

28. "Some people think," says Joseph Stalin, "that socialism can be consolidated by a certain equalization of people's material conditions, based on a poor man's standard of living. This is not true. . . . In point of fact, socialism can succeed only on the basis of a high productivity of labor, higher than under capitalism, on the basis of an abundance of products and of articles of consumption of all kinds, on the basis of a prosperous and cultured life for all members of the society" (*Leninism* [New York, 1942], p. 367).

29. On this score Max Eastman apparently makes a questionable reference to Karl Marx: "Marx was the first to see . . . that the evolution of private capitalism with its free market had been a precondition for the evolution of all democratic freedoms. It never occurred to him . . . that if this was so, these other freedoms might disappear with the abolition of the free market" (quoted by Becker, *Freedom and Responsibility,* p. 89).

30. Hayek, *Road to Serfdom,* p. 31.

31. Lord Acton is responsible for some considerable part of the abstract thinking about freedom. He conceives of freedom as a supra-social phenomenon instinctively sought after in all times and places as "the highest political end" by men of good will, but frequently withheld or defeated by the wicked. Thus, without much regard to the social origin of beliefs, Acton asserts: "By liberty I mean the assurance that every man shall be protected in doing what he believes his duty against the influence of authority and majorities, custom and opinion" (*The History of Freedom,* p. 3).

The following is an argument by James Burnham based upon "human nature" as a static, instinctual phenomenon out of which "freedom" or "despotism" unfolds: "A considerable degree of liberty is not usual in human society. If we review the history of humanity, so far as we know it, it is apparent that despotic regimes are far more frequent than free regimes, and it would therefore seem that despotism is more nearly than freedom in accord with human nature" (*The Machiavellians,* p. 250).

32. J. A. Hobson, *Democracy and a Changing Civilization* (London, 1934), p. 13.

33. Henry Pratt Fairchild, *Profits or Prosperity* (New York, 1932), p. 199.

34. So, indeed, for example, J. Ellis Baker, historian of the Netherlands, has already done in his criticism of the Dutch burgher politicians of the seventeenth century: "All sense of national cohesion, of community of interest, of responsibility, of duty and of self-sacrifice, had been killed, by an anti-national and immoral policy pursued by [the burghers], which, in the name of individualism and of utilitarianism, had elevated the part above the whole, had created universal anarchy,

and had inculcated deliberate and sordid selfishness in all by teaching that each individual should work for his own profit, thus increasing to the utmost the vice of selfishness" (*The Rise and Decline of the Netherlands*, p. 391).

35. Not even Henry A. Wallace, who wrote a book to emphasize the trend toward human welfare in modern society, has been able to abandon one of the horns of this dilemma. "Can economic mechanisms be found," he inquires, "which will enable all of us over a great continent to work not only for our own ends but for the general welfare? . . . Can this be done without losing the personal privileges and liberties which we prize as the essence of democracy?" And he answers: "The philosophy of the future will endeavour to reconcile the good which is in the competitive, individualistic, and libertarian concept of the nineteenth century and the cooperative concepts which . . . seem destined to dominate the late twentieth century" (*Whose Constitution* [New York, 1936], pp. 308, 311).

36. Hayek, *Road to Serfdom*, p. 62.

37. Ibid., p. 64.

38. Ibid., p. 67.

39. Ibid., p. 29; cited in Peter Drucker, *The End of Economic Man* (New York, 1939), p. 230.

40. Since this device of Hayek and his authority seems to be part of a system of anti-Russian antagonism, we shall cite John Strachey's summary of persistent capitalist aggression as a means of setting it in its proper perspective: "It is largely we [the British] and the other capitalist States of the world who have made Russia tough. First we made war on her; then we subsidized all the Russian landowners and capital owners who had been turned out, to make war on her; then we drew what we called a 'sanitary cordon' round her; then we boycotted her; then we refused her all credits; then we refused to make common cause with her against the Nazis, hoping they would attack her. And now people are surprised because she is very tough, pretty rough, depends on nobody but herself, and trusts nobody but herself.

Russia has been through unspeakable difficulties and sufferings, of which the German invasion was only the last: but she has been through them, and has come out one of the strongest nations on earth. This giant strength of Russia is built on the concrete foundations of a socialist economic system," Strachey, *Socialism Looks Forward*, p. 129, n. 40).

41. Hayek, *Road to Serfdom*, pp. 29–30 (emphasis added). But observe how Professor Carl L. Becker compares the two systems: "Communism is democratic—that is, the dictatorship is regarded as temporary, a necessary device for carrying through the revolution, to be replaced ultimately by a government of, by, and for the people; Fascism is antidemocratic—the dictatorship and the suppression of individual liberties are regarded as permanent. Communism is international—it preaches the brotherhood of man and the equality of nations; Fascism

is anti-international—it denies the equality of nations as well as the equality of individuals, and preaches the supremacy of the nation or of the master-race. Communism is pro-intellectual—it declares that social progress rests on knowledge, and that knowledge can be attained only by the disinterested search for truth; Fascisim is anti-intellectual—it regards science and the search for truth as of no importance, except in so far as they can be used for the attainment of immediate political ends" (*Freedom and Responsibility,* p. 104).

| IV |

A World-System Perspective on Capitalism

During the late 1950s and early 1960s Cox published three major books on capitalism: *The Foundations of Capitalism* (1959), *Capitalism and American Leadership* (1962), and *Capitalism as a System* (1964). In these works he traces the origin, growth, and development of capitalism as a world system, from what he argued were its beginnings in medieval Venice to its present form in the United States. These books were a logical outgrowth of Cox's attempt to understand present-day capitalism and the manner in which it gave rise to the problems faced by black people. As part of this effort, he examined how successive capitalist societies achieved leadership of the world capitalist system, focusing on those structural features and tendencies common to the organization, development, and ultimately the decline of capitalism. He linked two levels of analysis, examining both the internal organization of national units and the wider international system; the two together, he argued, constitute the world capitalist system. Thus in the introduction to *Capitalism as a System* the sequence of development has been predominantly from the wider system to the national society: "The internal societal organization seems to depend upon demands and imperatives arising chiefly from a play of circumstances peculiar to the system. Furthermore, historically the system has, on the whole, preceded its component societies, which were gradually included as the system expanded."

Obviously, the depth and range of the discussion contained in these three volumes cannot be captured in the following selections, but they do make available a major aspect of Cox's sociology, especially important since all three books are currently out of print.

223

As these selections show, Cox's conception of capitalism presages by almost two decades much of the current work on world-systems theory, and shows how he addressed some of the critical issues now fashionable among world-systems theorists. Unfortunately, the contemporary world-systems literature contains few references to any of Cox's books and even fewer attempts to evaluate the quality of his contribution.

Cox was nevertheless at the forefront of the development of a theory of the political economy of the world system. The first selection, "Capitalist Cities" (taken from *The Foundations of Capitalism*), introduces a typology, or model, of a hierarchical global system, as a guide to the more substantial discussion in later chapters of the book. He lists five types of capitalist cities and towns that make up the system—the *national,* the *dependent-subject,* the *fairs,* the *kontors* or *staples,* and the *emporia* areas—with the degree of sovereignty achieved by each being a key factor in determining its position in the system. The next two selections, "Venice the Progenitor" and "The Economic Underpinning of Venice," illustrate the analytical strategy Cox pursued in *The Foundations of Capitalism.* Here Cox investigates the social organization of a number of medieval societies, including Venice, in order to demonstrate how certain features in some of them were peculiar to capitalism. Through chance events, Venice was the place that capitalism first emerged and flourished—not capitalism as a mature system but capitalism as the prototype for future capitalist societies. As a city-state, Venice was assured its leading role in the system by its commercial domination of the Mediterranean region. The degree of development of its governmental structure and political sovereignty, the preeminence of the merchant class, and the constitutional rights afforded to Venetian citizens—and other attributes—distinguished Venice (and other early cities) from both ancient and feudal societies and set it on the road to capitalism.

A concise theoretical reprise of several of the themes discussed in both *The Foundations of Capitalism* and *Capitalism as a System*—from which it is taken—is found in the fourth selection, "Structure of the System." Here Cox revises his classification of city-states in the light of his examination of the subsequent development of the capitalist system, and proposes a model of the structure and territorial organization of the world capitalist system during the first two decades of this century, when Great Britain, the United States, and Germany became the key competitors for leadership. He also includes a discussion of the unequal commercial relationships that existed between the Hanseatic League and Venice, the two societies that dominated trade in their respective regions in the thirteenth century, and the subordinate fairs and backward towns and countries of Europe. He argues that societies have changed their relative position over time, as one replaces a former rival for leadership. Several general principles are constant, however: "The nations, colonies, and dependent communities . . . tend to form a commercial and power-status gradient with its most energetic and prestigious component at the top." Moreover, the opportunities for the accumulation of wealth by leader nations rests on the imbalance in the world market situation.

The fifth and sixth selections, taken from *Capitalism and American Leadership* and *Capitalism as a System,* offer additional insights into many of the ideas first put forward in *The Foundations of Capitalism.* In "Assumptions of Leadership," Cox analyzes the factors that have contributed to the ascendancy of the United States as the leading capitalist nation. Of particular importance is the similarity between early and present-day capitalism: while U.S. businessmen, like the early capitalists, recognized that domestic manufacturing had to be tied to the production of raw materials in the less-developed countries, they also knew that the American people and government had to be used to promote the expansion of U.S. exports and investments abroad. In "Imperialism," Cox argues further that because foreign trade is necessary for any capitalist city-state or nation-state to maintain its position, imperialism is a basic "structural underpinning" of the capitalist system. Imperialism involves winning trading rights and privileges by gaining access to native rulers who, to enhance their own economic well-being, open their countries to foreign exploitation without being fully aware of the exploitative capacity of the system to which they are granting concessions. By virtue of its very existence, imperialism does not allow backward countries to assume the economic, political, and cultural status of the leading capitalist nations. Backwardness means, Cox argues, that developing nations will be perpetually subordinant to the commercial politics and aims of the imperialist powers. Cox's discussion predates much subsequent thinking about imperialism, world capitalism, and underdevelopment, but his work has been just as neglected in this sphere of scholarship as in that of race relations and world-systems theory. No mention of his work appears in any of the leading texts on the subject, by such scholars as Paul Baran, Andre Gunder Frank, Immanuel Wallerstein, and Albert Szymanski, to mention only a few of those working on the subject.

As the last selection, "Movements Toward Change" (also from

Capitalism as a System), demonstrates, Cox's emphasis on the world capitalist system did not mean that he abandoned his earlier emphasis on political-class struggle. Here Cox examines capitalism from the standpoint of the dynamics of a single society and in terms of its dynamic as a system, attempting to integrate the two levels of analysis into a single theory of social change. Thus he argues that social change can be promoted, or impeded, through indigenous class antagonisms, either within the advanced capitalist nations or the backward countries, or between the nations that are the components of the world capitalist system. A major condition affecting the nature of the class struggle, however, is the position of the country in the wider system—so that the "higher the nation stands in the system, the greater the consequences of its class struggle upon universal capitalism." Although Cox does not discount the reformist political and economic advances made by labor in the leading nations, he argues that the historically privileged status of workers in the advanced capitalist nations makes it more likely that they will advocate reform rather than revolution, and be more antagonistic to the demands of working-class groups in the backward countries. If radical change is to come about, it will therefore emerge from the people in the backward countries of the world, the real proletariat.

14

Capitalist Cities

To understand the nature of the capitalist system it is necessary to examine the characteristics and the processes of development of medieval and early modern European cities. This is so because the cities cradled the system, hence its traits may be recognized far more simply in them than in the more complex modern nation.

It is important to recognize, however, that communities known as medieval cities involved quite different types of social organization, so that a description of one may not serve as a significant characterization of another. Moreover, medieval cities have not always been distinguished significantly from such ancient urban centers as Rhodes, Athens, Carthage, Delos, Alexandria, and the vestiges of Roman towns particularly in Italy. We shall, therefore, begin by attempting a typology of these cities.

Of course, there may be different bases of classification. Perhaps the most obvious of these is geographical. Cities tend to grow at strategic trading points. "Every kind of trade," observes [Henri] Pirenne, "necessarily implies the existence of certain points of concentration, which are determined by the configuration or contours of the land, inasmuch as they correspond to the necessities of the social organization and the development of means of communication. The ends of gulfs, the mouths of rivers, the confluence between two rivers, the spot at which a stream ceases to be navigable, are places designed by nature for halting places in transit."[1]

It is possible, then, to account for the growth of cities and their relative importance by indicating the natural incidence of their location. The existence of such cities as Antwerp, Pisa, Milan, London, Ypres, Ghent, and virtually all others of any considerable size may be explained in this way. Thus says C. W. Previté-Orton in further support of this criterion:

> While the medieval towns are obviously akin, the divergences among them in character and history are deep and wide; and most aberrant from the rest, if the most pronounced and perfect of the type, are the

Italian city-states. Like their congeners, indeed, they owed their florescence ultimately to geographical factors. Some, like Venice and Pisa, were ports on the sea; others were halting-places at the fords or junction of rivers, like Cremona; others, like Verona, were at the mouths of passes; others punctuated the immemorial roads, like Siena or Bologna; others, perhaps, were merely safe centres in a fertile land, clots of population, which could produce un-bled by feudal tyranny.[2]

And yet, geographical criteria do not distinguish meaningfully between ancient and modern trading places. For certain purposes the cities may be classified otherwise according to the extent to which they were either manufacturing, trading, or financial centers, or even by their type of manufacturing or trading specialty. Religious centers such as Rome, Cologne, and Liège differed in certain more or less important respects from Lübeck, London, and Venice. Moreover, the cities may be grouped according to the similarity of their charters or constitutions, which were frequently adopted from certain acceptable models, such as, for example, those of Venice, Lübeck, or Rouen.[3]

Our typology, however, centers about certain indispensable conditions of capitalist development, the degree of sovereignty of the cities or their related dependent functions [see Table 1]. From this point of view, as shown in the following scheme, the structural pattern of the capitalist system may already begin to appear. There is some overlapping in the classification, but it is intended to emphasize dominant traits; and no attempt, of course, is made to include all the cities which may be defined by these categories.

The national cities were the center of capitalist organization and action; they constituted the true home of capitalists. They succeeded to a very high degree in isolating themselves from feudalism and in developing a distinct system of law and economic order. Thus, the stronger the feudal lord and the more uninterrupted his dominion, the greater was the difficulty of organizing national-capitalist cities. The French and English cities, caught up in the stream of developing capitalism, remained relatively dependent and subject particularly because of the settled state of their feudal overlordship.

The fair towns were the foci of commerce and financial transaction; it was in those communities that the most advanced principles and techniques of the market of the capitalist system were largely worked out. They depended, however, principally on the commercial activities and patronage of the national capital cities for their

Table 1
Types of Capitalist Cities

NATIONAL............	Sovereign: Venice, Amalfi. Autonomous: Florence, Genoa, and other Tuscan republics Autonomous Leagues: Hanseatic cities—Lübeck, Hamburg, Bremen, Brunswick, Cologne Sovereign Federal: Amsterdam and the cities of the United Provinces
DEPENDENT-SUBJECT	Communes English Boroughs London
FAIRS.................	Periodical: Fair Towns of Champagne (Provins, Troyes, Lagny and Bar-Sur-Aube), Lyons Permanent: Bruges, Antwerp
KONTORS OR STAPLES	Concessionary: Constantinople, Novgorod, London (before 1450) Subject: Tyre, Calais, Bergen, Goa (c. 1580), Shanghai
EMPORIA..............	Wisby, Lisbon, Seville, Ormuz, Hong Kong

prosperity. They were not, therefore, initiators of capitalist commerce.

The *kontors* or staples, on the other hand, were trading outposts particularly of the national-capitalist cities. The trade here was more elementary and less sophisticated than at the fairs, involving mainly primary collection and distribution of goods. They are distinguished in this classification from the *emporia* in that the latter constituted essentially great marts and warehouses patronized or established by the national cities.[. . .]

Notes

1. Henri Pirenne, in *Cambridge Medieval History* (Cambridge, 1924), vol. VI, p. 512.
2. C. W. Previté-Orton, in *Cambridge Medieval History,* vol. V, p. 208; cf. Pierre Clerget, "Urbanism: A Historic, Geographic, and Economic Study," *Annual Report of the Board of Regents of the Smithsonian Institution, 1912* (Washington, 1913), pp. 653–67; and Edward Ullman, "A Theory of Location for Cities," *The American Journal of Sociology* 46 (1941): 853–64. The author examines and generally accepts Walter Christaller's "central-place" theory of the location of cities, which conceives of modern urban communities as service centers for their immediate environs.
3. One popular classification which could lead to vast misunderstandings about the progress of modern urbanism is that of representing the industrial revolution as a historical break, introducing factors so completely distinct that all previous cities in Europe, Asia, or Africa before the eighteenth century may be classed together as having essentially the same characteristics. The "prime difference" being "industrialism" or its absence in one or the other of the categories. Cf. Gideon Sjoberg, "The Preindustrial City," *The American Journal of Sociology* 60 (March 1955): 438–45; and Kingsley Davis, "The Origin and Growth of Urbanization in the World," ibid., pp. 429–33. See also Eric E. Lampard, "The History of Cities in the Economically Advanced Areas," *Economic Development and Cultural Change* 3, no 2 (January 1955): 81–136; and for a discussion of theories, Ullman, "A Theory of Location for Cities," ibid., pp. 853–64.

15

Venice the Progenitor

Considerable emphasis has been put upon the geographic position of Venice as a base for commerce between the East and western Europe. It is situated at the estuaries of many great rivers—the Po, the Adige, the Brenta—which penetrate into Italy and lead to Alpine passes into Germany. This fact was undoubtedly of great significance for the commercial development of Venice, and yet there were other places on the northwestern curve of the Adriatic which would have been geographically more suitable to that commerce than Venice.[1] For centuries before the invasions of the Roman Empire the lagoons had remained an inhospitable area virtually unpopulated.[2] Indeed the very physical limitations of Venetian topography, its barrenness and inaccessibility, became the decisive factors in providing that isolation and security needed for the early nurture of a new culture. Ships of superior draft had difficult access to Venetian ports, so that only seamen with considerable knowledge of the tides and currents could navigate successfully the meandering waters.

Far from being an inviting and obviously choice location for making a living, the numerous sand-banked islands which constituted Venice gained their first significant population by accident and virtually by force. The people who were to form the first permanent inhabitants were repeatedly driven there from the mainland during the fifth and sixth centuries by the invading tribes from the north. The place was so desolate, however—without a supply of fresh water or space for agriculture—that it was considered initially only a temporary refuge to be abandoned as soon as the mainland appeared settled enough for a safe return. Horatio F. Brown recounts briefly this movement:

> The year 568 is the second great landmark in the early history of the lagoons; in that year Alboin and his Lombards invaded Italy from Pannonia. The mainland north of Venice was put to fire and sword. Once again the inhabitants of three of the ruined cities sought refuge

231

in the estuary. This time they resolved to remain there. . . . What Attila began, [in 452 A.D.] Alboin completed. Venetian history is the history of the people who, under stress of repeated invasion between the years 452 and 568, were thus gathered together in the lagoons.[3]

What kind of people were these refugees? They seem to have come in extraordinary proportion from the upper classes. It was against these groups particularly that the depredations of the terrible invaders were directed. The great masses of nonpolitical working people were left largely undisturbed by the new rulers.[4] Moreover, as has been indicated, with successive displacements of conquerors—Huns, Goths, Lombards, and Franks—on the mainland, some of each group of the vanquished found shelter in the lagoons.[5] Venice, then, began with a dispossessed but energetic and culturally mixed people. "Men of all classes were found among them," says Romanin, "especially of the wealthy and educated classes, who had more to fear and to lose under the dominion of the barbarians and who consequently abhorred it more."[6]

The new situation actually called for all the imagination and ingenuity that these educated classes could afford. They could not continue here their old way of life with agriculture as its base; there were few traditions to guide them; even the physical structure of the community had to be built from the ground up. To be sure, life here was not completely new, but old elements had to be brought together in a new way. Artisans came with their skills[7] and the Adriatic was already known to traders. For their building they had available the timber of the forests of the mainland; hence they readily constructed ships to trade with the surrounding country. At length, they settled on one great industry, salt-making, which became the staple of their sea and river-borne commerce.

Historians have concluded that as early as the sixth century the Venetian islands were well populated, "that their inhabitants were already undertaking long voyages by sea and up the rivers, that they had great fleets and extensive commerce, especially in salt, and that they had admirable ability in the construction of their dwellings."[8]

An Interstitial Zone

[. . .] Venice was situated in an interstitial power zone, at the unstable margins between the conquering but relatively uncultured Lombard Lords in Italy and the Eastern Roman Empire with its seat at Constantinople. Her major diplomatic achievement in those early days—and insofar as capitalism is concerned, an indispensable accomplishment—was to steer such a course that neither of these powers was able to establish political dominance over the inhabitants of the lagoons. At that time such a policy by a relatively impotent group of people was unique.[9]

Two factors contributed to its accomplishment: (a) the peculiar situation of the islands, which had been looked upon traditionally as desert spots of no particular value to feudal production, and (b) the unceasing hostility between the two great emergent powers of the East and West. Venice played a completely self-interested game, a most daring innovation, in dealing with these antagonists.[10]

By law all the unconquered land in Italy belonged to the Roman Empire in the East; therefore Venice was subject to the eastern emperor.[11] But the distant ruler, while consolidating his position in the East, had to relax his hold on the lords in the West; hence the rise there of a variety of power organizations.[. . .]

Quite early in her career Venice discovered the importance of sea power. She was frequently called on by her suzerain in the East for help in the defense of the western dominion; she was, however, outspoken in her intent to protect her own interests against Constantinople. It has been recorded that when, in 584, Longinus, the exarch of the Eastern empire in Italy, demanded that the Venetians declare themselves subjects of the Empire, they answered "that they themselves had made the lagoon-islands; that they had withstood the incursions of Attila, the Eruli, the Goths, and the Lombards; [and that] . . . 'this second Venice, which we have raised in the lagoons, is a mighty habitation for us. No power of Emperors or Prince can reach us save by sea, and of them we have no fear.'"[12]

[. . .] The Venetians in 742 used their fleet to aid in expelling the Lombards from Ravenna, a part of the Italian domains of the empire. It should not be supposed, however, that at this time Constantinople was powerless on the sea; her navy, in fact, ruled the Mediterranean. It came to the rescue of Venice in the first great attempt of the feudal powers on the mainland to subjugate her. This mission was directed by no less a figure than Charles the Great; and his son, Pepin, King of the Lombards, was chosen to lead the attack. The general attitude of hatred for the selfish people of the lagoons shows that the latter had already developed basic capitalist traits.[. . .]

Constantinople answered an appeal for help by sending a detachment of warships to the Venetians in the year 809, and thus the struggle began. The combined fleet led an attack on the mainland in an attempt to disperse Pepin's gathering forces, but its troops were defeated in a battle at the city of Comacchio. The ships had to retire in haste to the islands where they alerted the people for their defense. This time, however, the king had to cross the sea, and here the Venetian seamen proved their mettle. Caught in the treacherous shoals of the lagoons, most of his navy was crippled and destroyed. Such was the issue of this futile enterprise. A year later, before other plans to subdue Venice could materialize, Pepin died; and although future monarchs, Otto II and Frederick Barbarossa, had similar ambitions, none went so far as to attempt an invasion of the islands.

It should be emphasized that at this time, even with Venice demonstrating her ability to stand alone, the idea of so small a territory existing as an independent power had not become established. In the peace treaty which followed in 812, the contending emperors agreed that Venice should continue to be a part of the Eastern Empire. "The two great Empires did not seem to allow in their neighborhood any independent state."[13] However, the Republic continued her own way of life, one which could not be merged into that of either great state.[. . .]

It was not so much the fact that Venice was the "meeting place of two civilizations," as that she contrived to make herself the dynamic center of those civilizations. Byzantine and feudal society were cultures in different states of development. This cultural imbalance resulted in a natural tendency to movement of commerce between the areas, and Venice sought to organize and dominate it. In the process she developed a type of self-centeredness which was to become the precursor of modern nationalism.[. . .]

Relationship with the Byzantine Empire

In describing this early period of capitalist development it is necessary to relate the phenomena to Constantinople. The empire in the West was the lesser power both in cultural advancement and in priority of status. The seat of the authentic Roman Empire was at Constantinople, the most elaborately developed city of the Mediterranean and probably of the world. But, as we shall indicate later, it was not capitalistically organized, and Venice profited from this fact.

One outstanding trait of capitalist society is its enormous capacity for cultural assimilation, a characteristic which Venice had already begun to demonstrate. She was able selectively to imitate and copy the arts and commercial practices of the great city and frequently to improve on them. Indeed, this is so obvious that many modern writers have concluded that Venetian culture was merely taken over from the East.[. . .]

And yet, it was precisely a difference in "government," in social organization, that the two societies presented categorically distinct social orders. Their systems of values and economic means of existence differed fundamentally. This fact is brought out clearly as we follow the relationship between the two communities up to the spectacular Fourth Crusade, which reveals inverse trends of power and diplomatic development.

As early as the eighth century, Venice had become fully conscious of the value of commerce as an exceedingly productive way of life, while Constantinople had been organizing its commerce as a means of provisioning the empire. This was the great opportunity for the Venetians; therefore, as Daru observes: "They established themselves nearer to the source of their objects, and such was the success of their activity and courage that they became first the merchants and then the masters of the commerce of the luxurious Constantinople."[14]

In the last quarter of the eleventh century the nature of this mastery was strikingly evinced. The Normans had established themselves in Sicily and southern Italy, and had now decided to move east in conquest of the wealthy empire. This brought them face to face with Venetian interests and consequently into inevitable opposition from the latter. By this time, however, the empire, after having been subjected for centuries to the deadening touch of commercial exploitation, was prepared to see the Venetians take the typical lion's share of capitalist nations in such situations. Molmenti gives the following summary of this:

> When the old and decrepit Eastern empire, threatened by the adventurous Normans, already lords of lower Italy, turned to the growing nation of the lagoons for help, the Venetians at once perceived that if Greece fell, as Apulia had fallen, into the hands of the Northmen, their trade with the East, the chief source of all their wealth, was at an end. They had every reason, therefore, to wish to curb the Norman power; and on the promise of ample recompense, they accepted the Emperor Alexius' invitation (1082). After a long struggle, carried on with varying fortune, Byzantium was saved by Venice, which received, as a reward, privileges of the widest character (1084): her dominion over Dalmatia and Croatia was confirmed; she was granted a special quarter in Constantinople; many concessions were made to the clergy and to churches; Venetians were free to

trade, in all manner of goods, in every part of the empire except Crete and Cyprus without paying customs, wharfing, or other dues.[15]

The point to observe here is not that Constantinople was already so physically weakened that Venice could invade and subjugate her; the time was not yet ripe for anything of the sort. What is significant is that Venice was able to secure such augmentation of her commercial privileges in the empire as no capitalistically sophisticated power would have dared to grant. Indeed, Constantiople had no clear idea of the nature of capitalist commerce, its power to bleed white a foreign nation; hence she remained, on the whole, friendly to the Venetians. She had frequently suspected the lagoon-men of trading with her relentless enemy, the Mohammedans in the Levant, but it was only with the coming of the Crusades that she began to sense real danger. The Venetians became associated with feudal groups in conquest of the borders of the eastern Mediterranean where they established staples for trading directly with the East. From the beginning, however, the emperors mistrusted the territorial ambitions of the Crusaders. And now the claim to sovereign staple rights embroiled Venice directly in a conflict of interests.

The first Crusade brought two relatively new trading cities, Genoa and Pisa, into prominence. They had assisted in transporting the Crusaders to the Levant and were also rewarded with trading posts and privileges in that area. Furthermore, during the course of the twelfth century they moved into Byzantium and established themselves in Constantinople. From this time on the most effective strategem [. . .] the Emperors could devise to hold the ambitions of Venice in check was to favor Genoa and Pisa with competitive commercial opportunities and privileges. It was this policy together with a popular uprising instigated by the uneasy sovereign against the overbearing Venitian community[16] of some ten thousand in Constantinople, which, in 1171, led Venice to declare war aginst the empire. Although this aggression proved abortive, it nevertheless underlined the fatal weakness of the eastern power. Its economic structure had become dependent on the foreign trade of a few Italian cities whose interests involved the undermining of that structure.

The emperors might attempt to restrain the Venetians, but it was a problem of a quite different sort to dispense with them altogether. When a noncapitalist people of the presocialist variety establishes commercial relations with a capitalist power, it enters into a system from which it can seldom extricate itself. Its economy tends to be dependently geared to that of the capitalist network; and unless it is able effectively to imitate the social organization of the dominant units of the latter, it may find itself sinking to the point of complete national subordination. Ordinarily, the victim cannot escape by attempting to play capitalist rivals off against each other.[. . .]

The great city Constantinople eventually caved in, thus becoming a symbol of the first great noncapitalist civilization to be exploited and sapped by the systematic commerce of a capitalist nation.[. . .]

Organization

We shall now attempt to sketch the remarkable governmental organization of Venice, which, we think, constituted the kernel of her capitalist innovations. Venice never held a charter from an overlord; indeed, her situation was such that only after a gradual constitutional development did the nature and value of a charter become apparent. Her political experience, therefore, became the subject of future urban charters. According to Horatio Brown: "The Venetian constitution, which, on account of its stability and efficiency, compelled the envy and admiration of all Italian and numerous foreign statesmen, was the product of the growth of Venice, slowly evolved to meet the growing needs of the growing state."[17]

An important difference between early Venice and the great countries to the east and west of her was that she had no traditionally established form of social organization. In the East, the powerful institutions of the Roman Empire persisted under the new emperors; in the West, feudalism, with its stabilizing religious sanctions, spread rapidly. The Venetians, it is true, learned much from the Roman law practiced at Constantinople, but neither of these two patterns of social organization suited their purpose. They had to improvise. Unlike the situation of later nationalist cities, they were never faced with the problem of reducing an established feudal order.[. . .]

As we should expect, the very situation of the Venetians, demanding originality on a vast scale, engendered serious problems which sometimes flared into sharp internal conflict.[. . .] The settlement of the islands was accomplished not only at different times but also by groups largely from different traditional areas of the mainland. At intervals, common danger from outside readily brought them together for common defense, but acute interisland rivalries soon developed and threatened the stability of the entire community. Says Molmenti: "Each [major] island was a separate center, a settlement as it were, with its own government and its own magistrates."[18] Here, then, was presented a situation which later has confronted virtually every leading capitalist nation—even down to the United States with its factious liberated colonies and then states' rights. The Venetian solution has been uniformly followed.

This solution was made possible, however, by the nature of the Venetian economy. It was based not upon land, but upon industry and commerce—and, what was of crucial significance, upon *foreign* commerce. Power in this type of economy tends to be associated with wealth which is acquirable by the economic ingenuity of individuals in their relations with foreign peoples. Thus, the tendency here was toward internal cooperation of producers of wealth for opportunistic foreign transactions. Even without actual aggression from abroad the conflict of interests at home called for "rules" and impartial leadership. This need, as opposed to a latent desire for hereditary rulership, was recognized quite early in the history of the archipelago, and from time to time representatives from the various townships assembled to devise methods of government. Brown dates the beginning of Venetian independence from 466 (before the ultimate fall of Rome in 476), when representatives from the island-townships met at Grado, a town at the northern tip of Venice, to "elect officers, with the title of Tribunes, to govern the affairs of each island."[19]

The tribunate went through a series of changes. Its importance increased as Byzantine power on the mainland decreased. In the townships it "wielded both military and civil authority" and the office had some tendency to become hereditary.[20] Its national organization finally developed into an incipient parliamentary institution, thus according to Molmenti:

> The primitive *tribuni marittimi,* having been proved inadequate to the growing needs of the State, gave place to tribunes elected yearly, for the most part, in each lagoon island and in each center of population. The tribunes themselves soon felt the need for meeting together to discuss the common interests of the State, and thus gave rise to the *consociazione,* the germ of the famous commune of Venice.[21]

The next great step in the formation of the Venetian constitution was the election of a head of state, a doge or duke.[. . .] "They elected Paoluccio Anafesto their Doge . . . and gave him almost absolute authority over the administration of the army, and also over ecclesiastical appointments. The tribunes were retained but merely as local officers. The *arrengo* [or popular assembly of citizens] alone stood as a check on the Doge's autocracy."[22] The power of the state was now embodied in a supreme chief magistrate; and, it may be said, a sort of federal government was established. The voluntary yielding of local authority contributed to the cohesion of the state and the more effective defense of it.

And yet, the power of the dogate was not without its temptations. Of these, the most insidious were the attempts of some of the executives not only to perpetuate themselves in the dogeship but also to make the office hereditary. The determined opposition of the Venetians to this tendency, at a time when hereditary rulership was almost everywhere the custom, showed them to have been decided on a crucial trait of capitalist government: elected, controlled leadership. The usual procedure of the usurpers was to associate with them one or more of their relatives in the conduct of the office so that at death or superannuation the dogeship could be easily taken over.

[. . .] In 814 the seat of government was finally established on the Rialto group of islands. There the famous palace of the doge, his chapel and other public buildings, all of which finally came to be known as Saint Mark, symbolized the authority of the people. These structures, moreover, represented the continuity of the state; the doge lived in his luxurious residence by authority of the state as its first servant. Ultimate power, therefore, resided in no single person but increasingly in a class of Venetian citizens.

This class of citizens constitutes one of the most remarkable traits of capitalist organization; and nowhere else in the history of capitalist development do we find the ruling class so clearly delineated as in Venice. This fact is due primarily to the purity of the social situation in which it developed. There was no other significant, competing social system with established class-interests to complicate the rule of her major capitalists. As elements of the society itself, however, there were two other possible sources of power: that inherent in the masses of the people and in the potential dictatorial rule of the doge. In a fashion typical of all future capitalist communities, the ruling class subdued and restrained both these forces.[. . .]

In some capitalist communities the ruling class may lead by controlling only certain areas of the legislature and administration or the behavior of legislators who themselves may not be identified with the ruling class. In Venice, however, the ruling class openly took over the membership of the national legislature, achieving thereby such a degree of consistency between capitalist economic power and the law as has never been matched in the annals of capitalism.

Frequently, in the literature on the beginnings of the constitution, we come on the idea that "the people" in their general assembly or *arrengo* elected the tribunes and the doges; it is still not exactly clear, however, who "the people" were—whether there were age, economic, or other restrictions to their political participation.[. . .] Nevertheless, it is certain that "the people," whoever they were, were more and more excluded from participation in law making and in administrative functions of the state. In the process the qualifications for office holding became more exacting and clearly defined.

[. . .] Industry and commerce constituted the source of wealth in Venice, but this wealth was far from evenly distributed among the people. It tended increasingly to concentrate in the hands of relatively few of the citizens and so also went power in the state. At length the welfare of the state became identified with the interests of its wealthy class. In discussing the formation of this capitalist oligarchy, George B. McClellan observes:

> There were no feudal seigneurs in the Venetian aristocracy, no landowners, no rulers of castles or of towns, no soldiers. All were merchants engaged in the pursuit of wealth, through commerce. For them the acquisition of wealth was the sole and necessary path to eminence and power. For them wealth and power and wealth and success became synonymous. They appreciated the fact that the prosperity of the individual merchant depended upon the welfare of the commercial class as a whole; and that for benefit of the class everything else must be subordinated.[23]

[. . .] The crucial instrument of the Venetian ruling class was its parliament, its Great Council; here resided this sovereign power of the state. And the extent to which this power was preempted has ever been the envy and aspiration of all future capitalist classes. "The Great Council was the legislature of the Republic; unrestricted by any written constitution, it could enact, amend, or repeal any law upon any subject. Being absolute, it could not only delegate its authority but could revoke authority already granted."[24] Although the membership of the oligarchy continued to establish its exclusiveness, the rule of Venice by its great businessmen engaged in foreign trade became a settled fact by the third quarter of the twelfth century. Under the sagacious leadership of this group Venice became a world power and model of capitalist culture.

[. . .] The Great Council was at first a body of superior capitalists representing various communities of the republic. However, a major event, of preeminent significance for understanding the nature of the expansive traits of capitalism, resulted in focusing on Venice the entire commercial wealth of the Near East. In 1204 the Venetians redirected the Fourth Crusaders against Constantinople, captured and forced it to disgorge its treasures, and reorganized the empire in its own commercial interests. This fabulous windfall further increased the disparity of wealth between the Venetian aristocracy and the lesser merchants, to say nothing of the common people. The tendency now was to bring into line a concentration of power consistent with that of wealth, and its culmination was the closing of the Great Council. This act "made it impossible for any outsider to become a member of the aristocracy, except by consent of the aristocracy itself."[25] Finally, in 1506, an official roll of those eligible to membership was compiled, thus bringing to its final completion the definition of a capitalist ruling class. It has been estimated that this class constituted less than 2 percent of the population.[26]

In 1310, apparently because of a recognition of the unwieldiness of the Great Council in times of emergency, a smaller body, the famous Council of Ten, was created. Elected by the Great Council itself, the Ten readily assumed wide juridical and administrative powers. As Horatio F. Brown puts it: "The Ten were competent to cite cases before their tribunal; to make special and secret expenditures; to give private instructions to ambassadors; in short, the Council became the real master of Venice."[27] It provided maneuverability for the sovereign authority inherent in the great parliament.

This, then, was the nature of the power structure of the Venetians. Between the Great Council and the doge there were various other groups—the senators, the ducal councilors, the Forty—forming without precedent the most efficient and stable government of early capitalism.[28] Coming down to the very end of the eighteenth century, it outlasted most of its imitators. Perhaps the crowning political achievement of Venice was her establishment of a stable government by law and not by persons, albeit in the interest of her major wealthy producers, the upper capitalist class.[29] [. . .]

The very nature of the Venetian social order necessitated a relatively elaborate system of civil, criminal, and international law. The law of property and commerce, of course, oriented that of all other relationships.[30] Certain attempts have been made to codify the laws, but there is extant nothing approaching a complete code.

Roman law, the legal heritage of the community, formed the basis of the structure developed to facilitate the requirements of the new social order.[31] There is, however, a significant difference in spirit between the two systems. Sanctity of property dominates Venetian law. Thus Molmenti observes:

> While Venetian penal legislation displays a great care for property, we find, on the other hand, that crimes of violence against the person were punished by a single fine to the government and to the victim. This mildness towards crimes of personal violence proves that the early laws of Venice diverged widely from the Roman Code; but it also proves that the islanders, jealous of their hard-earned possessions, were determined to defend them against robbery by the severity of the penalties attaching to thefts.[32]

Perhaps it was rather the peculiar role of "property" in the capitalist social order than any superior difficulty of acquiring it which determined its importance in the law. This trait has tended to persist in all future capitalist societies.

And yet it should not be assumed that no interest was taken in social legislation.[. . .] There were child-labor laws to guard against certain employments of children, sanitary and food inspection laws, and other ordinances for the welfare of the people.[33] Individuals as such, then, had *rights* in Venice. But it was in her laws of contract and inheritance that Venice developed her rules of business transactions, the primary concern of her way of life. Moreover, as early as 1167 reference has been made to Venetian "nautical statutes" employed in international treaty engagements.[34]

No feudal courts existed in Venice and the jurisdiction of canon law was highly restricted; the clergy were tried in secular courts for criminal offenses.[35] The importance of judge-made law derived from the procedures of the "judges, councillors, tribunes, gastaldi, delegates, ripari, constables, juries, and notaries" was recognized.[36] Thus a tradition of the law was provided for. And yet in extreme cases, where some offending individual of extraordinary status had contrived to defy the law, resort to the dagger or poison vial was not beneath the dignity of the highest councils.[. . .]

Citizenship

Perhaps as significant a social component as any in capitalist society is the peculiar definition and role which it allows to individuals known as citizens. In final analysis the citizen becomes legally related to a territory and is identified with the interests and fate of the total community. Citizens have *rights* and obligations, and the distinguishing feature of capitalist citizenship inheres in the nature of these attributes. Venice demonstrated that it is possible to administer effectively a capitalist society without any appreciable participation of the masses. Indeed she was able to do so without serious objection from this group, to say nothing of revolt.[37] The ruling class, however, promulgated the typical capitalist conception of democracy: "They gloried in their democracy to the end, even when their government was a rigid oligarchy."[38] In fact the oligarchy readily conceived of its interests as the ideal of the people and offered its chosen leaders to them as if such leadership had sprung from their very optimum desires.[. . .]

The Venetian held his citizenship either by right or by favor; but citizens were not of all the same status. Persons who were born in Venice or had resided there for a certain number of years, except the manumitted and slaves, had the right to citizenship; while the Senate through its subordinate office, the *Provveditori di Comune*, bestowed this right by decree upon certain other persons who sought it—even on foreigners.[39] Citizens were divided into two general classes: the upper group or *intus et extra* and the lower or *de intus*. The patrician class stood out as specially privileged citizens. Ordinarily lesser merchants, the petit-bourgeoisie, constituted the class of "de extra" citizens since no person who practiced a mechanical trade or had such a tradition in his paternal ancestors for three generations could belong to it. Members of this class could aspire to important political offices.[40] Above all, they had the right to sail under the protection of the Venetian flag and to trade in Venetian markets.[41]

De intus citizenship was the heritage of the common people, tradesmen of all kinds who were tax-payers. This type of citizenship was also granted to the numerous skilled workers who were encouraged to come to Venice. Among these, Molmenti observes, "We find natives of all parts of Italy, and of the most various trades, from the simplest to the most highly skilled."[42]

The population of Venice, at 180,000 to 190,000 at the height of the city's power,[43] was divided into three principal types of citizens: the upper commercial class or patricians, the middle, and the workers. The middle class, especially at its upper reaches, was also called original citizens or *cittadini originarii*, and considerable latitude for social and economic development was available to it. In the government it was represented by its "grand chancellor." [. . .]

However, in any leading capitalist nation citizenship itself tends to be a valuable privilege; even the common people may come to realize this fact. In Venice wages and conditions of work were better than in the surrounding area; and the oligarchy, knowing the importance of successful industry to their own economic welfare,[44] sought "to remove all causes of discontent" among the artisans so that on the whole the two classes reached a satisfactory accommodation. Moreover, there was room here for social mobility. . . . Molmenti points this out in saying: "The aristocracy, though jealous of its privileges, did not suppress the development of the people, and we find examples of men of humble and obscure birth rapidly acquiring great riches."[45] The lower class, therefore, found advantages here that were relatively superior to those of their congeners in other parts of Italy.

And yet the ultimate value of Venetian citizenship derived from the privilege of carrying on foreign commerce under the regulations and protection of Venice. This was the enviable source of wealth and power of the people, and they guarded it jealously against foreign usurpation. Thus says Comte Daru:

> The Venetian legislation relative to foreigners, in all that concerned their commerce, was hard . . . and jealous of their advantages. The laws guarded against even the receiving of any foreign merchants on Venetian vessels. Foreigners paid duties twice as heavy as that of Venetian nationals. In the former's disputes with citizens, it was necessary that they bear the expense of obtaining a slow justice. It was neither possible to have constructed in nor to buy ships from the ports of the Republic. The ships, the patrons, the owners of the merchandise—all must be Venetian. . . . Foreigners did not have these privileges and protection and, as a consequence, the benefits available . . . to citizens because they were the rights attached to the quality of the citizen of Venice; thus this kind of condition designated by the estimate of citizenship was brought into being."[46]

In Venice the capitalist citizen thus emerged as an active, self-seeking, responsible individual with a direct material interest in the state and a passionate allegiance to the country.

Notes

1. If geography is to account for the development of cities in this region, Constantinople should take the palm. Her easily defensible position at the crossroads of commerce attracted not only the Roman Empire but also Venice itself, which, even after the islands had become a built-up community, debated seriously the proposition of moving its capital to

the city on the Bosporus. This was in 1221, after Venice had surpassed Constantinople in power and importance.

2. In Roman times "Venice" referred especially to the mainland opposite the lagoons, the Augustan region Venetia. Pompeo Molmenti describes the general development of the area: "In the year 215 B.C. the Veniti allied themselves to the Romans to fight their neighbors the Gauls, and in 183 they voluntarily made submission to the mighty empire of Rome, accepting its religion, law, culture and language. Under Roman dominion the Venetian territory formed, with Gallia Cisalpina, a single province. Ancient writers draw a pleasant picture of the great cities, the fruitful soil, the riches of Venetia, which was both an ornament and a source of strength to the capital. Even in the days of the decline, Venetia and Insurbia were able to bear heavy taxation, thanks to their commerce and their sea trade" (*Venice: Its Individual Growth from the Earliest Beginnings to the Fall of the Republic* [Chicago, 1906], vol. 1, pt. 1, p. 4).

3. Horatio F. Brown, *Venice, an Historical Sketch of the Republic* (1893), pp. 9–10.

4. "We must understand," Professor Ferdinand Schevill points out, "that these three terms, slaves, serfs, landlords, describe the outstanding social elements of the late-Roman agrarian system. The Lombards had only to get rid of the landlord class, either by outright murder or by driving its members into exile, and success was theirs. Without further ado they would acquire title to the expropriated fields, while the slaves and serfs, left undisturbed, would work the farms exactly as before except that the surplus product of their labor would now go to another set of masters" (*History of Florence: From the Founding of the City Through the Renaissance* [New York 1936], p. 18).

5. Cf. Pompeo Molmenti, *Venice: Its Individual Growth from the Earliest Beginnings to the Fall of the Republic*, trans. Horatia F. Brown (Chicago, 1906), vol. 1, p. 71.

6. Samuele Romanin, *Storia Documentata di Venezia* (Venezia, 1861), vol. 1, p. 60.

7. "Of the Venetian Arts, many are recorded on Padovan stones (or gravestones), others can be reasonably conjectured from the state of things. All however were grouped in corporations from the beginning, according to Roman custom. Thus are recorded the blacksmiths, the patch-work workers or weavers of rough cloth (monk's cloth always manufactured in a special way in Venice), the fullers or cleaners of cloth . . . the manufacturers of cards (which alludes to the working of woolens), the merchants, the storekeepers, the chiselers, the potters, the manufacturers of ointments, the gamblers, etc. Nor were the painters lacking among the fugitives, which explains how painting and works in mosaic came to flower so early in Venice; at first naturally with Romano-byzantine forms" (ibid., p. 61).

8. Ibid., p. 70.

9. "It was in this regard," says W. Heyd, "a great advance over all the

other cities of Italy" (*Histoire du Commerce du Levant au Moyen-Age* [Leipzig, 1885], vol. I, p. 109).

10. Cf. F. C. Hodgson, *The Early History of Venice* (London, 1901), pp. 135–36.

11. Schevill emphasizes this: "It is a fact of the greatest importance for the history of medieval Italy first, that the empire of the East did not for many centuries cease to lay claim to the peninsula, and second, that for many generations after Justinian's time it retained within its grasp, even though that grasp was steadily weakening, scattered segments of the Italian coastal area. In short, in one way or another the Eastern empire continued to figure as an element in the complicated play of Italian medieval forces which must always be reckoned with" (*History of Florence*, p. 13). Justinian, (518–565), in his attempt to re-establish the authority of the old Roman emperors, reconquered much of the old Roman territory, including Italy.

12. Horatio F. Brown, *Venice*, p. 15. William Roscue Thayer makes the following comment on this issue: "Longinus freely acknowledged that their habitation was indeed mighty, and that they need fear neither prince nor emperor, but he coaxed them so pleasantly to send an embassy to Constantinople, promising that no formal oath should be exacted of them, that they complied. In due season their envoys returned, bringing the first treaty with the Venetians, as a separate state, negotiated with a foreign power" (*A Short History of Venice* [New York, 1905], p. 11).

13. Comte Daru, *Histoire de la République de Venise* (1840), vol. 1, p. 34; cf. also Heyd, *Histoire du Commerce du Levent*, p. 108.

14. Ibid., p. 81. On this opposite movement of power relationships Charles Diehl quotes Nicephorus Gregoras, a fourteenth-century Greek writer, as follows: "While the Latins steadily increased their profits and their power, the Greeks grew weaker, and every day added fresh calamity to past misfortune. . . . [They] have taken possession not only of all the wealth of the Byzantines, and almost all the revenues from the sea, but also of all the resources that replenish the sovereign's treasury" (*Byzantium: Greatness and Decline* [1919], pp. 195–96). By this time Genoa had already become the leading capitalist competitor of Venice in the exploitation of the Empire.

15. Molmenti, *Venice: Its Individual Growth from the Earliest Beginnings to the Fall of the Republic*, vol. 1, pt. 1, pp. 118–19. "It was in 992 that Venice secured her first formal treaty guaranteeing commercial privileges in the Empire. The 1084 grant was a valuable extension of them" (Diehl, *Byzantium*, pp. 191ff).

16. This capitalist attitude of contempt for exploited peoples, from which race prejudice develops, is described by Charles Diehl: "They made no effort to disguise their mercenary greed or their arrogance and treated not only the lower classes with insolent disdain, but also those of high rank; even the Emperor himself was not spared their insults. 'They treated citizens like slaves,' said a twelfth-century Greek chron-

icler. 'Their boldness and impudence increased with their wealth,' wrote Nicetas, 'until they not only detested the Romans but even defied the threats and commands of the Emperor.' In time they became altogether insufferable" (*Byzantium*, p. 192).

17. Horatio Brown, *Cambridge Modern History*, vol. I, p. 270.

18. Molmenti, *Venice*, p. 18. See also *Cambridge Modern History*, vol. IV, p. 386.

19. Brown, *Venice*, p. 5.

20. *Cambridge Modern History*, vol. IV, p. 387.

21. Molmenti, *Venice*, vol. 1, pt. 1, p. 72.

22. Thayer, *A Short History of Venice*, pp. 14–15.

23. George B. McClellan, *The Oligarchy of Venice*, p. 15. As Comte Daru among others points out, the Venetian nobility "continued to be merchants up to the time when the republic had already fallen from the power and splendor of its commerce" (*Histoire*, vol. IV., p. 79).

24. Ibid., pp. 158–59.

25. Ibid., p. 16. The law of 1297 classified the citizens, giving preference to those who had been already members of the Council. "It divided the citizens into three classes: those who had never been, and whose ancestors had never been, in the Great Council—in numbers by far the largest class; those who were now members; and lastly, those who could point to either a father or an ancestor in the Great Council" (Thayer, *A Short History of Venice*, p. 106).

26. Thayer, *A Short History of Venice*, p. 213.

27. Brown, *Venice*, p. 399.

28. See W. Carew Hazlitt, *The Venetian Republic* (London, 1900), vol. 2, pp. 435 ff., for a discussion of the machinery of state.

29. On this point Hazlitt observes: "It is interesting to contemplate, through the medium of the Coronation Oath of Dandolo, the development and dignity already given to a Common Law, which was archetypical of the Common Law of all other modern European societies" (ibid., p. 406).

30. In the following summary Comte Daru catches the spirit of the Venetian laws: "During the eight centuries, that is to say up to the time when the Venetians wished to become conquerors of the mainland of Italy, the legislation, the politics, had for their principal object the advancement of commerce. Privileges among foreigners, security among them, facilities for the transport of men, commodities, and capital, the establishment of banks, the improvement of monies the encouragement of industry and manufacture, police supervision without being incommodious, religious toleration then little known among other nations, all worked together in the making of a unique Venetian commerce, and they were, of all the men of the world, those who had the greatest freedom to employ their faculties in augmenting their well-being" (*Histoire*, vol. IV, pp. 78–79).

31. Romanin, *Storia Documentata*, vol. 1, p. 337 *passim*.

32. Molmenti, *Venice*, vol. 1, pt. 1, p. 113.

33. "Her declared object," says Horatio F. Brown, "was to win the heart and the affection of her people, and this could only be brought about by attention to their interests" (*Cambridge Modern History*, vol. 1, p. 283).
34. Romanin, *Storia Documentata*, vol. 2, p. 136.
35. Ibid., vol. I, pp. 340–41. But see on the matter of canon law Brown's summary in *Cambridge Modern History*, vol. 1, pp. 268ff. "In one important matter," writes Thayer, "Venice stood firm: she refused to allow civil or mixed causes to be tried in the ecclesiastical court. This was in accordance with her rigid separation of the State from the Church. Even in consenting to the introduction of the Inquisition (1289), she took care to protect herself and her citizens from its tyranny by insisting that the Papal Nuncio, the Patriarch, and the Father Inquisitor, who directed the Holy Office, must be approved by the Doge, and must report without reserve their proceedings to him and to the Senate" (*A Short History of Venice*, p. 222).
36. "All the law-suits and acts relating to accusations, testimony, defense and sentences were registered by the lawyers through two notaries in a special book, which, jealousy guarded, gave proof of the regularity of the judgments. Finally, it was the duty of the *Lawyers of the Commune*, as of all the other magistrates, to present on leaving office, which usually lasted from one year to sixteen months, a memorial of the observation made and the reforms and improvements which needed to be introduced into that branch of administration, a provision which one can never commend enough and which shows a very real desire for betterment in the government, an admirable care in order to profit from experience and to aid progress" (Romanin, *Storia Documentata*, vol. 2, p. 360).
37. In the following, William R. Thayer suggests with what determination the oligarchy excluded even better class people from the administration: "The closing of the Great Council was not accomplished without some protest. The story goes that in 1300 Marin Bocconio, a rich citizen not entitled to nomination to the Council, gathered a few score sympathizers and marched to the Palace, where they knocked boldly on the door and demanded to be admitted to take part in their country's affairs. They were admitted one by one . . . and immediately executed. . . . A more likely account states that the Doge got wind of the plot and had the troop of protestants arrested and tried . . . the ringleaders hanged, head downwards between the columns in the Piazetta" (*A Short History of Venice*, pp. 111–12).
38. Ibid., pp. 29–30.
39. "From the days when Venice began to rule the seas and to claim the respect and admiration of Europe for her political constitution, the privilege of citizenship was eagerly sought by foreigners not merely as an honour but also on account of its utility. The conditions of navigation were at that time wretched, but under the banner of San Marco every one journeyed safely. Even foreign princes and the most il-

lustrious personages of foreign countries sought Venetian citizenship to safeguard their trade and to command, when necessary the protection of Venice" (Molmenti, *Venice*, vol. 1, pt. 1, p. 175).

40. "In order to belong to it," says Romanin, "it was necessary to prove legitimate and honorable birth . . . that one's name had never appeared in the criminal records, and that one was a financial supporter and contributor to the city government. The members of this class had the right to run for ducal posts, up to the ambitious dignity of Great Chancellor. . . , for notary offices, for co-adjutant . . . etc." (*Storia Documentata*, vol. 4, pp. 469–470).

41. Molmenti, *Venice*, vol. 1, pt. 1, pp. 169–70.

42. Ibid., vol. 1, pt. 1, p. 173.

43. Romanin, *Storia Documentata*, vol. 4, p. 468. Cf. Brown in *Cambridge Modern History*, vol. I, p. 257.

44. "It was in short a rule of the Republic to burden the citizens as little as possible and to promote their comfort, since from this depended the true wealth of the State" (Romanin, *Storia Documentata*, vol. 2, p. 388).

45. Molmenti, *Venice*, vol. 1, pt. 2, p. 46.

46. Daru, *Histoire de la République de Venice*, vol. IV, pp. 106–7. This point seems significant enough to be emphasized: "In order to enjoy the favors which the government accorded to commerce, it was necessary to have acquired this right; thus one sees a great number of rich merchants of other nations registered on the list of citizens of Venice. One may cite on this subject a King of Serbia, who, on his departure from Venice, was so afraid of the amount of taxes on the commodities which he imported, that he sought the rights of the Venetian citizen in order to dispense with the payment of these duties. The citizens of the Republic were objects of jealousy in the capital; the merchandise of luxury and even the things of prime necessity could only be supplied by Venetians. To establish a factory (fabrique) outside the dogado it was necessary to obtain a privilege, and for a long time the cities of the mainland could not export their merchandise to foreigners unless they passed through Venice where they paid duty" (p. 107).

16

Economic Underpinning of Venice

Commerce

The trade of Venice [. . .] was dynamic and "worldwide."[1] It had characteristics which differentiated it from all previous systems of commerce. As Brown sees it: "The city was a great reservoir of merchandise constantly filled and constantly emptied again, with eastern luxuries flowing westward and western commodities flowing east."[2] It was to be expected that the government should have an immediate interest in the direction of this commerce. Since the world was not yet organized for capitalist commerce, problems of security and of capital accumulation for distant trade had to be met in part by the state itself. Ships most suited to navigation in different waters were built by the state and sent regularly to various regions with goods and their merchants who hired space in them:

> These fleets were called after their destinations: for example, the Tana fleet, which made for the Black Sea and traded with Russians and Tartars; the Syrian fleet, which dealt with Asia Minor; the Roumanian fleet, destined for Constantinople and the ports of Greece and Roumania; the Egyptian fleet, touching at the ports of Egypt, and lastly the Flanders fleet, which sailed by Tripoli and Tangiers, touched Spain, passed the Straits of Gibraltar, coasted Morocco, and then passing up the shores of Portugal and France, reached Bruges, Antwerp, and London.[3]

The most famous of these argosies was the Flanders fleet, which, [. . .] after calling at many Mediterranean and African ports, sailed through Gibraltar for the great marts of the north; London, Bruges and Antwerp.[4]

In the heyday of Venetian commerce, however, her relationship with Germany was of particular significance. The celebrated Hanseatic League was not only stimulated and educated by this commerce but also had its prosperity centered in it. Until the early fourteenth century (1317), when the Venetian galleys first reached Bruges,[5] the main routes of Venetian goods into Germany were across the Alpine passes [. . .] Before the crusades, however, trade with the emergent German cities did not extend far beyond the Alps, and it is pertinent that German merchants took the initiative in coming to the centers of exchange for their goods. [. . .] The end result of this relationship was the division of early capitalism into two areas of leadership: Venice in the Adriatic and the Hansa in the Baltic. By 1228 the Germans had been established their great trading house the *Fondaco dei Tedeschi* in Venice and, with the Venetians in authority, many rules regulating the division of commerce were laid down.[6] At this period trade with the English was on a quite different basis. Before the rise of the Tudors, Venetian trade in England was typically that of capitalist-feudal relationships.[7] Indeed, Venice has already passed from leadership when England began her ascendancy to capitalist status.

[. . .] Although the Venetians traded mainly in foreign products, their own staples were by no means of trifling concern. Salt, fish, and some manufactures such as glass and cloth formed a nucleus about which the great commercial structure centered. She sought vigorously to monopolize the production of salt in as wide an area as possible. In her immediate vicinity, she either smashed the salt-pans of other peoples or regulated production. In distant areas she bought up salt and thus controlled the market. "It is incredible," says Daru, "how much treasure this sole branch of commerce brought the Venetians."[8] A suggestion of this is given in Molmenti's observation that "not only Italy but also distant lands, depended on Venice for their salt. Caravans numbering forty thousand horses came every year from Hungary, Croatia, and eastern Germany to fetch Venetian salt from Istria."[9] She perfected the art of its manufacture; hence her own product, which she separated from foreign grades, was of the finest quality.[10]

It has been pointed out that the Venetian slave trade was the first capitalistically organized commerce in human beings. Slavery, to be sure, existed from time immemorial, but early in her career Venice brought the traffic within the system of her commodity exchanges and defended it against sporadic moral attacks, principally from the church at Rome. The Venetians bought and sold Christians and infidels alike![11] "They bought slaves, mostly Slavs, Georgians, and Circassians, at Tana and Kaffa in the Crimea, and sold the men in Egypt and the women to the Christians of Western Europe. . . . Venice followed the common practice of enslaving prisoners captured in war, their usual doom being to man the oars of the galleys."[12] This slave trade continued well into the sixteenth century.

Like every other leading capitalist nation, a major share of the carrying trade was indispensable to Venice. From the beginning this trade became a fruitful source of profit and, as she grew, she expanded her interest in it, so that it may be said the Venetians were "the carriers of the world."[13] In this way her shipping remained active and advanced, while she kept her hands on the passenger and freight movements of many other communities.[14] For a long time she was a leading carrier of Florentine manufactures.

In discussing the nature of capitalist society we shall frequently refer to the place of the sea in its organization. Pompeo Molmenti is emphatic in saying: "The Venetians drew all their prosperity from the sea, and to the sea they devoted their whole attention and care."[15] The Venetians, at any rate, were outstanding seamen. The importance of long-range commerce and the relative cheapness of water transportation impels a capitalist people to mastery of this vehicle. But water routes, like land routes, must be established and protected, hence the "lifeline" becomes a typical capitalist phenomenon. The home end of the Venetian lifeline was the Adriatic Sea, and Venice ultimately established such mastery over it as only inland lakes were elsewhere subjected to. The Hansa never went so far on the Baltic.

At first the lagoon-men had to clean out the pirates from the borders of the gulf, especially those on the eastern shores, the Delmatian coast, and then to establish their right to control its shipping. This right was emphasized in 1296 by the imposition of a tax upon all merchandise and vessels navigating its waters, and every ship entering or leaving was vigorously examined. Other cities like Pisa and Genoa complained but without effect, while the weaker communities on its borders submitted docilely to the duty. The Venetians claimed that freedom of the sea had to be produced at a cost, and only Venice was strong enough to maintain that freedom.[. . .]

All this power and skill in shipping [. . .] centered in the Arsenal, the most celebrated shipyard of all time. The state itself controlled it. "The Arsenal was considered the foundation of the power of Venice, the heart of the state. The College, the Senate, and the Council of Ten participated directly in its management."[16] Here outstanding shipwrights were given an opportunity to exercise their ingenuity and to merit the recognition of the state. They built several kinds of ships "according to the requirements of cruising, distant-trade, river navigation . . . and war."[17] They were always conscious of the fact that it was the power and excellence of the fleet which "gave to Venice that commanding position which enabled her to secure commercial advantages to which no other maritime state could pretend."[18]

We shall be continually brought to emphasize the point, even though a demonstration of it must come later, that foreign commerce is indispensable to a capitalist nation. The capitalist nation must trade or perish. This fact is exemplified in Venetian experience, as it is in vital international problems of our own day, by her attitude toward the question of "trading with the enemy." [. . .] The persistent enemy in the East was the Saracens—opposed by all Christendom and, immediately, especially by Constantinople. But the Arabs in the Levant controlled the spice and luxury routes. To secure this trade Venice had to offer in exchange what was demanded, and the Saracens particularly wanted construction materials for war purposes. The eastern emperors knew this; they therefore prohibited such Venetian trade under pain of severe punishment. In 971, as a climax to many earlier warnings, they sent ambassadors to the Republic

> with terrible menaces declaring that if the Venetians continued to trade with the Saracens to the detriment of the empire, all the ships that would be found loaded with iron or other war material, would be burned together with the cargo and ship's crew; that it was therefore necessary to put an immediate stop to the disorder, and remove a sin that deserved divine punishment and rendered the nation ignominious. Then all vowed for themselves and for their successors that they would no longer take arms, wood for building, armour, or iron to the Saracens, nor anything that might be used in war.[19]

And yet, as Heyd observes, "The Venetians had become so accustomed to this commerce that it became for them a vital necessity."[20] In their dilemma, then, they decided to trade surreptitiously with the Moslems. So this commerce, carried on sometimes openly, sometimes in secret, but always morally opposed in the West, continued down to the declining days of the republic. Even during her inevitable wars with the Turks, her tendency was toward peaceful trade with them.

Another important aspect of capitalist commerce is that of "provisioning." Provisioning, simply defined, involves the securing of the consumptive needs of a people mainly through official action. One of the most dramatic instances of this goes back to the story of Joseph's prediction of famine in Egypt, and the storing of corn against the event. At any rate, the provisioning of another people, especially a noncapitalist people, by a capitalist nation is a quite different economic transaction from that of a capitalist nation provisioning itself—indeed from that of a noncapitalist nation provisioning itself.[. . .]

Colonization

Venice herself was territorially far more destitute of the means of subsistence than the empire, but she would not have tolerated for a moment the supplying of these to her by some other nation. In fact, in the very process of provisioning herself, she brought the provisions of others under her control. In principle, when a given consumptive need has been brought into the stream of commerce of a capitalist nation, domestic provisioning tends to take care of itself. For example, Venice had no land for the production of corn; and yet, through her foreign trade, she became most abundantly supplied with it.[. . .]

But there are other provisioning needs of a more dynamic type characteristic of capitalist peoples. They are those demanded by industry: the call for raw materials. This particular requirement tends to gear the economic existence of other communities with which the capitalist nation comes into commercial contact to the demands of capitalist industry. "Venice was not content to go and buy from the foreigners the raw material which she needed; she tried to force those countries to produce her needs. She recruited gangs of workers in Palestine, and sent them into the mountains of Austrian Istria; she covered the land of Friuli with mulberry trees; she tried to grow the sugar cane in the islands of the Levant."[21] Indeed, there is a tendency to go beyond the organization of the economic existence of others to the point of conquest and control of their territory as production areas.[. . .]

There is, then, a capitalist strain toward colonization, the essentials of which should be distinguished from colonization among the ancients. Venice, now a developed capitalist state, forsook individual enterprise in this field, making colonization the business of the government as it was to be later that of the Dutch and British.[22] After the fall of Constantinople in 1204, the Venetians came into possession of many islands in the Aegean Sea, including Salonika and Crete. This territory was administered in true colonial fashion, the control of the economic activities of the natives in the interest of businessmen at home, though with some feudal concessions in favor of that control. It has been pointed out in summary that "the Republic displayed at once the governing ideas of her colonial policy, namely to interfere as little as possible with local institutions; to develop the resources of the country; to encourage trade with the metropolis; to retain only the very highest military and civil appointments in her own hands as a symbol and guarantee of her supremacy.[. . .]"23

It was [also] inevitable that, with her increase in power, Venice should be driven to territorial expansion into the relatively non-capitalist lands to her west. In her earlier days she could be satisfied with treaties for the navigation of the Italian rivers and for other commercial concessions, but now, particularly since the vanquishing of the Genoese at the end of the fourteenth century [. . .], her commercial and industrial demands had become far greater and more insistent: she had to control this critical area.24 And yet, to move in that direction with its endless chain of feudal interrelationships was to embark upon an exhausting and ultimately disastrous conquest. But stagnation was intolerable, hence she reluctantly entered continental diplomacy and war. The vicissitudes of her experience here need not detain us: she made huge gains on the mainland, suffered defeats, became involved with the pope over territorial rights, governed her possessions with liberality and tact so that she held much of them even through her declining days,25 but was never able to organize that territory into a larger Venetian nation.

Industry

Studies on the rise of capitalism have commonly referred to the phenomena which we have been discussing as "commercial capitalism." In due course, however, we shall attempt to demonstrate that all capitalism is essentially commercial. Industry has an important but peculiar place in capitalist society, and the Venetians recognized clearly this importance. They went to great lengths in fostering home industries;26 everywhere, among peoples with whom they traded, they studied carefully the techniques of production: "They saw the sumptuous edifices [of the East]; they entered the workshops where textiles were made, which the West envied without knowing how to imitate; and they perfected their naval architecture in the school of the Greeks, who were then the masters of this art."[27] Moreover, they had the typical capitalist proclivity to import raw materials and export finished products. "They brought to their islands the raw products of others at high cost and were able to increase them greatly in value; such as, for example, linen and hemp to make the riggings of ships and iron for anchors and arms. Greater still were the worth bestowed upon the more precious materials: wool, cotton, silk, silver and gold."[28] Although Venice had many specialties, she was probably most celebrated for the fineness of her glass products. Leading capitalist peoples typically excel in bookmaking, and thus as we should expect, Venice initially showed this trait: "Immediately after the discovery of printing, the Venetian press became celebrated among the scholars of the world."[29]

Although capitalist peoples strive to include and to monopolize an unlimited number of industries, they usually recognize some one or a relatively few of them as traditionally peculiar to their economic order. Pickled herrings played a dominant role in the organization of both the Hanseatic League and the United Provinces; wool was at the heart of Florentine industry and it fostered the rise of capitalism in England, while Venice was indebted to salt.[. . .]

It was, however, in the shipbuilding industry that Venice evinced most clearly the strains of capitalist industrial enterprise. Here emerged large-scale organization for efficient factory production with specialization of skills, under the direction of both private and state enterprise.[. . .]

Her famous plant, the Arsenal,[30] was founded early in the twelfth century, and it gradually became the world's largest industrial organization, employing thousands of workers and spreading over sixty acres of "ground and water." In the fourteenth century it had a capacity of some 40 galleys per year,[31] besides the manufacture of small arms and artillery. As to the size of the vessels, F. C. Lane observes: "The climax of the growth of the great galleys of Venice was reached about the middle of the fifteenth century. Thereafter the merchant galleys for the great trading voyages were practically all of the one large design, able to load about 250 tons below deck."[32] For rapid construction, parts were standardized; and there was some approach to the efficiency of the modern assembly line. A system of bell ringing regulated the time of the workers, who were closely watched for maximum production.[. . .]

Labor

Like all future leading capitalist nations, Venice continually attracted foreign workers. Because of her extensive control of markets, her demand for labor was greater. The coming of the skilled workers from Lucca is not unlike the later immigration of the Huguenots into the capitalist towns of northern Europe. To put it in modern terms, Venice, in her day, was "God's country." Everybody participated in her general prosperity, hence labor was extraordinarily contented. Says Daru:

> The general well-being of the population, the affluence of foreigners in the capital, the tribute of the Orient, the increase of luxury, the interior and exterior movement, the consumption of troops, the arming of flats, all became an occasion of work for the poor, a source of wealth for the speculator and for the State; and this source increased from day to day, because each effect became a cause.[33]

Venice had none of the great uprisings of workers which took place in Florence and in certain of the free cities of Germany and the Low Countries. Besides mere prosperity, however, as we shall attempt to show later, the source of Venetian wealth tended to determine the attitude of workers.

Venice, to be sure, had her labor disputes even though they were not revolutionary. The galley slaves were certainly not a happy lot,[34] and the employers of free labor would not have been true to their tradition if they did not take some opportunity to drive their employees wages down to subsistence. An instance of how this was done is presented in the complaint of a certain society of caulkers "that the shipowners agreed together, ten or twelve of them, not to pay more than a certain wage. Thus they drove wages so low that the caulkers could not make a living. If the caulkers objected and attempted to force higher wages by mutual agreement on their part, the shipowners accused them of conspiracy."[35] The Venetian oligarchy was so powerful that organized labor could not make its weight felt.

Skilled workers were organized into guilds; but, compared to those of other cities, they were politically insignificant. They performed many religious and social services for their members, protected their craft monopoly, and participated with verve in national celebrations but they could not bring employers to terms. During the great state pageants the workers, from the richest guilds to the day laborers, took their places according to status.[36] The constitutions of the guilds were modeled on that of the state with its system of privileged families and doge.[37]

Business Enterprise

Businessmen were at home in Venice, the land of supreme opportunity. Among them there were, as in all subsequent leading capitalist nations, the great aristocrats of foreign trade and the much larger number of lesser merchants and traders who participated mainly in derived domestic commerce. Capitalism, set in motion by its foreign trade, produced all sorts of consumptive demands at home, which [were] naturally satisfied by the trader. Venetian industry created demand for labor and supplied buying power. "Industrial activity," says Daru, "augmented the population; the increase in population augmented consumption of all kinds; and this consumption, still more extended, became a new source of speculation and profit."[38] More specifically it has been observed that "thousands of persons . . . derived a livelihood from the woolen trade, mainly through the large and continual demand by the staff of the Arsenal and by seafarers."[39] In a single lifetime it was possible to move up "from rags to riches" in this society where individual initiative counted. Max Weber's sketch of the rise of the successful businessman may be taken as typical:

> He began as a trader, that is a retailer; then he proceeded to travel overseas, securing from the upper class families a credit of money or good which he turned over in the Levant, sharing his profit on his return with those who provided the loan. If he was successful he got himself into the Venetian circle either by way of land or ships. As a ship owner or land owner the way was open for his ascent into the nobility, down to the closing of the Great Council.[40]

Commerce centered about the activities of the great business leaders; and yet, it is important to note, the power of none of these superseded that of the state. There were no Medici or Fugger in Venice; the Venetians, quite early, saw to that. The establishment and transactions of the great merchants are depicted for us by Romanin:

> One of the principal houses of commerce at the end of the XIV century was that of Albano and Marco Morosini. They traded in their own merchandise and in that of others for a commission. In Aleppo, they owned a branch office from where they covered the markets of various cities: Damascus, Beirut and other shops in Syria, including

Famagosta and Nicosia in Cyprus. Besides the patronage of many foreign businesses in Venice, about fifty Venetian noblemen [commercial nobility] had commercial transactions with the firm; some of the latter had branch offices of their own in other places. The Morosini brothers kept in Aleppo and elsewhere as administrators, two agents besides interpreters, brokers, and a chaplain who had the privilege granted by the two agents to conduct some small business affairs of their own.[41]

Galleys carried the commodities of the West to this port and returned to Venice with Levantine products. Like most foreign traders of the time this mercantile concern dealt also in currency exchange.

In Venice private enterprise was limited only by the apparent requirements of the capitalist society itself. The state galleys did not put the state into business but rather provided means for the expansion of private foreign trade. In fact, privately owned ships, though less well organized and spectacular, did most of the trade.[. . .]

Finance

Although the practice of some sort of money holding and money changing, like trading itself, may be discovered in ancient times, banking and money have assumed vital and characteristic roles in capitalist societies. Money, of course, was indispensable to this trading community, but coinage had to be delayed until its acceptability could be assured. At first, then, the coins of other great states— Franks, Lombards, Eastern Romans—and barter were employed. It is believed that the first Venetian mint was established in the reign of Charlemagne.[42] Thenceforward the city continued to issue coins of increasing importance in world trade until in 1284 the famous gold ducat was minted.[43] Concern about the quality of its currency is a trait of leading capitalist nations; accordingly Romanin observes: "The golden ducat . . . remained always the outstanding coin of the Venetians, distinguished for its purity, its flexibility and color, for the stability of its value and size which it maintained without change, so that it was sought after at all times and everywhere."[44] As we should expect, Venetian money became standard in international trade.

It was characteristic also that the republic should take leadership in banking. In 1160 the state in extremity had to borrow 150,000 silver marks from a group of merchants. This event produced a national debt, and, incidentally, the basis of the Bank of Venice. Indeed, the event was rather similar to that of the founding, centuries later, of the Bank of England, while the Venetian principle of funding that debt has become a commonplace in capitalist communities.[. . .]

The fact of significance for us here is that in this project an important institution of capital accumulation was incidentally established. It gradually evolved fundamental banking practices; its stock circulated as obligations ultimately backed by the state; and it served as a source of investments. It is, furthermore, a characteristic of leading capitalist nations that investment capital tends to flow toward them; hence foreigners sought, as a privilege, to invest in these gilt-edge securities. "The confidence which was almost universally felt in the stability and good faith of Venice, encouraged an extensive resort to [this market]. Foreign princes and capitalists of all nationalities deposited their money in the Funds as the securest investment which could be made."[45] Banking, it is true, did not have its most significant development in Venice, but it had important origins there. Florence, Barcelona, and Genoa made notable early contributions; yet the precedence of Venetian banking has been recognized.[46]

The income of the state was secured principally by taxation of industry and commerce. There was a duty on both imports and exports, on the use of port facilities, on salt and certain other consumption goods, besides profits from banking activities.[47]

Notes

1. Samuele Romanin, *Storia documentata di Venezia* (Venezia, 1861), vol. I, p. 334; see also H. F. Brown, *Venice* (London, 1893), p. 81.
2. Brown, in *Cambridge Modern History*, vol. I, p. 278. "The traffic of the civilized world centered at Rialto," says Pompeo Molmenti, *Venice: Its Individual Growth from the Earliest Beginnings to the Fall of the Republic* (Chicago, 1906), vol. 1, pt. 1, p. 38.
3. Molmenti, *Venice*, p. 134. According to Brown: "The State built the ships, let them out to the highest bidder at auction. Every year six fleets were organised and dispatched: (1) to the Black Sea, (2) to Greece and Constantinople, (3) to the Syrian ports, (4) to Egypt, (5) to Barbary and the north coast of Africa, (6) to England and Flanders. The route and general instructions for each fleet (muda) were carefully discussed in the Senate. Every officer was bound by oath to observe these instructions and to maintain on all occasions the honour of the Republic" (*Cambridge Modern History*, vol. I, p. 277).

4. See Alexandre Pinchart, "Essai sur les relations commerciales des Belges avec le nord de l'Italie et particulièrement avec les Vénetiens, depuis le XIIe jusqu'au XVIe siècle," *Messager des Sciences Historiques, des arts et de la Bibliographie de Belgique* (Gand, 1851), pp. 9–25, and W. C. Hazlitt, *The Venetian Republic* (London, 1900), vol. 2, pp. 568 ff.

5. Of this date Emma Gurney-Salter says, "The first document relating to the Flanders galleys is of 1273, and an Act of 1304 granting the Venetians the right of free trade in England and Flanders is preserved in the *Libri Commemoriali* of the Venetian Archives. The first recorded 'Flanders voyage' was made in 1317 by a 'small' fleet" (*Tudor England Through Venetian Eyes* [London, 1930], p. 21).

6. Cf. Romanin, *Storia Documentata*, vol. 2, p. 372.

7. "In [1340] Edward III, being desirous of prosecuting with vigor his war against France . . . prayed his serenity [the Doge] to lend him his cooperation by organizing at his cost a squadron of forty galleys, which might harass the maritime frontier of the enemy. He granted the Venetians full leave to name their own terms; and he pledged himself to discharge the debt within the twelvemonth in 'gold, silver, and merchandise' [which the Venetians diplomatically refused]. This episode belongs to a time when Venice was more to England than England to Venice; when a Venetian fleet ascending the Thames, could have readily taken London, if London had been worth taking; and when the Venetians looked upon the [English] as a people whose products and manufactures rendered their friendship highly valuable, but scarcely as valuable as the friendship of Bruges or the friendship of Marseilles" (Hazlitt, *Venetian Republic*, vol. 2, pp. 576–78).

8. Comte Daru, *Histoire de la République de Venise* (Brussels, 1840), vol. IV, p. 78.

9. Molmenti, *Venice*, vol. 1, pt. 1, p. 124.

10. Romanin, *Storia Documentata*, vol. 2, p. 135.

11. H. F. Brown emphasizes his capitalist trait of Venice thus: "She trained herself in that egotistical policy which is usually characteristic of a commercial race; her conduct was guided . . . by a consideration of her own sole interest. Frank, Saracen, or Greek, believer or infidel, were alike indifferent to her, except in so far as they affected for the moment her own prospects of aggrandisement" (*Venice*, p. 41).

12. W. R. Thayer, *A Short History of Venice*, p. 227; see also Molmenti, *Venice*, vol. 1, pt. 1, pp. 124–25.

13. Hazlitt, *Venetian Repubic*, vol. 2, pp. 563–64.

14. See Romanin, *Storia Documentata*, vol. 1, p. 335.

15. Molmenti; *Venice*, vol. 1, pt. 1, p. 122.

16. F. C. Lane, *Venetian Ships and Shipbuilders of the Renaissance* (Baltimore, 1943), p. 152.

17. Romanin, *Storia Documentata*, vol. 1, p. 336.

18. Brown, *Venice*, p. 64.

19. Romanin, *Storia Documentata*, vol. 1, p. 248. For a translation of the

Doge's equivocal answer to this 971 complaint see: R. S. Lopez and
I. W. Raymond, *Trade in the Mediterranean World: Illustrative Documents*
(New York, 1955), pp. 333–35.

20. W. Heyd, *Histeire du Commerce du Levant au Moyen-Age* (Leipzig, 1885),
pp. 113–14. "Trade with Moslem areas," says Archibald R. Lewis, "was
their economic lifeblood" (*Naval Power and Trade in the Mediterranean,
A.D. 500–1100* [Princeton, 1951], p. 95). In discussing the continuing
nature of this problem F. C. Hodgson argues that "if the European
states were not prepared to forego all trade with the East—to do
without silk, and pepper, and camphor, and cinnamon—they must
needs traffic with Mussulmans, or depend upon the long and difficult
caravan routes that led over the steppes of Central Asia to the Volga
and the Black Sea. All the easiest and best known routes from the East
to the West passed through territories subject to the successors of the
Prophet. . . . The Church itself was in part responsible for this intercourse with the unbelievers. There was a constant demand in the
West, especially at Rome, for pearls and precious stones to adorn
crosses and vestments, and for incense for the Church services; all
these commodities came from the East" (*The Early History of Venice*
[London, 1901], pp. 160 and 164).

21. Daru, *Histoire de la Republique de Venise*, vol. IV, p. 111.

22. Jacob Strieder reaches a similar conclusion in saying: "The Italian city
states developed a colonial system in the Mediterranean, a system
which was a precursor and a prototype for Spain and Portugal in the
fifteenth and sixteenth centuries, and even for Holland in the seventeenth" (*Jacob Fugger the Rich* [New York, 1931], p. 13).

23. Brown, *Cambridge Modern History*, Vol. I, p. 256.

24. In the following explanation by Brown a typical situation of the capitalist nation emerges: "Without a provision-yielding district at her
back, any maritime reverse rendered Venice liable to blockade and
starvation. . . . Another consideration . . . rendered it difficult for
Venice to avoid acquiring mainland territory; that was the question of
the passes. Had the mainland to the foot of the Alps and the passes
over the Alps into Germany been in the hands of a power other than
Venice, that power would, even in times of peace, indubitably have
reaped a large share of Venetian commercial profits by imposing taxes
for transit; and in time of war would have been able to check Venetian
land traffic entirely. It seems, then, that it was hardly possible for
Venice to have avoided occupying mainland territory" (*Venice*,
pp. 262–63).

25. See Cecilia M. Ady in *Cambridge Medieval History*, vol. I, pp. 230–31;
and Brown, *Venice*, pp. 248–49.

26. Daru, *Histoire de la Republique de Venise*, vol. IV, pp. 123–24.

27. Ibid., vol. I, p. 39.

38. Ibid., vol. IV, pp. 110–11. Brown says: "Among the most important
industries of Venice we find metal work, both copper and iron, and
the art of bell-founding among the earliest. . . . The silk trade was

introduced from Lucca . . . Cloth of gold, wrought leather, and above all, bead making, glass blowing, and the manufacture of mirrors" (*Venice*, p. 154). Great staple industries, however, were salt making, salt fish, and shipbuilding. See also, for other industries, Romanin, *Storia Documentata*, vol. 1, p. 335.

29. Daru, *Histoire de la Republique de Venise*, vol. IV, p. 126; see also Hazlitt, *Venetian Republic*, vol. 2, pp. 717ff.

30. On the origin of the name Romanin says: "Having enlarged the pools and excavated there a deep lake, the Venetians called the place by a name taken from the Arabs, among whom such enclosures were probably first in use, *Darsana* and corruptly *Arsana*, finally *Arsenale*" (*Storia Documentata*, vol. 2, p. 34).

31. J. H. Clapham in *Cambridge Medieval History*, vol. VI, p. 501. Says Hazlitt: "The numerical complement of vessels in the arsenal at the time of the greatest prosperity—about 1450—has been computed at 3300, manned by 35,000 hands, and employing in their maintenance and renewal a staff of 16,000 skilled operatives" (*Venetian Republic*, vol. 1, p. 130).

32. Lane, *Venetian Ships and Shipbuilders*, p. 15.

33. Daru, *Histoire de la République de Venise*, vol. IV, p. 111. See also Romanin, *Storia Documentata*, vol. 2, pp. 392–93.

34. It should not be supposed that slave labor formed the basis of Venetian wealth; as Lane points out: "The toiling oarsmen of the Venetian galleys were not, before the sixteenth century, slaves chained to their benches, but free citizens ready to exchange their oars for their weapons when battle was joined" (*Venetian Ships and Shipbuilders*, p. 6).

35. Ibid., pp. 80–81.

36. Ibid., p. 74.

37. See Molmenti, *Venice*, vol. 1, pt. 1, p. 185.

38. Daru, *Histoire de la République de Venise*, vol. IV, p. 111.

39. Hazlitt, *Venetian Republic*, vol. 2, p. 650.

40. Max Weber, *General Economic History*, trans. Frank H. Knight (London, 1923), p. 324.

41. Romanin, *Storia Documentata*, vol. 2, pp. 341–42.

42. See Romanin, *Storia Documentata*, vol. 1, pp. 225–26; cf. Molmenti, vol. 1, pt. 1, pp. 152–53 and 155; and Brown, *Venice*, pp. 55–56.

43. Florence had already issued her gold Florin in 1252.

44. Romanin, *Storia Documentata*, vol. 2, p. 320; see also p. 342. On the same point Molmenti writes: "This, the finest and most highly valued coin of Venice . . . was not called the sequin till 1543. The name of 'ducat' was then applied to the silver coin of 1561" (*Venice*, vol. 1, pt. 1, p. 157).

45. Hazlitt, *Venetian Republic*, vol. 2, pp. 643ff.

46. In a note for 1171 David Macpherson writes: "New ideas suggested by the vast increase in Venetian commerce, gradually produced the bank of Venice, which is generally acknowledged to be the most ancient establishment of kind banks, which were set up, first in some other

commercial cities on the coast of the Mediterranean Sea, and in process of time in almost every city and town in Europe" (*Annals of Commerce* [London, 1805], vol. 1, p. 342. See also James W. Thompson, *Economic History of the Later Middle Ages* (New York and London, 1931), p. 422; Frederick C. Lane, "Venetian Bankers, 1496–1533," *Journal of Political Economy* 45 (1937): 187–206.

47. See Hazlitt, *Venetian Republic*, vol. 2, pp. 650ff.; Romanin, *Storia Documentata*, vol. 2, p. 387, and vol. 3, pp. 350–51; and Brown, *Venice*, pp. 255–256.

| 17 |

Structure of the System

We may regard the elementary structure of the capitalist system as constituted of the whole network of its territorial units and their interrelationships. The nations, colonies, and dependent communities thus related tend to form a commercial and power-status gradient with its most energetic and prestigious component at the top. In this matrix, economic and political positions are in constant flux, the rate depending largely on the vicissitudes of the leader. The latter maintains its position in competition with other major aspirants. Thus, apart from war and diplomacy, international competition takes place in a variety of internal and external market situations, ordinarily with entrepreneurs and business enterprises initiating the transactions.

It may be shown, then, that from the very inception of capitalism in Europe, the internal structure of the system has been formed by a continually readjusting and expanding constellation of economically interlocking entities. The system first became irreversibly organized at about the opening of the thirteenth century with two dominating centers: one in the Mediterranean and the other in the Baltic. Then, with the discovery of the New World, Holland gradually emerged as leader of a more unified structure. Later, under the leadership of Great Britain, the process of expansion and unification continued until practically the whole world became integrated into an interdependent rhythmic unity with a single major nucleus. The system apparently reached its highest state of perfection between 1870 and the First World War.

Among many criteria which might be used in classifying the units of the system, the extent to which a community has been able to control its foreign commercial relations seems crucial. The leader nation is normally least subject to the economic restraints and plans of other nations, while it is most influential in altering the affairs of others in its own interests. This does not mean, however, that the leader is ever completely independent. Indeed, leadership has meant greater and greater dependence upon the rest of the system, but this dependence is characterized by progressive diversification. There are no closed capitalist societies, and any disruption of the system must be reflected as a disruption of capitalism itself. Recently, in an address before an assembly of outstanding businessmen, this point was emphasized by one of their congeners:

> The capitalist system is essentially an international system. If it cannot function internationally, it will break down completely. . . . Capitalism, even in modified form—that is, with the essentials of private initiative in economic activity maintained—must be recognized as only possible in an integrated world society with full facilities for a maximum of international economic activity assured.[1]

Thus, despite the apparent exclusiveness of capitalist nations, they are in fact closely bound together in a logical system of universal market relationships.

The Integral Order

If we think of this system as it functioned during, say, the decade before 1914 and perhaps during its period of unstable resuscitation in the 1920s we can recognize its territorial structure headed by a pace-setting nation, Great Britain or the United States, followed by a few advanced European nations and Japan, each with varying potentialities for growth and differing competitive capacities. In the face of the United States and Germany, no other country could then reasonably aspire to world leadership. Although some sought to imitate the nationalistic pretension of the *leaders,* in reality they were more or less resigned *subsidiaries.*

Then, in a relatively subordinate position to these subsidiaries, came a group of "new nations"—the British dominions and Argentina—each with large stocks of natural resources relative to population and with ambitions and capabilities for development somewhat similar to those of the United States. These may be called the *progressives.* The progressives, however, did not have the same open road to success as the United States had, and their growth was already limited by plethoric industrial capacity in Europe and the United States. Basic industries in Canada and Latin America, for example, were mostly financed by U.S. capital and managed by American corporations.

In the fourth and fifth categories fell the great areas of capitalist exploitation. Pre-revolutionary Russia,[2] China, the Near East, and the rest of South America were considered *dependent* communities with relatively little self-initiative in foreign commerce and subject to the immediate, self-interested, economic calculations of the great powers.[. . .]

The *dependents* tended to be included in the so-called spheres of influence of the leading powers. While, however, there was some question as to whether it was sound capitalist strategy to seize direct control of the economic resources of the dependents, no such question arose concerning the *passives,* the lowest group. The passives constituted virtually all of Africa, the rest of Asia, the West Indies, and the islands of the Pacific. They were regarded by the leading powers as having no international rights. Their peoples were thus voiceless, and their resources were organized directly with a view to the enhancement of the economic welfare of any active capitalist nation that was able to establish and maintain control.[3]

Although the structural pattern here described developed historically, through an interplay of economic, military, and diplomatic forces, into a nicely adjusted mechanism, it was, in fact, a social process continually in flux. Any classification such as I have presented may thus be open to question, especially at the margins. But attempts at absolute precision may detract from the purpose of classification.[4] Figure 1 is intended to suggest the position of the groups and their relative population weights in percentages.

Market Situations

Capitalist production is production for markets and not immediately for consumption. The fundamental opportunities for the accumulation of wealth by leader nations in the capitalist systems rests in the imbalance of the world market situations. These situations may be characterized in terms of degrees of sophistication, power of self-determination, and kinds of resources. The basic and most coveted market relation is that between leading, highly sophisticated, capitalist nations and backward areas with extensive resources. It is mainly in such markets that trade among the active capitalist nations acquires its momentum. A leading nation may thus actually encourage another nation to exploit a backward country in the interest of greater and more profitable commerce with the secondary country. Already the trade of thirteenth- and fourteenth-century capitalism had evolved five essential market situations, namely: (a) that between the advanced capitalist cities and

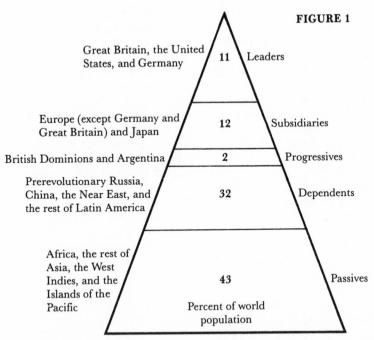

FIGURE 1

Great Britain, the United States, and Germany — 11 — Leaders

Europe (except Germany and Great Britain) and Japan — 12 — Subsidiaries

British Dominions and Argentina — 2 — Progressives

Prerevolutionary Russia, China, the Near East, and the rest of Latin America — 32 — Dependents

Africa, the rest of Asia, the West Indies, and the Islands of the Pacific — 43 — Passives

Percent of world population

noncapitalist peoples; (b) among the advanced capitalist cities; (c) between the advanced cities and minor European towns; (d) in the highly competitive situation at the fairs; and (e) in domestic transactions. The commercial network which had Venice and the Hanseatic League as focal points may be indicated by Figure 2.

. . . Although the trade with any one of the backward communities may have amounted to less in value than between Venice and the League, the total trade with the unsophisticated peoples was indispensable to the commerce between these two major national cities (if we may call the organization of the Hanse a city). Indeed, it seems that capitalism itself depends pivotally neither upon the market situation among advanced capitalist nations, nor upon domestic transactions, but rather upon the economic and political relations developing between the major capitalist nations and the backward peoples. Here lies the heart of the imbalance and elasticity of capitalist market situations. There is no substitute for it. When Venice lost its eastern trade and the Hansa its *kontors*, they both lost their traditional status as capitalist powers. Both needed the products which each acquired abroad, not particularly for domestic consumption but to support their profitable circle of

FIGURE 2

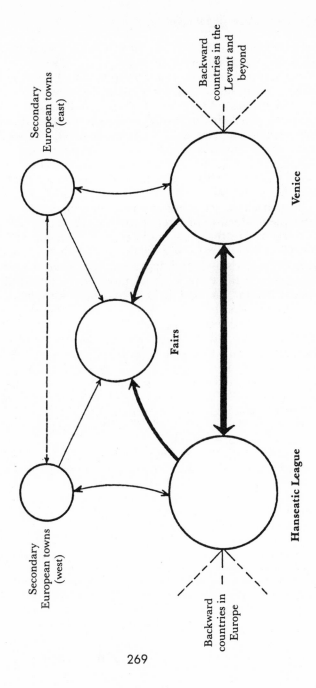

Secondary European towns (east)

Venice

Backward countries in the Levant and beyond

Fairs

Secondary European towns (west)

Hanseatic League

Backward countries in Europe

external commerce. Moreover, the economic principles involved in each of these market situations must [. . .] be distinct.

Even in this elementary though fundamental pattern of capitalist commerce, the home market tends to become increasingly complex. The masses are kept busy with the handling and processing of goods; the availability of foreign markets stimulates domestic manufacture; and the city, as a reservoir of profits, expands its consumption of goods and increases its expenditure on science, learning, art, religion, recreation, and so on. The home market becomes, consequently, highly intricate, interdependent, and speciously self-sufficient.

The market structure of the fully developed capitalist system under the leadership of Great Britain was more complicated than that organized by the cities, but its essential elements were retained. The axis of the structure was still the market situation of the leader, Great Britain, vis-à-vis the dependent and passive countries situated mainly in the tropics. The United States, as a leading power opposite Britain, also had major transactions with the tropics, and, as might be expected, with Britain and the dominions as well.[5] Germany, a third focus of capitalist commerce, traded precariously with the tropics and the dominions on the one hand and, on the other, largely with European countries, [that is,] with the subsidiaries. The weak arm of the German market situation, as this country moved toward a dominant position in the capitalist system, was her tenuous access to the resources of backward territories.[6] And, like Genoa vis-à-vis Venice in another age, she fought desperately against Great Britain and the United States to a frustrating finish for a master's share of them.[7]

The place of the fairs was eventually taken largely by the Bank of England and the great stock and commodity exchanges in London, New York, Chicago, Paris, Berlin, and Tokyo.[8] The major changes in the home market situation centered in the increasing role of technology in the processing and manufacture of goods. It seems to me that any formulation of capitalist economic principles which ignores the importance of these differential market situations of capitalist commerce must remain inadequate as an explanation of economic reality.

The Business Enterprise

The representative capitalist enterprise is thus an international business organization. The validity of this statement may be most clearly recognized if it is regarded in the light of the experience of the early capitalist cities, and Holland and England. In a capitalist society, enterprises with exclusively domestic interests such as those concerned with internal transportation and communication, service, and provisioning may be thought of as complementary to essentially capitalist enterprises. This is another way of saying that in the absence of capitalist businesses identified with foreign relations, there can be no capitalist system. The critical enterprise is thus the domestic unit in whose economic interest the capitalist state fashions its foreign policy. It must follow, therefore, that the national interest in the international relations of an active capitalist state will be represented mainly by the consensus of the leadership of its domestic enterprises engaged in, or immediately affected by, foreign trade. It is in this tightly woven in-group of businessmen that nationalism in the capitalist state has its being.

In leading nations, the capitalist business enterprise is a relatively large, profit-making organization contrived by private citizens in their own interest and yielding its wealth chiefly through the commercial or industrial ingenuity of its contrivers. Nevertheless, it abides by the traditions, rules, and laws of the state. Werner Sombart called it an "abstract unity," an "intellectual construct."⁹ The capitalist enterprise cannot, therefore, thrive outside a capitalist society. Indeed, the capitalist society develops essentially in response to the peculiar needs of its dominant business enterprises.

The enterprise is accordingly more than an isolated venture. It embodies a more or less permanent structure and system of relationships through which the plans and actions of an entrepreneur may be effectuated. It tends, furthermore, to have objective reality, and to persist beyond the lifetime of the businessman. Since, indeed, the welfare of the capitalist state depends on the success of its enterprises, the state naturally has an interest in this continuity. The durability of the enterprise tends to establish permanent sources of wealth not only for single individuals, but also for generations of families; it becomes the basis of a multiplicity of urban dynasties. In his study of this phenomenon as it occurs in the United States, Henry H. Klein concludes:

> Dynastic Europe is dead, but the dynasties in America flourish. There are more dynasties in the United States than ever existed in the old world; and their wealth-power is greater than all the king-power combined. Theirs is the power of life and death over the whole human race. There is the Dynasty of Oil and the Dynasty of Copper, the Dynasty of Beef and the Dynasty of Coal, the Dynasty of Steel and the Dynasty of Ships, the Dynasty of Tobacco, the Dynasty

of Rubber, the Dynasty of Sugar, the Dynasty of Telephone and
Telegraph, and the dynasties of a hundred other things in essential
use by the people."[10]

The dynastic element in the enterprise, of course, has frequently
developed even more strikingly in certain capitalist communities of
Europe; for example, the Medici, Fugger, and Rothschild financial
dynasties.[11] In recent times, however, continuity has been increasingly lodged in the great corporation.

As I have indicated, a peculiar trait of the capitalist enterprise, as
distinct from what has been called passive commercial establishments, is its tendency to be organized internationally. With head-
quarters at home, it sets up branches or commissions for
regularized transactions in foreign communities. This ordinarily
leads to protective involvements of the parent state: to the maintenance abroad of embassies, consulates, and even military stations.
Feudalism knew no such system of foreign representation, and
Rome was permanently represented only within her empire.

Under capitalism, the average business enterprise has tended to
increase in size. In foreign trade, the control of ever larger quantities of capital is likely to be an important factor. It was in this trade
that the modern corporation, both regulated and joint-stock, first
became established. The corporation facilitated the necessary
amassing of capital for the exploitation of distant markets. It was
also in foreign commerce that wholesale enterprise had its critical
origins. The great merchants of the medieval capitalist cities ordinarily left retailing to domestic shopkeepers. As Pirenne says of
these merchants, "It is in gross that they export and import."[12]

In the capitalist nation, businesses tend to constitute an informal
hierarchy. The great industries and financial houses on the one
hand, and the retail enterprises—the private community groceries,
haberdasheries, and so on—on the other, fall into opposite positions of economic power and national significance. The greater the
extent of capitalist organization for the production of consumer
goods, the less the private community businessman can influence
the market for them—hence the familiar phenomenon of commercial, industrial, and financial leadership. Prices are ordinarily determined by the leaders. The tendency toward monopoly is thus ever
present in the system. Professor J. W. Markham observes: "Nearly
every major industry in the American economy has, in its initial
stages of development, been dominated by a single firm—the Slater
Mill in cotton textiles, the Firestone Company in rubber tires,
Birdseye in frozen foods, the American Viscose Corporation in
rayon yarn, etc."[13]

The small community businessman is typically a distributor of goods, the prices of which he can do very little to influence. By the opening of the seventeenth century, at least, all the major forms of business organization—the individual proprietorship, the partnership, and the corporation—were in operation. The joint-stock company, the most advanced of these forms, probably goes back to fourteenth-century Italy.[14] Its advantages have been frequently listed: its greater capacity for survival, its power to accumulate and to impersonalize capital, and the relative security of uncommitted assets of stockholders from legal involvement, especially in bankruptcy proceedings, have made it ideally suited to capitalist needs.

In all the leading nations since the rise of Holland, the corporation has had a dominant position. In England, as I have intimated, it was perfected before the industrial revolution, mainly in the fields of foreign commerce, banking, and speculation. Its tendency to expand, apparently without limit, has sometimes brought it into sharp political conflict with its home government. Capitalist society abhors the rise of any uncontrollable power within its jurisdiction; this was true of the early capitalist cities and it is so today. In their investigation of the American experience, Professors Berle and Means conclude:

> The rise of the modern corporation has brought a concentration of economic power which can compete on equal terms with the modern state—economic power versus political power, each strong in its own field. The state seeks in some aspects to regulate the corporation, while the corporation, steadily becoming more powerful, makes every effort to avoid such regulation. Where its own interests are concerned, it even attempts to dominate the state. The future may see the economic organism, now typified by the corporation, not only on an equal plane with the state, but possibly even superseding it as the dominant form of social organization. The law of the corporations, accordingly, might well be considered as a potential constitutional law for the new economic state.[15]

But perhaps the authors have gone too far in their speculations. The political organization is the societal instrument. If any business enterprise, or group of enterprises, were to become so large and powerful that it could attempt to dominate the state, it would then be matching political power with political power, not economic with political. In the event that the state should lose such an opposition, capitalist society would break down.[. . .]

At any rate, I have quoted the statement by Professors Berle and Means at length because it describes vigorously an inherent relationship between the enterprise and the state. As I noted earlier, however, the interests of the capitalist state tend to coincide with those of its larger enterprises; there is thus no fundamental antagonism between state and business. What appear to be categorical conflicts may in fact be only factional disputes, or the reaction of some individual firm to the consensus of the others. The Sherman Anti-Trust Act, for instance, is not an anticorporation law; it is rather a businessmen's regulation in the interest of wider opportunity for a larger group of corporations. And this accounts in part for the looseness with which the law is enforced, especially in foreign trade relations.

Technique of the Enterprise

Business technique may be considered [. . .] as part of the structure of the enterprise; it is available to the entrepreneur as an instrument. Of the various business methods and practices, double-entry bookkeeping has ordinarily been given first place. In fact, some students have come very close to ascribing the major influence in the rise of capitalism to the development of bookkeeping.[16] Double-entry bookkeeping, however, seems to be but one result of the application of capitalist rationalism to the systematization of business accounts. That this need is an inherent and continuing one is indicated by the concomitant growth in complexity of accounting methods and the technology allocated to its service.

Double-entry bookkeeping evolved in Italy in the first half of the fourteenth century, far in advance of imitations in the North. According to Dr. Florence Edler: "Venice took the lead in the development of the science of bookkeeping and set the style for most of Italy and northern Europe. Indeed, bookkeeping by double entry was popularly known in the sixteenth century as 'bookkeeping according to the method of Venice.'"[17] The scientific keeping of books allows the entrepreneur to gauge accurately the results of his transactions.

Another primary instrument of capitalist enterprise is the bill of exchange, which the Florentines used in their various foreign transactions.[18] It has since become indispensable to leading capitalist nations. The bill of exchange increased the fluidity of capitalist transactions and served increasingly as the principal means of international commercial settlement.[19] At a time when the Dutch had become the leading innovators of techniques in business, Sir Josiah Child, who never missed an opportunity to observe advanced practices in that country, had this to say regarding the advantages of the bill of exchange:

> The law that is in use among them [allows] for transferring of bills for debt from one man to another; this is of extraordinary advantage to them in their commerce; by means of which, they can turn their stocks twice or thrice in trade, for once that we can in England; because having sold our foreign goods here, we cannot buy again to advantage, till we are possest of our money; which perhaps, we shall be six, nine, or twelve months in recovering: and if what we sell be considerable, it is a good man's work all the year to be following vintners and shopkeepers for money, whereas, were the law for transferring bills in practice with us, we could presently after sale of our goods, dispose of our bills, and close up our accounts, to do which, the advantage, ease, and accommodations it would be to trade, is so great, that none but merchants who have lived where that custom is in use, can value to its due proportion.[20]

Incidentally, Child's distinction between "vintners and shop-keepers" on the one hand, and "merchants" on the other, is an elementary one which needs to be constantly kept in mind in any analysis of capitalist development.

Commercial banking grew hand in hand with the increasing currency of these credit instruments. The development, furthermore, of risk-bearing institutions in the capitalist cities added still another pillar to the structure of the enterprise. Insurance in various forms helped to stabilize business. It goes without saying that a reliable monetary system constituted the primary matrix of commercial relations.

Notes

1. Henry F. Grady, address before the National Foreign Trade Convention, in *Report of the 29th N.F.T. Convention* (1942), pp. 462–63.
2. It could be argued with reason that Russia before World War I should not be placed so low in this scheme, for she was herself imperialistically aggressive among Asiatic and Balkan peoples. But Russia did not yet have its capitalist revolution; Western capitalists could still make deals directly with its feudalistic Czar; its industrialization was relatively backward; its oil, coal, and steel were heavily controlled by Anglo-French interests; and it was looked upon by England, France, Germany, and even Japan, as an area open not only to investment, but also to territorial conquest.
3. "Even today," wrote Gustav Schmoller before the turn of the century,

"economic powers seek to utilize their economic superiority in all their international relations, and to retain weaker nations in dependence; even today any half-civilized nation or tribe, among whom the English or French establish themselves, is in danger, first, of a sort of slavery for debt and an unfavourable balance of trade, and, following closely in the wake, of political annexation and economic exploitation" (*The Mercantile System* [New York, 1896], p. 63; see also Leonard Woolf, *Empire and Commerce in Africa* [London, 1919], pp. 53–54).

4. For some comparative figures see Merrill K. Bennett, "Population, Food, and Economic Progress," *The Rice Institute Pamphlet*, July 1952, p. 68.

5. Cf. Richard W. Van Alstyne, *The Rising American Empire* (New York, 1940), chap. VII.

6. For a more detailed and statistical presentation of this subject see League of Nations, *The Network of World Trade* (Geneva, 1942); also Folke Hilgerdt, "The Case of Multilateral Trade," *American Economic Review*, Supplement 33, no. 1 (March 1943), 391–407.

7. Cf. Parker T. Moon, *Imperialism and World Politics* (New York, 1932), p. 475.

8. Cf. Oliver C. Cox, *The Foundations of Capitalism* (New York, 1959), pp. 262ff.

9. Werner Sombart, *Der Moderne Kapitalismus*, vol. I (Munich and Leipzig, 1928), p. 321; and "Capitalism," *Encyclopedia of the Social Sciences*.

10. Henry H. Klein, *Dynastic America and Those Who Run It* (New York, 1921), p. 11.

11. In his research on the Fugger family, Jacob Strieder gives particular attention to the problem of the family's providing for succession to leadership in the business, see *Jacob Fugger the Rich*, trans. M. L. Hartsough (New York, 1921).

12. Henri Pirenne, "The Stages in the Social History of Capitalism," *The American Historical Review*, vol. 29, p. 504; cf. James W. Thompson, *Economic and Social History of Europe in the Later Middle Ages* (New York and London, 1931), p. 586.

13. J. W. Markham, "The Nature and Significance of Price Leadership," *American Economic Review* 51 (December 1951): 895–96.

14. Cf. W. Miller, "The Genoese in Chios, 1346–1566," *English Historical Review* XXX (1915): 418–32.

15. Adolf A. Berle, Jr., and Gardiner C. Means, *The Modern Corporation and Private Property* (New York, 1932), p. 357. See also Edward S. Mason, ed., *The Corporation in Modern Society* (Cambridge, Mass., 1960), pp. xii and 169ff.

16. Cf. B. S. Yamey, "Scientific Bookkeeping and the Rise of Capitalism," *Economic History Review* 1, nos. 2 and 3 (London, 1949): 99–113; also J. W. Thompson, *Economic and Social History of Europe in the Later Middle Ages* (New York and London, 1931), p. 449.

17. Florence Edler, "The Oldest Example of Double Entry Bookkeeping," *Bulletin of the Business Historical Society* 4, no. 4 (June 1930): 13.

18. Cox, *The Foundations of Capitalism*, p. 166.
19. Professor J. W. Thompson lists some of the early forms of the bill as follows: "The bill payable to order, and the promissory note; the ordinary bill drawn in the money of the country where it was payable, and the bill payable in another country at the rate current when due; the bill payable in a place specified, or where cargo was discharged; the bill to mature at date fixed, or the draft. The birth of the concept of credit and its conversion to usages of business surely is one of the most important events in European economic history" (*Economic and Social History of Europe in the Later Middle Ages*, p. 433).
20. Josiah Child, *A New Discourse of Trade*, 5th ed. (Glasgow, 1751), p. 5.

Assumption of Leadership

Nature of the Role

The confident assumption of leadership of the capitalist system by American commerce was one of the "natural" expectations of capitalism. Long before the industrial revolution, English mercantilists, as we have noticed elsewhere,[1] predicted this event; and from time to time since then, even at the height of Britain's hegemony, the coming of American ascendance was conceded. Furthermore, the pattern of development in the system was always such that there was never any significant alliance among other nations to obstruct her forward march. In the last quarter of the nineteenth century Mr. Gladstone is reported to have said as part of a general conviction that the British have "no more title" against the American right to leadership "than Venice, or Genoa, or Holland had against us."[2] To be sure, there were always important reservations as to when and how the torch would be taken, but the dominant tendency followed a definable logic of the system.

Three factors seem to have decided the competitive position of the United States as compared to, say, that of Brazil, Russia, or India: its superb capitalist organization, its freedom to employ the most advanced capitalist techniques, and its vast natural resources. Given comparable forms of capitalist societal organization, the basis of victory in the international struggle for markets had now clearly become supremacy in mass industrial production. The relative size of the domestic market, making it possible to apply capitalist techniques in production to an ever larger number of commodities and continually to perfect existing methods, gave the United States a singular advantage over her competitors. The market was supported in part by an upward trend in wages.[3]

It should be emphasized, however, that the American market was always tied into the global system.[4] In this respect it differed in degree and character from, say, the even larger potential Russian or Chinese market. The accession to leadership did not mean greater capacity to endure economic isolation; to the contrary, leadership meant embarkation upon a more complete and responsive integration of the domestic productive processes with production in foreign countries. In other words, the leader role involved in its totality a continually increasing dependence upon foreign economic relations. This situation was clearly recognized by the major American business community. In 1922, for instance, James S. Alexander, President of the National Bank of Commerce in New York, observed:

> There is much to suggest the increased importance of the United States in the economy of the world. Granting all this, however, we must not forget that growth in importance does not necessarily mean growth in independence. On the contrary if there is one thing that is now clear in the light of recent evidence, it is that with the growing importance of the United States has come growing and unmistakable dependence upon the rest of the world.[5]

Leadership thus enmeshed the leader ever more closely and fatefully into the universal network of disparate economies.

The Quest of Peace

Although at the end of [World War I] the American business community opposed the country's entry into the League of Nations because it seemed to involve too many "foreign entanglements," businessmen recognized nevertheless a vital need to ensure world economic stability. It became apparent that the advantages of leadership could be most effectively utilized only in a universal pax Americana similar to the nineteenth-century British peace. There was at this time, however, no comparable political structure capable of engendering forces sufficient to limit the free play of national economic ambitions. Therefore, although both the Treaty of Versailles and the Covenant of the League of Nations had recognized the necessity of working for a "reduction of national armaments,"[6] and indeed some work had already been done toward the end of producing a disarmament program, American conservatives proceeded to agitate for independent action to restrict the war-making potentials of the world. The following declaration in 1921 by Frank H. Taylor, President of the S. S. White Dental Manufacturing Co., may be taken as representative of the consensus of this community:

> In times of peace, foreign accounts have sooner or later been paid. Fundamentally the great credit risk has always been war. We ought to

unite in a great nation-wide call upon Washington to limit armament. We should apply ourselves to this end with all our definitive power, not stopping at mere declaration. It is a specious argument to assert that man is a fighting animal, that because we have always had war we always will have wars.[7]

The war-weary American public was quite ready to move with alacrity behind almost any program for peace, hence all sections of the population welcomed and supported the calling of the Washington Disarmament Conference in the summer of 1921. The Conference dealt chiefly with the limitation of naval power among the Great Powers, especially Great Britain, Japan, France, and the United States. Its positive accomplishments did not, of course, remove the basis of all future wars, but they included workable agreements to reduce the number and capacity of battleships, and they set a pattern for similar conferences both in Europe and the United States.

The disarmament movement was thus the American way of establishing peace for the system. The alternative would have been to build up military structures superior to those of any other power. Indeed, the fact that everyone knew the United States had the resources to realize the latter course made her program acceptable to the other nations. It has been observed that when Mr. Charles E. Hughes, the American secretary of state and chairman of the conference, presented the original plan, "his position was so strong and American naval supremacy was so inevitable if his proposal should be rejected, that his program was at once accepted in principle."[8]

The world view of Americans thus became capitalistically pacific but not, as has been sometimes believed, isolationist. Peace among the leading nations had become a condition of expansion. There was at this time, let it be remembered, still no reliance upon militarization as a vital element in capitalism. Reliance was put upon traditional means.

New Emphasis on the Role of Manufacture

Active capitalist nations, as far back as the early city-states, have always been solicitous about the progress of their manufactures. [. . .] Because of the extent of its natural resources, however, the [United States] was still able to profit from relatively large exports of raw materials especially to the more advanced capitalist nations where there was earlier and greater concentration on manufacture. Even so, there was a continuous rise in both the capacity to satisfy domestic consumptive demand for finished products and the proportion of manufactured goods in total exports. To illustrate, in 1850 the dollar value of finished products exported was 20 percent of the value of crude materials exported, in 1880 it was 38 percent, and in 1913, 104 percent. On the other hand, the value of finished manufactures imported decreased from 760 percent of the value of crude materials imported in 1850 to about 60 percent in 1913.

On the assumption of leadership, American business leaders considered this trend far too lethargic. Thus they insisted that some form of direct action should be taken to discourage the export of "natural resources in their raw state." "We must," said one advocate, "export cotton in fabrics and not in the bale; iron and steel in machinery and implements; leather in shoes and other finished articles; use our coal under our own factory boilers; and in every way multiply the over-seas movement of products of hand and brain."[9]

But the drive for leadership in the export of manufactures was more systematic than this statement would imply. Leading nations have been at the same time both the largest importers and exporters of manufactured goods. What the leader controls is "key" manufacturing industries, and the character of these [has] been changing with the progress of capitalism. It was in the so-called heavy industries, based upon iron, steel, copper, aluminum, petroleum, and so on that the nation sought to excel. In 1921 the following were considered as particularly representative of "American manufacturing genius": "Agricultural machinery and tools; locomotives and certain types of motor cars; machine tools and labor-saving devices; textile and sewing machines; typewriters, calculating machines, and cash registers; printing and composing machines; padlocks and pens; boots and shoes."[10]

Having decided upon capturing the key industries, which always dominate the most wanted class of manufactured goods in foreign trade, the country was in a position to support a vast proliferation of minor industries. In other words, command of the markets for major products served as a multiplier of enterprises which might otherwise have been too weak to embark on their own. [. . .]

New National "Needs"

National needs, of course, constituted chiefly raw materials produced in the backward countries of the world. Many of these products seemed "indispensable" to the growth of the economy, hence concern for their continued inflow became a matter of prime urgency. They included both consumption and production goods, but the latter [were] of far greater moment. In 1918, to illustrate, Robert H. Patchin, manager of the famous trading firm W. R. Grace and Co., asserted that the United States normally required at least "fifteen indispensable imports, of which ten are the following manufacturing materials: wool, silk, fibers, cotton, rubber, hides, copper and other ores including manganese, tin, gums, and nitrates; while five are foodstuffs: sugar, coffee, tea, cocoa and fruits. None are entirely luxuries except certain fruits."[11] Since these imports were considered indispensable, to limit or to cut them off would necessarily involve some degree of national peril, and thus might have even become *casus belli*.

Indeed, once the nation assumed dominant status in competitive manufacturing, its needs tended to become limitless. Accordingly, many foreign countries were converted into more or less specialists in production of raw materials for American factories and thus made dependent upon the latter for manufactured consumption goods.[12] It is inevitable that domestic needs and shortages abroad should develop together. By the very process of expanding the market for finished products, "insatiable" demands upon foreign commodities materialized. In an elaborate analysis of America's future "needs" an important government report, [. . .] reached the ultimate conclusion that "the United States' appetite for materials is gargantuan—and so far, insatiable."[13]

It is an inherent prerogative of the leader nation to have first choice in the world market for the major raw materials. Whether it will import, oil, or iron ore, or copper may depend more on market price—and the leader may not always be passive in the determination of what that price shall be—than upon domestic availability. Indeed, even such products as are unavailable at home may be imported in far greater quantities than necessary for final domestic consumption. Thus, from the point of view of the necessity to feed the nation's manufactures as its markets actually expanded and as expectations of further expansion mounted, the industrial calculations of needs were well founded.

Perhaps we can now see even more plainly how capitalist leadership involves a definable process that renders the leader increasingly dependent upon the system. The dominant tendency in this process is to make the leader itself a specialist, even though the amplitude of its specialization necessarily becomes greater than that of any other member of the system. To the extent, of course, that protective tariffs are removed, to that extent also the movement is intensified. [. . .]

[. . .]The generality of business executives hardly seemed to have realized that the operation of the capitalist system was not then exactly the same as that over which Great Britain had presided. Because of the profound changes in the system, their approach to national leadership should have been redefined. They were assuming primacy in the system at a point where important markets for manufactured goods could be secured only through large investments in the very foreign projects calling for use of those goods. Investments had thus to produce the means of purchasing in the domestic markets of the leader nation.

Argument and Campaign for Foreign Investment

The United States, as we all know, was not a "traditional" foreign investor when it reached its new determination to expand abroad. The country was a debtor nation before the first World War; such nations as Great Britain, France, and Germany were even then exporting capital in far greater amounts.[14] The way in which invested capital was accumulated by the latter countries, and the areas and interests which attracted it, were not the same as those now available to America. Notwithstanding these altered conditions for the export of capital, American business leadership proceeded characteristically to convince its own community, the public, and the government that they must invest abroad or "stagnate." We shall attempt to indicate here the logic of the argument used in this campaign.

Investment, A Prerequisite to Major Foreign Commerce

Although the movement began in moderate tempo, it was nonetheless decided and resolute. As one government official put it:

> American investment seems to be a necessity for creation of an 'open door' policy in many of the projects required by future industrial development. It is true that our public has not acquired the foreign investment habit, but it is reasonable to expect that with a greater development of foreign commerce and encouragement of American mercantile success abroad, this tendency will assert itself.[15]

The essential argument was that the greater the foreign lending, the greater also the sale of American products abroad; hence it was stressed that "not only are our manufacturers, farmers, and merchants assured of prompt payment for their products but we enhance the purchasing power of our customers to at least the amount of the loans granted and enable them to make further necessary purchases from us."[16] The fact of "further purchases" is important, because it was seen that the actual loan served as a sort of nest egg, which, by tying the foreign economy in its major projects to the industries of the United States, channeled other business in the direction of this country. It is a point we have already alluded to, but it should be emphasized here to indicate its peculiar involvement with imperialistic forces. The foreign traders realized that the country making loans for large construction projects such as railways acquired thereby prior rights of maintenance, which in turn called for the sending out of many skilled workers and managers who established communities in the borrowing country. The growth of these communities

> invites new enterprises, such as the building of power plants, for the supply of electric light, urban and interurban traction, the opening of banks and of merchandising establishments. . . . And so step by step commercial control is obtained of a certain section of country, from which foreign competition . . . is barred more effectively than by a Chinese Wall.[17]

There was some consideration given to the relative value of various types of loans, especially as they might be classified as direct or portfolio investment.[18] But the principal criterion of their usefulness remained the question whether sale of American manufactures derived from export of capital. It was thus held that "foreign government loans made to defray administrative expenditures or for the carrying out of economic or monetary reforms can be of no direct benefit to our industries or general commerce."[19]

By about 1920, then, the consensus among major American businesses was that foreign investments had to precede or at least accompany the expansion of exports. The government, too, had acknowledged this. Indeed, the Federal Trade Commission had already argued before a committee of the House that commerce should be granted legislative assistance so that it might compete effectively with other nations in the foreign loan market.[20]

Investment Areas

As the movement for investment abroad gained momentum, persistent questions arose as to the most favorable economic situations and areas for the export of American capital. Although we have already taken notice of this fact in another connection, it seems to be of sufficient importance to merit more specific consideration. Two major areas, Europe and the underdeveloped countries, were constantly in view. To most foreign lenders the backward countries and especially South America seemed to have first claim on American investments; it was there that permanent markets could be won. They were the great source of raw materials. Thus, Percival Farquhar of the Brazil Railway Company contended:

> It is to our advantage to make our foreign investments preferentially in South America, and to make it as far as possible our source of supply of raw materials and articles for which we must go abroad, so as to risk the least derangement to our business through outbreak of war or other circumstances over which we have no control.[21]

South America and the Caribbean area were thus looked on as a critical sphere of American capitalist interests. However, it was sometimes realized that the backward regions both in this hemisphere and in Asia did not possess the political order and commercial organization of dynamic capitalist nations. There was very little established credit machinery in them for converting investments into profit-bearing industries such as that which existed in the United States during its earlier period. In spite of their other cultural accomplishments, therefore, these countries, under capitalism, seemed destined to remain exporters of primary goods: meat, grain, fruit, coffee, wool, hides, fine woods and dye woods, rubber and minerals. It was not always clear whether this fact was to be preferred by American capitalists.

Besides, the aftermath of war seriously complicated the traditional pattern of the movement of investment funds in the capitalist system. Europe, for "reconstruction" purposes, became not only an extraordinarily large importer of American goods but also a borrower with a peculiarly uncapitalist claim to American capital. [. . .]

An old capitalist area thus became a prime attraction to new investments because, as J. T. Holdsworth explained further to his business colleagues in 1922: "The great outstanding problem of the world today is the restoration of the normal producing and consuming power of Europe and, whether she wishes it or not, America is intimately and profoundly concerned in the solution of that problem." Paradoxically, the principal way suggested of helping Europe to pay her debts was to make additional loans to her. Thus

Holdsworth continued: "Europe's progress towards the correction of its unfavorable trade balance and the liquidation of its debts to America will be determined measurably by our willingness to assist her by further advances of capital and credit."[22] Only incidentally a voice, at that time going largely unheeded, was heard to say that lending to Europe was, on the whole, like lending to a permanent bankrupt.[23] Eventually, it seemed generally agreed that all markets should be entered, and favorable political and diplomatic action conveniently paved the way for a vast outpouring of American capital, especially into Europe and South America.

Role of the Public in the Investments

But there remained a vital question regarding the source of investment funds. It was contended by business leaders, probably for the first time in the annals of capitalism, that the people, primarily, should provide the capital. This they should do because, in final analysis, the benefits accrued to them. It was insisted, furthermore, that they should be educated regarding this obligation through the great media of public information. They should first be made to comprehend the nature of their stake in foreign commerce and then shown how the latter inevitably depends upon foreign investments. Accordingly, in 1920, James A. Farrell, president of United States Steel, declared:

> The American people generally must understand their personal relation to the international commerce of the country as a whole; they must realize that it is not only those connected with foreign trade, but every inhabitant of the land, wherever located and however occupied, that shares in its benefits and bears a direct responsibility for its continued success. In other words, the whole people must be prepared to join in giving sustained and intelligent support to the efforts of those who, whether in Government employ or in private enterprise, are charged with the obligation of directing and maintaining this increasingly important factor in our common life.[24]

[. . .] The new "capitalist mind" thus sought to be developed among the people required indoctrination in the principles of international commerce. The American vision that was previously turned "west" had now to be urgently refocused overseas. [. . .]

The major business community subscribed enthusiastically to this program of educating the people to their apparent interests in foreign commerce. Beyond providing morale for the movement, however, their education had to reach the point at which they would be willing to "finance the sale" of goods abroad. The advocates of this role for the public ordinarily made a distinction between "money market" transactions involving short-term loans for the purpose of financing immediate movements of goods, and long-term investments made in more permanent foreign projects. It was the latter that the people were asked to support principally by their purchase of debentures. Willard Straight, for instance, explained this in terms [. . .] the masses could easily grasp as follows:

> In great development schemes, such as railways, where vast quantities of material are required; in the construction of arsenals and electric lighting plants, street railways, etc., the community or the country which is being developed, in all probability, has not the funds with which to meet the expense involved and must, therefore, borrow. It cannot borrow from the bank, because the bank must make a turnover of its capital, and the result is, that instead of discounting a 90-day bill, or getting six months' credit on a call loan, that community or that country issues bonds for ten, or fifteen, or twenty five, or thirty years, and borrows from the public, not from the banks. That is the problem of foreign loans. Its solution depends, not upon the Government nor upon banks, but upon the public who have to buy the bonds.[25]

The public was thus asked and encouraged to be the creditors of the purchasers of American manufactures for large, long-time foreign ventures. Apparently there was no limit to the variety of approaches to this design. "It is," asserted the banker Fred I. Kent, "for the purpose of enabling the huge general investment fund of the United States to take a safe and satisfactory part in the foreign trade of our country that the idea of a debenture-issuing Edge corporation was born. Banking and manufacturing interests have extended credits to the full limits that they should, and the investment public must be brought into the situation."[26] According to some leaders of American capitalism, then, the prosperity of the United States depended upon the use of the savings of the American people in financing the purchase of American products by foreigners. It was never so starkly put by the dominant class in any previous leader capitalist nation.

But this imputed beneficence of the people in lending their savings was thought of as something more than a mere money-making enterprise; it was, in addition, advocated in terms of the duties of citizenship. Alert American citizens had a responsibility to invest in foreign bonds, because, as it was said, "back of America's ability to extend credits stands the ability and willingness of our people to fill the role of citizens of a creditor nation."²⁷ This obligation was emphatically expressed in the following terms:

> Every American, to be a good citizen, should understand and appreciate the importance of our foreign trade to the nation. It makes no difference what one's sex, occupation, age, politics, or religion may be; one's education is incomplete without it. A citizen cannot properly perform his or her obligations without understanding the fundamentals of foreign trade . . . our dependence for life's fullest happiness upon it. Almost every move we make, from dawn 'til dark, is affected by this great commerce. We cannot dress, nor eat, nor read, nor travel, nor telephone, nor do the hundred and one things unconsciously performed each day without the aid of foreign goods.²⁸

Indeed, the idea of financing the war and that of foreign investments were coupled. Thus J. T. Holdsworth declared: "It took a great war threatening world destruction to teach the American people to invest largely in the obligations of their own Government. This experience prepared them to buy the bonds of other governments."²⁹ It was expected, also, that a convinced and psychologically involved public would in turn influence Congress to give more direct aid in the enlargement of opportunities for foreign investment and commerce.³⁰

Role of Government

[. . .] The business community [also] felt that government should enter positively into the domestic campaign to sell foreign bonds and even into actual negotiation of loans abroad. The government could help at home by making "authoritative statements" to the effect that overseas investments will be protected. It had a sound basis for doing this because, it was asserted, "the general prosperity of the country and the strength of the Government itself depend upon the development of commerce and industry and finance." In rendering assistance abroad, the Department of State could at least busy itself negotiating advantageous commercial treaties. E. P. Thomas of U.S. Steel put the argument in this way:

> If the government is the servant of the whole people, there is no impropriety in its acting as chief agent of that great number of its people who are so vitally affected by foreign trade. Consistently therewith it might employ its representatives accredited to foreign countries not merely in the acquisition of commercial information of more or less hypothetical trade prospects, but in the actual negotiation or assistance in the negotiation of loans and like credit facilities

predicated on the development of national resources and capable of producing such effectual returns as would be unlikely under any ordinary conditions to require governmental assistance in collecting the principal or interest.[31]

Examples were replete of other governments, especially those of the German and the Japanese, securing foreign commercial privileges for their businessmen; hence their experience was cited here as further grounds for asking the state to assume more direct obligations.[32]

The Achievement

By 1929 American commercial interests had apparently achieved all their major objectives. From the time of her rise to leadership at the end of the war to about that date, the United States had become the outstanding foreign trading nation and had outdistanced Great Britain by far as the leading world source of credit. Professor Madden and his associates refer to this American effort as "the most remarkable period of foreign lending in the history of the world."[33] The author also presents data showing conveniently that for the interval between 1920 and 1931 the American capital market disposed of over $11.6 billion of foreign securities or $9.9 billion exclusive of refunding; while for the same period Great Britain exported $6.4 billion exclusive of refunding. The magnitude of this change in position may be indicated by the figures for long-term investments of these two countries in 1914. It has been estimated that at the latter date the total foreign investment of the United States was $3.5 billion and of Great Britain $19.5.[34] Furthermore, the United States, not having had its industrial system disrupted by the war, was in a still stronger position as a foreign competitor.

According to plan, the investors achieved their goal of selling the public the idea of the urgency of foreign investment. As far back as 1921 the final Declaration of the National Foreign Trade Convention said in regard to progress of the educational campaign: "We commend efforts to acquaint our investing public with the necessity of purchasing debentures issued by such institutions against approved foreign securities for this purpose, so that eventually every community will serve its own vital interest in furthering our foreign commerce as a necessary component of domestic prosperity."[35] And early in 1929 Mr. Julius Klein, a ranking member of the Department of Commerce, stated with obvious gratification:

"Our fourteen billions of oversea investments are owned, not in concentrated blocks by a few large bankers, but by tens of thousands of small investors scattered all over this broad land."[36] It was an important part of the achievement, then, that the American public became deeply involved as holders of foreign securities.

Exports, of course, responded to the investments. Nevertheless, even then, the specter of repayment began to loom. The foreign investments were sometimes thought of as the best kind of imports especially because they did not enter into competition with American industrial production. The argument ran thus:

> In view of the fact that the importation of foreign securities has not been attended by any considerable outflow of gold, it is evident that the proceeds have been used to purchase American exports. This then is a class of imports which counts as much as any other in the restoration of the trade balance. Moreover, these invisible imports do not directly compete with other American products as sometimes in the case with visible imports, but serve American industry and agriculture by stimulating exports."[37]

Simple calculations were frequently made showing the difference between total exports and imports with the conclusion that the "favorable balance" must have been offset by new investments in foreign securities; and the larger the investments, the greater was the commendation of the American purchasers of foreign paper for their role in contributing to national prosperity.

During this period there was also an expected upward trend in the export of finished manufactures and a similar movement in imports of raw materials. Those branches of industry in which the nation was particularly efficient, involving standardized mass production, were continually enlarged partly in response to foreign demand. On this point Dr. Cleona Lewis observes:

> These [foreign] loans and contracts provided a considerable market for American materials and services. The road building contracts, for example, expanded the demand for American steam shovels and grading machinery; and also called for cement and asphalt from the South American and Cuban subsidiaries of American companies. The building of sanitation, gas, and waterworks systems called for metal pipes and plumbing supplies. Railway building called for steel rails, engines, and cars. The execution of all these contracts gave employment abroad to a large number of American engineers, and also called for additional numbers of employees in the home offices of the companies concerned. . . . So long as American lending continued, practically all types of industry and all parts of the United States were more or less conscious of its supporting influence.[38]

It is probably clear, then, that American factory output responded directly to the activities of the salesmen of investments abroad. But that was not all these salesmen seemed to have accomplished. By 1929 Europe was regarded as having been satisfactorily restored. American loans had apparently provided the bridge over which European capitalism had passed to unprecedented heights of development. In 1928 an outstanding American industrialist said to his fellows assembled: "The renaissance of Europe, in a brief decade, to a point where, in many lines of exports and imports it is participating to a much greater extent than prior to the War, is due in large part to these American investments in its securities."[39]

[. . .] With Europe thus admittedly recovered and climbing to new heights of capitalist achievement, the system seemed to be again in regular motion, and, apparently, more vigorously so than ever. The United States was riding one of its greatest prosperity crests; unemployment was at the lowest point for the decade; and it was generally thought that the country had fully caught up with the postwar excess capacity that produced the 1921–1922 depression. Only ineffectual voices could be heard to question the soundness of the economic mechanism.

Notes

1. Oliver C. Cox, *Foundations of Capitalism* (New York, 1959), p. 387.
2. Cf. W. T. Stead, *The Americanization of the World* (1902), p. 343.
3. Cf. on the importance of the "size of the economy": Erwin Rothbarth, "Causes of the Superior Efficiency of U.S.A. Industry as Compared with British Industry," *The Economic Journal* 56 (1946): 383–90.
4. Cf. Emory R. Johnson et al., *History of Domestic and Foreign Commerce of the United States* (Washington, D.C., 1915), vol. II, chaps. 23 and 24.
5. James S. Alexander, in *Report of the 9th N.F.T. Convention*, p. 50. Without a more detailed analysis of the foreign-trade ratios presented by Simon S. Kuznets (*Economic Growth* [Glencoe, 1959], pp. 101–03), which tends to show the contrary, we may be left with a false impression.
6. For the official record see David H. Miller, *The Drafting of the Covenant*, 2 vols. (New York, 1928).
7. Frank H. Taylor, in *Report of the 8th N.F.T. Convention*, p. 38.
8. Charles P. Howland, ed., *Survey of American Foreign Relations* (1928), p. 527.
9. *Report of the 2nd N.F.T. Convention*, pp. 160–61.
10. Frank H. Taylor, "Problems of Exporters to Europe," in *Report of the*

8th N.F.T. Convention (1921), pp. 32–33. For relative values of imports and exports of crude materials and finished manufactures, see *Statistical Abstract of the United States*, 1955, table 1115.

11. Robert H. Patchin, *Report of the 5th N.F.T. Convention*, pp. 529–30.
12. Referring to the expansion of American business enterprise in South America before 1930 Professor James W. Angell observes: "The movement substantially influenced the pattern of our own economic life; and . . . in certain cases it completely revolutionized the social and economic structures of the foreign countries involved" (*Financial Foreign Policy of the United States*, p. 83).
13. The President's Materials Policy Commission, *Resources for Freedom* (1952), vol. 1, p. 4.
14. *Report of the 1st N.F.T. Convention* (1915), pp. 284–85. Cf. Eugene Staley, *War and the Private Investor*, pp. 5ff. See, for U.S. creditor and debtor position from 1843 to 1951: *Historical Statistics of the United States 1789–1945*, Series M 1-1, and *Continuation Historical Statistics to 1952*, p. 31.
15. Edward N. Hurley, in *Report of the 1st N.F.T. Convention* (1915), pp. 293–94.
16. Charles M. Muchnic, "Relation of Investment to South American Trade," *Proceedings of the Academy of Political Science* 6, p. 139.
17. Ibid., pp. 141–42.
18. See, for instance, Willard Straight's analysis in the *Report of the 1st N.F.T. Convention*, pp. 178ff.
19. Muchnic, "Relation of Investment," p. 139.
20. Said the Federal Trade Commission: "Though now increasing, American investments abroad are comparatively small. British, German and other foreign traders, on the other hand, enjoy a peculiar advantage from the billions of dollars of investments made by their fellow nationals in foreign lands, frequently on the express condition that supplies and equipment should be purchased in the country furnishing the funds. British and German investments in South American railways and public utilities, French investments in Turkey, and Japanese investments in China and Manchuria are typical examples. In consequence, time and again American manufacturers have found it impossible to sell their products abroad because the prospective customer was forced to purchase from or through the interested investors" (*Congressional Record*, 65th Congress, 1st Session, V-55, pt. 4, 1917, p. 3,576).
21. Percival Farquhar, in *Report of the 3rd N.F.T. Convention* (1916), pp. 28–30.
22. J. T. Holdsworth, in *Report of the 9th N.F.T. Convention*, p. 11.
23. Dr. Walter Lichtenstein, a trained economist and executive secretary of the First National Bank of Chicago, said in 1920: "If Europe now borrows very large sums from us, it means that part of her exports must be used to make good interest payments. This will of necessity cut down her imports, and so reduce in the long run her standard of living. This is the reason for saying that as a permanent matter credit

can be extended only to new countries, where there is for long periods of time a surplus of exports over imports, out of which payments for interest and capital can be made without cutting down needed imports. I do not see any possibility of this in Europe. . . . It is for the reasons outlined above that I come to the conclusion that, while some readjustments must be made in Europe with our aid, and we must forgive them their debts just as we do in the case of any insolvent concern which we wish to have continue in business, it will be impossible for us to undertake too much as far as Europe is concerned" *(Report of the 9th N.F.T. Convention,* p. 390).

24. James A. Farrell, in *Report of the 7th N.F.T. Convention,* p. 14. Farrell had earlier uttered the feelings of his group as follows: "There is no issue of more vital importance to the welfare of American industrial enterprise and labor than stimulation of our commerce abroad, as it is a recognized fact that extensive trade overseas tends to stabilize industry, by ensuring to manufacturers and producers a larger sphere of activity. . . . Every business house, every firm, whether in trade or in the professions, every chamber of commerce, board of trade and commercial organization—in fact, every man, woman and child in these United States has a vital personal interest in the furthering of our export trade. It has yearly assumed a more important position among the factors which determine the material welfare of this country" *(Report of the 1st N.F.T. Convention,* pp. 33–34).

25. Willard Straight, in *Report of the 1st N.F.T. Convention,* pp. 174–75.

26. Fred I. Kent, in *Report of the 8th N.F.T. Convention* (1921), p. 13.

27. J. G. Geddes in *Report of the 8th N.F.T. Convention* (1921), p. 107.

28. W. E. Butterbough, in *Report of the 13th N.F.T. Convention* (1926), p. 82.

29. Holdsworth, in *Report of the 9th N.F.T. Convention* (1922), p. 13.

30. Said J. Walter Drake of the Hupp Motor Car Co.: "As a nation, we must recognize and acknowledge the fundamental necessity of foreign trade. There must be built up in this country a body of public opinion behind this idea that will, if necessary, force Congress to accept it as part of our national policy and provide for its adequate support as for other essential parts of the government program. This of course, means the education of the public and Congress to this end. Foreign trade is a long road, with national business stability as the destination" *(Report of the 8th N.F.T. Convention* [1921], pp. 221–22).

31. E. P. Thomas, *Proceedings of the Academy of Political Science* 6 (1915–1916): 158–59.

32. For a study of actual participation of the U.S. Government, see Angell, *Financial Foreign Policy of the United States.*

33. Madden, *America's Experience as a Creditor Nation,* p. 68.

34. Cf. Staley, *War and the Private Investor,* p. 523. Compare figures for U.S. foreign investments in *Historical Statistics of the United States 1789–1945,* and later Series M 1–5; and *Survey of Current Business,* August 1956, p. 15. See the Royal Institute of International Affairs, *The Problem of International Investment* (1937), p. 338.

35. *Report of the 8th N.F.T. Convention,* p. viii.
36. Julius Klein, quoted in *Frontiers of Trade,* p. xi. Klein pointed out further: "In the early months of 1921 the Department of Commerce was receiving about 700 requests for information on foreign commercial matters every day. At present the daily average is in excess of 11,000 such queries. The significant feature of this great and ever-rising tide of nation-wide interest in oversea commerce is the fact that the bulk of these queries originate with small merchants and manufacturers to a degree undreamed of even a few years ago. It would seem that today, as never before in the nation's history, our foreign economic relations are the direct concern of vast numbers of our citizens and not simply of a few leaders in commerce, finance and public affairs" (p. xii).
37. Holdsworth, in *Report of the 9th N.F.T. Convention* (1922), p. 12.
38. Cleona Lewis, *America's Stake in International Investments,* pp. 379–380.
39. E. P. Thomas, in *Report of the 15th N.F.T. Convention,* p. 9.

| 19 |

Imperialism

Imperialism [. . .] seems to be an abiding attribute of capitalism. It is not, as sometimes thought, a late-nineteenth-century development; rather, it has gone hand in hand with the rise of the capitalist system as a necessary component.

Necessity of Imperialism

Capitalist foreign trade, especially as it serves dominant nations, proceeds directly into imperialistic relations; hence all the leaders, ranging from the national cities to the United States, have been imperialists. The expansion of capitalist commerce tends to set up relationships abroad that involve the very means of existence of the capitalist nation, which then becomes obligated to protect the markets upon which its internal economy is built.[1] This ordinarily leads to some form of control in foreign territory. Moreover, actual or potential rivalry among capitalist nations sometimes compels them to preempt market situations either by an annexation of territory or by acquisition of commercial and political influence over foreign peoples. Even during the days of the city-state system of capitalism, it was clearly apparent that no national city would rise to eminence without an assured complement of backward areas and their resources.

The intrinsic expansionist drive and the cultural capacity to make it effective thus tend to be irresistible forces in capitalist development. Wherever the resources of backward peoples become unduly exposed, the roving ships of the mercantile state will not pass them up.[2] Since capitalists are not mere wandering traders and pirates, however, their more or less permanent control of these resources becomes a natural means of extracting from them a maximum of wealth.

When the Dutch and English began to retrace the old Spanish

295

and Portuguese trade routes, they had principally commerce and plunder as their objectives. And yet, almost from their original voyages, the forces of imperialism came into play. Opportunities for profits were so great that the trade could not be reasonably abandoned. Instead, it had to be made secure. The long journey to the East called for permanent way stations; and in the great markets themselves, "factories" had to be set up in order to assure cargoes. In the West, especially in the West Indies, sugar was gold; to get it, however, the islands had to be appropriated and labor supplied.[3] Concerning the evolution of the economic role of the British East India merchants, John Bruce, an official of the company [. . .] asserted: "It ought to be remembered that the relation of Great Britain to its Asiatic dominions is of a mixed and novel kind. It began with commerce; it was reared up by arms; it has terminated in the acquisition of territories, by treaties and by conquests."[4] Indeed, in an important sense, we may think of imperialism as a vital means by which outstanding capitalist nations seek to stabilize and expand their commercial opportunities. This indispensability of imperialist acquisitions, as it related to Great Britain, was starkly enunciated in a foreign policy address by Joseph Chamberlain, illustrious exponent of his country's interests:

> The Empire . . . is commerce. It was created by commerce, it is founded on commerce, and it could not exist a day without commerce. . . . If I were to ask myself the oft-repeated question, whether the Empire is destined to follow the empires of antiquity and to perish, and the memory of it to be forgotten, or whether we are to sink like some of our rivals into a condition of mediocrity or obscurity, I confess my answer would depend not so much upon what may be done or said by the population of these small islands, but rather upon the eventual determination of that greater Britain which forms . . . the larger portion of the Empire. . . . We in this country are . . . pretty well convinced of the assured future of our colonies and our dependencies.[5]

Imperialism, therefore, is by no means a nugatory excrescence of capitalism; it has, on the contrary, provided its very base, its broad structural underpinning. Accordingly, then, this realization has led all leading capitalist nations properly to associate their imperialist position with their destiny. Since leader nations always seek to secure the lion's share in all new ventures abroad, there can be no room for contentment with existing possessions. Competition for leadership will not allow it. Again, Chamberlain seems to be in point:

I am convinced that it is a necessity as well as a duty for us to uphold the dominion and empire which we now possess. For these reasons, among others, I would never lose the hold which we have over our great Indian dependency, by far the greatest and most valuable of all the customers we have or ever shall have in this country. For the same reasons I approve of the continued occupation of Egypt; and for the same reasons I have urged upon this Government . . . the necessity for using every legitimate opportunity to extend our influence and control in that great African continent which is now being opened up to . . . commerce; and, lastly, it is for the same reasons that I hold that our navy should be strengthened. . . . Imperial defence is only another name for the protection of Imperial commerce.[6]

The Backward Peoples

Inasmuch as capitalist commerce thrives upon systemization and efficiency, it abhors the nontechnical, irrational economic traits of precapitalist peoples, who must consequently be brought under the influence of the market and made to conform to its rules. Peoples whose culture is such that they cannot make the effort independently will be "taken over" and subjected to the "civilizing" discipline of capitalist nations. The urge in this direction has been overwhelming. In 1915, Willard Straight, president of the American Asiatic Association, made the following analysis of the Chinese situation:

> In China . . . the government is, and has been, weak. There is constant pressure on all sides. One legation insists that a certain contract should be concluded with this person, another demands that the contract should be concluded with that firm. In many cases the contract is awarded to the people whose diplomatic representatives have brought the strongest influences to bear. The situation is unfortunate. It would be much better for all concerned if the Chinese government were not so weak, if it could withstand demands of this sort and consider proposals submitted on their commercial merit alone.[7]

This sort of weakness tends to be an open invitation to the major powers to come in and set the house in order: to the United States in South America, to Great Britain and France in the Middle East, to Japan in China, to all the leaders hastily in Africa, and so on.[8] One of the earliest "scrambles" for the territory of a backward people was that between the French and English for India. The fate of that country was decided when the following situation arose:

During the war which terminated in 1748, France began to form the bold scheme of becoming one of the sovereign powers in Hindoostan. The nature of this undertaking, and the probable success of it, with reason alarmed the English company, who now saw that the seats of their ancient commerce in the East were in danger of falling into the hands of an European rival: and that those profits, which they had for so many years drawn from their trade, might, in a moment, be swept away from them by the united arms of their Indian and French enemies. These alarms were, in appearance, dispelled by the peace of Aix la Chapelle, in 1748, which restored their Indian factories to the French and English nations. It was impossible, however, that either of these powers could be indifferent to a prize of such value as a territory in Hindoostan, which might afford a revenue sufficient to support the force required to defend it, and a surplus sum for the purchase of investments for the European market.[9]

The outcome of this British anxiety is, of course, well known to all of us. The imperialist scramble involves a situation in which rival capitalist nations find a native ruler so impotent that he cannot even guarantee the privileges and concessions [. . .] they are able to extort from him. The rivals thus come into conflict over what seems to be their rightful interests in the area. The process apparently follows a logic of its own, with the major prizes settling eventually in the hands of the most powerful nation.

Nature of Imperialism

Capitalist imperialism, then, is a vital part of good business. Specific imperialist projects may default, but on the whole imperialism provides the most lucrative and capitalistically significant branch of business enterprise. The early chartered companies for example, kept books; and they determined that their investments should continue to pay handsomely. The relatively recent *direct involvement* of the state as imperialist may have obscured this fact. Feudalistic states tended to be apathetic and unconcerned about their subjects' drive for preferential commercial positions abroad; they seldom, if ever, went to war over trading concessions. But the very earliest capitalist communities, Venice and Genoa, for example, fought each other as nations because of antagonistic imperialist claims in the Eastern Empire and in the Levant. It was largely private business organizations, however, which laid the foundations of the British, Dutch, and French empires. And, as we know, it took time before the British, French, and German nations could identify themselves completely with the interests of their businessmen.

When this happened, the nations themselves began to feel the same desperate urgency in their imperialist position as did their businessmen all along.

The Germans and Japanese were slow to achieve capitalist nationhood. But their bid for a stake in the backward countries, say after 1880, did not begin "the imperialistic stage" of capitalism; it simply intensified international rivalry and induced new fears about survival among the old colonial powers. The scramble for China was consequently speeded up, and Africa was finally "partitioned." "The governments," observes Grover Clark, "took over the expenses involved in protecting the interests which already had developed and in expanding the opportunities for further trade. But they did not take over the trade itself. That remained in private hands."[10] The governments could well afford to pay these expenses, however, for they now exploited new sources of revenue in the foreign countries.

The role of imperialism as a fundamental component of the economies of leading capitalist nations has not changed in essence. It serves to maximize and stabilize domestic income at the expense of more or less backward peoples.

Exploitation

The essence of imperialism, therefore, is exploitation. Domination facilitates exploitation. It is here that the capitalist uses of the persons and property of others in the interest of domestic enterprise may be observed in their purest forms—that is, the "distinctive parasitic" relation of capitalist groups to backward peoples.[11] Of the many illusions concerning the nature of imperialism, one of the most deceptive is that at some time after the American Revolution a "new colonial policy" of capitalist nations transformed fundamentally the imperialist intent of leading nations. Following the American secession, it gradually became evident that the colonies of European settlement could not be held in complete subservience to the mother country; they were, therefore, granted progressively larger measures of self-government. But this was not a fundamental change in colonial policy; it was rather an expedient within that policy. The drive to exploit yielded only in the face of opposition; it remained intact where opposition was weak. In 1897, for instance, Mr. Chamberlain put it in this way:

> The British Empire is not confined to the self-governing colonies
> and the United Kingdom. It includes a much greater area, a much

more numerous population in tropical climes, where no considerable European settlement is possible, and where the native population must always vastly outnumber the white inhabitants; and in these cases also the same change has come over the Imperial idea. Here also the sense of possession has given place to a different sentiment—the sense of obligation.[12]

That this "sense of obligation" was not new is indicated by the views of the great colonial secretary himself. In the more concrete situation of a Parliamentary debate, he gave his reasons for encouraging the colonization of East Africa. "We shall," he said, "get from this country gum and rubber, and perhaps even wheat, and in return we shall send out large quantities of manufactures";[13] which is, of course, precisely what seventeenth-century mercantilists thought colonies were good for. As Parker T. Moon observes: "In addition to the Dominions there is still the Empire."[14] Even in our own day, the granting of formal self-government to a number of non-European countries does not mean that colonialism in the tropics ias all but ended. Other peoples will doubtless be forced to achieve their freedom by making it appear that they are determined and able to take it for themselves.

The Technique

Imperialism rests ultimately on the peculiar capitalist use of superior power and deception among backward peoples. Moreover, these peoples, unlike even the weakest European nations, tend to fall outside international law and civilized morality: *They have no rights.* In the dealings of capitalist traders with them, a matter of prime importance has been the form of their political organization. Almost without exception, this organization has been highly autocratic. The nonpolitical masses lived mainly by agriculture, with minor trade and industry serving chiefly domestic consumer needs. In none of these countries, not even in pre-1860 Japan, did the native merchants hold positions of influence among the ruling classes. This general type of social structure was thus made to order for invasions by capitalist agents.

Unlike ordinary wandering traders, the representatives of capitalism sought immediate access to the rulers of native governments. They ordinarily approached the latter as genuine ambassadors, with greetings and sometimes presents from their own sovereign. What the merchants wanted then, as previously noted, was *trading rights;* and, usually, the native chief was able to grant these without limit. It was in this peaceful way that a bare handful of capitalist merchants succeeded in striking off the heads of some of the most powerful backward states.

Few, if any, of the non-European rulers knew the difference between the capitalist entrepreneur and the traditional wandering trader. Hence they could not perceive that free commercial concessions to capitalists involved also a grant of their own authority over their subjects and resources. From the moment such concessions were made and utilized, the economic and social order of the backward country began to deteriorate and to be subjected to a new kind of organization. Most important of all, the native economy entered an international system of markets operating in the interests of capitalists and virtually closed to the comprehension and creative reach of the natives.

Sooner or later, by one means or another, the natives and their leaders became conscious of the disintegrating effects of the new commerce, and attempted to resist it. The way in which imperialists have dealt with this reaction has been determined by specific conditions in given situations. The range of these conditions has been such as to call for either direct suppression, various compromises, or even temporary withdrawal. But usually the contact has already made the native ruler dependent upon the new merchants for economic support, thus estranging him from his own people. He presently came to realize that he had pressing needs for money to provide for such things as his personal consumption and the maintenance of an army, and that the merchants had money in abundance. The society, having lost forever its traditional cohesion could now be held together only by the ingenious authors of its disintegration. [. . .]

Situations of Exploitation

In defining imperialist exploitative situations, three major factors should be taken into account: (1) the position of the imperialist nation in the structure of the capitalist system; (2) the historical epoch; and (3) the cultural condition and political posture of the host country.

1. Only leader capitalist nations can make fullest use of the resources of backward peoples. If, through historical accident, retarded countries such as Spain or Portugal come into possession of valuable exploitable areas, the leader nations will ordinarily seek to establish control over those resources either by prying away the

territory itself or by working through the authority of the weaker countries and thus pyramiding the exploitation. In the latter event, forces tending to the elimination of the secondary power come into play insistently and cumulatively. With the rise in effectiveness of technology, small or inefficient nations have become less and less able to make the best use of the raw-material capacity of their colonial possessions; and some, like Portugal, Belgium, and Holland before [. . .] World War [II], held their possessions mainly because of economic rivalry among the great powers.

Diplomatic and military actions relating to indirect exploitation are usually very complicated. When it seems profitable and convenient, the most powerful capitalist nation will guarantee the integrity of the subordinate nations' foreign possessions;[15] or it may encourage the "independence" of those possessions when direct relations with them seem more advantageous. Great Britain followed both policies in regard to the Spanish and Turkish empires. It is the implicit policy of the United States today to uphold and protect the stability of all imperialist holdings even against the resistance of the natives. The minerals of the former Belgian Congo, one of the most severely exploited colonies, are of use particularly to American industries. In 1945, Fred I. Kent, director of the Bankers Trust Company of New York, said in point:

> We know that in the old days they [the Dutch] met their obligations extremely well. But we know another thing: that Holland imported from us more than we imported from Holland; and that the difference was made up largely from imports which we took from the Dutch East Indies. So that, as I recall it, in one year before the war we exported ninety-eight millions to Holland and imported only something like forty millions and took in something like sixty-two millions from the Dutch East Indies. That is one thing to think about.[16]

Exploitation of colonies by nonleader nations tends to be more severe. Among the causes for this is that the secondary nation itself may be looked upon as exploitable by the leaders; hence, the pressures of exploitation may be multiplied in its effects upon the natives. Moreover, the typical exploitative devices—the withholding of modern education, discouragement of political participation, promotion of "cultural parallelism," racial intimidation and coercion—are likely to be more extensively used in the pyramid situation. Because of its positions as a less efficient, intermediary interest between the major economic power and the ultimate laboring masses, the secondary imperialist nation tends to absorb the share of income which might otherwise go to the natives. We should expect that the people of Angola, for example, would fare better as colonials of the United States than as Portuguese subjects exploited by U.S. interests; or, indeed, under any circumstance, than as Portuguese colonial subjects.

2. The historical epoch of imperialist exploitation involves mainly broad changes in available opportunities and in national justification for imperialist action. If we disregard earlier imperialist expansion in Europe itself, there seem to be four major movements with respect to opportunities: (a) the gathering of large quantities of loose or hoarded wealth in America, Asia, and Africa; (b) the occupation of the choicest areas in these continents and their islands, sometimes for settlement and sometimes for exploitation of their labor and resources; (c) the division and redivision of the peoples and resources of the backward countries between about 1880 and [. . .] World War [II]; and (d) reaction among the backward peoples, beginning effectively after [. . .] World War [I] and continuing since with increasing energy. These movements—not precisely defined as stages, of course—show that capitalist nations have been finding it more and more difficult to maintain imperialist opportunities.

At first, imperialism was justified virtually as a religious duty; then, by about 1600, as a right shared by all nations to participate in the "commerce" and settlement of the world; later, with the coming of the Victorian expansion, as a duty to civilize the backward peoples; and finally, as a "sacred trust of civilization"—a trust to be held until the people are "able to stand by themselves under the strenuous conditions of the modern world." This latter is a principle laid down in Article XXII of the Treaty of Versailles. More recently, one important index that a backward people is not yet strong enough to stand by itself has been any sign that it intends to put itself beyond the reach of capitalist exploitation.

The morality involved in rationalizing the capitalist uses of backward peoples thus becomes less and less convincing. Moreover, the previously voiceless peoples to whom these rationalizations have referred are increasingly making themselves heard.

3. As I have already intimated, the state of cultural development and the political posture of backward peoples have been factors determining their exploitative situation. If the people are nonliterate, small in mass, and militarily feeble, they are likely to be exterminated. If, however, they are densely settled, and their labor can be effectively organized, they will ordinarily be subjected to routine pressures of exploitation. In more advanced and complex cultures, exploitation has been limited; the upper classes have been able to avoid the use of manual subjection.

Economic rivalry among the capitalist nations, especially since the latter part of the nineteenth century, has yielded some protection to backward peoples. The "anticolonialism" and open-door policy of the United States before [. . .] World War [II] have probably attenuated colonial subjection, particularly in the Middle East and China. The system of "mandates" and "trusteeships" of the League of Nations and the United Nations respectively are the outcome of two capitalist wars waged principally to settle rights to resources in underdeveloped countries, and they have doubtlessly contributed to the mitigation of imperialist action.

Meaning of "Backward Peoples"

A word should be said about the meaning of the terms "backward peoples" and "underdeveloped" countries. The early imperialists usually referred to their host peoples, virtually all nonwhites and living mainly in the tropics, as "heathens," "pagans," "primitives," "savages," and so on. These pejorative terms had the desired effect of helping to vindicate the uses which "civilization" might make of the subjects. The more modern designations, which I also have been using, convey the idea of the movement of these peoples toward the cultural and political status of leading capitalist nations; they may even suggest that these nations are doing all in their power to bring about this happy state.[17]

With the exception of Japan, however, whose case seems unique, no backward people subject to European imperialism has become a recognized capitalist nation. The overwhelming burden of fact seems to show that imperialist nations have gone as far as they could, consistent with their capitalist interests, to maintain backwardness among their hosts. Indeed, an indiscriminate transmission of capitalist culture would speedily produce the means of expelling the imperialists. In a roughly decreasing order of severity, the Belgians in the Congo, the Dutch in Indonesia and in South Africa, the French in Asia and Africa, the English all over the world, have resisted the cultural ambitions of the exploited peoples. In the midst of these peoples the imperialists have segregated themselves; rationed out education strategically and in very much smaller quantities than at home; barred the natives from an education in the schools at home as the Belgians do; and sometimes even withheld the use of modern languages from them.

And yet, paradoxically, imperialism ordinarily can be fully productive only if capitalist order is established in the situation. Natives must be taught the law, they must ordinarily be given military and police training, hygienic training, and even engineering and technological skills. They are, however, never taught native nationalism and the essential foreign commercial aggressiveness of the imperialists themselves.

But the economic conditions imposed upon backward peoples tend to freeze their situation. No backward people under imperialist control has ever been transformed from an essentially agricultural and mining nation to an essentially manufacturing one. Technological progress has never become a positive movement in countries subject to imperialism. Backwardness for most of the people of the world thus seems to be a relatively permanent condition of the mature capitalist system. It is largely through this imbalance of cultural and political status that the world's wealth has been funneled into the leading capitalist nations. We should not expect these leaders now to create, voluntarily, any conditions among their exploited peoples which counteract this flow.[. . .]

Contributions of Imperialism

The outstanding argument of imperialists, even to our own day, has been that imperialism civilizes backward peoples. They point to achievements ranging all the way from elimination of head-hunting and cannibalism—and, somehow, most backward peoples before the coming of the imperialists seem to have been involved with cannibalism—to the introduction of literacy and stable governments. There can be no question about the truth of some of these assertions. Capitalist culture could not be fully withheld even from its victims. I do not regard the word "victim" here as an exaggeration. At an earlier day the English, though they received some of their basic education in capitalism from the Hanseatic League, were insistent on describing themselves as the prey of "those Germans." The British, in turn, thought that they had given the American colonists a priceless heritage of social organization as well as military protection, and that this should have at least merited them the gratitude of the Americans. Nevertheless, the latter resisted with all their might the essential purpose for which the recognized benefits were granted.

Indeed, in virtually every colonial situation the imperial power may be able to show some residual contribution to the native culture. For example, a railway in Africa connecting an inland copper mine to a modern seaport may be viewed as a priceless addition to the civilization of the natives. The driver of its locomotive may be an African whose traditional mode of carriage had been his own bare foot and back. For certain purposes it could be argued that it required tens or even hundreds of years for Europeans to develop the steam locomotive, whereas the imperialists gratuitously bestowed it on the Africans. The benefits to the people of the region through which it runs may thus be considered as of such importance that its original purpose becomes thoroughly obscured.

It is not that imperialism makes no positive cultural contributions to backward peoples, but that, insofar as the welfare of these peoples is concerned, it is rather the motive from which such contributions are derived which is of ultimate significance. By understanding this motive, we are able to see why most subject peoples—English, American, Chinese, Indian, African—have resisted with all their energy the presence of imperialists. Let us recall that even modern slavery has been justified as a civilizing force. What seems particularly to incite revolt against imperialism is the fundamental exploitative design of the imperialists, the inherent disregard of the welfare of native peoples, and the necessarily incidental, or even reluctant, way by which the relatively meager cultural contributions are made. Since, therefore, "civilization" cannot be the dominant purpose of imperialists—since indeed such a purpose will ordinarily be considered an impediment to the realization of their interests—it cannot be counted as an intention of imperialism. Accordingly, as its major economic motives dictate, the same imperialist interest which has brought literacy to one backward people under certain circumstances has made the dissemination of literacy a criminal offense under different conditions. Native peoples may always expect their welfare to be disregarded when it comes into conflict with the dominant imperialist interests.

Furthermore, imperialism invariably carries with it contempt for the exploited group. This social fact constitutes the primary source of modern race prejudice and antagonism. It would be next to impossible for, say, the British in East Africa to conceive of the masses as normal human beings and yet maintain their exploitative designs toward them. Because the natives tend to resist this debasing attitude with increasing determination, the imperialist situation remains charged with insoluble intergroup conflict.[18]

Notes

1. On the movement of European nations into the backward areas of the world, Alfred Lyall observes: "The value of the prize for which they were competing was even then perfectly well known; and subsequent history has proved that the wealth, liberties, and political predominance at home of the contending nations depended considerably on their failure or success. It was the foreign imports that brought the revenue which maintained the great fleets and armies of Spain; it was maritime trade that fed the stubborn power of resistance displayed by the Dutch Republic; and the greatness of England has been manifestly founded upon her world-ranging commerce" (*The Rise and Expansion of the British Dominion in India* [London, 1911], pp. 19–20).

2. There could be little doubt, to cite an early instance, about the intent and effect of the following story brought back from Calicut at the opening of the sixteenth century: "When I was in that place, the King lived rather in a state of grief, both on account of the war in which he was engaged with the Portuguese and because he was afflicted by the veneral disease which had got into his throat; yet his ears, hands, legs, and feet, were richly garnished with all sorts of jewels and precious stones, absolutely beyond description. His treasure is so vast, that it cannot be contained in two immense cellars or warehouses, consisting of precious stones, plates of gold, and other rich ornaments, besides so much gold coin as might load a hundred mules, as was reported by the Bramins, to whom these things are best known. This treasure is said to have been hoarded by 12 kings, his predecessors. In this treasury there is said to be a coffer three spans long and two broad, entirely full of precious stones of inestimable value" ("Travels of Lewes Vertomannus, Gentleman of Rome, in the year 1503," in *A General History and Collection of Voyages and Travels*, ed. Robert Kerr and F. A. S. Edin, [London, 1824], vol. VII, pp. 96–97).

3. For the role of imperialism in the West Indies, see Lowell J. Ragatz, *The Fall of the Planter Class in the British Caribbean, 1763–1833* (New York, 1928); Frank W. Pitman, *The Development of the British West Indies, 1700–1863* (New Haven, 1917); and Eric Williams, *Capitalism and Slavery* (Chapel Hill, 1944).

4. John Bruce, *Historical View of Plans for the Government of British India and Regulation of Trade to the East Indies* (London, 1793), p. 5. On this point, Sir Alfred Lyall quotes from a letter to Lord Clive, the company's servant in India, and adds his own comment: "The time now approaches when we may be able to determine whether our remaining as merchants, subjected to the jurisdiction, encroachments, and insults of the Country Government, or the supporting your privileges and possessions by the sword, are likely to prove more beneficial to the Company;—in other words, whether the Company should openly take up an attitude of independent authority. And he decided, rightly,

that nothing else would give them a stable or legitimate position" (*The Rise and Expansion of the British Dominion in India*, p. 157).

5. Joseph Chamberlain, *Foreign and Colonial Speeches* (London, 1897), pp. 102–03.

6. Ibid., pp. 132 and 180. Further, in a speech, "The British Occupation of Egypt," in 1890, he defines the position which still carries tremendous force: "A nation is like an individual; it has duties which it must fulfill, or else it cannot live honored and respected as a nation; and I hope that as we have been singled out for the performance of this great duty, the whole nation without distinction of party, will resolve to carry it to a triumphant issue" (ibid., pp. 43–44; cf. Julius W. Pratt, *America's Colonial Experiments* [New York, 1950], chap. I).

7. Willard Straight, "Governmental Policy and Trade Relations with the Far East," *Proceedings of the Academy of Political Science* 6 (1915–1916): 152.

8. What really happens to these backward countries is that, after contact with capitalist nations, their older order falls to pieces. Referring to the collapse in China as early as 1833, Professor Michael Greenberg observes: "A century earlier, by both Voltaire and the Jesuit missionaries, China had been praised as the most civilized and well-governed country in the world. Now the Mandarin Empire seemed but a 'wretched burlesque,' incapable of resisting the new 'princes' of Europe, the spearheads of an industrial West" (*British Trade and the Opening of China, 1800–1842* [Cambridge, 1951], p. 215). Egypt having fallen into the same state of helplessness by the turn of the nineteenth century, induced the Earl of Cromer to remark that the "difficulty is to decide who is to interfere, on the assumption that some foreign interference is indispensable. . . . If England did not interfere, some other power would do so" (*Modern Egypt*, vol. II [New York, 1908], pp. 565–66).

9. Bruce, *Historical View of Plans for the Government of British India*, pp. 12–13.

10. Grover Clark, *A Place in the Sun* (New York, 1936), p. 13. It is obviously a developed stage of national imperialism to which Richard Koebner refers in the following definition: "The term 'economic imperialism'—this much should be clear—has a meaning only when the 'interests' belong to the spheres of trade, industry, or investment; when these 'interests' are in the hands of discernible groups of capitalists who put the dependency to their own use; when they form an essential part of the economic interests to which the home government (the 'imperial' government) must pay attention. Only if all these conditions are fulfilled can there be reason for saying that the government and the nation which make themselves responsible for the dependency have become 'tools of capitalism'" ("The Concept of Economic Imperialism," *The Economic History Review* 2, no. 1 [1949]: 10). One should note, however, that an imperialist nation is not a "tool"; and for the simple reason that the interests of the state and those of its imperialists

are identical. The fate of the imperialist state is intermeshed with the success of its foreign exploitation. It is in this sense that Cecil Rhodes made the following familiar remark: "These islands can only support six millions out of their 36 millions. [. . .] We cannot afford to part with one inch of the world's surface which affords a free and open market to the manufactures of our countrymen" (quoted by Sarah Gertrude Millin, *Rhodes* [London, 1937], p. 174).

11. Cf. J. A Hobson, *Imperialism* (London, 1938), p. 262. What parasitism means may be indicated by the following journalistic observation of Basil Davidson, distinguished student of African affairs: "Just as in South Africa—and in every other mineral-bearing territory in Africa—so in the Rhodesias have mining companies continued, year in year out, to dig up their minerals and export them overseas, pocketing their mammoth profits and never giving a thought to the welfare or the future of the territories they were ravaging. Attitudes of contempt toward the African inhabitants enabled the mining companies—and the imperialist peoples for the most part—to rob these territories of their natural wealth (and, in doing so, to ruin the health of a respectable proportion of the inhabitants as if by right, as if these territories had no claim to what was taken from them). And so it comes about that although Northern Rhodesia, for example, has enjoyed the blessings of white man's government for 50 years, it has managed so far to produce only two African graduates with arts degrees, and not a single one with a science degree, not a single African lawyer, not a single African doctor" ("Empire Building: 1953 Style," *Monthly Review,* August 1953, p. 177).

12. Chamberlain, *Mr. Chamberlain's Speeches,* ed. C. W. Boyd, vol. II (London, 1914), pp. 2–3.

14. Joseph Chamberlain, *Foreign and Colonial Speeches* (London, 1897), p. 127. I. C. Greaves concluded in 1935 that "the state which exercises control over a backward territory expects to perform three functions: to maintain the supply of exports from the territory, to protect the profitability of foreign investments in the territory, and to develop among the natives a market for its own manufactured exports" (*Modern Production among Backward Peoples* [London, 1935], p. 31).

14. Parker T. Moon, *Imperialism and World Politics* (New York, 1932), p. 522.

15. When, in 1919, Japan's intention with respect to the exploitation of China had become clear, Frederick J. Koster, president of the San Francisco Chamber of Commerce, said: "We, being the larger and richer, and the more powerful, owe the greater obligation of understanding and of generosity in attitude, and I maintain that while we must recognize the fact that there is much antagonism in China toward Japan, because Japan has not always dealt wisely with her big neighbour; yet, if the Japanese were not, out of their own necessity, and therefore of their own volition, interesting themselves in the raising of slumbering China, the task of development there is so

tremendous that we would almost find it necessary to urge Japan to help us in the work" (*Report of the 6th National Foreign Trade Convention* [New York, 1919], p. 295).

16. Fred I. Kent, *Report of the 32nd National Foreign Trade Convention* (New York, 1946), p. 202. A Frenchman, Capt. Pierre Lantz, assistant general secretary of *Direction Générale des Services Français*, speaking before an earlier meeting of this very assembly in 1919, made the following suggestion: "I would not like to end without making a brief reference to the new countries whose agricultural and mineral resources are rapidly being developed under French control. I have in mind especially northern Africa, Tunis, Algiers, Morocco, whose climate is very similar to the southern California one. They will be called to play an interesting part in the economic life of Europe, and America should not overlook this extension of the French market, which can absorb a good many American products, including agricultural implements (*Report of the 6th National Foreign Trade Convention* [New York, 1919], pp. 529–30; see also Basil Davidson, "Cashing in on Old Imperialism," *The Nation*, September 13, 1952).

17. The terms "underdeveloped," "developing," and "less-developed" have become increasingly popular as designations acceptable to the backward countries. For a discussion of the history and purport of these concepts, see Charles Malik in "Report of the First National Conference on International Economic and Social Development," *World Neighbors Working Together for Peace and Plenty* (Washington, 1952), p. 20.

18. For a discussion of "the native's place," see Ida C. Greaves, *Modern Production among Backward Peoples* (London, 1935), pp, 126–27; also Oliver C. Cox, *Caste, Class, and Race* (New York, 1948), pp. 317ff.; and Louis L. Snyder, *Race, A History of Ethnic Theories* (New York, 1939).

20

Movements Toward Change

Fundamental changes in human society have seldom occurred without the intervention of social groups. But most societies resist with tremendous tenacity utopian schemes for their reorganization. Yet change is possible. Indeed, compared to the quasi societies of lower creatures, the crucially differentiating characteristic of human society is probably its changeability. It is, no doubt, this happy trait of societal plasticity that allows the human being scope for imagining a better way of life and a more advanced civilization than his own.

Since a society of any considerable magnitude can hardly be changed fundamentally by artificial design, such mutations as do take place by group implementation are ordinarily encouraged by internal or external cultural developments. These developments tend to be determined by the pattern of the existing social organization. The capacities of different societies for action and reaction are not only distinct, but also sometimes predictable. We should not expect, for example, a feudal society to sustain such a continuous chain of technological inventions as that which culminated in the industrial revolution; neither should we expect to find in that type of society any basic change in social organization as a result of political class action.

Viability of Capitalism

Fundamental societal changes, then, are not erratic and unexplainable; they are explainable by the peculiar tendencies of social situations in given societies. Perhaps no major civilization has been more subject to endogenous social change than capitalism. The system itself, notwithstanding, is an extremely viable form of culture. By contact, it has revolutionized every other civilization on earth, without being itself significantly transformed in the process.

311

The extraneous cultural objects [. . .] it has sometimes freely borrowed from other systems have been assimilated and made strictly to serve its own ends. Capitalism's extraordinary ability to transform what it touches has resulted in the wholesale disintegration of traditional cultures as they became involved with it. Native groups everywhere have been put under a desperate necessity to substitute capitalist cultural traits for their own. Thus, even though there are still important survivals of other systems, the way of life characteristic of modern Western nations has become the cultural nucleus of the world.

The fact that capitalism has been violently aggressive does not of itself explain its spread. In the past, conquerors have been absorbed by the conquered. But capitalism has never been in any such danger.

Nature of the Change

Although the system has stood up powerfully in the face of other cultures, it has been subject to its own order of development and decline. Presently, we shall be concerned with the group action directed against the system's very existence. Generally speaking, this opposition has been principally directed not against the culture as a whole, but rather toward its inadequacies and its system of exploitation. But since exploitation constitutes the fulcrum of capitalism, its elimination anywhere must [. . .] involve some reconstitution of the system itself.

It is important to note that the opposition groups are indigenous to the system itself. They constitute, mainly, the *classes* that are more or less organized around the opposite poles of the productive process. The peoples of the backward countries may conceive of themselves as occupying one of these poles.

Class organization is a complex phenomenon, varying with the position of the country in the hierarchy of the capitalist system, as well as with the system's own historical stage of development. Moreover, the chances of success of the opposition class are not the same in different countries and at different times. The struggle necessarily involves not only a particular country, but also the entire system. One may generalize that the higher the nation stands in the system, the greater the consequences of its class struggle upon universal capitalism. Taking into consideration the period, then, an overthrow of the ruling class in the leader nation would doubtless result in the overthrow of the global system. There are, however, conditions in leader nations which give them relatively greater power of resistance to direct class action.

The Classes

We have seen that classes and class struggle are a characteristic of capitalist society. Unless we are interested in the generalized phenomena of social conflict, it is of no particular significance to identify class struggle in capitalist society with intergroup antagonisms occurring in other patterns of social organization. The incidence and process of class conflict in the capitalist system are peculiar to the system, and hence can be understood only with respect to the immanent social situations. Both the social-status hierarchy and the divergent communities of power constituted by interest groups are generally referred to as "the class system." The two are not identical, however. The structures are related only insofar as honor and prestige tend to increase directly with the power attributes of the interest groups; otherwise, they are distinct in their organizational and functional characteristics.

Although it may also include more or less significant marginal interest groups, the society of leading capitalist nations (or cities) is inherently composed of two principal political classes. This fact is determined by the nature of the productive process. The critical capitalist method of utilizing resources with increasing efficiency as a means of producing income defines the larger part of the people in the society as a utilizable factor of production. And, like any other factor, the extent to which this human component can be manipulated in the interest of larger output, to that extent also income may be maximized.

Whether given members of the masses of people are in actual employment or not, the fact that they are in an exploitable position engenders certain utilitarian attitudes toward them. The necessities of exploitation tend also to require their docility. The two groups thus tend to be divided both in interests and feelings. This major conflict of attitudes, as we have seen, occurred in every capitalist city of early capitalism.[. . .]

Aims of the Exploited Class

It is possible, through violent uprising, to overthrow the ruling class—that is, the exploiter group—and then discover that the society has fallen back into its traditional mold of social organization. After this happens, any constituted government of workers will inevitably find itself sloughed off. Workers at the head of a capitalist state are in an absurd position; they almost always assume the very attitudes and behavior of the displaced ruling class. This is because the established attitudes and behavior of national leaders are essentially socioeconomic, and not merely political. The class system, therefore, cannot be changed without revolutionizing the societal pattern itself.

But such a revolution is manifestly not a simple matter. Although a leading capitalist nation will insist on its sovereignty above all else, it is by no means independent or isolated. It is dependent upon a more or less universal network of external relationships for its income, and an overthrow of the society may result in a loss of its livelihood. The consequent economic situation may thus be vastly worse for the workers than the first. In capitalist entities such as Venice or Holland at their prime, the certain economic disaster which would have resulted from a radical overthrew of the oligarchy would have made any such action extremely unpopular.

The integration of individual societies into the capitalist system involves a variety of relations with which workers can hardly cope. They are, for example, confronted with hostilities from active capitalist units other than their own.[. . .] It was enough for the Diet of the Hanseatic League to threaten a boycott of some of its leading cities to secure the exclusion of artisans from participation in elections. Indeed, a country may be actually invaded by a sister capitalist nation for the purpose of putting down a worker government. Furthermore, workers of leader nations are contradictorily placed with reference to the established network of exploitative foreign relations. The aims of the working class, then, tend to be conditioned by its peculiar social situation.

Situations of Class Conflict

Situations of capitalist class conflict are defined essentially by the historical period in which they take place, by the position of the country in the system of nations, and by the social status and aims of the workers. The aims of workers have had two major tendencies: reform and revolution. The reformist position tends to be limited to struggle for a larger share of the national income and better working conditions. The revolutionary movement, on the other hand, attacks the social organization itself. There seems to be a correlation between the aims of the workers and the position of the nation in the system. First, however, let us consider the factor of history.

The historical period may be regarded as constituted by the era of capitalist development and that of its maturity. Up to about 1914, the expansive force of capitalism was so irresistible and the peoples of the backward countries still so unschooled as to the true nature of the forces impinging upon their traditional culture that in no part of the world was there a serious possibility of a worker or proletarian revolution; attempts at revolution constituted predetermined abortions. None of the countries of Europe was psychologically or economically able to endure a workers' state.

Besides, the class struggle of the world had no positive ideology until the latter part of the nineteenth century. Workers were not sure whether their salvation lay in emigration, in withdrawing to the little ideal communities of the Utopians, in anarchy, or in resignation to intermittent and sporadic conflict with employers and their police when occasion and opportunity arose to force a better deal.

As everyone knows, it was Karl Marx and his collaborator, Frederick Engels, who insisted that there was a social logic to the existing class struggle; that the heritage of the workers was inevitably the transformed capitalist system itself; and that this must be so because of the incapacity of the system to perpetuate itself vis-à-vis the unending antagonism it set up between workers and the ruling class. These thinkers argued, moreover, that workers possess a moral obligation to displace the capitalist oligarchy. Their teachings gave exploited peoples everywhere a logical core of ideas concerning their destiny.[1] These ideas became extremely stimulating and viable because they were grounded in observations of the actual processes of the capitalist society. Class struggle may thus be differentiated into pre- and post-Marxian conflicts.

[. . .] World War [I] may be taken as marking the age of mature capitalism; by that time it had filled up the important spaces of the earth. The people in the great backward countries were also awakened, and they had become equipped to read history in such a way as to circumvent the attractions of the proclaimed ideals of imperialism. The sordid facts of foreign exploitation, the spectacle of the leading nations fighting for rights to control the passive areas, the absence of any reasonable hope of themselves becoming advanced capitalist nations, plus the convincing prospects of socialism, presented strong inducements to revolution in the backward countries.

It had once been argued that the overturn of capitalism would most likely be initiated in the nations farthest advanced industrially. This, indeed, is a well-known conclusion derived from Marx's logic of social change. There is evidence, however, which seems to indicate major fallacies in this hypothesis. In the first place, the wealth of a leading capitalist nation is not entirely, or sometimes even mainly, accumulated from the exploitation of domestic workers. The ruling class of Holland, for example, by its systematic draining of foreign resources, was a manifest contributor to the income and welfare of the Dutch worker, who could not reasonably refer to that class as his exploiter without important reservations. In leading capitalist nations, therefore, workers tend to become participants in foreign exploitation. It should be recalled that Marx and Engels recognized this fact marginally. Thus in 1883, Engels wrote: "Apart from the unexpected, a really general workers' movement will only come into existence here when workers are made to feel the fact that England's world monopoly is broken. Participation in the domination of the world market was and is the basis of the political nullity of the English workers."[2] In such a country, discontent among the workers is likely to center on the size of their share of the general wealth. And, because the pie is available, a larger cut is possible. It is this fact to which Professor Lipson referred when he wrote:

> In the growing prosperity of the country the working class shared with other sections of the community. Its progress was revealed in the shorter hours of labour; in the advance in wages real as well as nominal; in the more abundant and varied articles of consumption; in the marked decline of intemperance; in the influence exerted upon social habits by the spread of education; in the mounting deposits of savings banks; in the provision—made by friendly societies (whose number even in the eighteenth century ran into thousands) with several million members—for the casualties of life; in building societies to enable working men to own their homes; in the institution of holidays; in the facilities for cheap travel; in the amenities afforded by public authorities, such as libraries, parks, etc.[3]

The important point here is that while British workers were improving their status and standard of living, workers in the colonies and dependent countries were being subjected to [. . .] economic pressures [. . .] so that in some cases even their traditionally low plane of living was further depressed. "If capitalism finds a partial escape in colonialism," Maurice Dobb remarks, "it may avoid forms of pressure on the working class of the metropolis to which it would otherwise have had to resort. Compared with the latter alternative, the metropolitan proletariat may be said to benefit from imperialism."[4]

The leading capitalist nation develops, in addition, an important class of workers vitally concerned with the administration of its foreign interests. Police and military personnel, civil servants, technicians, and employees in the foreign business bureaucracy tend to form a hard core of relatively well-to-do functionaries whose passion in favor of the status quo could ordinarily be depended on.[5] In Holland, Belgium, and Great Britain this group has been considerable and significant; it has been rapidly expanding in the United States.[6] The dependent and passive countries, of course, do not possess such a category of workers. Thus, while the "middle class" in leader nations tends to be bound closely to capitalist interests, the relatively few persons of middle-class *training* in backward countries tend to become identified with the discontented masses in opposition to foreign exploitation. This popular attitude is sometimes even transferred to the intermediary native capitalists, whose interests are associated with and ordinarily adjuvant to those of the foreigners.[. . .]

Affiliation of Classes

Like the proverbial goose, then, capitalism may inspire solicitude and protectiveness among workers. The remarkable nationalism displayed by this group in the leading capitalist nations has a real basis. It is not to be identified with the negative or defense nationalism of backward countries, but rather with the very ambitions and actions of ruling classes. And, once again, it rests on the workers' role as participants in the foreign exploits of these classes.

[. . .] The affiliation of workers with the ruling class is rooted deeply in the capitalist society. Although employers, because of their concern about minimizing costs, are in an antagonistic position to labor, they have always as a class exerted themselves to increase employment opportunities for domestic workers. The mercantilists were particularly solicitous in this respect. The income of workers is one primary source of business expansion; hence, capitalists have an abiding interest in its augmentation. Anything which enhances the consuming power of the masses *contributes* to business prosperity. "It is thus as much in the interest of the workman as of his employer," said James A. Farrell, president of the U.S. Steel Corporation, "that provision should be made for the steady sale abroad of the products of the mechanical industry of the United States. It is in the interest of both that the capital needed in that industry should be obtainable on easy terms."[7] Another American business leader identified the interest of workers and employers as follows:

> We seek the combining of all classes in a united effort to uphold our own labor, our industries, in the titanic struggle that the constant war of international commerce forces upon us.
>
> This war is inescapable. It is the result of huge masses of population in various parts of the planet. We invite people to come here; having arrived, we must afford them the means of sustenance; of supremest importance is the opportunity of steady employment.
>
> Steady employment of labor is impossible unless there be continuous run of manufacturing plants. Continuity of run is impossible unless there be continuity of disposal of the things made. The absorptive powers of our domestic trade being far in arrear of our productive capacity, the matter of vastly increased exports is not one of choice. It is a matter of industrial life or death.[8]

It should be pointed out again that workers in backward countries cannot be offered a like program to relieve their unemployment. In fact, the converse of the action taken by the advanced nations may be the aggravation of unemployment and the increase of pressure on the land among backward peoples.

Effects on Class Struggle

The working class in a leading nation, therefore, has sufficient reason to walk arm in arm with its oligarchy against the world. On imperialist questions, we should ordinarily expect this class to be nationalistic, because a threat to the imperial position of the nation tends to become a threat to its own welfare. The class struggle thus goes on at home, as I have indicated, for a larger share of the national income.[9] But it is a struggle that tends to stop at the water's edge where antagonisms with rival imperialists and exploited backward peoples begin. The working people of a leading capitalist nation are likely to rise up in wrath against those of their fellows who disclaim the imperialist actions of the government, regarding them as traitors. "Imperialism thus figures," says Hobson, "as an important and imposing feature of neo-capitalism, seeking to avert internal democratic struggles for economic equalitarianism by providing outlets for surplus goods and surplus population together with emotional appeals to the combatant predacity which animates a spirited foreign policy."[10]

We should not expect, then, that workers in leader nations will take a determined initiative in transforming their society to socialism. The initiative must come from still more disadvantaged groups abroad. The backward peoples are the real exploited and exploitable proletariat of the system. It is apparent that most of the advanced nations, especially the older, smaller ones, could not—at least in the short run—maintain their standard of living under socialism. That standard, as has been made plain, is based significantly on economic relations with backward countries. Hence, the abandonment of capitalism by a leader nation, involving as it does its hold on lesser economies, would expedite the collapse of the entire system.

There is no organized proletarian force in either Great Britain or the United States able or willing to challenge directly the position of the ruling class. What seems more likely, and indeed what is already in process, is that the stronger backward countries will throw off the "parasitic" grip of the imperialist nations and then proceed to develop through planning.

In these countries the class struggle is at the same time a nationalistic struggle against foreigners. Socialism, for them, is much more feasible because they have no valuable exploitative claims abroad to relinquish. To the contrary, socialism may provide the reason for expropriating the claims of foreigners, which may give some backward economies an initial material advantage. But this withdrawal from the system by backward areas removes the ultimate supports of leader capitalist nations, and thus generates situations in those nations conducive to the development of real socialism among their workers.

The class struggle thus becomes not simply a violent clash between workers in the most advanced capitalist nations and their ruling classes, but a conflict between the masses of people, mainly in the more organizable backward countries, led by native socialists or nationalists, and their weak, domestic bourgeoisie or feudality supported by the system. Nationalism and anticolonialism have implicitly come to mean anticapitalism.

Intraclass Antagonism

The two world wars, which were essentially intraclass conflicts, have given backward countries invaluable opportunities to extricate themselves from the capitalist system. Since World War II especially, many of these countries have been striving with increasing success—sometimes in the face of appalling violence from the leader nations—to take advantages of these opportunities. The economies of such countries as France and Japan, although they may still seem to possess their former blush of prosperity, have been undermined by this movement. In fact, the primary struggle to keep these nations from abandoning capitalism altogether is currently waged on their home territory principally through the military operations and encouragement of the leading capitalist power.

It is not, as some writers think, that the class struggle has changed its locus from the advanced nations to the backward countries.[11] The process involves a consistent movement within the capitalist system as a worldwide phenomenon. The economic situation was unfavorable to a workers' revolution in the early capitalist cities. The wealth of a city like Venice could neither have been created nor sustained by a proletarian society. In the new leader nations—Holland, England, the United States—workers became participants in the accumulation and use of wealth. They were thus always profoundly divided on the question of the goal of their struggle with the ruling class. In none of the leader nations—save, perhaps, in Florence—did they achieve the solidarity and resolution necessary to overthrow the ruling class. Indeed, they never seriously formulated such an intention.[12] They have been essentially reformists from the beginning, and perhaps more so in the mid-twentieth century than ever.

In all the leader nations, moreover, the working class has been divided into its well-known "conservative aristocracy," and its more radical masses. This aristocracy has identified itself with the masses only under pressure, and never wholeheartedly. The reasons for this seem clear. Unionization is indispensable in effective bargaining with employers; but workers strategically placed may more easily improve their status if they can dissassociate their unions from those of the masses. In the United States workers are still strongly divided by bargaining situations in which race has been a critical factor. In some parts of the nation the latter consideration serves effectively to limit the supply of skilled labor; consequently, the "aristocracy" has exploited the race issue with vigor and determination.

Workers have been divided not only domestically, but also internationally. The working-class leaders in the advanced capitalist nations, true to their traditional conservatism, have been loath to identify their interests with those of workers in contemporary socialist societies. They have, moreover, sought to guard their market area from competition with "substandard" workers abroad. For instance, Emil Rieve, president of the Textile Workers of America, argues in favor of excluding foreign textiles, as follows:

> This desire of foreign countries to secure a foothold in our textile market has been a real threat to the textile worker. Earnings in foreign countries have been relatively lower than those in this country, and working hours have been longer. Before the present war English and German textile workers were receiving one-half to one-third of the American standard, and Japanese workers were receiving only one-twentieth of the present American rate. While the standard working week in the United States was 40 hours, only a few European countries boasted of a similar work week and these have extended their working hours with the announcement of the present war. Working hours of Asiatic workers ranged from 9 to 11 per day, while most European countries observed a 48-hour week. Competition with these labor conditions is impossible.[13]

Proletarian thinkers in the advanced countries have seen perhaps correctly that the workers constitute the real revolutionary force, but the social situation in these countries has not been heretofore conducive to revolution. The revolutionary areas have been the backward countries; hence it seems more accurate to say that the critical proletariat of capitalism resides in the backward countries of the system. This does not mean that the last country in, say Africa, will have to revolt successfully before the capitalist system begins to undergo transformation. It has, indeed, already lost more of the colonial area than it can afford. The continued withdrawal of this area from capitalist uses seems to be the surest means of bringing about those conditions in the leading nations hospitable to a proletarian revolution. The continued employment of vast resources to oppose the trend toward withdrawal shows abundantly that this fact is recognized by capitalism's ruling classes.

I do not, therefore, conceive of the class conflict as having changed its locus from the advanced nations to the dependent and passive capitalist countries. The workers in the advanced nations have done all they could, or intended to do—which was always something short of revolution.[14] But the social situation in the major backward countries is such that revolution is not only indicated, but also feasible and largely profitable. Hence revolutionary solidarity seems far more easily attainable among them. Their success will bring not only a change in the economic orientation and organization of the advanced capitalist nations, but also a new perspective on the benefits of planned economies to workers everywhere.

Incidence of Change in Leader Nations

Although the social situation in leading nations tends to limit developments to radical societal change, it would be a mistake to underestimate the importance of radical movements in these countries. The continuing general dissatisfaction with the morality and operation of capitalism, the attempt to find ways out by utopian or by realistic socialists, the unrest of anarchists, and the parliamentary struggle of the common people for increments of democracy have reduced capitalist freedom of action at home and abroad. This movement provided not only an ideology, but also inspiration and encouragement for defiance of the imperialists by the subjected countries. Its existence, moreover, frequently helped to buy critical time for revolutionaries in those countries to consolidate socialist gains.

At times when certain exploited peoples were so completely submerged that their crying could not be heard in the world, it was from the pen, rostrum, and pulpit of anti-imperialists in the leading capitalist nations that the shame of capitalist methods was broadcast. Thus, within the very heart of the power structure, effective ideological blows against it were and are still being struck. Persons and groups engaged in this ideological battle ordinarily feel the counterblows in no uncertain ways.

Furthermore, the reformist political and economic advances made by labor in the leading nations should not be excessively discounted. Gradually and almost imperceptibly, the ruling classes in the leader nations have come to recognize a fundamental responsibility to the working people. The workers can no longer be effectively blamed for unemployment. They have been conceded the right to employment at an improving standard of living. In essence, this is clearly an increment of socialist transition, and any determined down-swing of the business cycle will undoubtedly intensify it. The climate for societal change appears to be far advanced beyond that of, say, the decade before World War I. The two movements, that in the backward economies and in the leader nations, thus supplement each other.

Notes

1. Cf. G. D. H. Cole and R. Postgate, *The Common People* (London, 1946), p. 686, for a discussion of the emergence of a "political mind" among British workers.
2. See Karl Marx and Frederick Engels, (Letter to Bebel, 30 August 1883), *Selected Correspondence* (New York, 1942), p. 420; and to the same effect, Frederick Engels, *The Condition of the Working Class in England* (London, 1949), pp. 246–47.
3. Ephraim Lipson, *The Growth of English Society* (London, 1949), p. 357. "Capitalist expansion," says Fritz Sternberg in a similar observation, "which led to a tremendous extension of markets abroad, was one of the main factors which created a situation in which the increasing productivity of labour was accompanied by rising profits *and* rising wages. Wages rose not merely for a few years, or even for a few decades, but for whole generations, and this was true not only for England, but of all big industrial countries" (*Capitalism and Socialism on Trial* [New York, 1952], p. 68; cf. Cole and Postgate, *The Common People*, pp. 500 and 648).
4. Maurice Dobb, *Political Economy and Capitalism* (London, 1937), p. 233.
5. Ibid., pp. 247–48.
6. "The most typically capitalist figure in the world," Professor Julius H. Boeke observes, "is the man who plays an economic role as a foreigner in a tropical environment. He has broken with the many traditional ties that more or less held him in check in his home surroundings; his thirst for money-making finds expression, unmixed and unimpeded; he can devote himself completely to the achievement of his economic object, concentrate his whole attention upon it. This applies particularly to men who, having come out to the East at the productive age, leave that country when their productive period is over" (*Economics and Economic Policy of Dual Societies* [New York, 1953], p. 79.
7. James A. Farrell, *Report of the 3rd National Foreign Trade Convention* (1916), p. 32. The following figures by the same author may call for refinement, but they show the satisfaction of businessmen with the participation of workers in the income of foreign trade: "Probably 80 percent of the value of two and one-half billion dollars of annual exports represents labor at some stage of their production, from the origin in the soil or farm, or in the mines, and all the subsequent processes of manufacture and preparation and finishing, up to shipment. In the final analysis, the bulk of the cost of all manufactures or production is the labor. The wages, which are paid in the production and distribution of the two and one-half billion dollars of exports, amount to approximately two billion dollars annually, and it may, therefore, be reasonably assumed that this involves the employment of two million men in the manufacture or production of exports. There is, therefore, engaged, directly or indirectly, in the production or

manufacture of material ultimately destined for the foreign trade, about one out of every ten men in this country" (*Report of the 1st National Foreign Trade Convention* [1914], p. 35).

8. P.H.W. Ross, in *Report of the 1st National Foreign Trade Convention* (1914), p. 140.

9. This fact disturbed Engels, who expected the English worker to be consistently revolutionary: "The English labour movement," he wrote to Bernstein on June 17, 1879, "has been revolving [now and] for a series of years in a narrow vicious circle of strikes for wages and shorter working hours, and this not merely as an expedient and a means of propaganda and organization, but as an end in itself" Marx and Engels, *Selected Correspondence*, p. 420.

10. J. A. Hobson, *Imperialism* (London, 1938), p. xxii.

11. "The twentieth century," says Professor Dobb, "was destined to witness a new historical phenomenon in the shape of national-democratic revolts in the province of Empire, to join with the proletarian revolt at the metropolis of which Marx has spoken, to shake the pillars at Capital's rule. In this new epoch it might well happen that the centre of gravity even would be shifted, and the former, rather than the latter, set the pace of events" (*Political Economy and Capitalism*, p. 249).

12. We are not unmindful of the sincerity of radical groups with histories as old as the Diggers and Babeuvists. But neither in France, Holland, Britain, nor the United States has the class struggle, even after World War II, developed the force of a progressive mass movement. The stirrings among the workers in the West in the 1840s, which frightened the rising bourgeoisie and provided the theme for the work of Karl Marx, soon lost their revolutionary character—perhaps, in the Marxian sense, never to be regained.

13. Emil Rieve, "Trade Agreements and Labor," *Proceedings of the Academy of Political Science* 19 (1940–1942): 30.

14. In a letter from Marx to Engels (October 8, 1858), an important deterrent to proletarian revolution in Europe was recognized. "The particular task of bourgeois society is the establishment of the world market, at least in outline, and of production based upon the world market. . . . The difficult question for us is this: on the continent the revolution is imminent and will also immediately assume a socialist character. Is it not bound to be crushed in this little corner, considering that in a far greater territory the movement of bourgeois society is still on the ascendent?" (*Selected Correspondence*, pp. 117–18).

A Bibliography of the Writings of Oliver C. Cox

Articles

"Farm Tenancy and Marital Status." *Social Forces* 19 (October 1940): 81–84.

"Sex Ratio and Marital Status Among Negroes" *American Sociological Review* 5 (December 1940): 937–47.

"Marital Status and Employment of Women." *Sociology and Social Research* 25 (December 1940): 157–65.

"Sex Ratio and Marriages in Rural Communities." *Rural Sociology* 5 (June 1940): 222–27.

"Provisions for Graduate Education Among Negroes." *Journal of Negro Education* 9 (January 1940): 22–31.

"Employment, Education, and Marriage of Young Negro Adults." *Journal of Negro Education* 10 (January 1941): 39–42.

"The Modern Caste School of Race Relations." *Social Forces* 21 (December 1942): 218–26.

"Race Relations." *Journal of Negro Education* 12 (Spring 1943): 144–53.

"The Political Class." *Bulletin: Society for Social Research,* January 1944.

"Racial Theories of Robert E. Park, et al.," *Journal of Negro Education* 13 (Fall 1944): 452–63.

"Class and Caste." *Journal of Negro Education* 13 (Spring 1944): 139–49.

"Race, Prejudice, and Intolerance." *Social Forces* 24 (Fall 1945): 216–19.

"Race and Caste: A Definition and a Distinction." *American Journal of Sociology* 50 (March 1945): 360–68.

"Lynchings and the Status Quo." *Journal of Negro Education* 14 (Spring 1945): 576–88."

"An American Dilemma." *Journal of Negro Education* 14 (Spring 1945): 132–48.

"Estates, Social Classes, and Political Classes." *American Sociological Review* 10 (August 1945): 464–69.

"The Nature of the Anti-Asiatic Movement on the Pacific Coast." *Journal of Negro Education* 15 (Fall 1946): 603–14.

"Race Prejudice: A Two-Edged Sword." *The Aryan Path* (Bombay, India) 7 (January 1946).

"The Nature of Race Relations: A Critique." *Journal of Negro Education* 16 (Fall 1947): 506–10.

"Modern Democracy and the Class Struggle." *Journal of Negro Education* 16 (Spring 1947): 155–64.

"Color Prejudice: A World Problem." *The Aryan Path* (Bombay, India), June 1947).

"The New Crisis in Leadership Among Negroes." *Journal of Negro Education* 19 (Fall 1950): 459–65.

"Max Weber on Social Stratification: A Critique." *American Sociological Review* 15 (April 1950): 223–27.

"Leadership Among Negroes in the United States." In *Studies in Leadership*, ed. Alvin W. Gouldner. New York: Harper and Brothers, 1950.

"Patterns of Race Relations." *Mid-West Journal* 3 (Winter 1950–51): 31–38.

"The Leadership of Booker T. Washington." *Social Forces* 30 (October 1951): 91–97.

"Vested Interests Involved in the Integration of Schools for Negroes." *Journal of Negro Education* 20 (1951): 112–14.

"The Program of Negro Civil Rights Organizations." *Journal of Negro Education* (Summer 1951): 354–66.

"The Medieval City: Its Relationship to Modern Culture." *Mid-West Journal* 7 (Summer 1955): 165–75.

"Berreman's "Caste in India and the United States." *American Journal of Sociology* 66 (January 1961): 510–12.

"The Preindustrial City Reconsidered." *Sociological Quarterly* 5 (Spring 1964): 133–44.

"Introduction." In *The Black Anglo-Saxons* by Nathan Hare. New York: Marzani and Munsell, 1965.

"The Question of Pluralism." *Race* 7 (April 1971); 386–99.

"The Problem of Societal Transition." *American Journal of Sociology* 79 (March 1974): 1120–33.

"Jewish Self-interest in Black Pluralism." *Sociological Quarterly* 14 (Spring 1974): 183–98.

Books

Caste, Class, and Race. New York: Doubleday and Co., 1948; Rept. ed., Monthly Review Press.

The Foundations of Capitalism. New York: Philosophical Library, 1959.

Capitalism and American Leadership. New York: Philosophical Library, 1962.

Capitalism as a System. New York: Monthly Review Press, 1964.

Race Relations: Elements and Social Dynamics. Detroit: Wayne State University Press, 1976.

Unpublished Material

"The Buying Power Movement Among Negroes in Chicago," 1932.

"Workingmen's Compensation in the U. S., With Critical Observations and Suggestions." Master's thesis, University of Chicago, June 1932.

"Factors Affecting the Marital Status of Negroes in the United States." Ph.D. diss. University of Chicago, August 1938.

"The Road to Civil Disobedience: Negro Citizens' Quest for Democracy Through Group Action," (n.d.).

"The Negro's Quest for Democracy," 1963.